Nodame Cantabile

1

TOMOKO NINOMIYA

TRANSLATED AND ADAPTED BY
David and Eriko Walsh

LETTERED BY
Michaelis/Carpelis Design

DEL REY

BALLANTINE BOOKS • NEW YORK

A Del Rey Books Trade Paperback Original

Copyright © 2005 by Tomoko Ninomiya

This publication—rights arranged through Kodansha Ltd.

Published in the United States by Del Rey Books, an imprint of The Random House Publishing Group, a division of Random House, Inc., New York.

Del Rey is a registered trademark and the Del Rey colophon is a trademark of Random House, Inc.

First published in Japan in 2002 by Kodansha Ltd., Tokyo.

ISBN 0-345-48172-0

Library of Congress Control Number: 2005921798

Printed in the United States of America

Del Rey Manga website: www.delreymanga.com

9 8 7 6

Lettering—Michaelis/Carpelis Design Associates Inc.

Contents

A Note from the Author
iv

Honorifics
v

Lesson 1
3

Lesson 2
35

Lesson 3
67

Lesson 4
95

Lesson 5
125

Lesson 6
153

Special Thanks
183

Translation Notes
184

Preview of Volume 2
189

A Note from the Author

I've always been envious of people who played the piano because they look so beautiful. But listening to classical music is very different from writing a comic about it. When I draw a picture of a piano in the comics, sometimes I get very frustrated. But I'll do my best!

Tomoko Ninomiya

Honorifics

Throughout the Del Rey Manga books, you will find Japanese honorifics left intact in the translations. For those not familiar with how the Japanese use honorifics and, more importantly, how they differ from American honorifics, we present this brief overview.

Politeness has always been a critical facet of Japanese culture. Ever since the feudal era, when Japan was a highly stratified society, use of honorifics—which can be defined as polite speech that indicates relationship or status—has played an essential role in the Japanese language. When addressing someone in Japanese, an honorific usually takes the form of a suffix attached to one's name (example: "Asuna-san"), or as a title at the end of one's name or in place of the name itself (example: "Negi-sensei," or simply "Sensei!").

Honorifics can be expressions of respect or endearment. In the context of manga and anime, honorifics give insight into the nature of the relationship between characters. Many translations into English leave out these important honorifics, and therefore distort the "feel" of the original Japanese. Because Japanese honorifics contain nuances that English honorifics lack, it is our policy at Del Rey not to translate them. Here, instead, is a guide to some of the honorifics you may encounter in Del Rey Manga.

-san: This is the most common honorific and is equivalent to Mr., Miss, Ms., or Mrs. It is the all-purpose honorific and can be used in any situation where politeness is required.

-sama: This is one level higher than "-san" and is used to confer great respect.

-dono: This comes from the word "tono," which means "lord." It is an even higher level than "-sama" and confers utmost respect.

-kun: This suffix is used at the end of boys' names to express familiarity or endearment. It is also sometimes used by men among friends, or when addressing someone younger or of a lower station.

-chan: This is used to express endearment, mostly toward girls. It is also used for little boys, pets, and even among lovers. It gives a sense of childish cuteness.

Bozu: This is an informal way to refer to a boy, similar to the English term "kid" or "squirt."

Sempai: This title suggests that the addressee is one's senior in a group or organization. It is most often used in a school setting, where underclassmen refer to their upperclassmen as "sempai." It can also be used in the workplace, such as when a newer employee addresses an employee who has seniority in the company.

Kohai: This is the opposite of "sempai" and is used toward under-classmen in school or newcomers in the workplace. It connotes that the addressee is of a lower station.

Sensei: Literally meaning "one who has come before," this title is used for teachers, doctors, or masters of any profession or art.

[blank]: Usually forgotten in these lists, but perhaps the most significant difference between Japanese and English. The lack of honorific means that the speaker has permission to address the person in a very intimate way. Usually, only family, spouses, or very close friends have this kind of permission. Known as *yobisute*, it can be gratifying when someone who has earned the intimacy starts to call one by one's name without an honorific. But when that intimacy hasn't been earned, it can be very insulting.

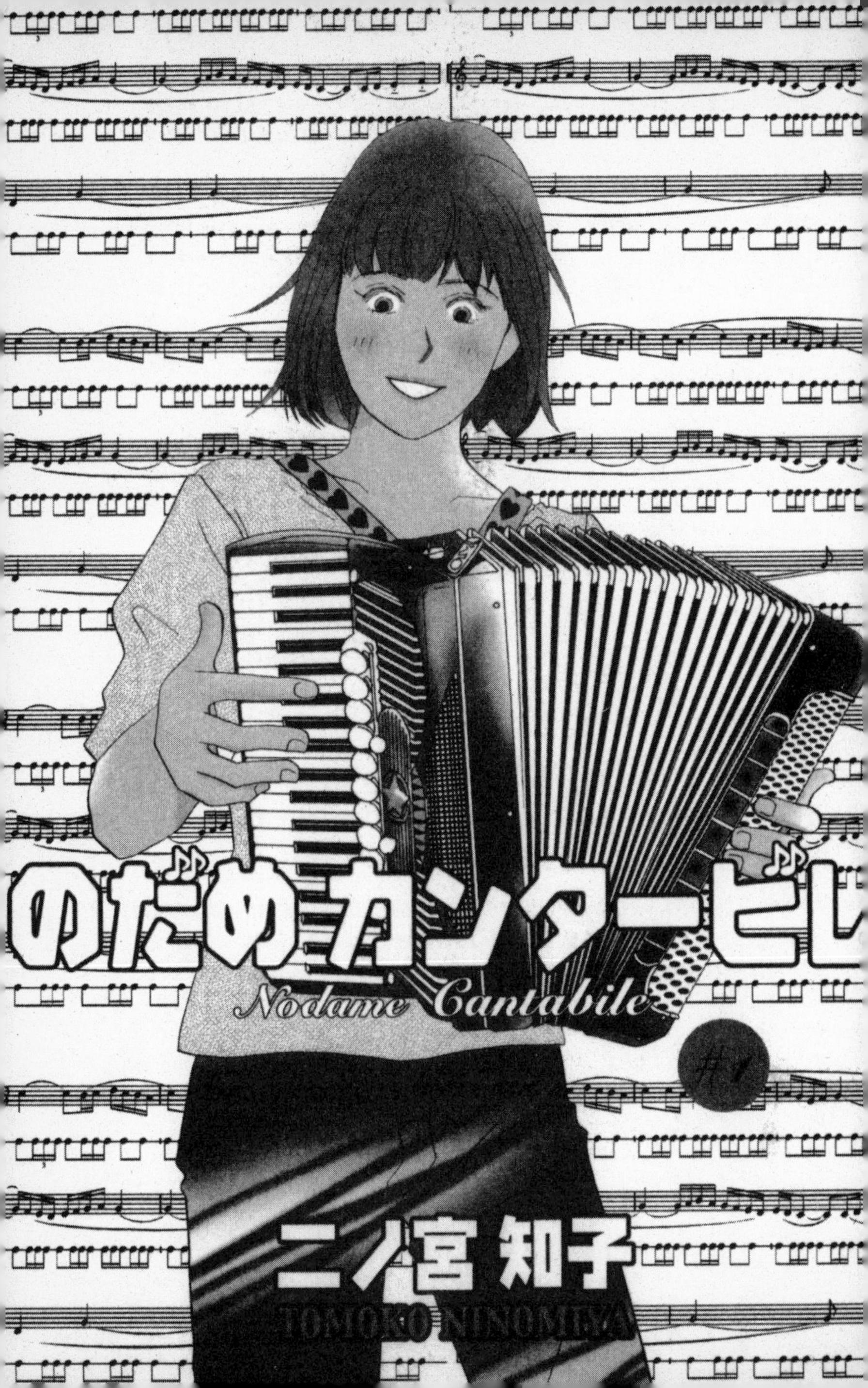

のだめカンタービレ
Nodame Cantabile
#1
二ノ宮知子
TOMOKO NINOMIYA

Nodame Cantabile

Contents

Lesson1 · · · · · · · 3

Lesson2 · · · · · · · 35

Lesson3 · · · · · · · 67

Lesson4 · · · · · · · 95

Lesson5 · · · · · · · 125

Lesson6 · · · · · · · 153

TOMOKO NINOMIYA

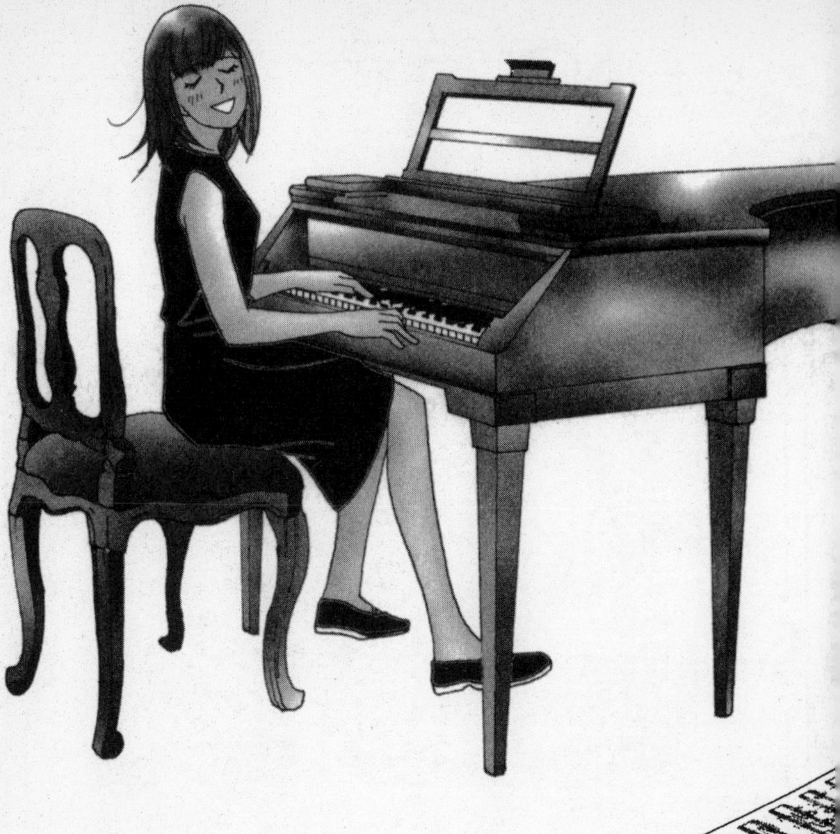

Lesson 1

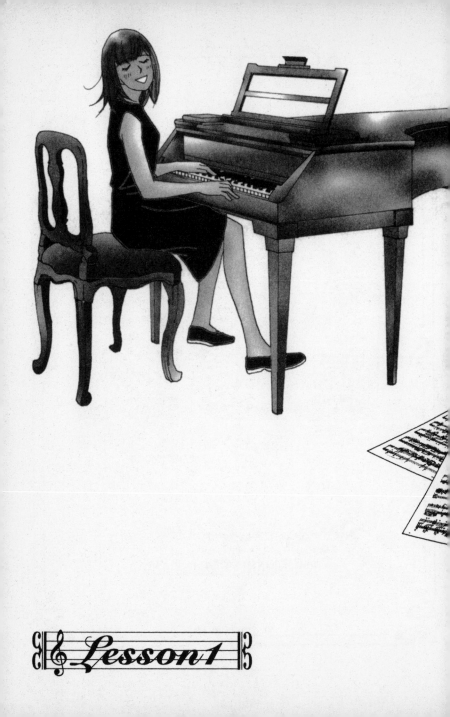

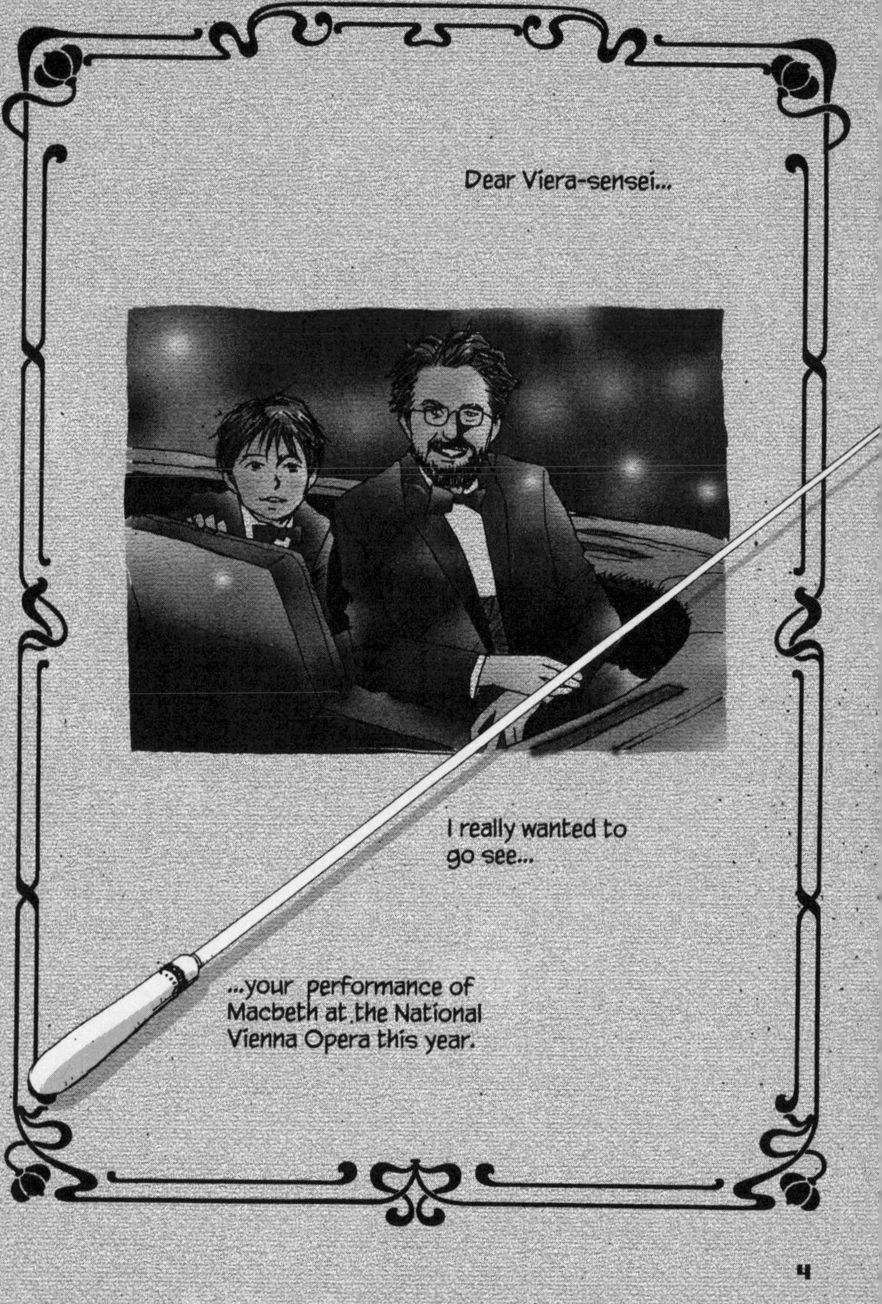
Dear Viera-sensei...
I really wanted to go see...
...your performance of Macbeth at the National Vienna Opera this year.

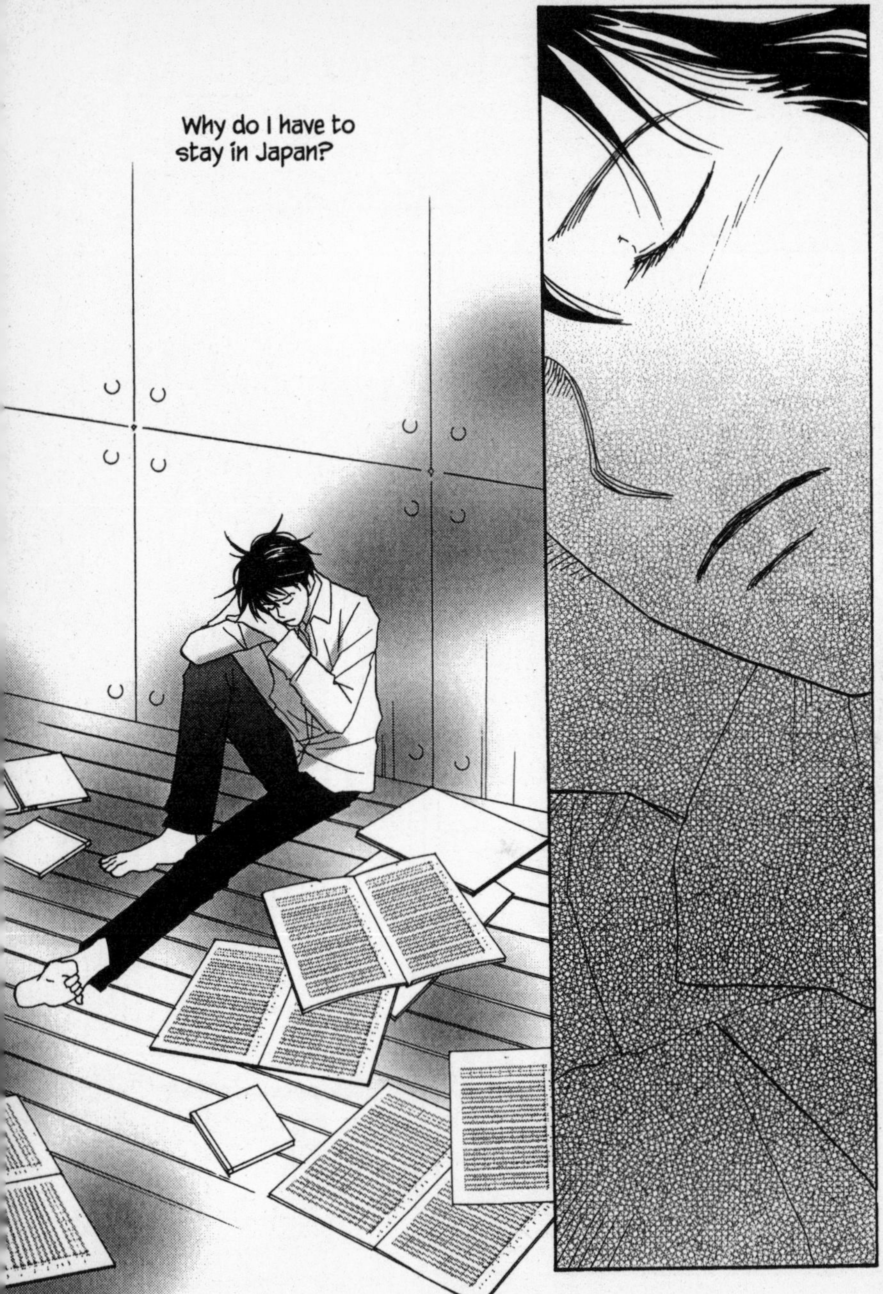
Why do I have to stay in Japan?

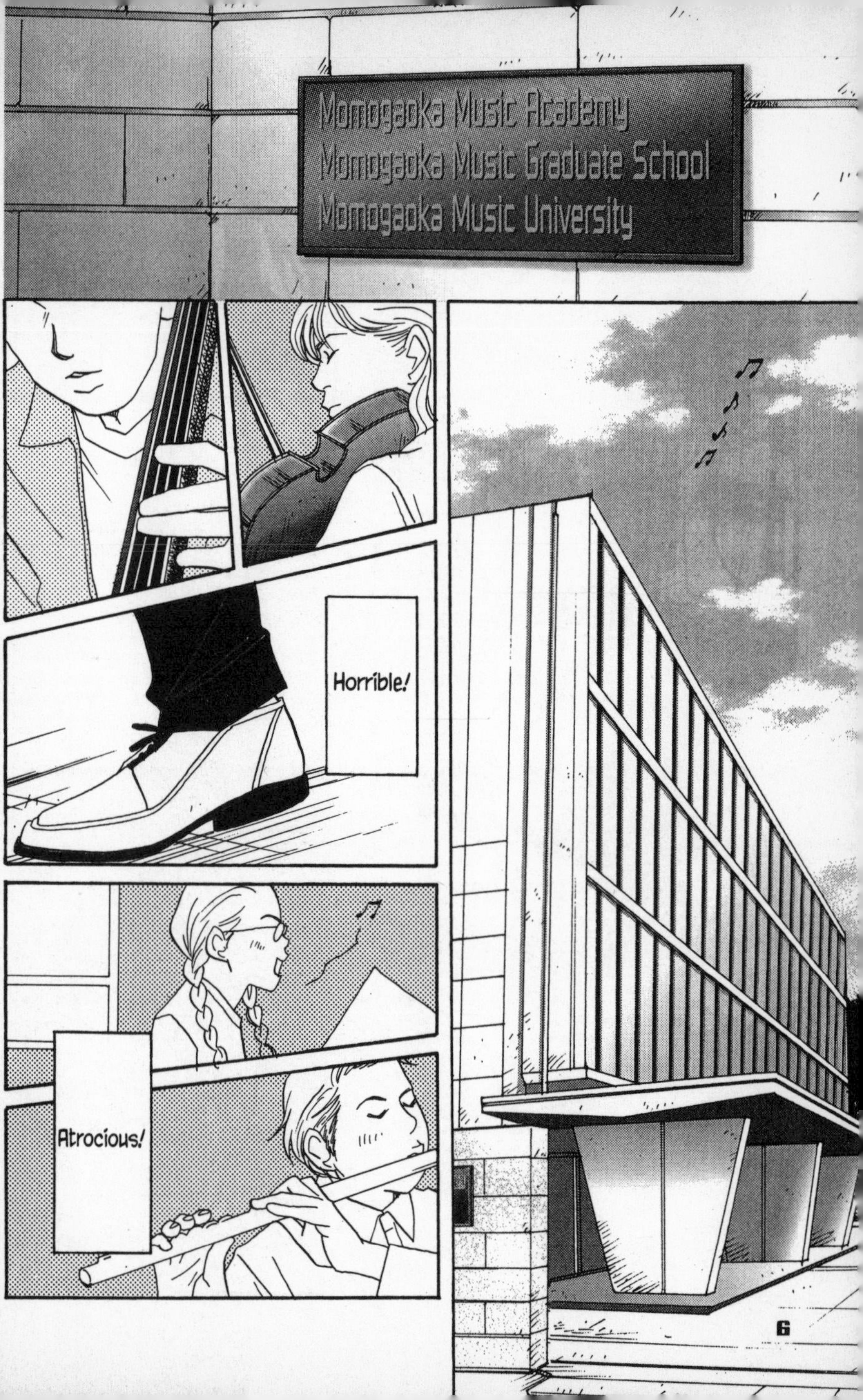
Momogaoka Music Academy
Momogaoka Music Graduate School
Momogaoka Music University
Horrible!
Atrocious!

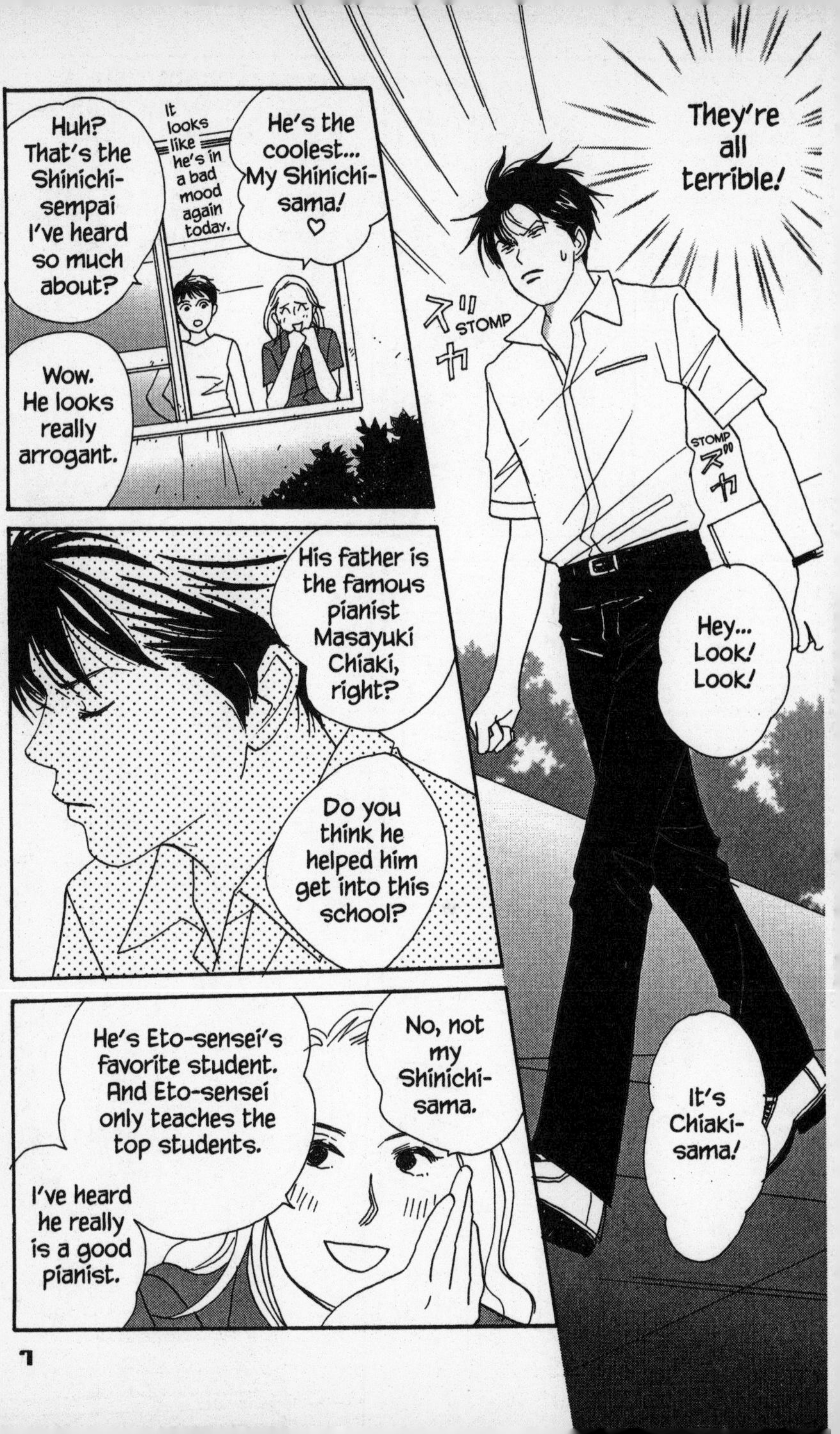
They're all terrible!
STOMP
STOMP
Hey... Look! Look!
It's Chiaki-sama!
He's the coolest... My Shinichi-sama! ♡
It looks like he's in a bad mood again today.
Huh? That's the Shinichi-sempai I've heard so much about?
Wow. He looks really arrogant.
His father is the famous pianist Masayuki Chiaki, right?
Do you think he helped him get into this school?
No, not my Shinichi-sama.
He's Eto-sensei's favorite student. And Eto-sensei only teaches the top students.
I've heard he really is a good pianist.

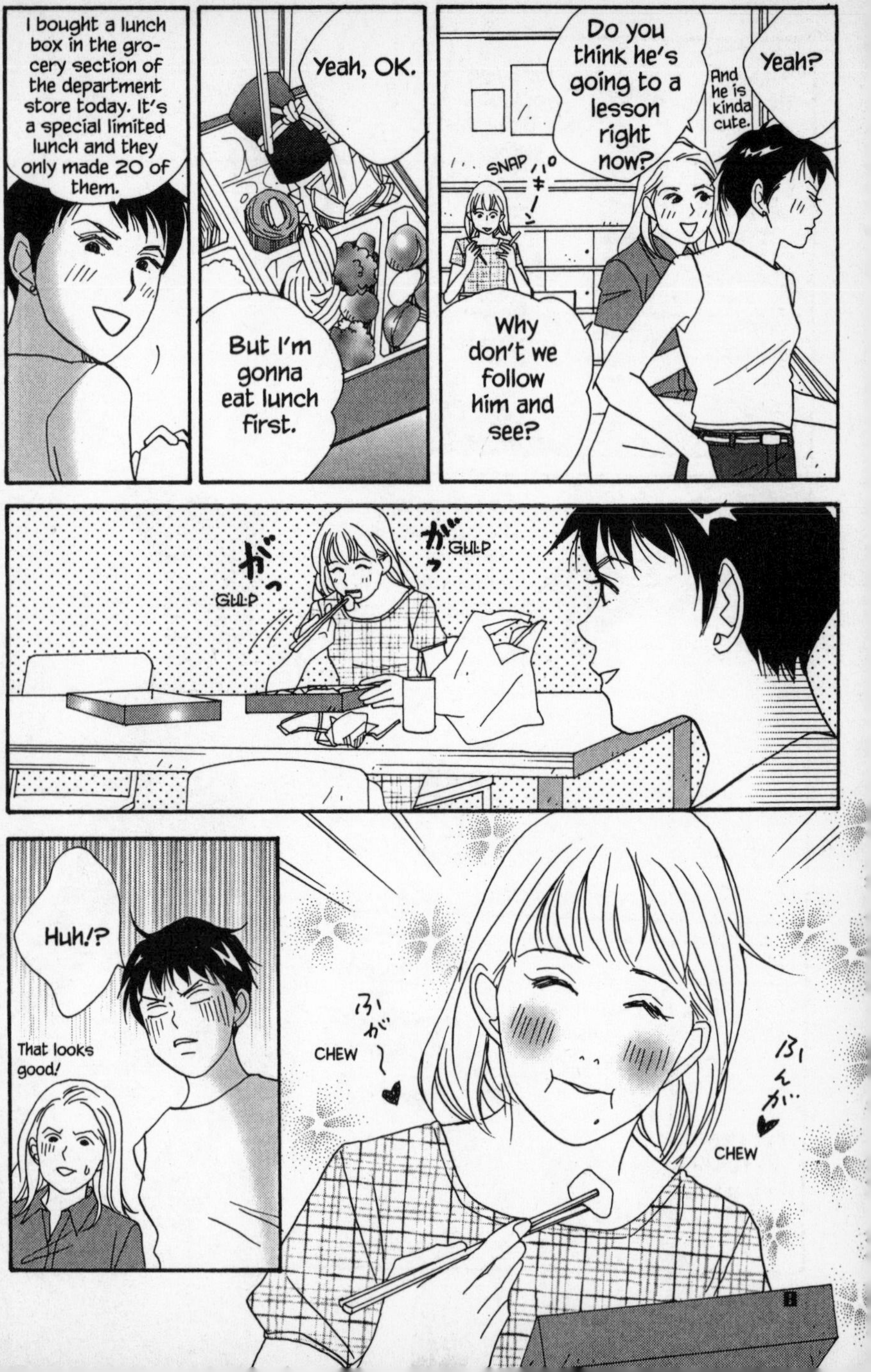
Yeah?
And he is kinda cute.
Do you think he's going to a lesson right now?
SNAP
Why don't we follow him and see?
Yeah, OK.
But I'm gonna eat lunch first.
I bought a lunch box in the grocery section of the department store today. It's a special limited lunch and they only made 20 of them.
GULP
GULP
CHEW
CHEW
Huh!?
That looks good!

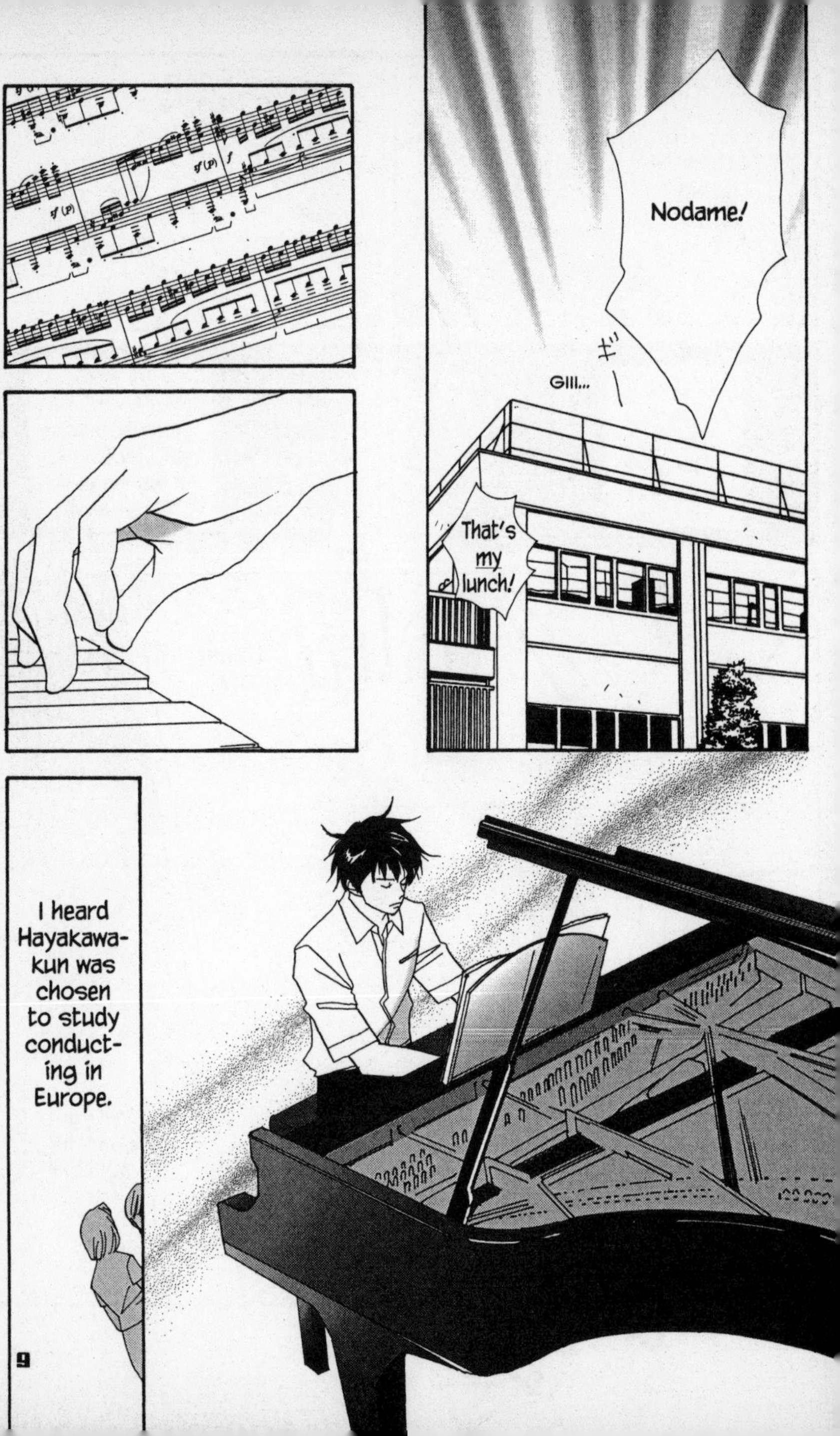

Nodame!
ギー
GIII...
That's my lunch!
I heard Hayakawa-kun was chosen to study conducting in Europe.

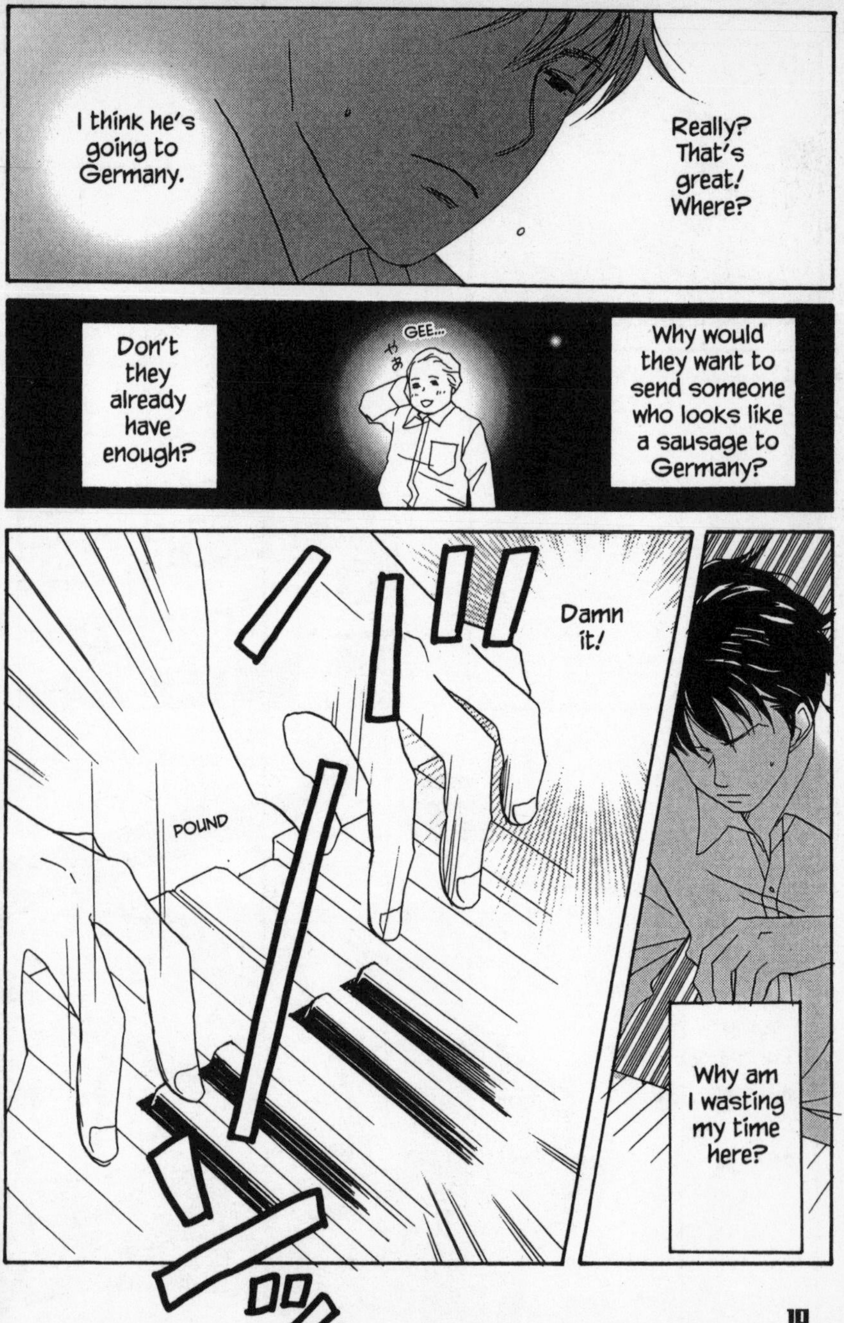
Really? That's great! Where?
I think he's going to Germany.
Why would they want to send someone who looks like a sausage to Germany?
GEE...
やぁ
Don't they already have enough?
Why am I wasting my time here?
Damn it!
POUND

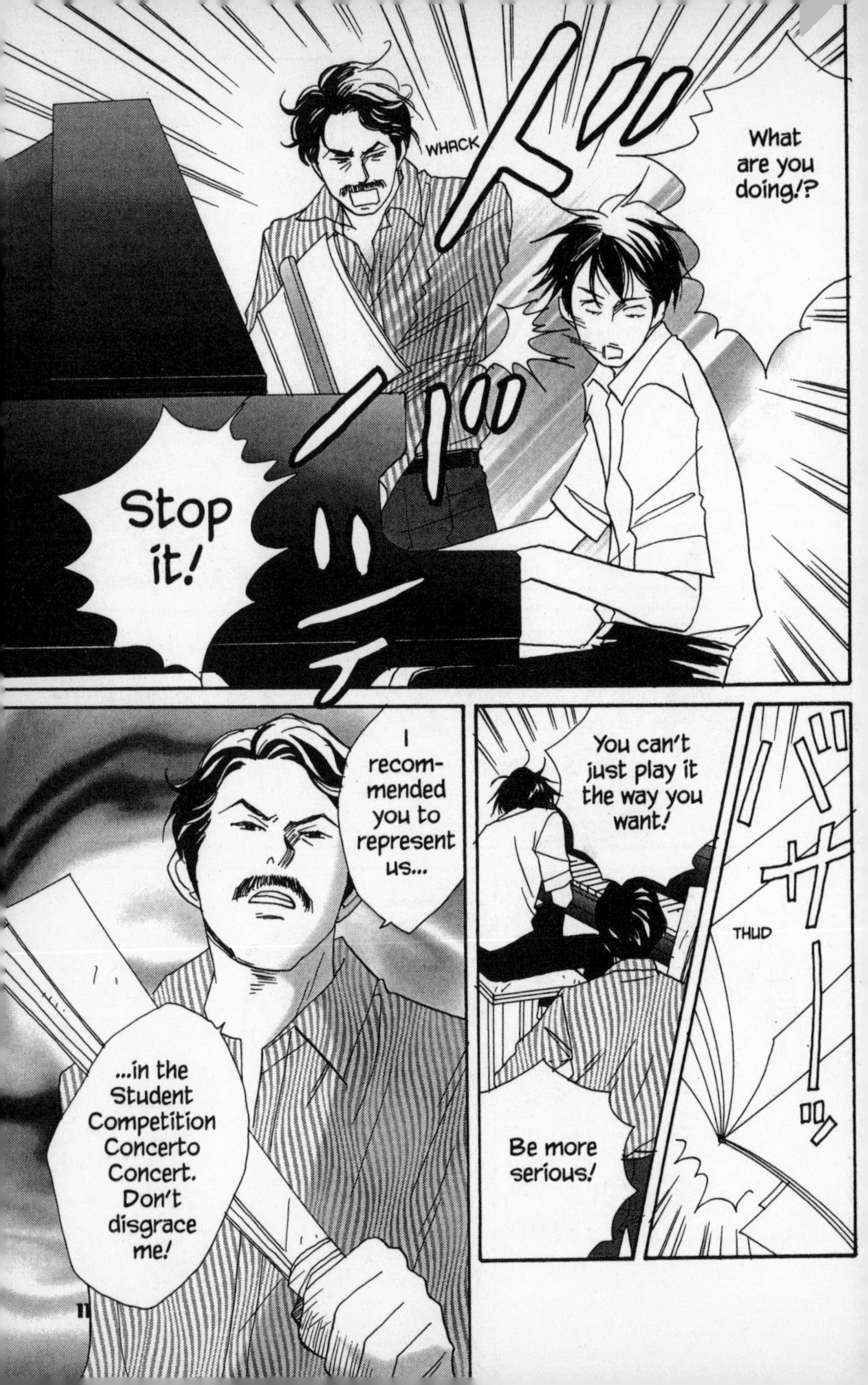
What are you doing!?
WHACK
Stop it!
You can't just play it the way you want!
THUD
Be more serious!
I recommended you to represent us...
...in the Student Competition Concerto Concert. Don't disgrace me!

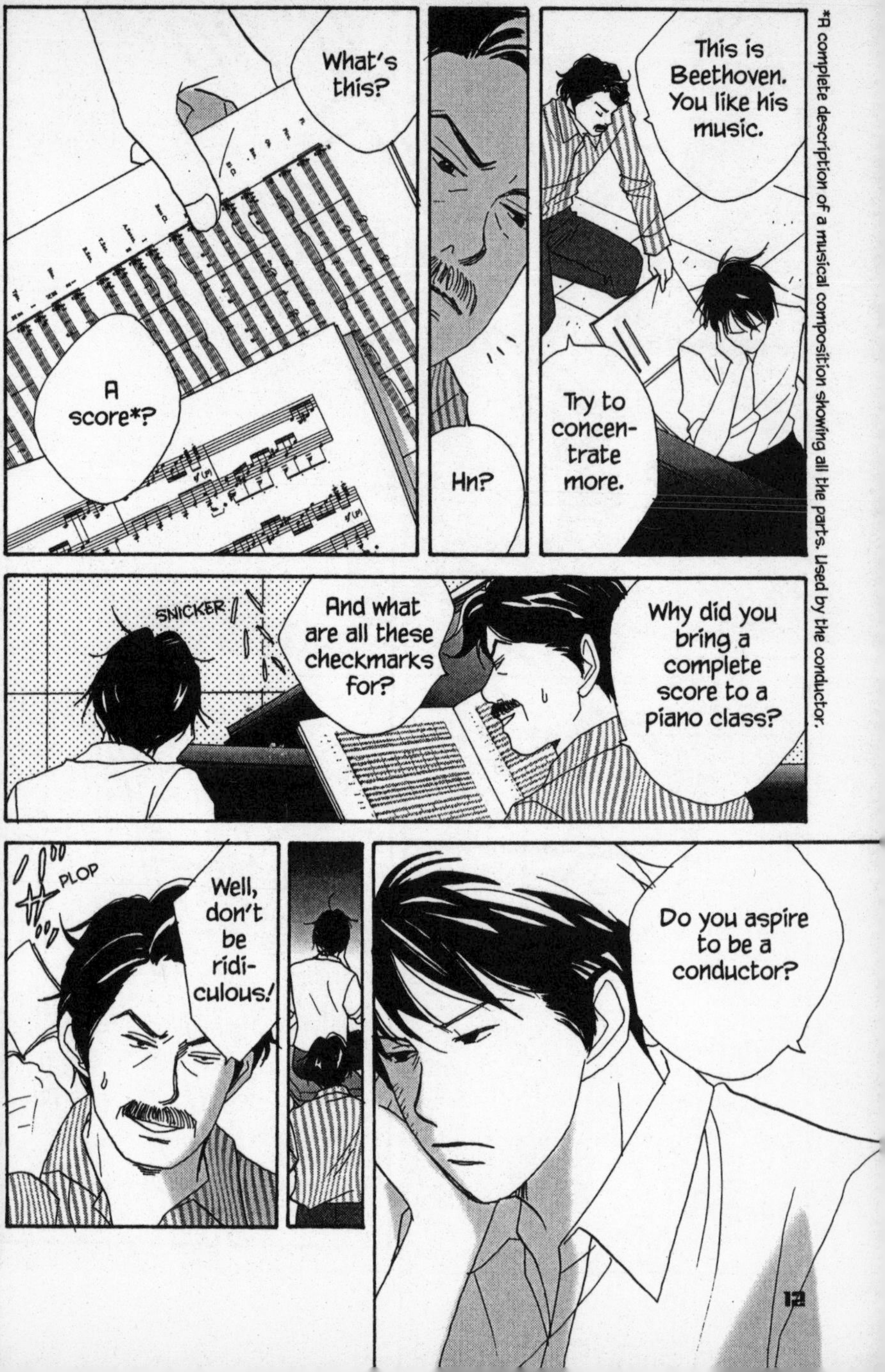
This is Beethoven. You like his music.
Try to concentrate more.
Hn?
What's this?
A score*?
Why did you bring a complete score to a piano class?
And what are all these checkmarks for?
SNICKER
Do you aspire to be a conductor?
Well, don't be ridiculous!
PLOP

*A complete description of a musical composition showing all the parts. Used by the conductor.

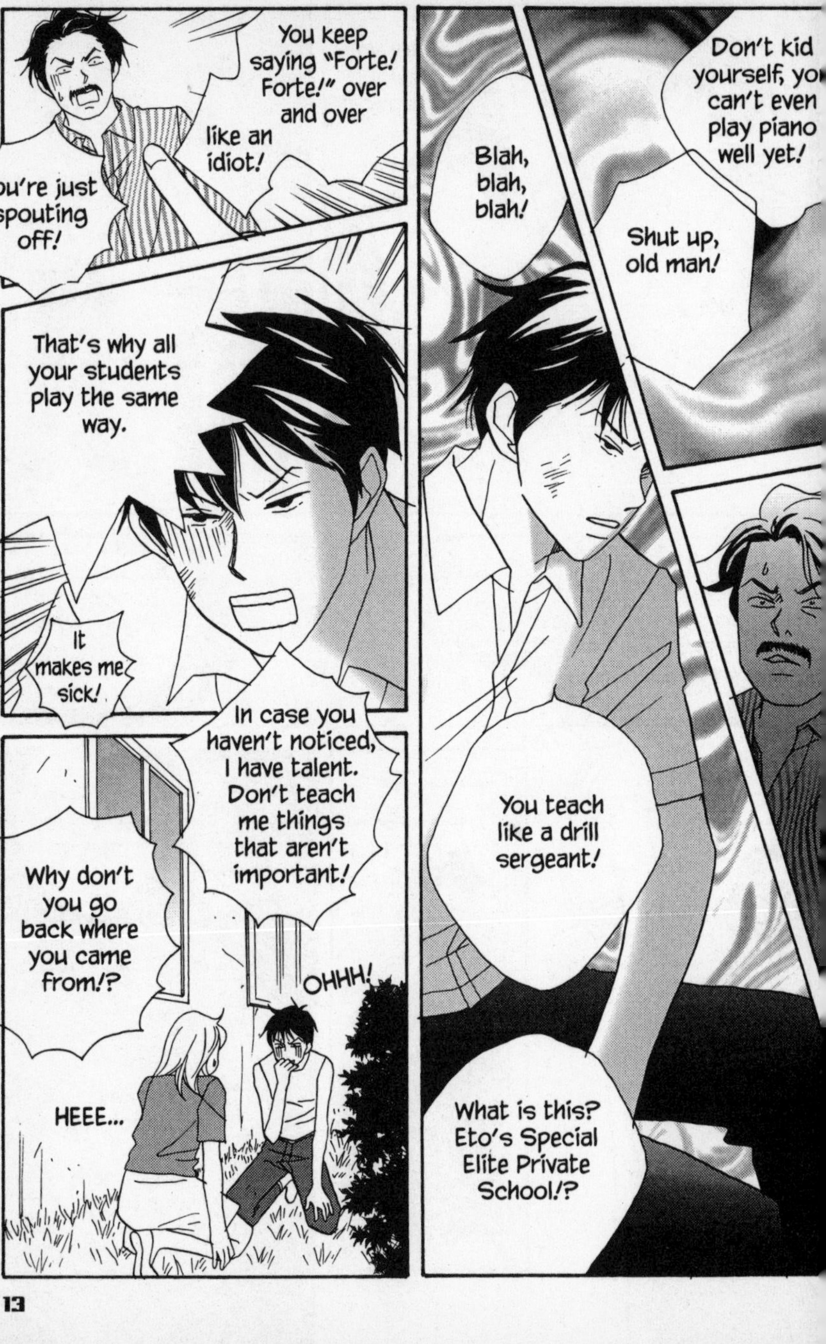
Don't kid yourself, yo can't even play piano well yet!
Shut up, old man!
Blah, blah, blah!
You teach like a drill sergeant!
What is this? Eto's Special Elite Private School!?
You keep saying "Forte! Forte!" over and over
like an idiot!
You're just spouting off!
That's why all your students play the same way.
It makes me sick!
In case you haven't noticed, I have talent. Don't teach me things that aren't important!
Why don't you go back where you came from!?
OHHH!
HEEE...

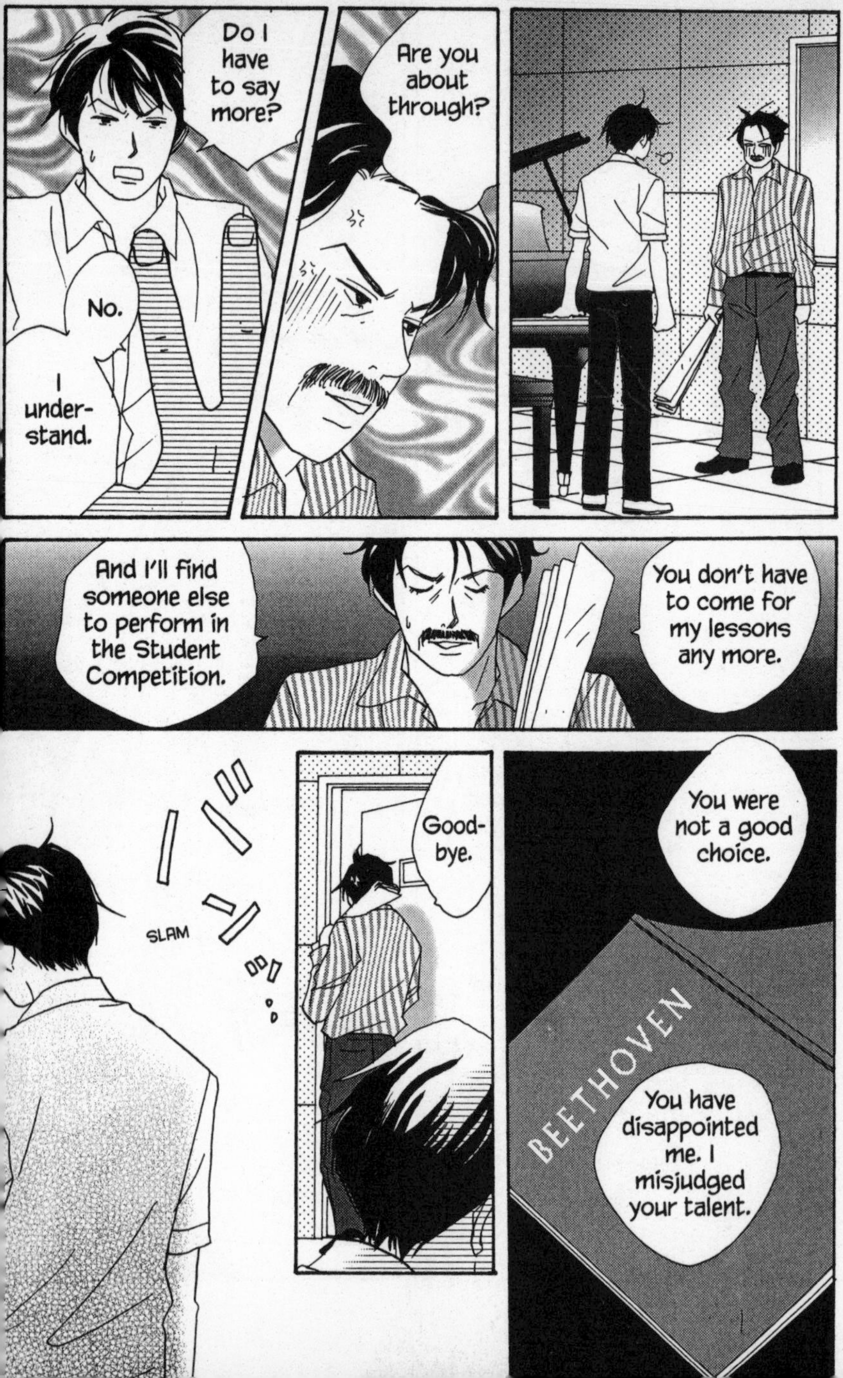
Are you about through?
Do I have to say more?
No.
I under-stand.
You don't have to come for my lessons any more.
And I'll find someone else to perform in the Student Competition.
You were not a good choice.
BEETHOVEN
You have disappointed me. I misjudged your talent.
Good-bye.
SLAM

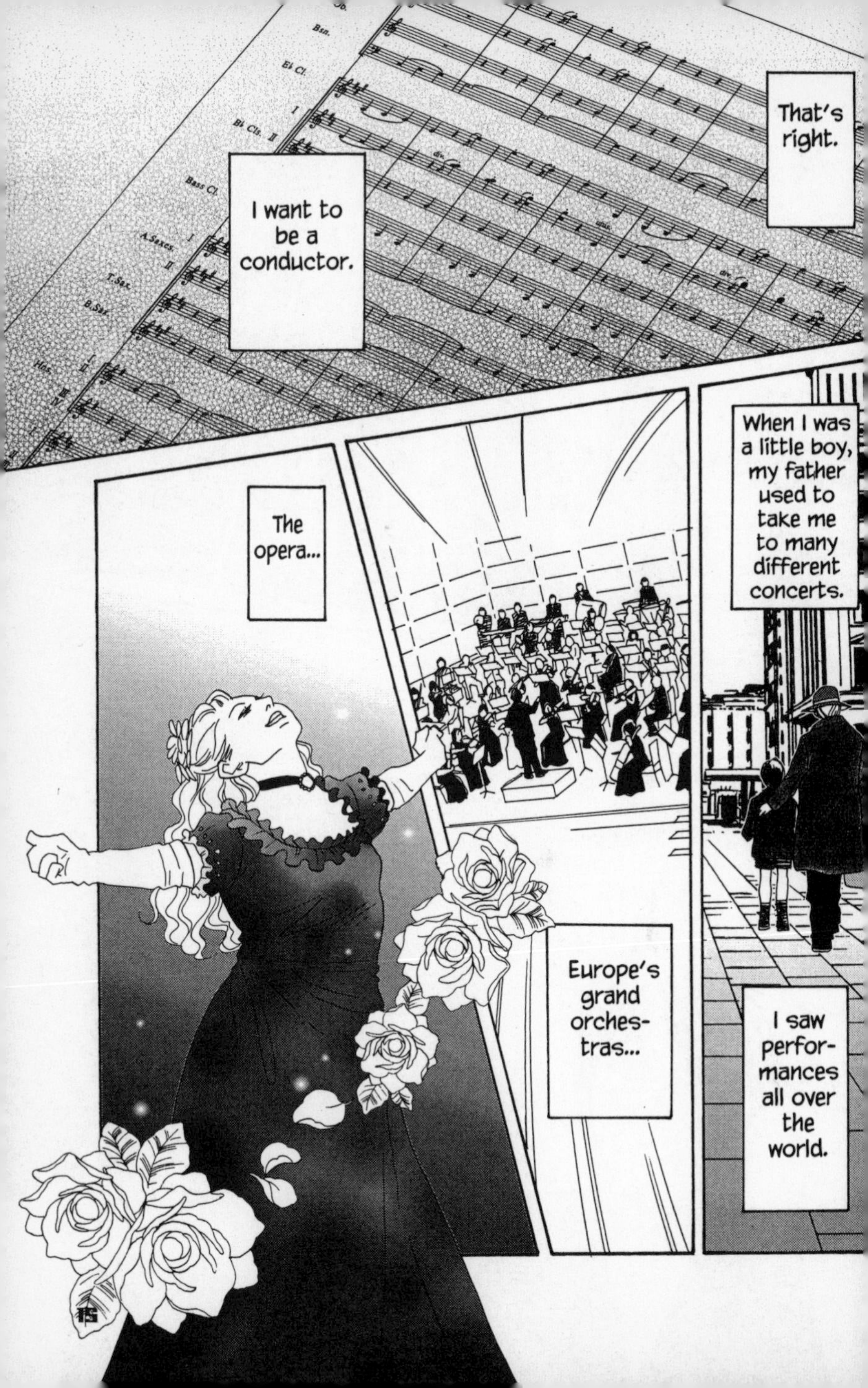
That's right.
I want to be a conductor.
When I was a little boy, my father used to take me to many different concerts.
I saw perfor-mances all over the world.
Europe's grand orches-tras...
The opera...

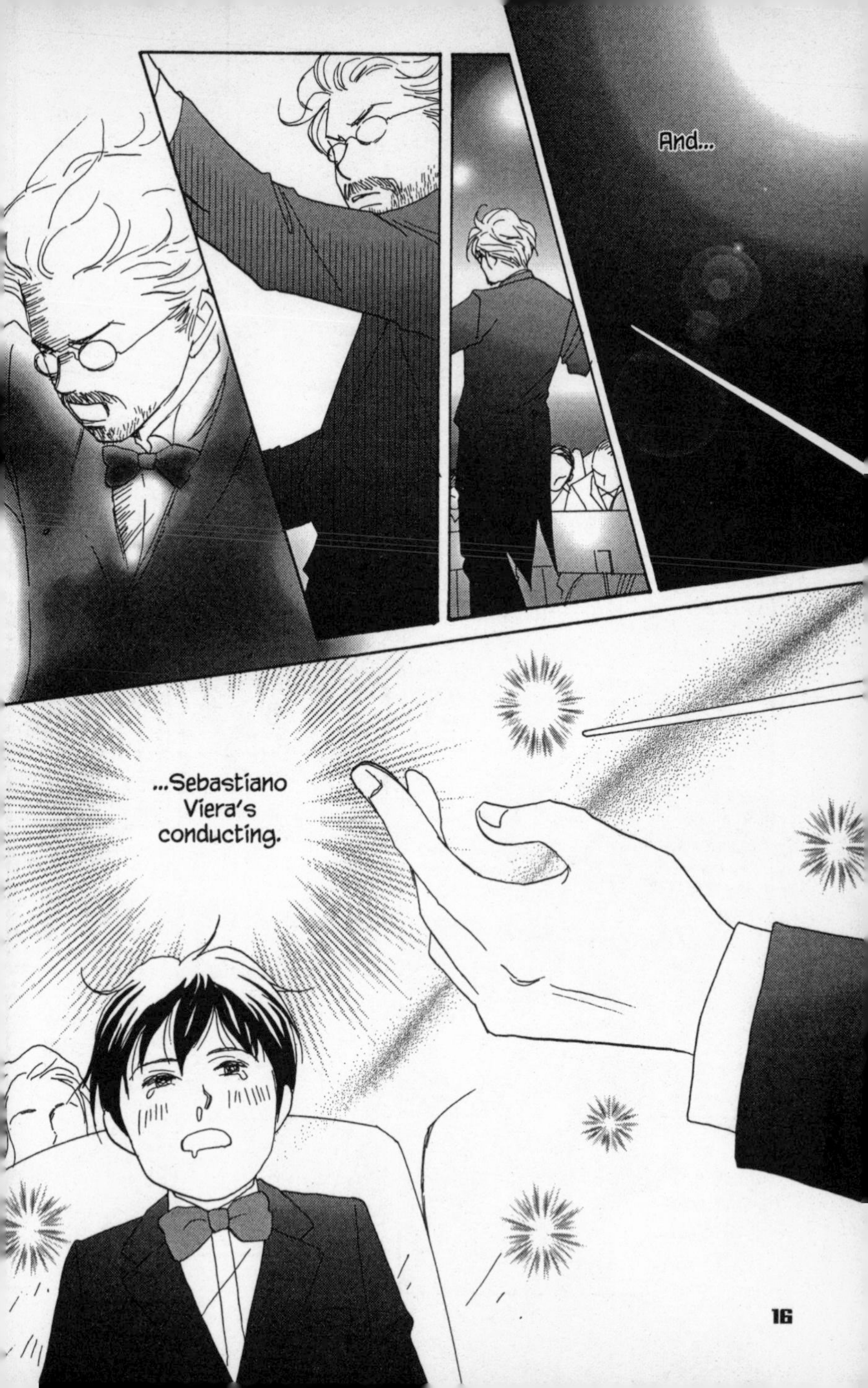
And...
...Sebastiano Viera's conducting.

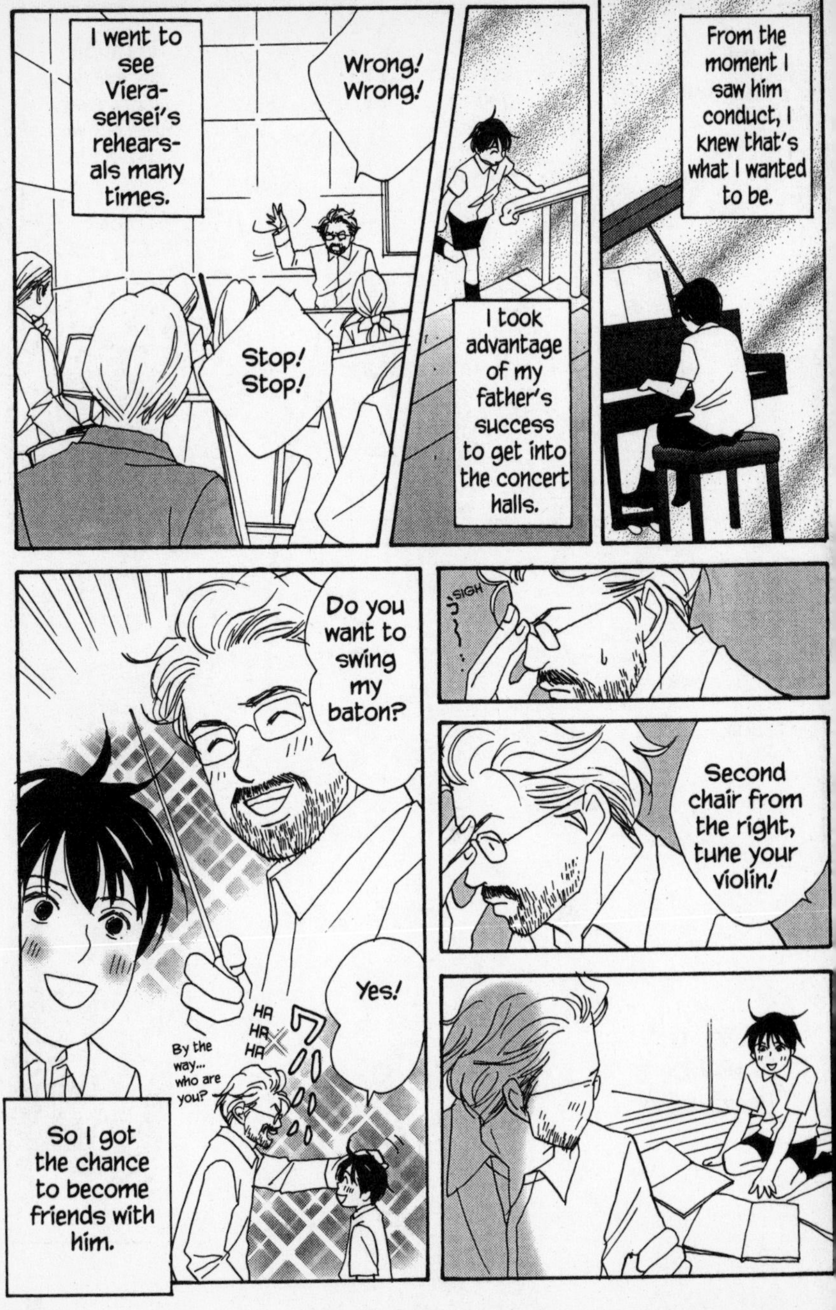
From the moment I saw him conduct, I knew that's what I wanted to be.
I took advantage of my father's success to get into the concert halls.
Wrong! Wrong!
I went to see Viera-sensei's rehearsals many times.
Stop! Stop!
SIGH
Second chair from the right, tune your violin!
Do you want to swing my baton?
Yes!
HA HA HA
By the way... who are you?
So I got the chance to become friends with him.

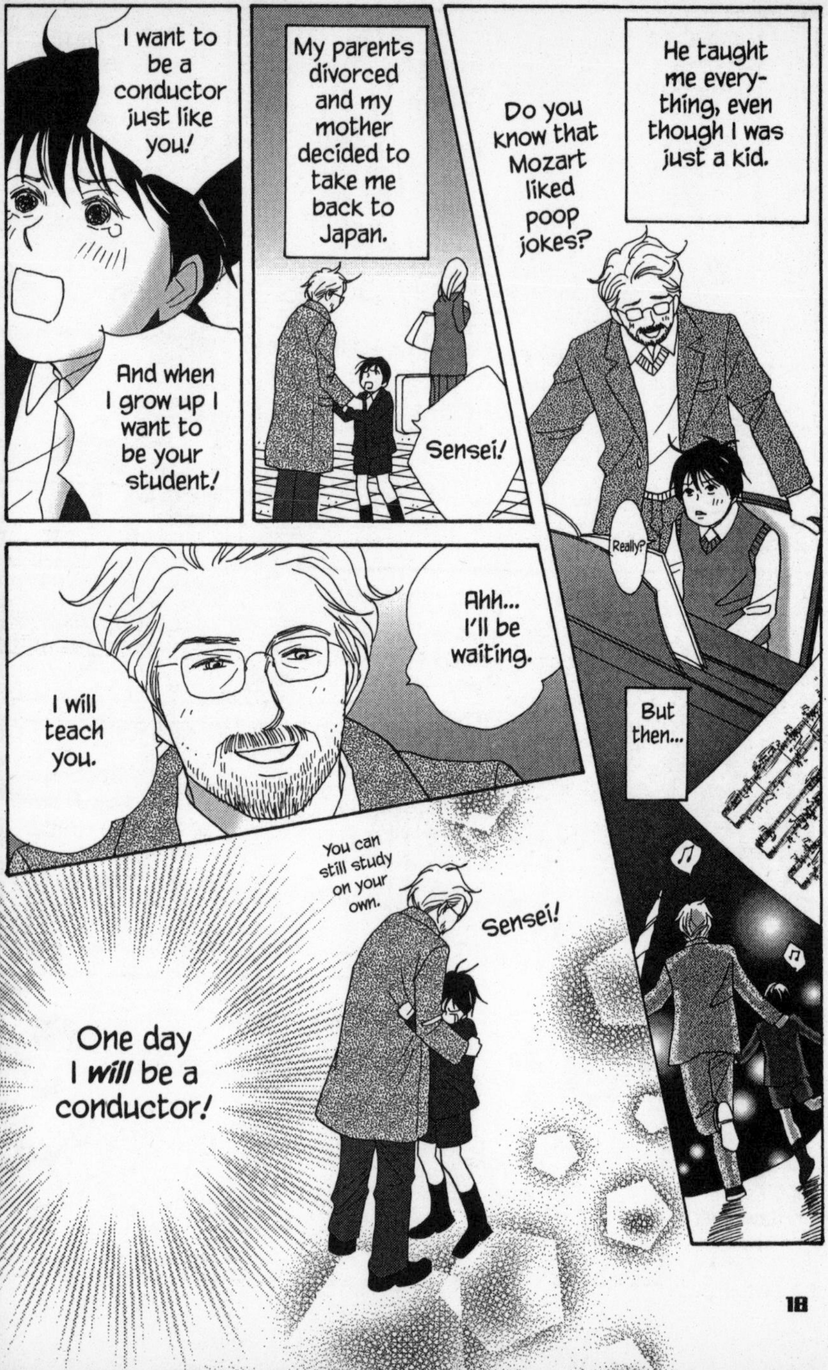
He taught me every-thing, even though I was just a kid.
Do you know that Mozart liked poop jokes?
Really?
But then...
My parents divorced and my mother decided to take me back to Japan.
Sensei!
I want to be a conductor just like you!
And when I grow up I want to be your student!
Ahh... I'll be waiting.
I will teach you.
Sensei!
You can still study on your own.
One day I *will* be a conductor!

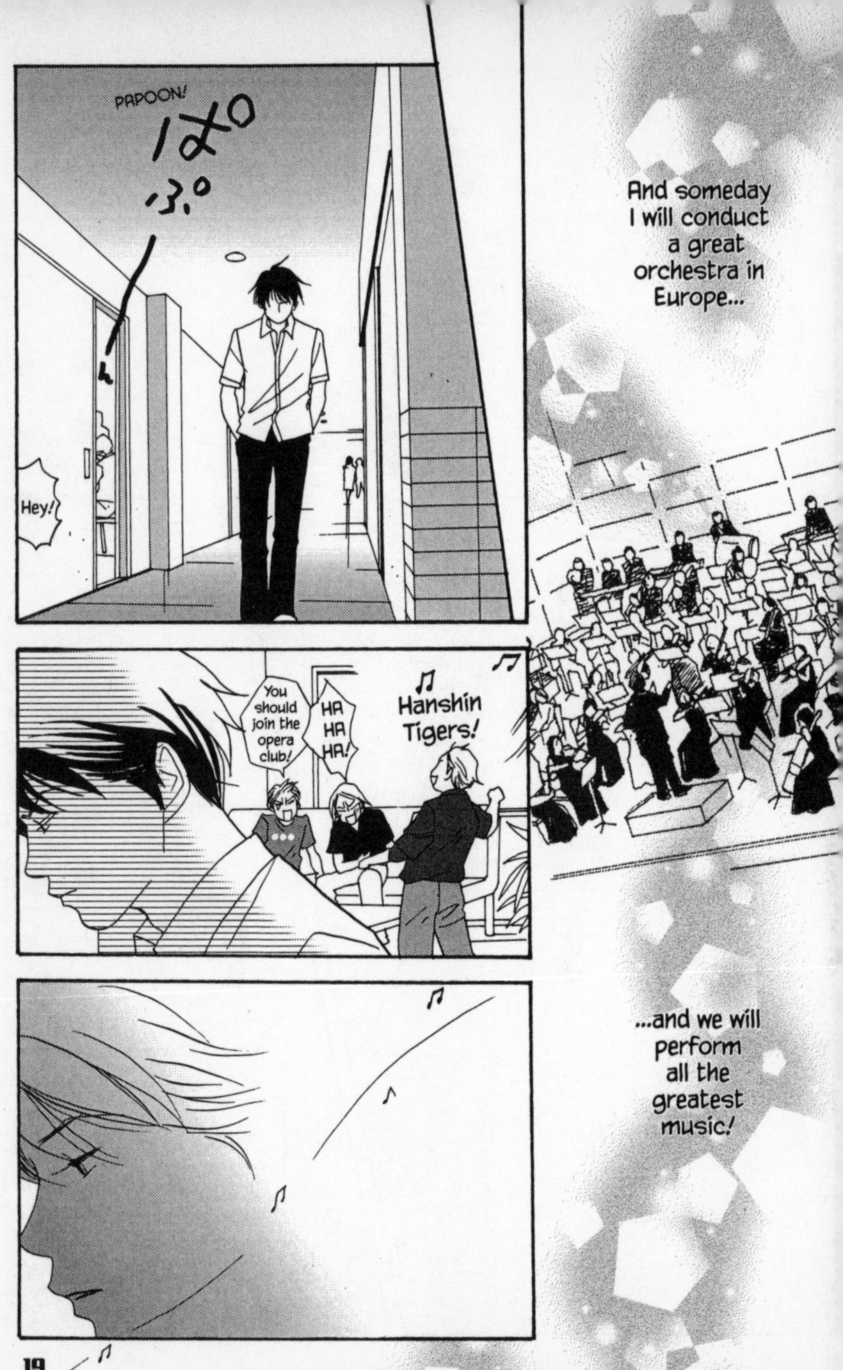
And someday I will conduct a great orchestra in Europe...
...and we will perform all the greatest music!
PAPOON!
Hey!
Hanshin Tigers!
HA HA HA!
You should join the opera club!

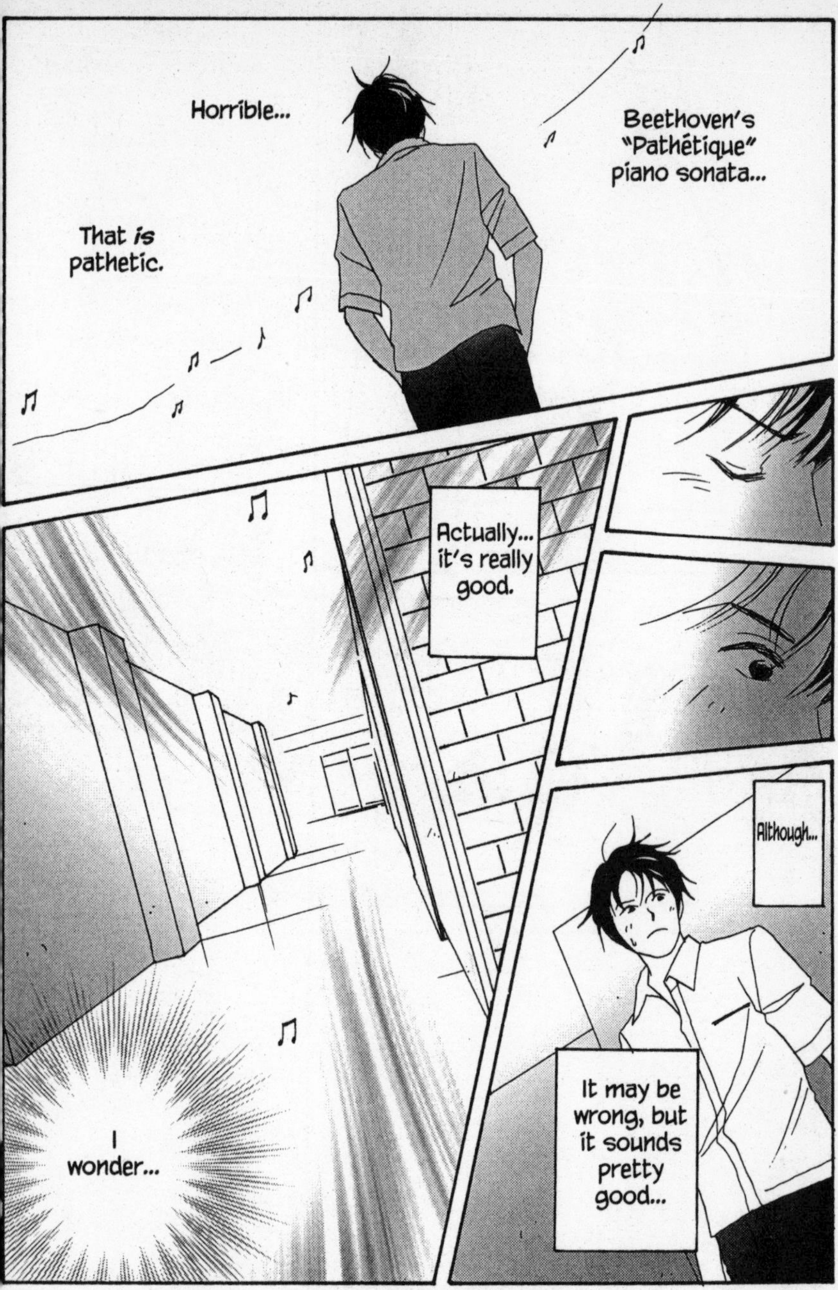
Beethoven's "Pathétique" piano sonata...
Horrible...
That *is* pathetic.
Although...
It may be wrong, but it sounds pretty good...
Actually... it's really good.
I wonder...

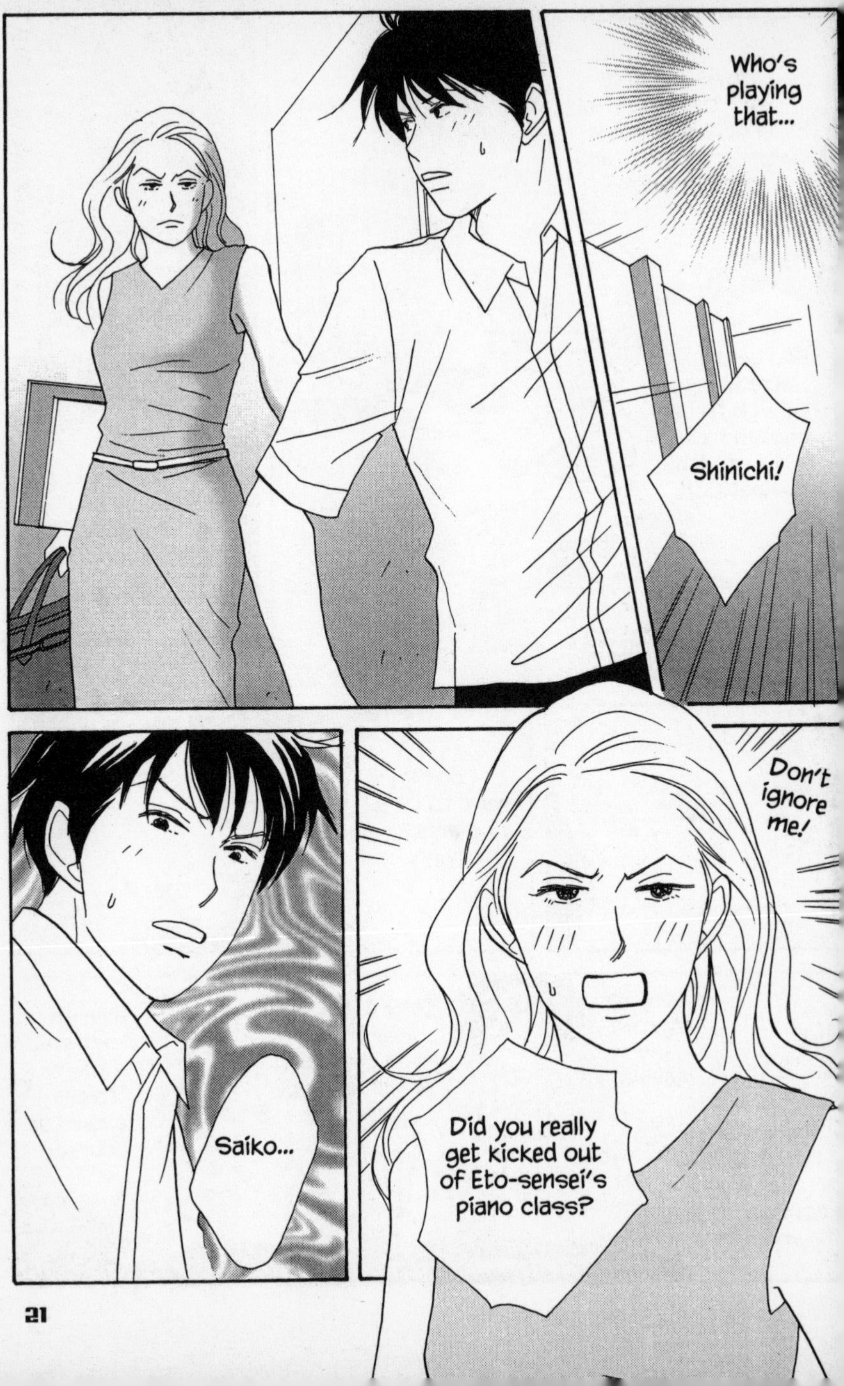
Who's playing that...
Shinichi!
Don't ignore me!
Did you really get kicked out of Eto-sensei's piano class?
Saiko...

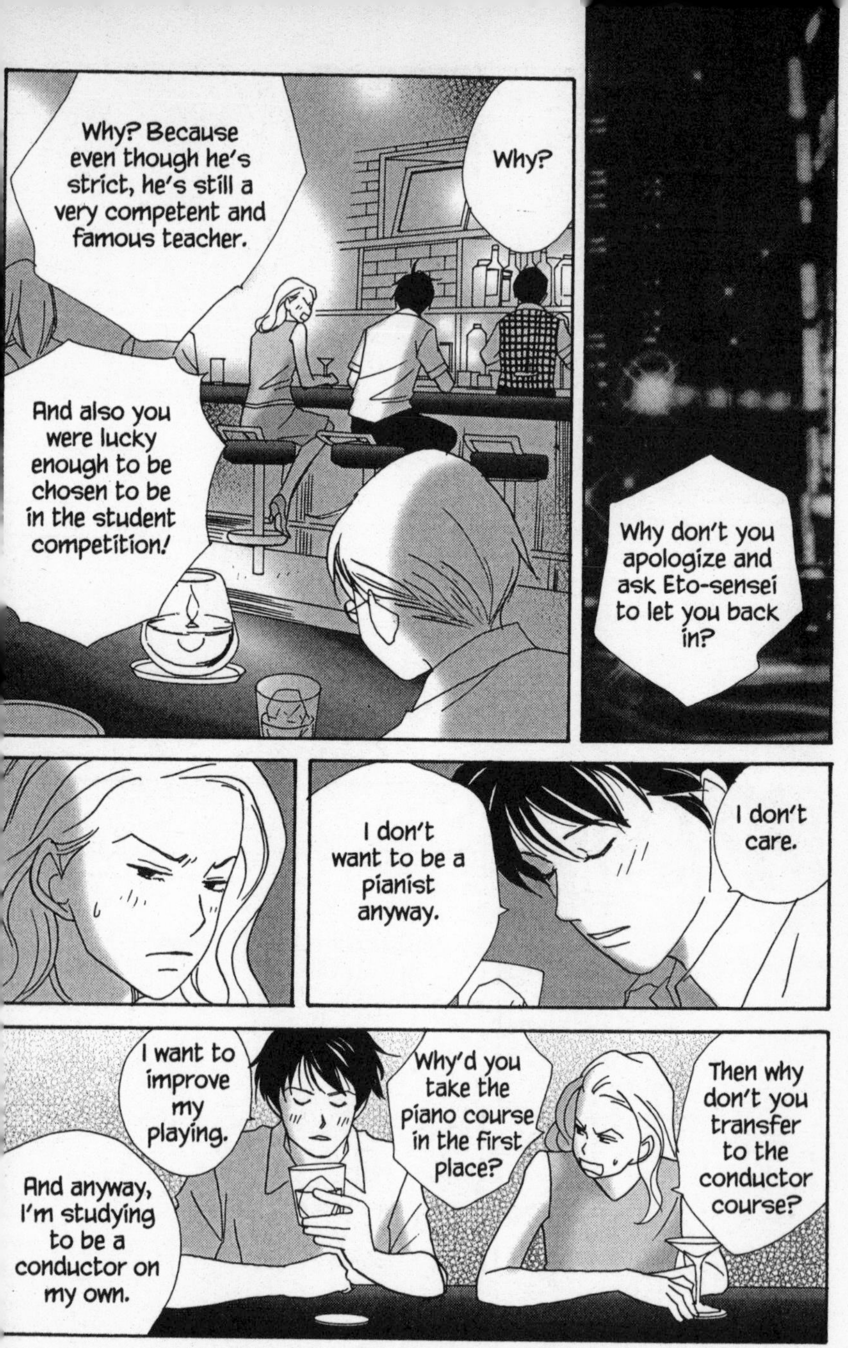
Why don't you apologize and ask Eto-sensei to let you back in?
Why?
Why? Because even though he's strict, he's still a very competent and famous teacher.
And also you were lucky enough to be chosen to be in the student competition!
I don't care.
I don't want to be a pianist anyway.
Then why don't you transfer to the conductor course?
Why'd you take the piano course in the first place?
I want to improve my playing.
And anyway, I'm studying to be a conductor on my own.

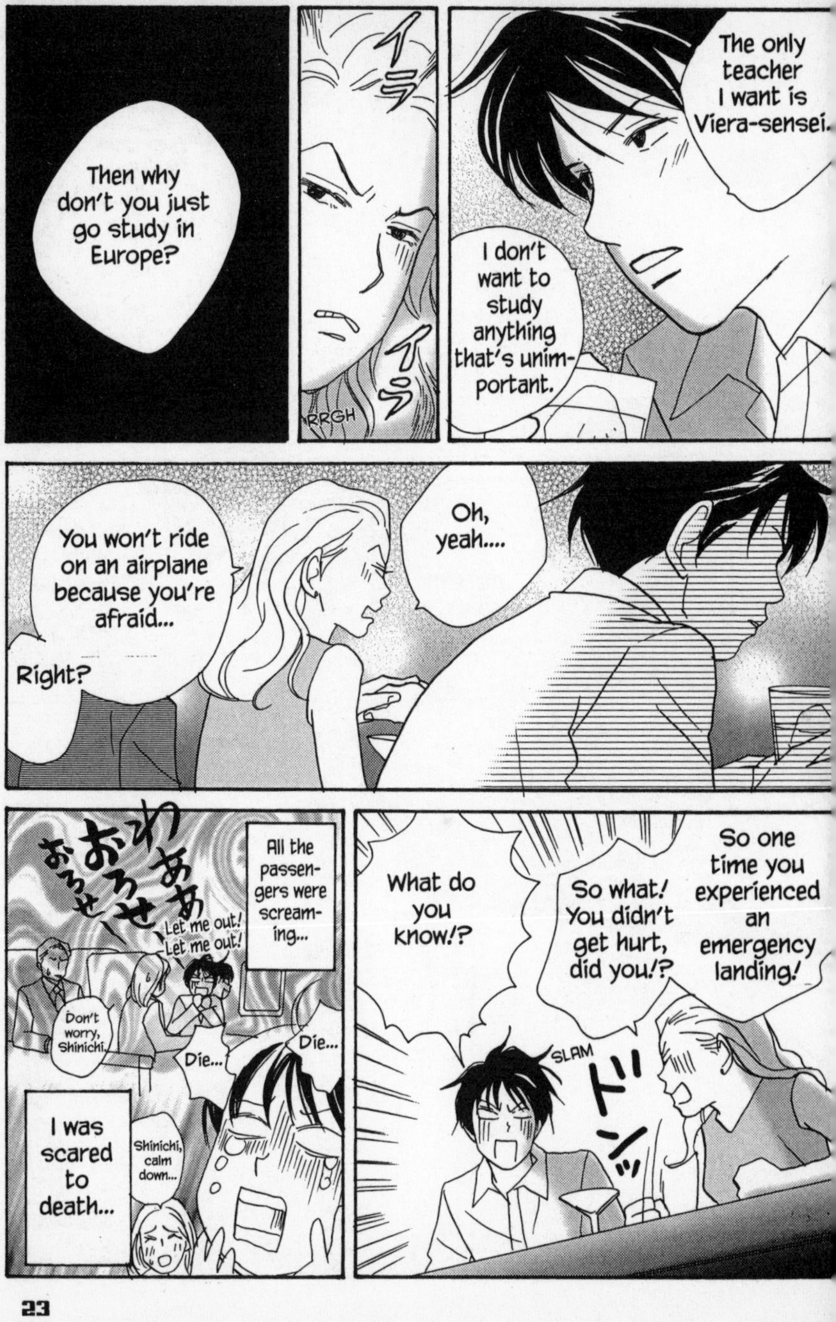
The only teacher I want is Viera-sensei.
I don't want to study anything that's unimportant.
イラ
イラ
RRGH
Then why don't you just go study in Europe?
Oh, yeah....
You won't ride on an airplane because you're afraid...
Right?
So one time you experienced an emergency landing!
So what! You didn't get hurt, did you!?
What do you know!?
SLAM
ドンッ
All the passengers were screaming...
Let me out! Let me out!
Don't worry, Shinichi.
Die...
Die...
I was scared to death...
Shinichi, calm down...

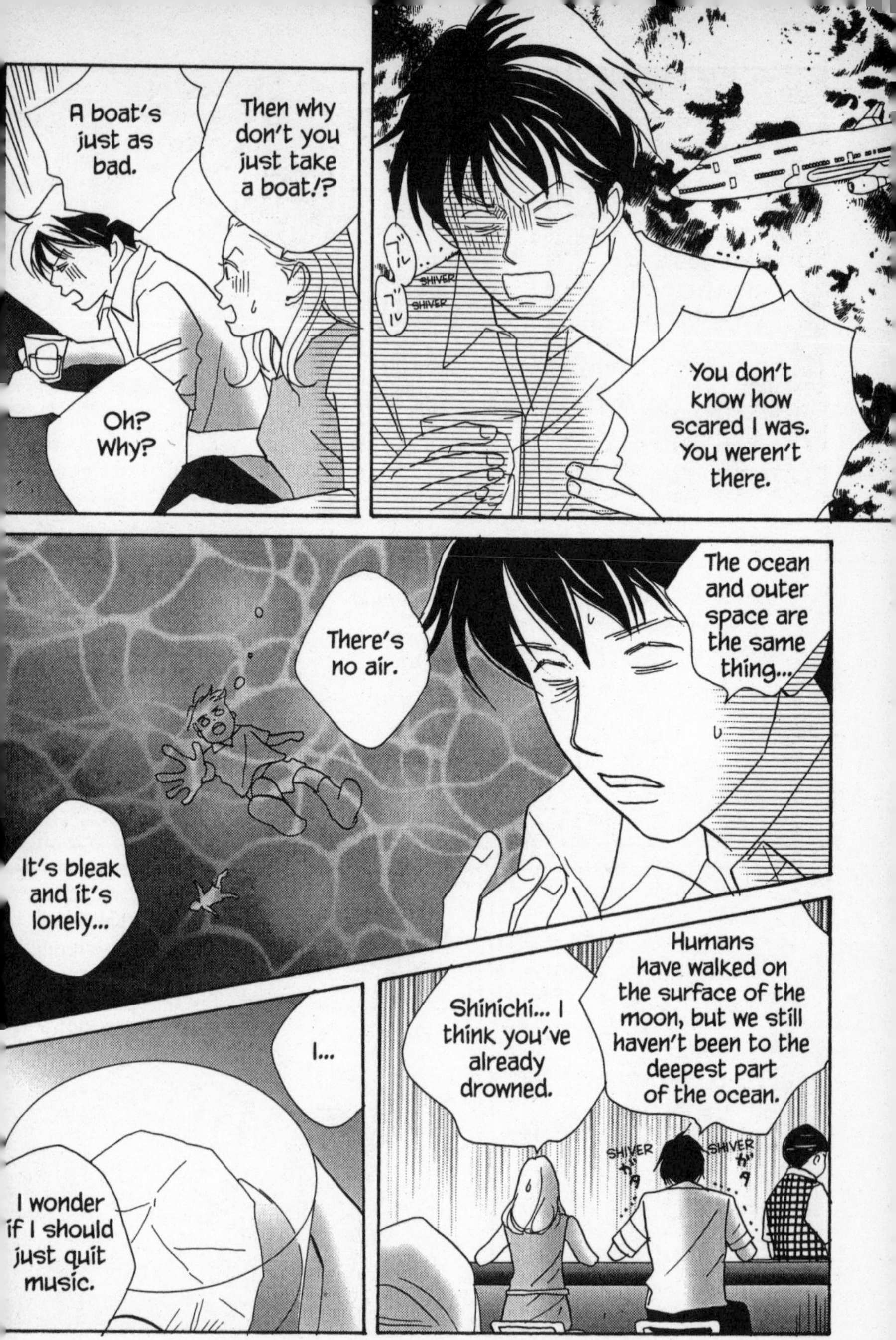
ブル
SHIVER
ブル
SHIVER
You don't know how scared I was. You weren't there.
Then why don't you just take a boat!?
A boat's just as bad.
Oh? Why?
The ocean and outer space are the same thing...
There's no air.
It's bleak and it's lonely...
Humans have walked on the surface of the moon, but we still haven't been to the deepest part of the ocean.
Shinichi... I think you've already drowned.
SHIVER
SHIVER
I...
I wonder if I should just quit music.

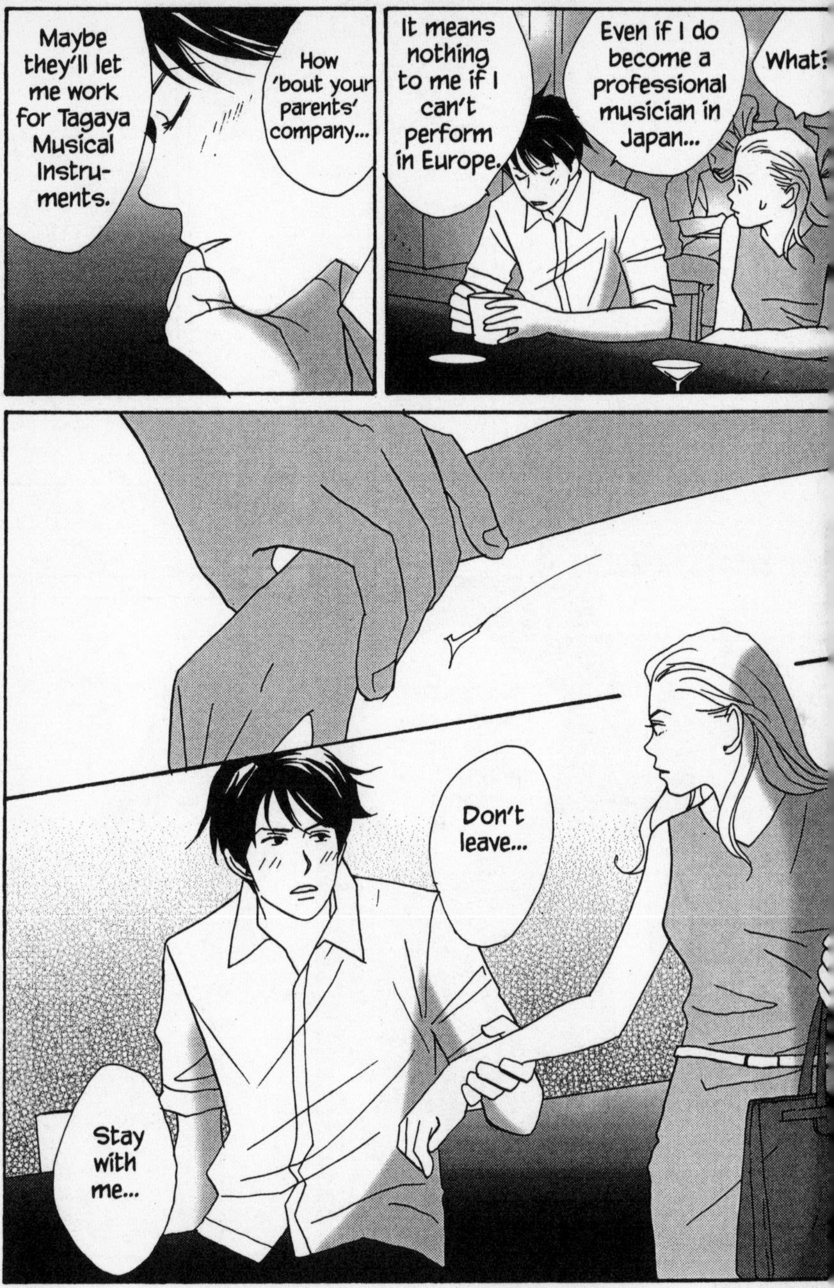
What?
Even if I do become a professional musician in Japan...
It means nothing to me if I can't perform in Europe.
How 'bout your parents' company...
Maybe they'll let me work for Tagaya Musical Instru-ments.
Don't leave...
Stay with me...

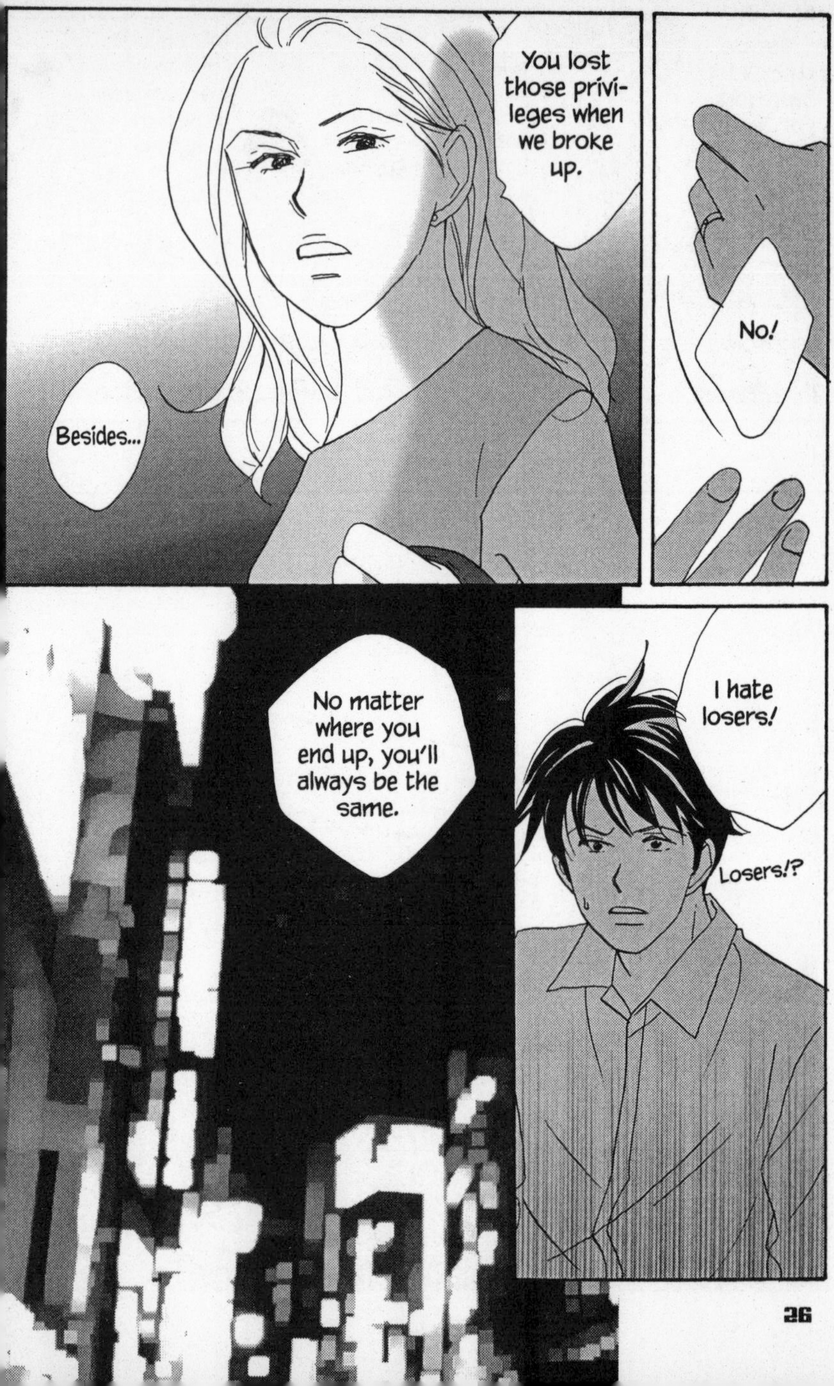
No!
You lost those privileges when we broke up.
Besides...
I hate losers!
Losers!?
No matter where you end up, you'll always be the same.

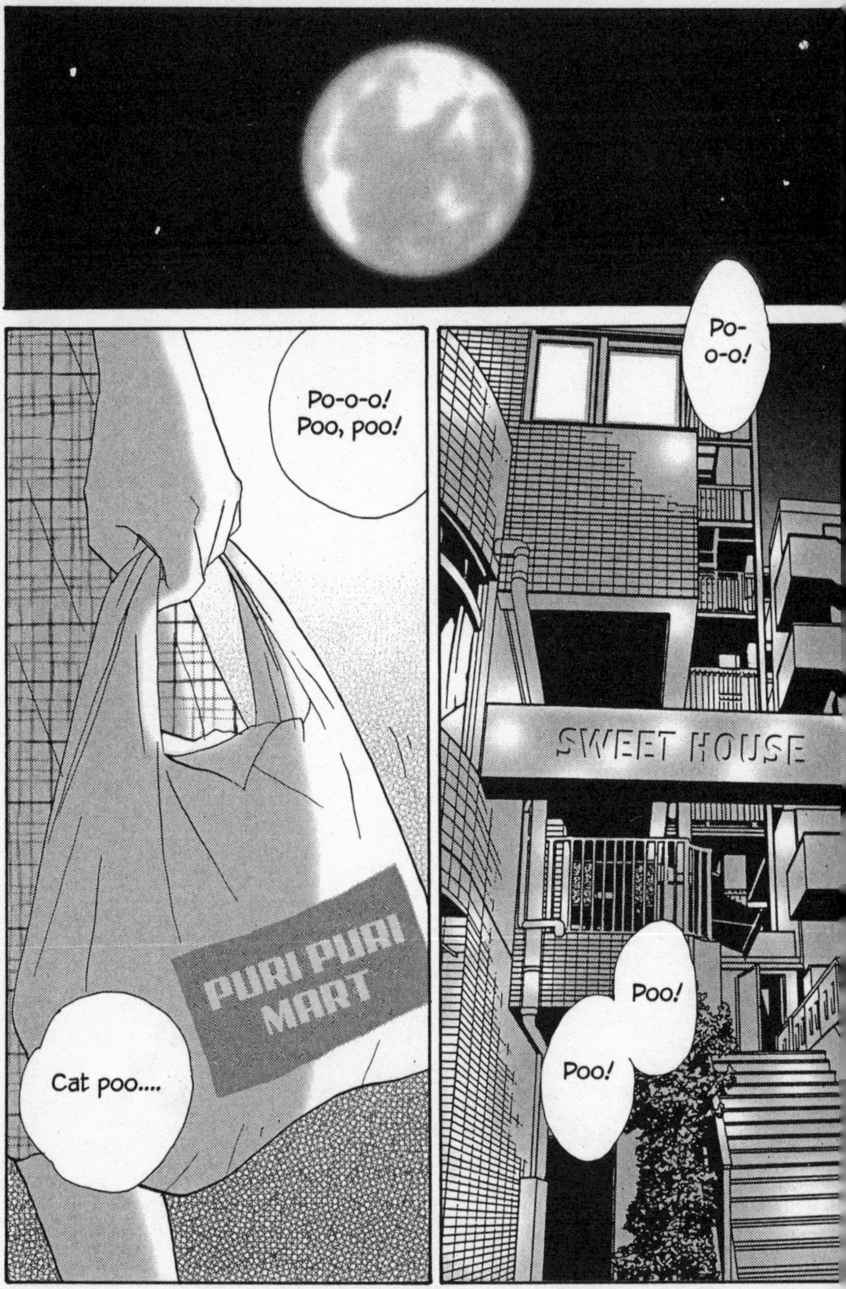
Po-o-o!
SWEET HOUSE
Poo!
Poo!
Po-o-o! Poo, poo!
PURI PURI MART
Cat poo....

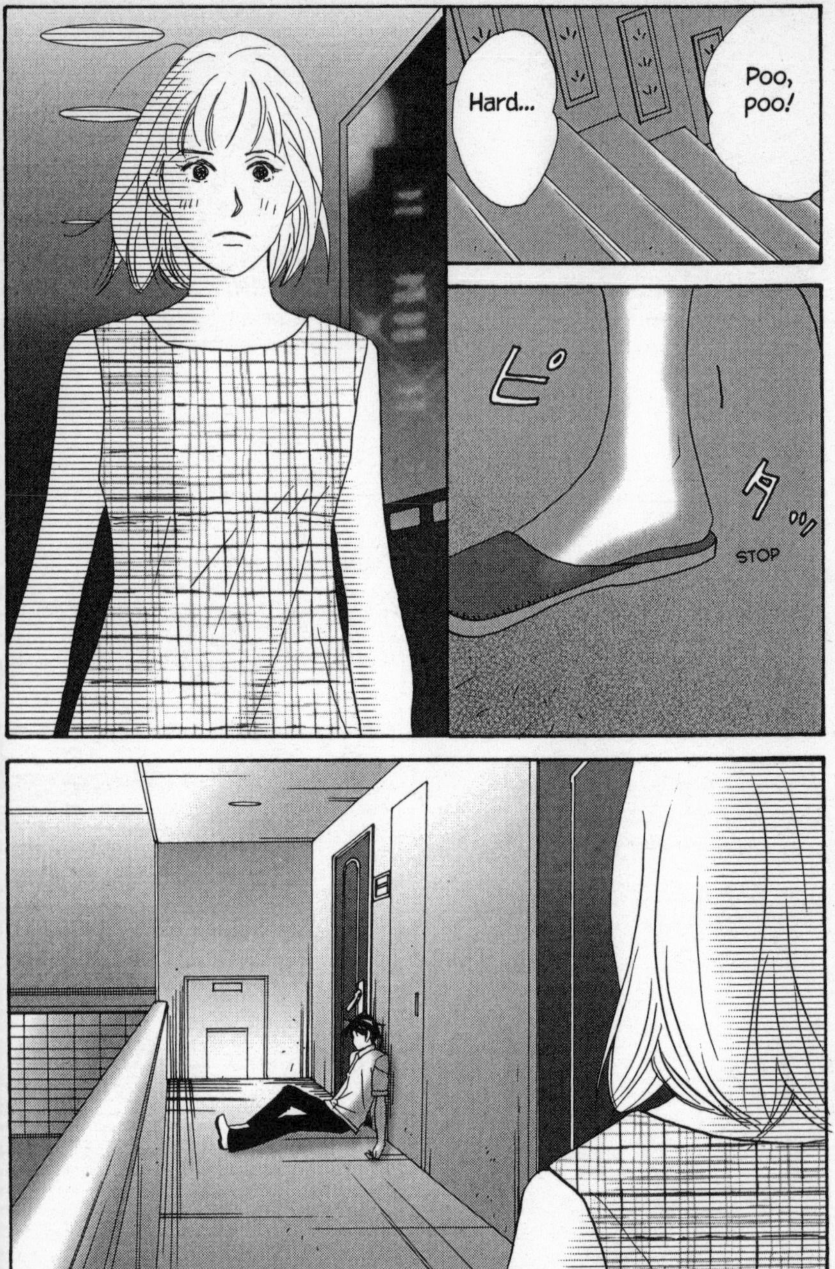
Poo, poo!
Hard...
ピタッ
STOP

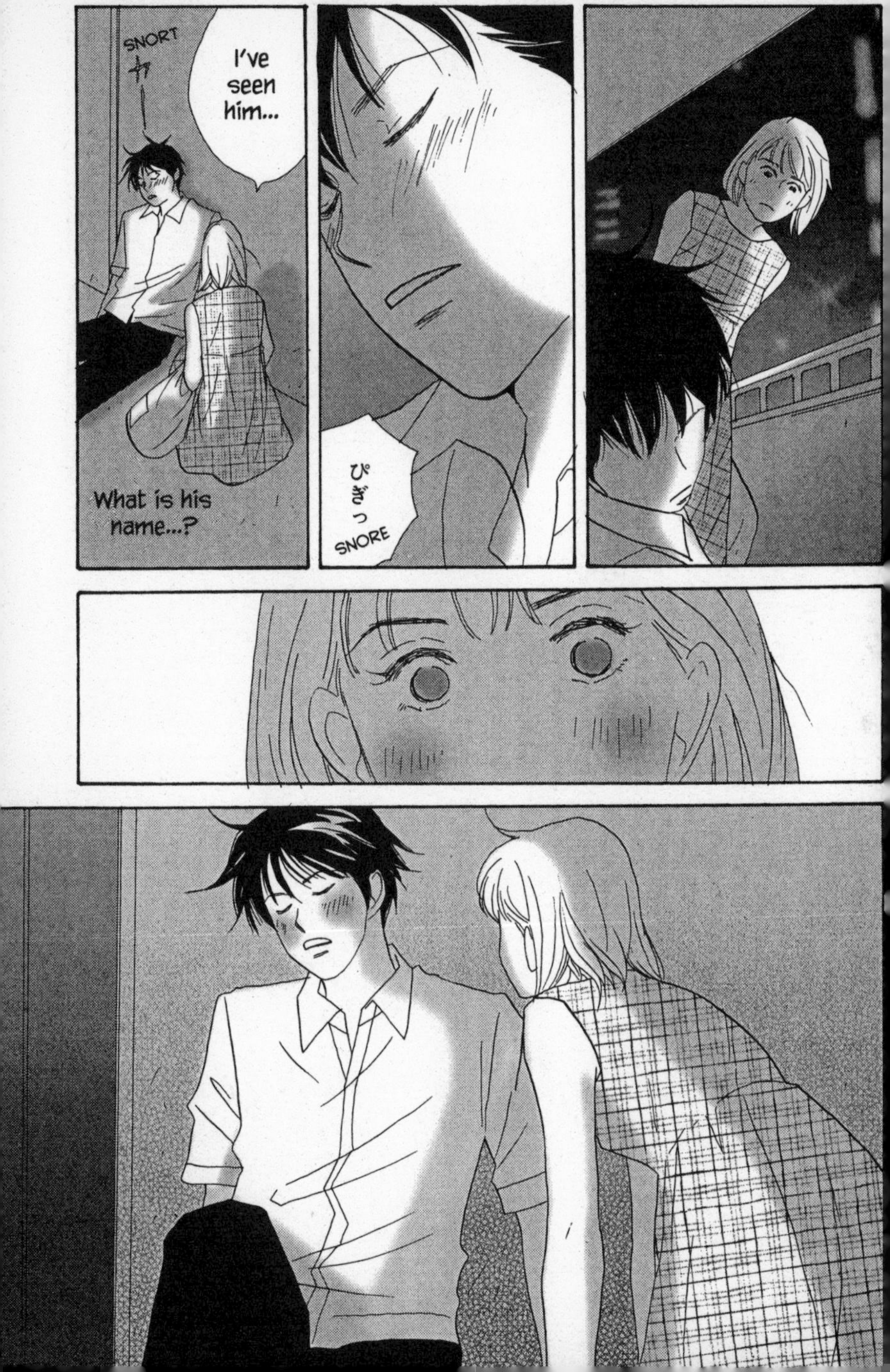
ぴぎっ
SNORE
SNORT
I've seen him...
What is his name...?

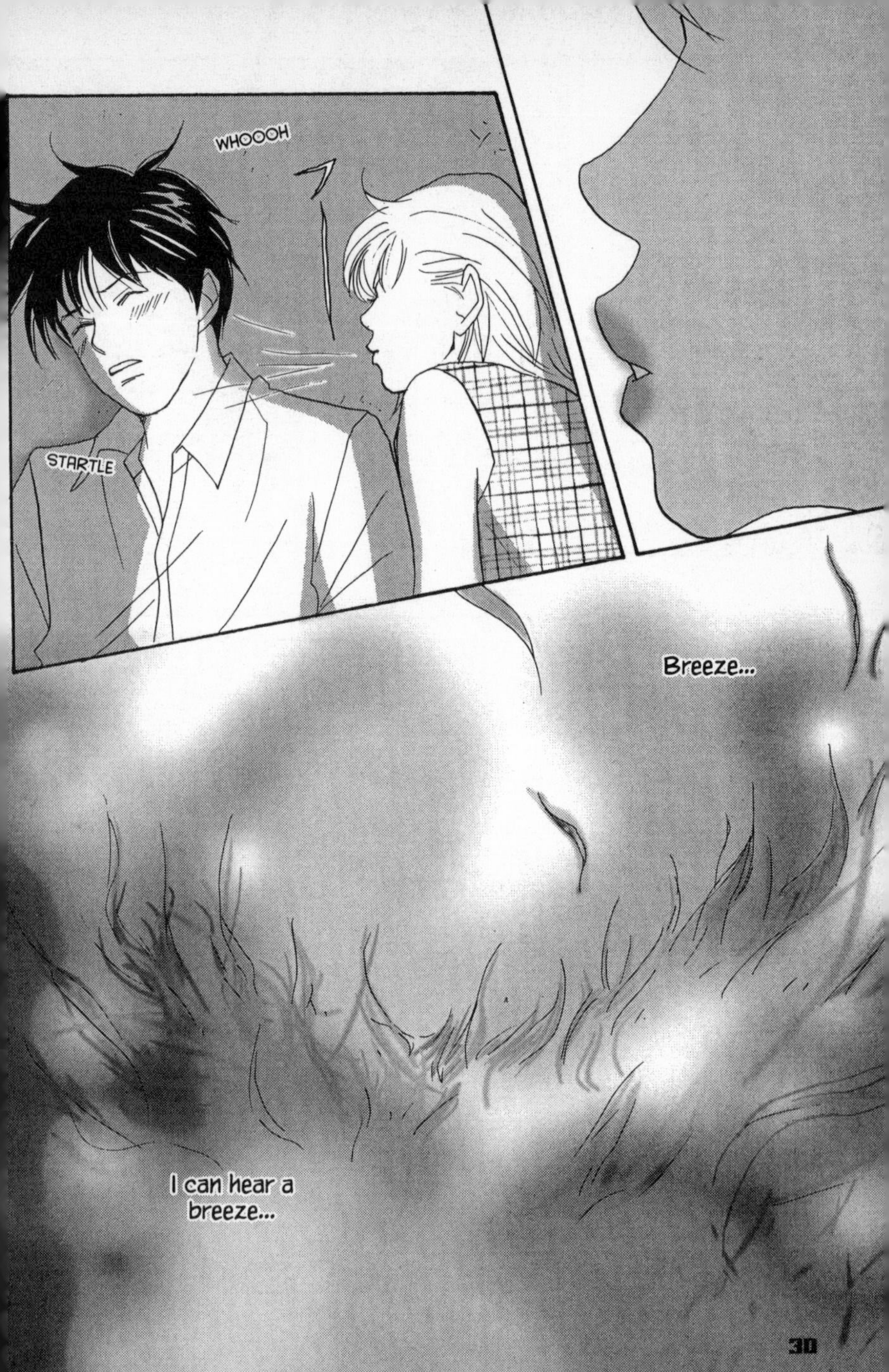
WHOOOOH
STARTLE
Breeze...
I can hear a breeze...

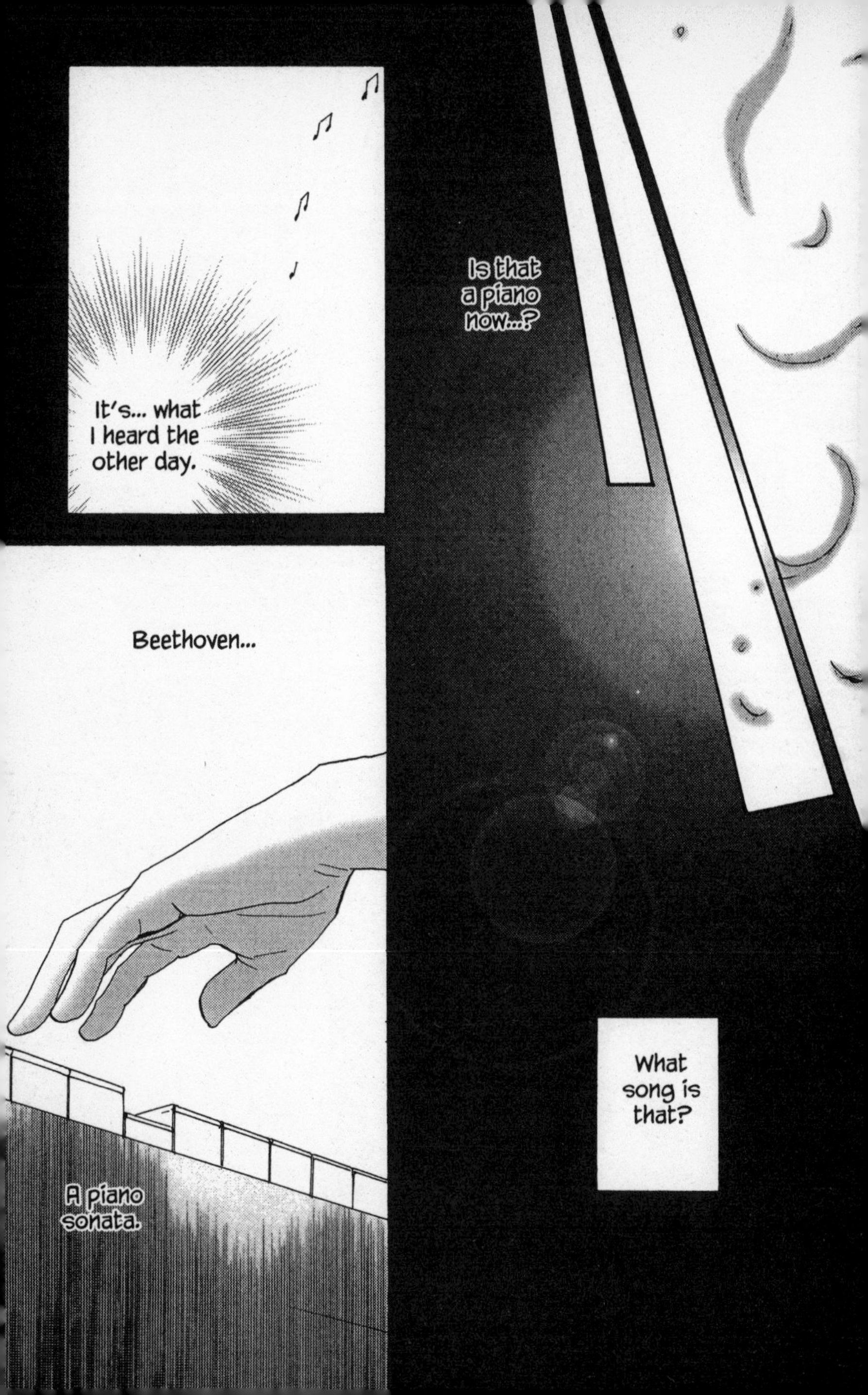
Is that a piano now...?
What song is that?
It's... what I heard the other day.
Beethoven...
A piano sonata.

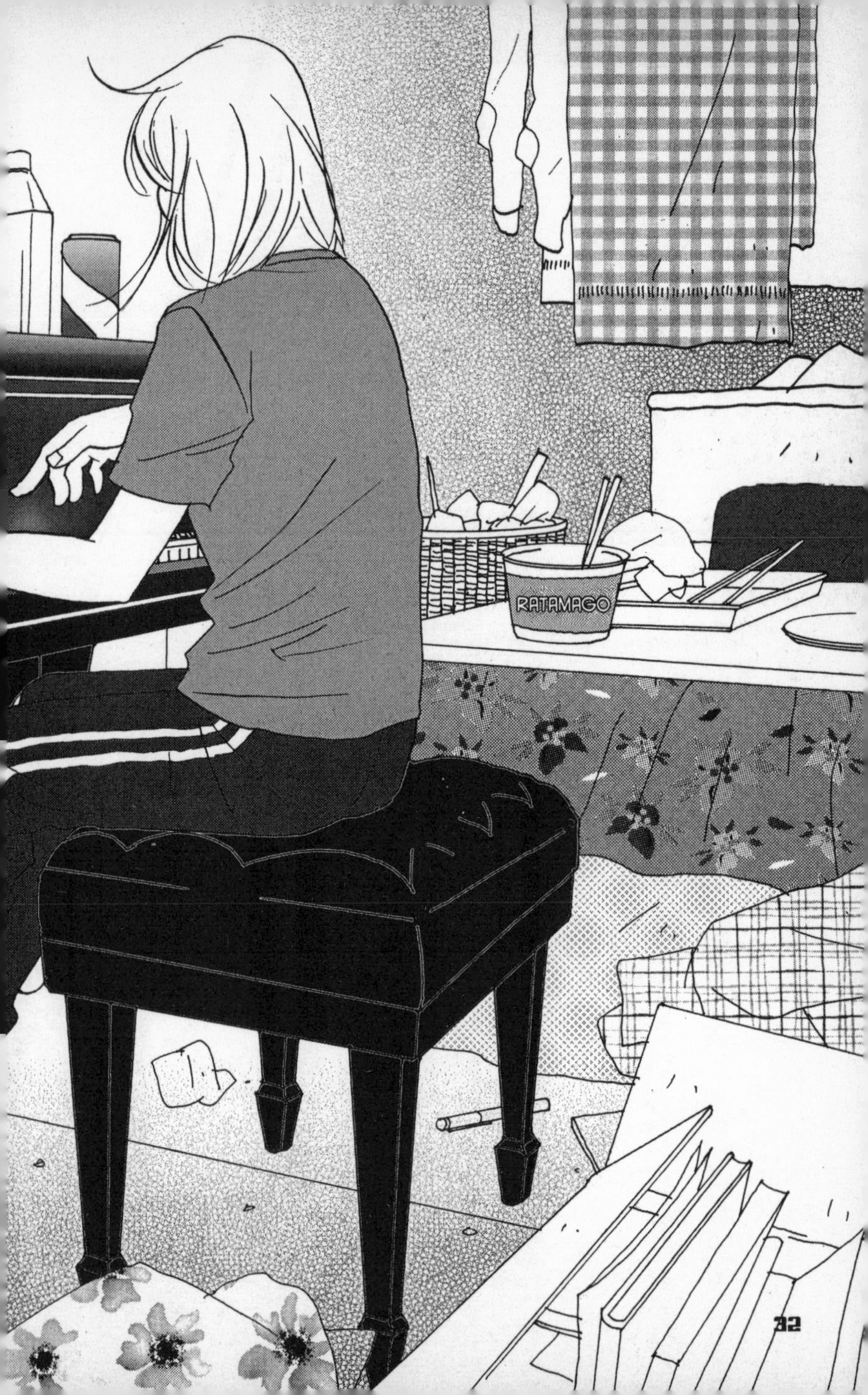
RATAMAGO

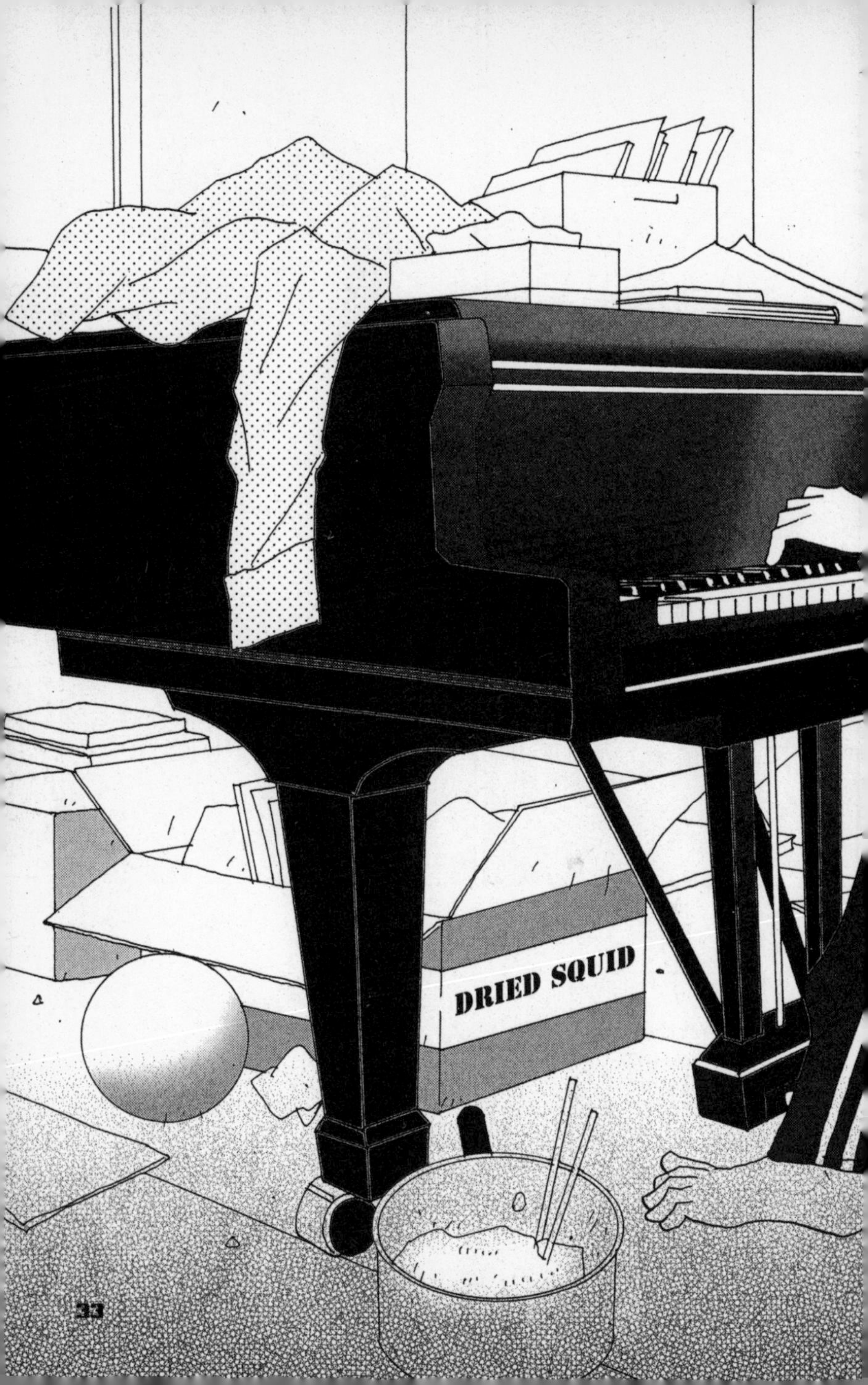
DRIED SQUID

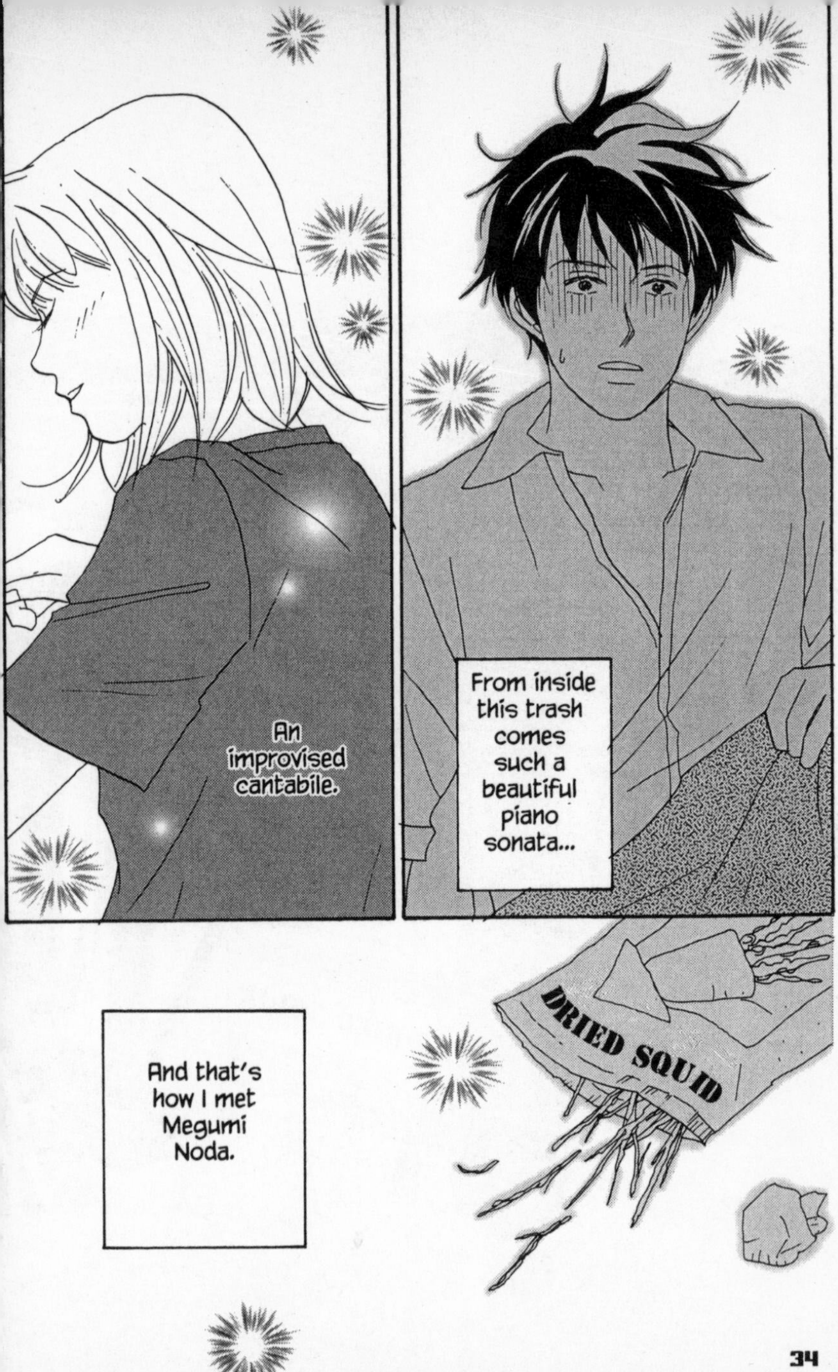
From inside this trash comes such a beautiful piano sonata...
An improvised cantabile.
DRIED SQUID
And that's how I met Megumi Noda.

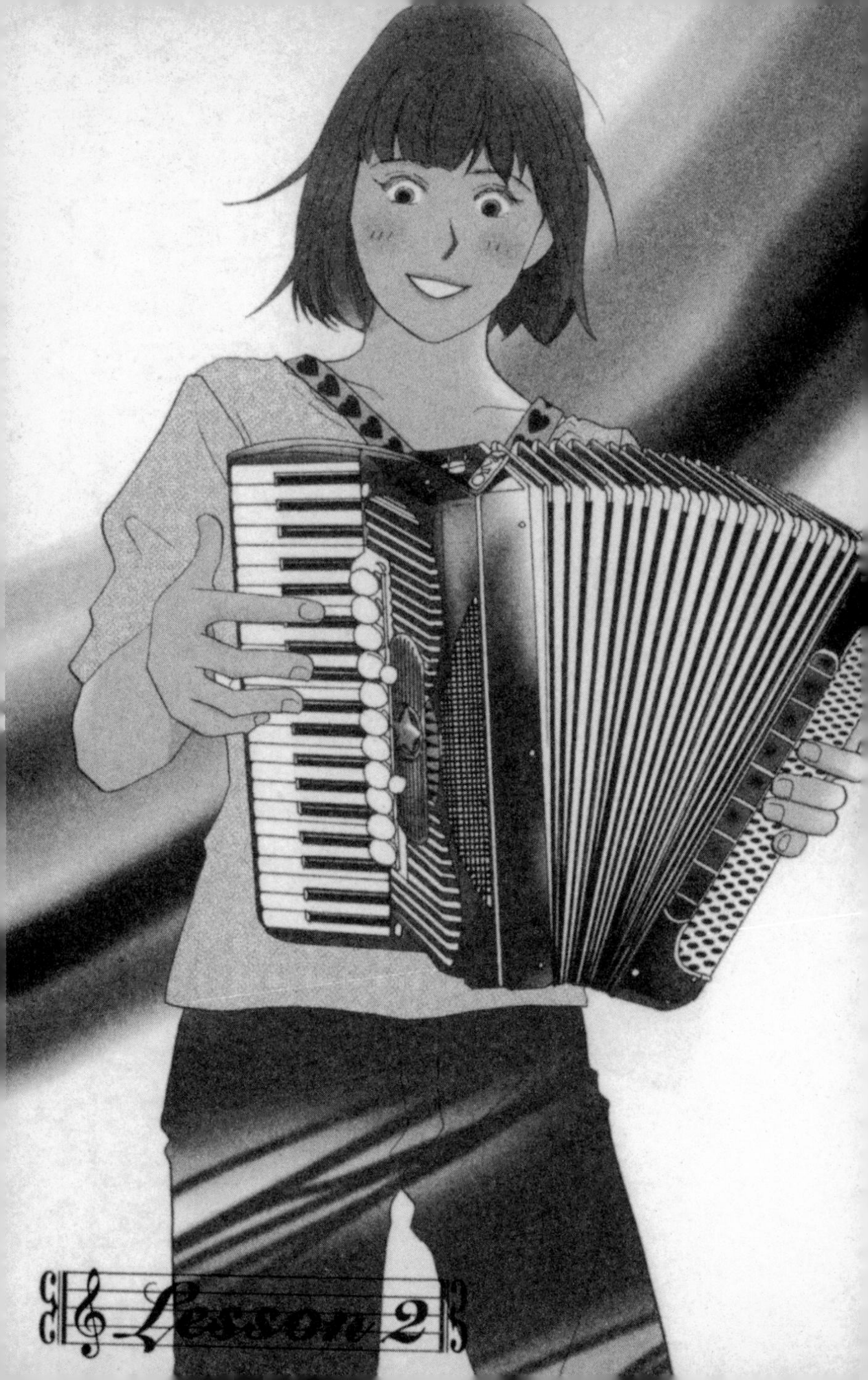
Lesson 2

NODAME CANTABILE

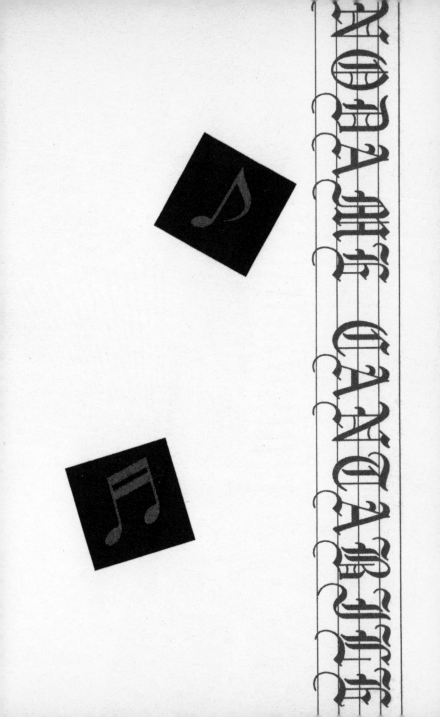

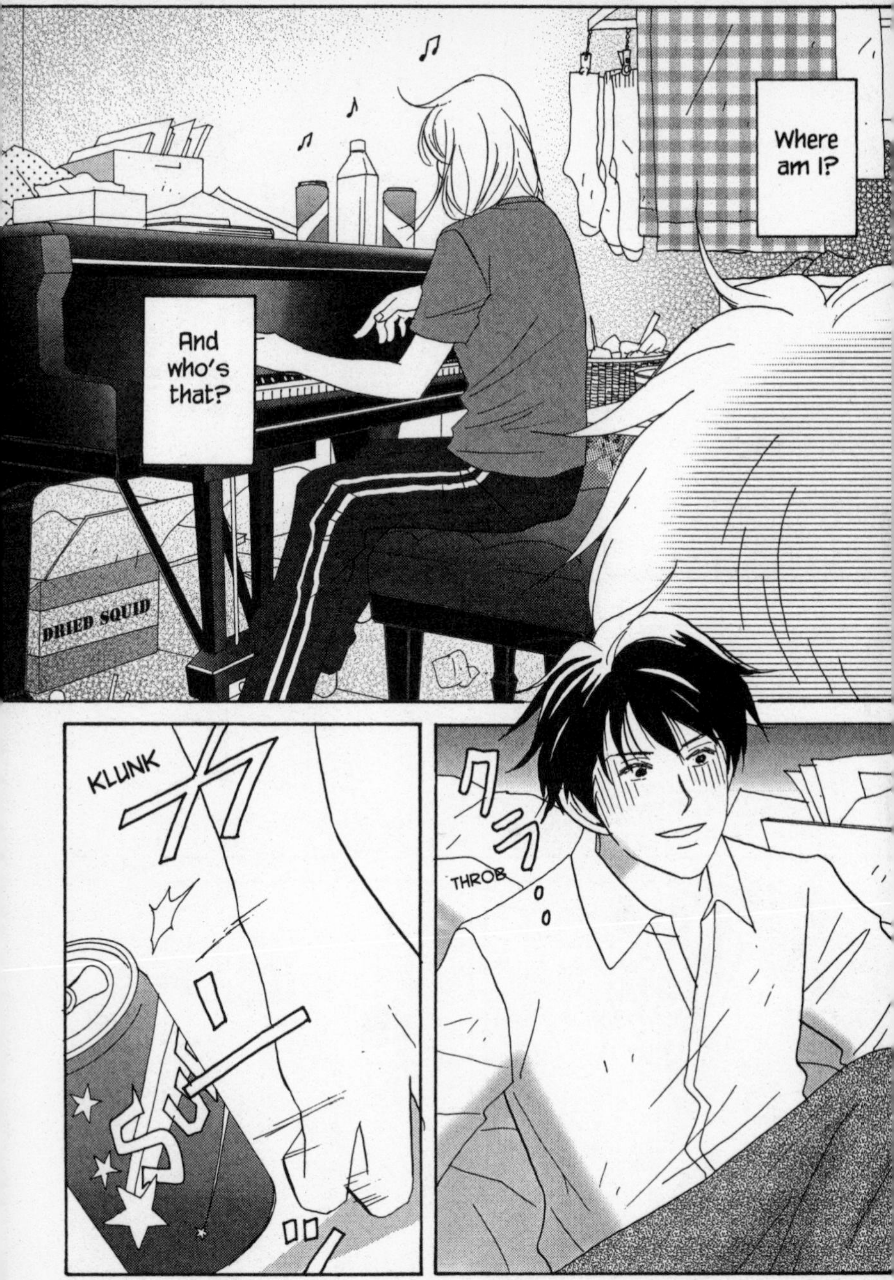
Where am I?
And who's that?
DRIED SQUID
THROB
KLUNK

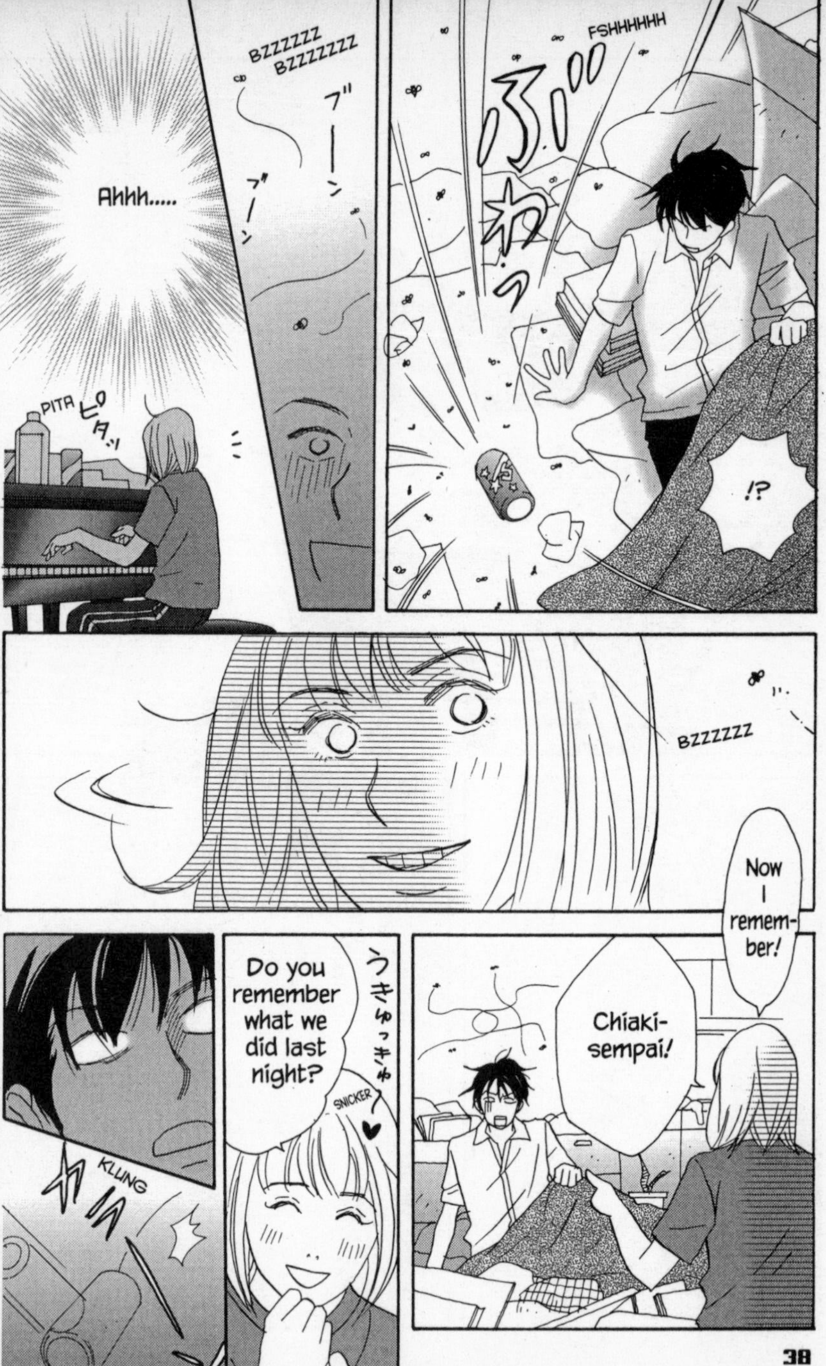

FSHHHHHH
ふわっ
!?
BZZZZZZ
BZZZZZZZ
ブーン
ブーン
Ahhh.....
PITA
ピタッ
BZZZZZZ
Now I remember!
Chiaki-sempai!
Do you remember what we did last night?
うきゅっきゅ
SNICKER
KLUNG

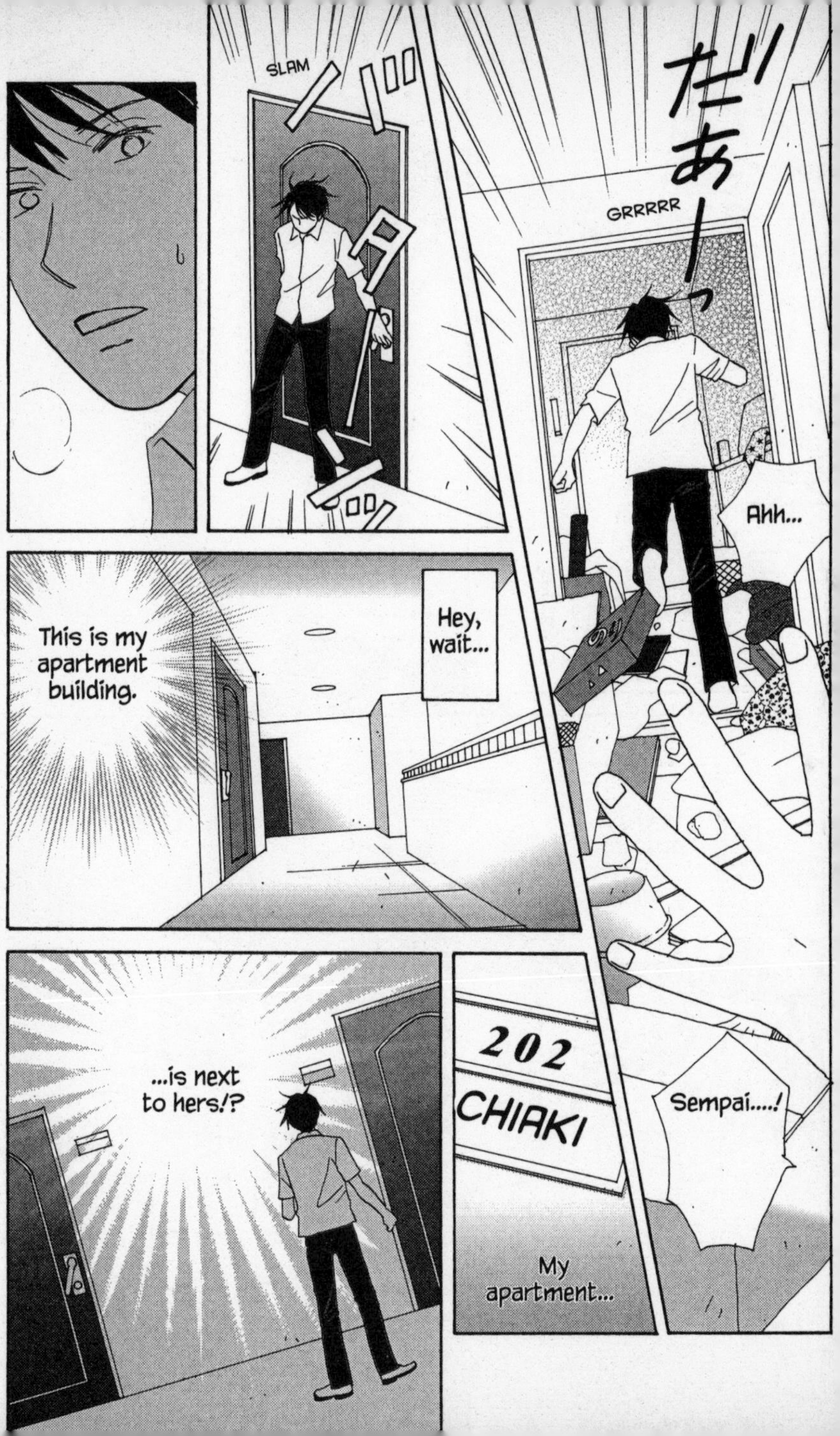
だあーっ
GRRRRR
Ahh...
Sempai....!
SLAM
Hey, wait...
This is my apartment building.
202
CHIAKI
My apartment...
...is next to hers!?

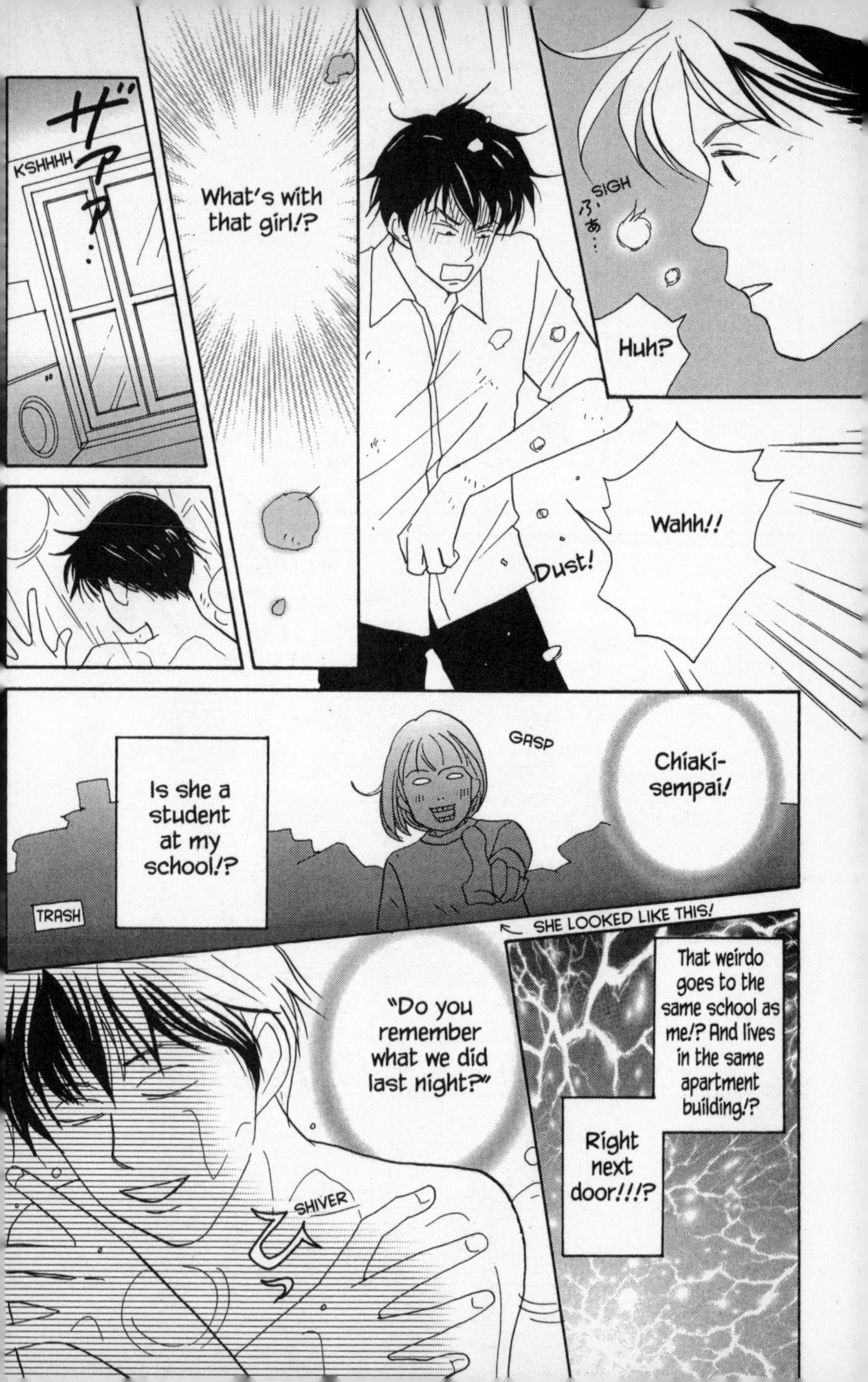
SIGH
ふぁ…
Huh?
What's with that girl!?
KSHHHH
ザァァ…
Wahh!!
Dust!
Chiaki-sempai!
GASP
Is she a student at my school!?
TRASH
SHE LOOKED LIKE THIS!
That weirdo goes to the same school as me!? And lives in the same apartment building!?
Right next door!!!?
"Do you remember what we did last night?"
SHIVER

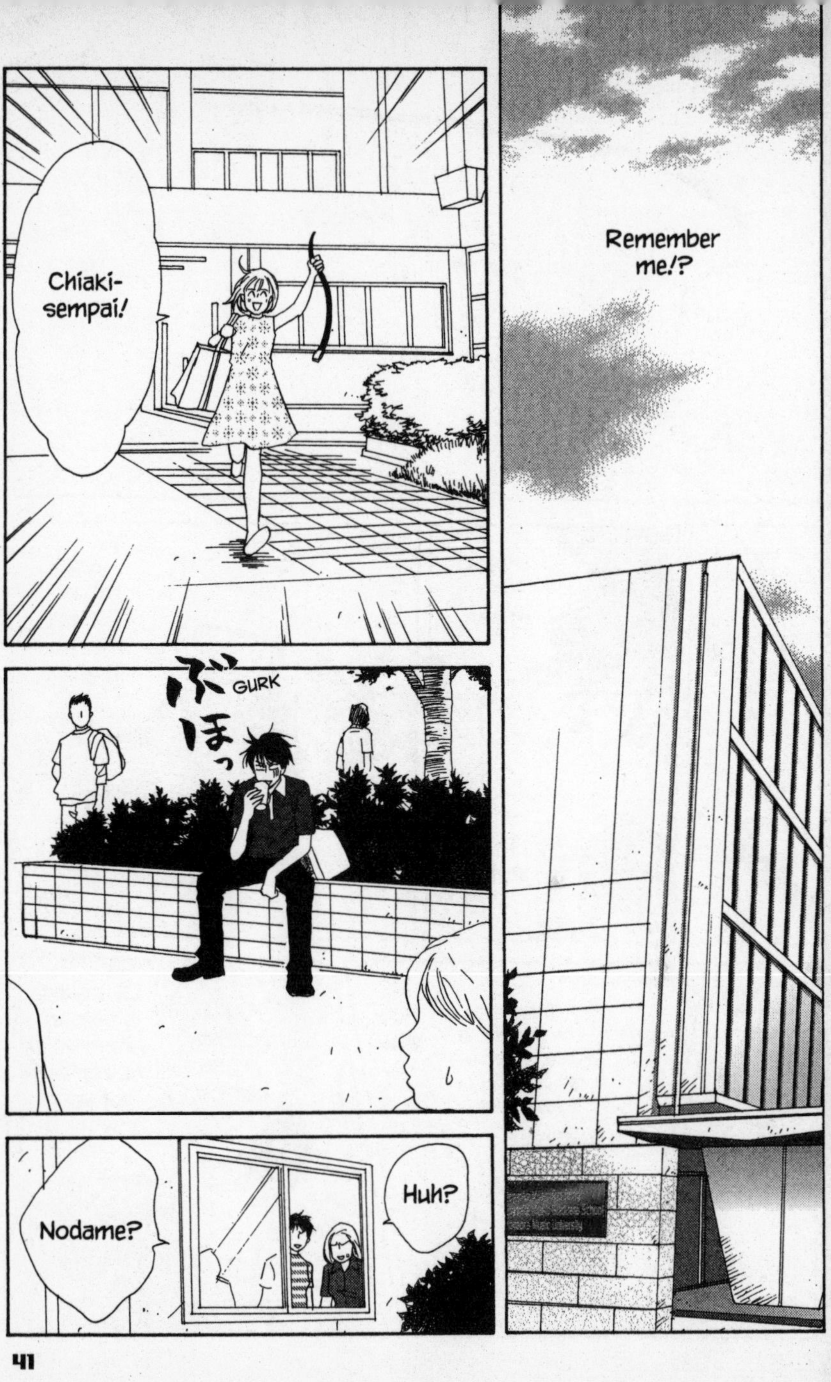
Remember me!?
Chiaki-sempai!
ぶほっ
GURK
Huh?
Nodame?

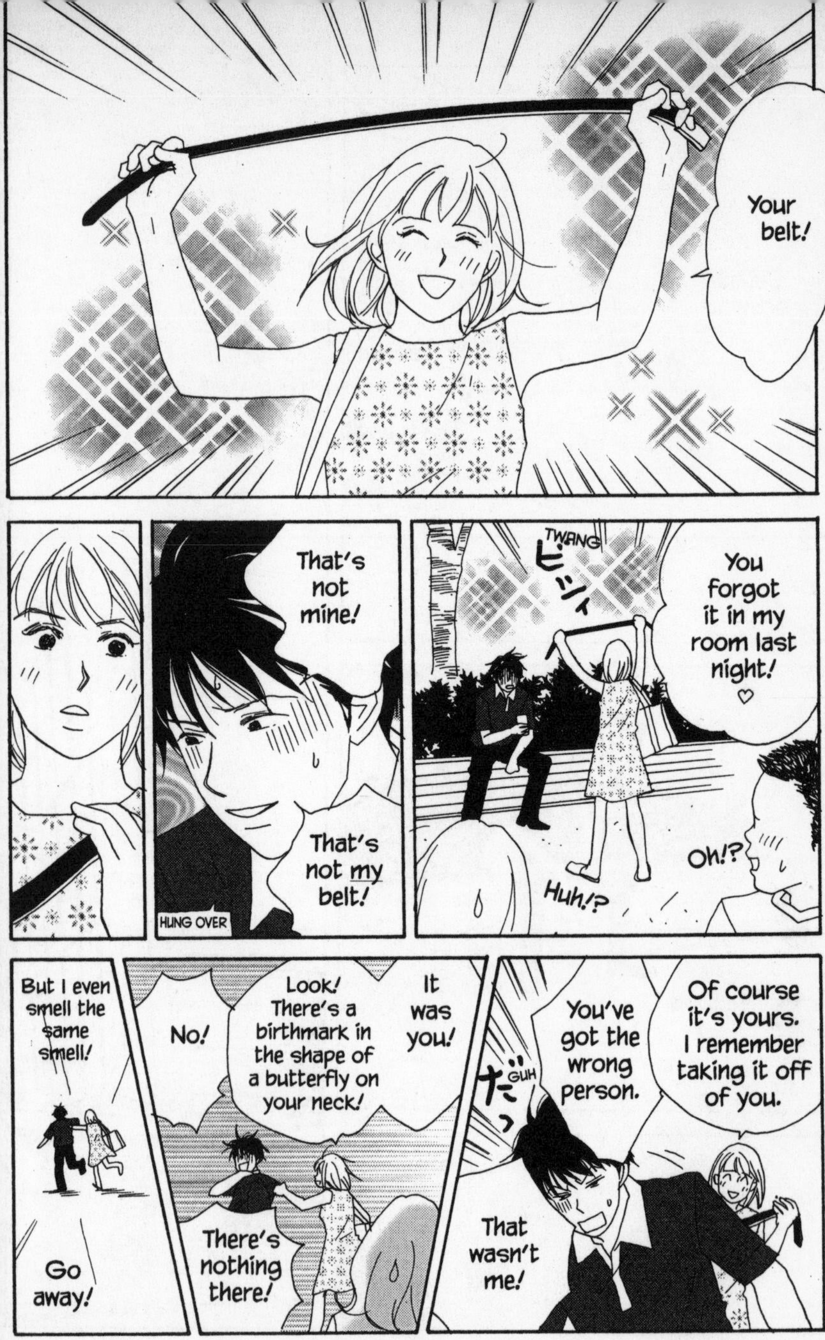
Your belt!
TWANG
ビッィ
You forgot it in my room last night! ♡
Oh!?
Huh!?
That's not mine!
That's not my belt!
HUNG OVER
Of course it's yours. I remember taking it off of you.
You've got the wrong person.
GUH
だっ
That wasn't me!
It was you!
Look! There's a birthmark in the shape of a butterfly on your neck!
No!
There's nothing there!
But I even smell the same smell!
Go away!

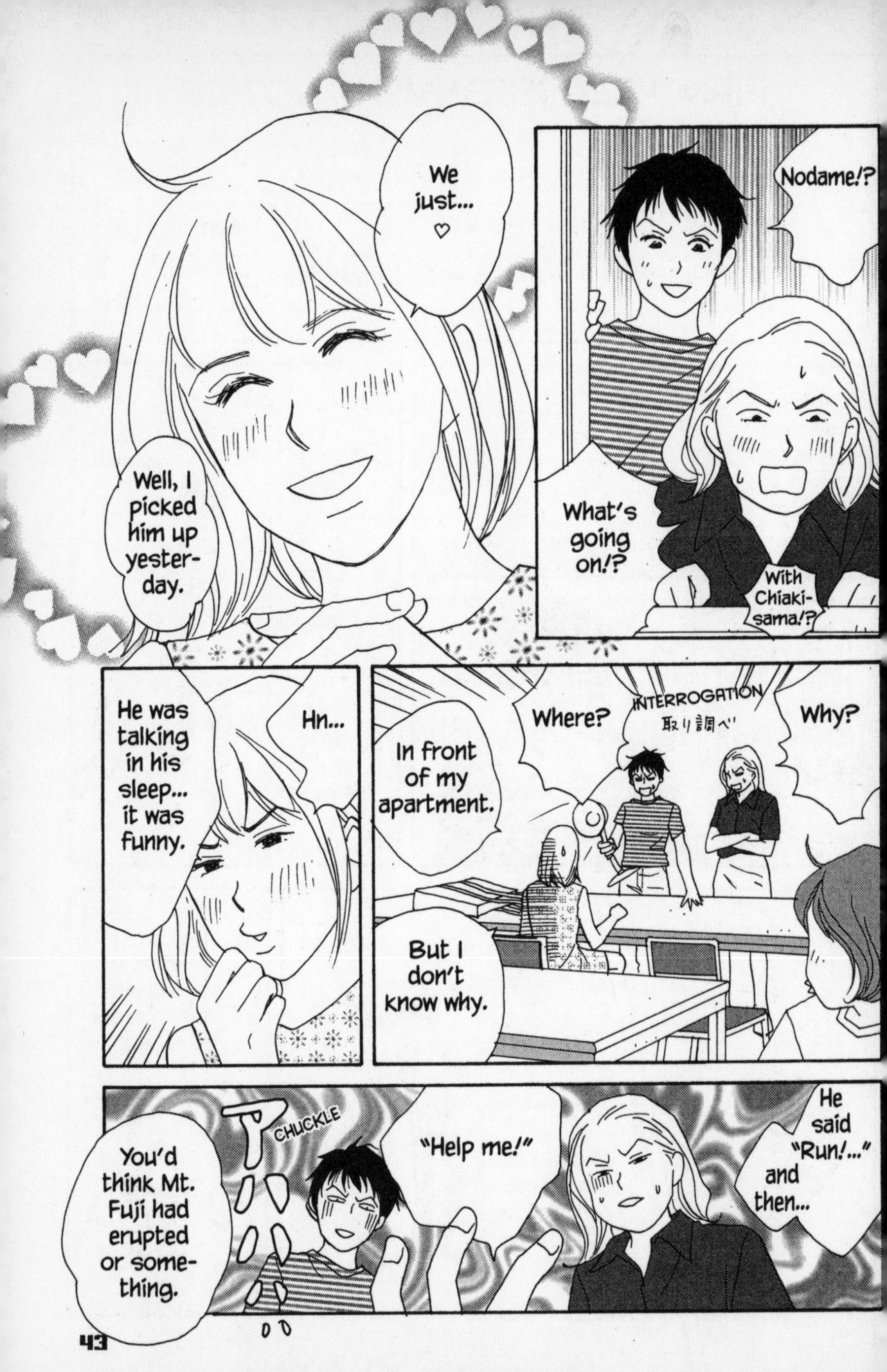
Nodame!?
What's going on!?
With Chiaki-sama!?
We just... ♡
Well, I picked him up yesterday.
Why?
Where?
INTERROGATION
取り調べ
In front of my apartment.
But I don't know why.
Hn...
He was talking in his sleep... it was funny.
He said "Run!..." and then...
"Help me!"
CHUCKLE
You'd think Mt. Fuji had erupted or something.

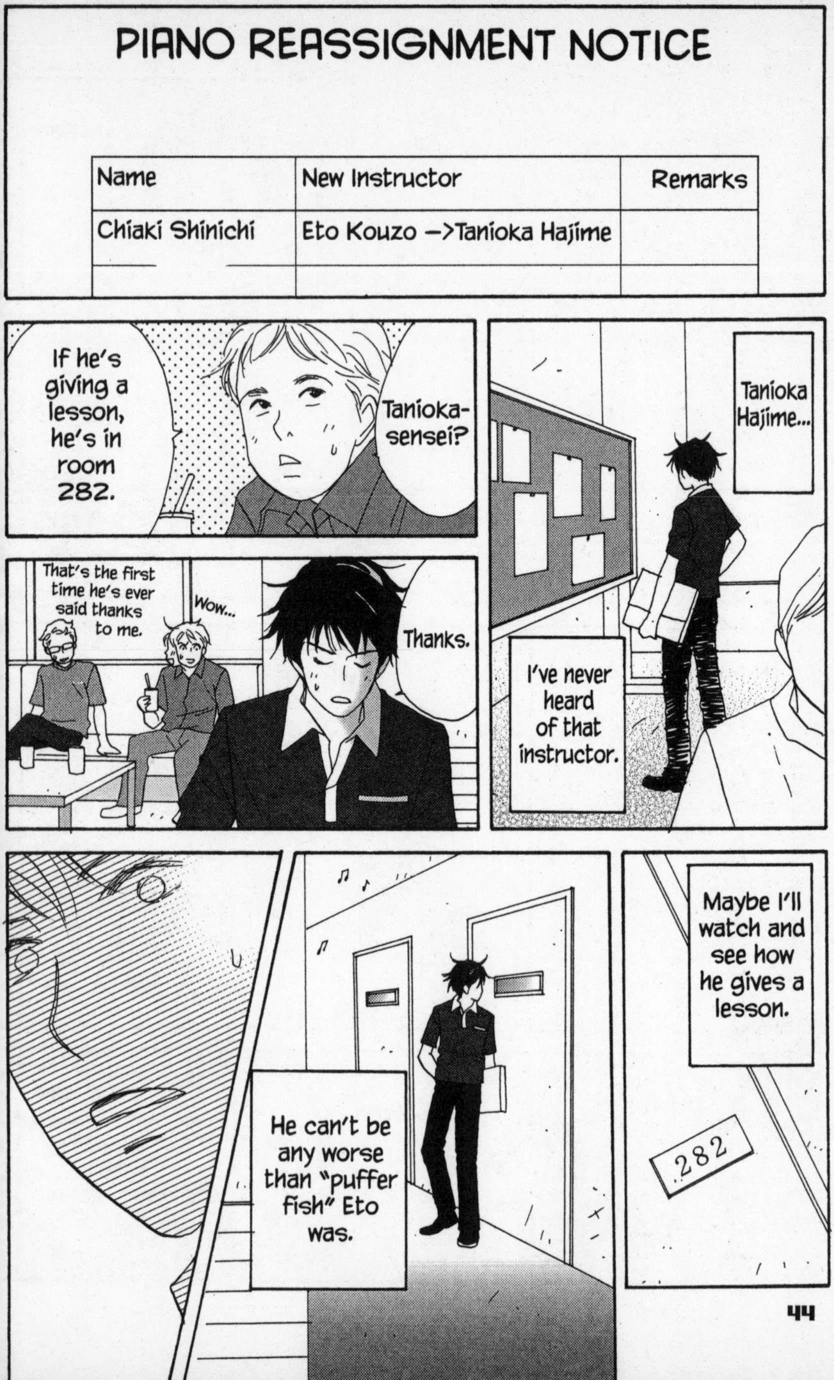
PIANO REASSIGNMENT NOTICE
Name | New Instructor | Remarks
Chiaki Shinichi | Eto Kouzo —>Tanioka Hajime
Tanioka Hajime...
I've never heard of that instructor.
Tanioka-sensei?
If he's giving a lesson, he's in room 282.
Thanks.
Wow...
That's the first time he's ever said thanks to me.
Maybe I'll watch and see how he gives a lesson.
282
He can't be any worse than "puffer fish" Eto was.

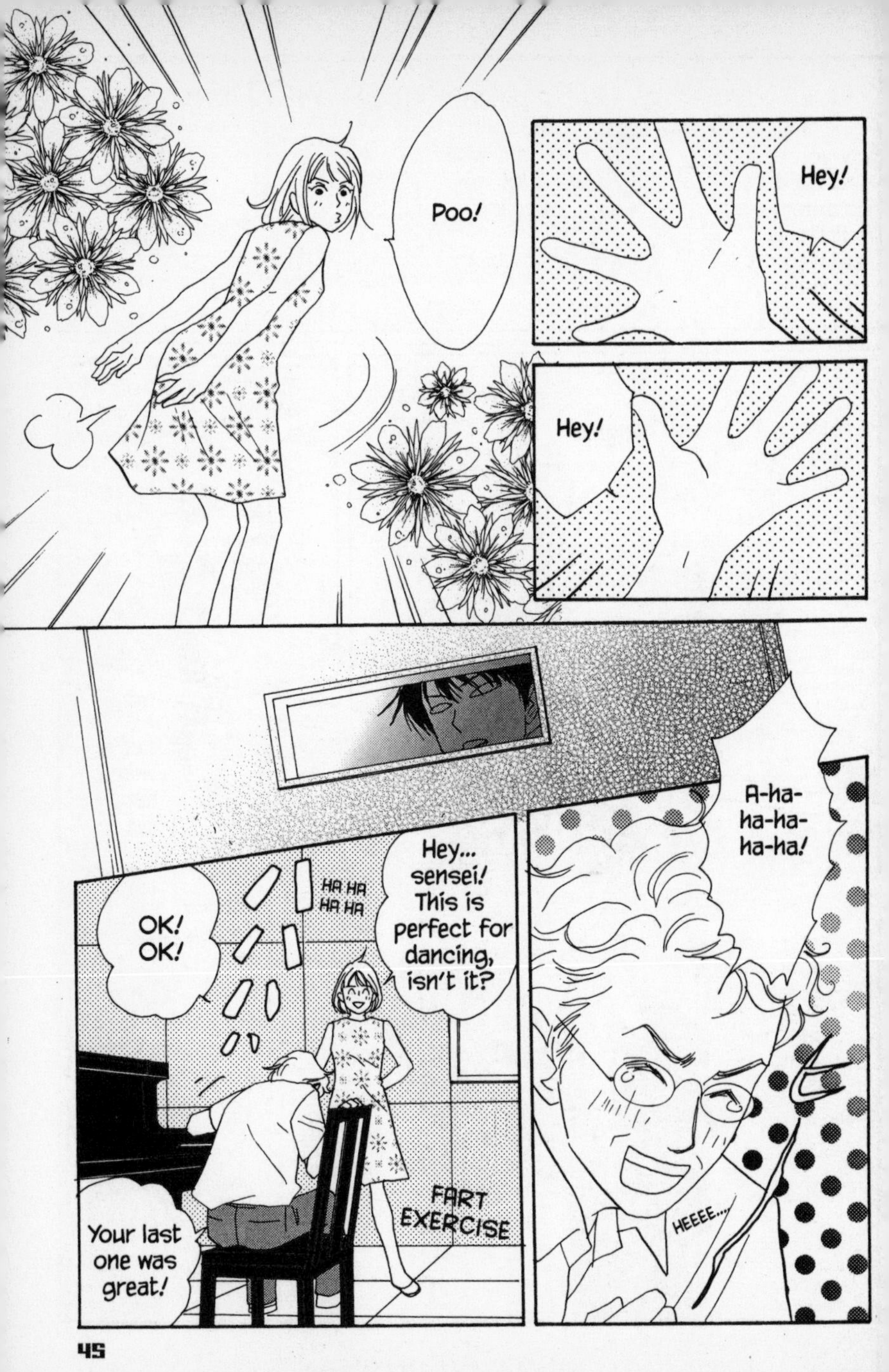
Hey!
Hey!
Poo!
A-ha-ha-ha-ha-ha!
HEEEE...
Hey... sensei! This is perfect for dancing, isn't it?
HA HA HA HA
OK! OK!
FART EXERCISE
Your last one was great!

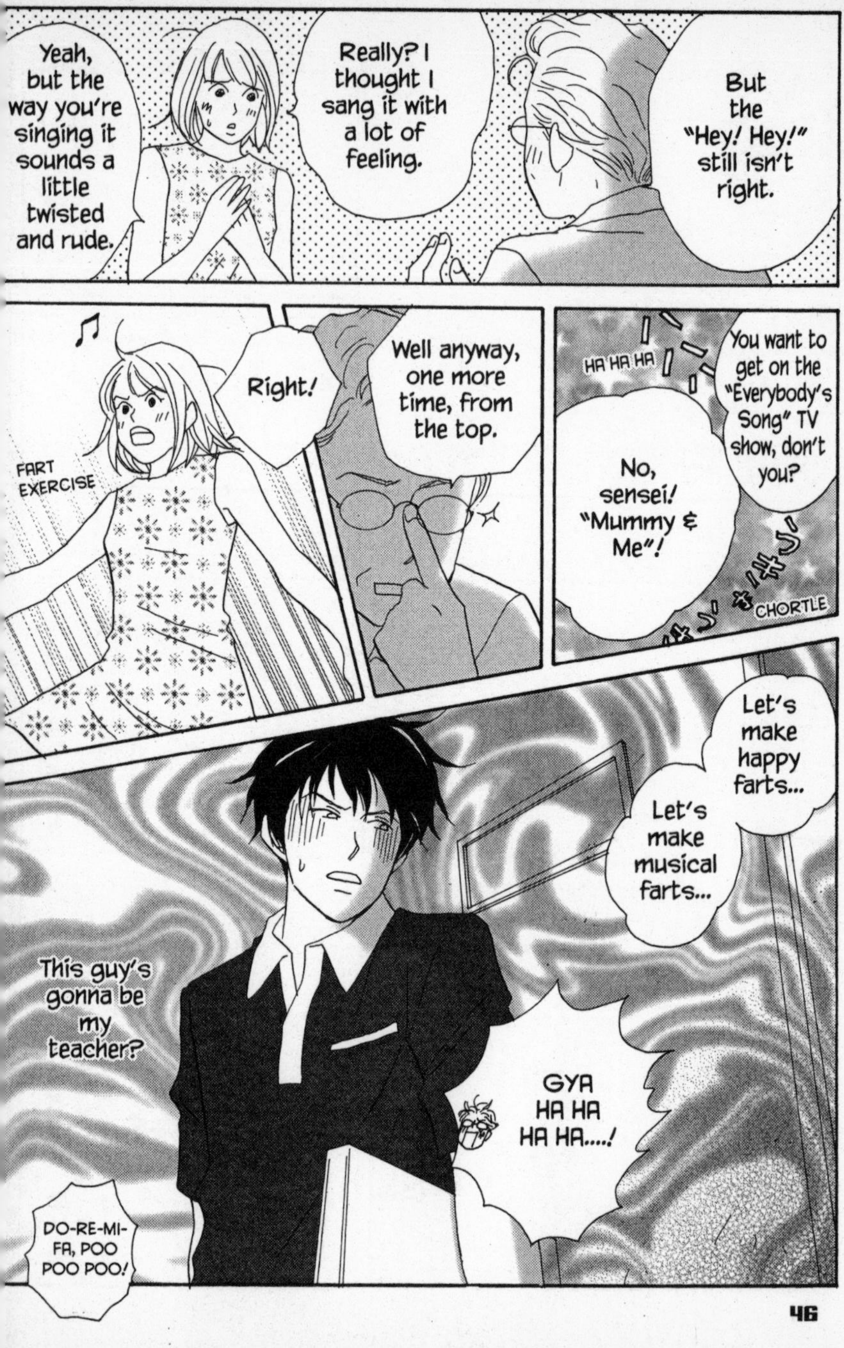
But the "Hey! Hey!" still isn't right.
Really? I thought I sang it with a lot of feeling.
Yeah, but the way you're singing it sounds a little twisted and rude.
You want to get on the "Everybody's Song" TV show, don't you?
HA HA HA
No, sensei! "Mummy & Me"!
CHORTLE
Well anyway, one more time, from the top.
Right!
FART EXERCISE
Let's make happy farts...
Let's make musical farts...
GYA HA HA HA HA....!
This guy's gonna be my teacher?
DO-RE-MI-FA, POO POO POO!

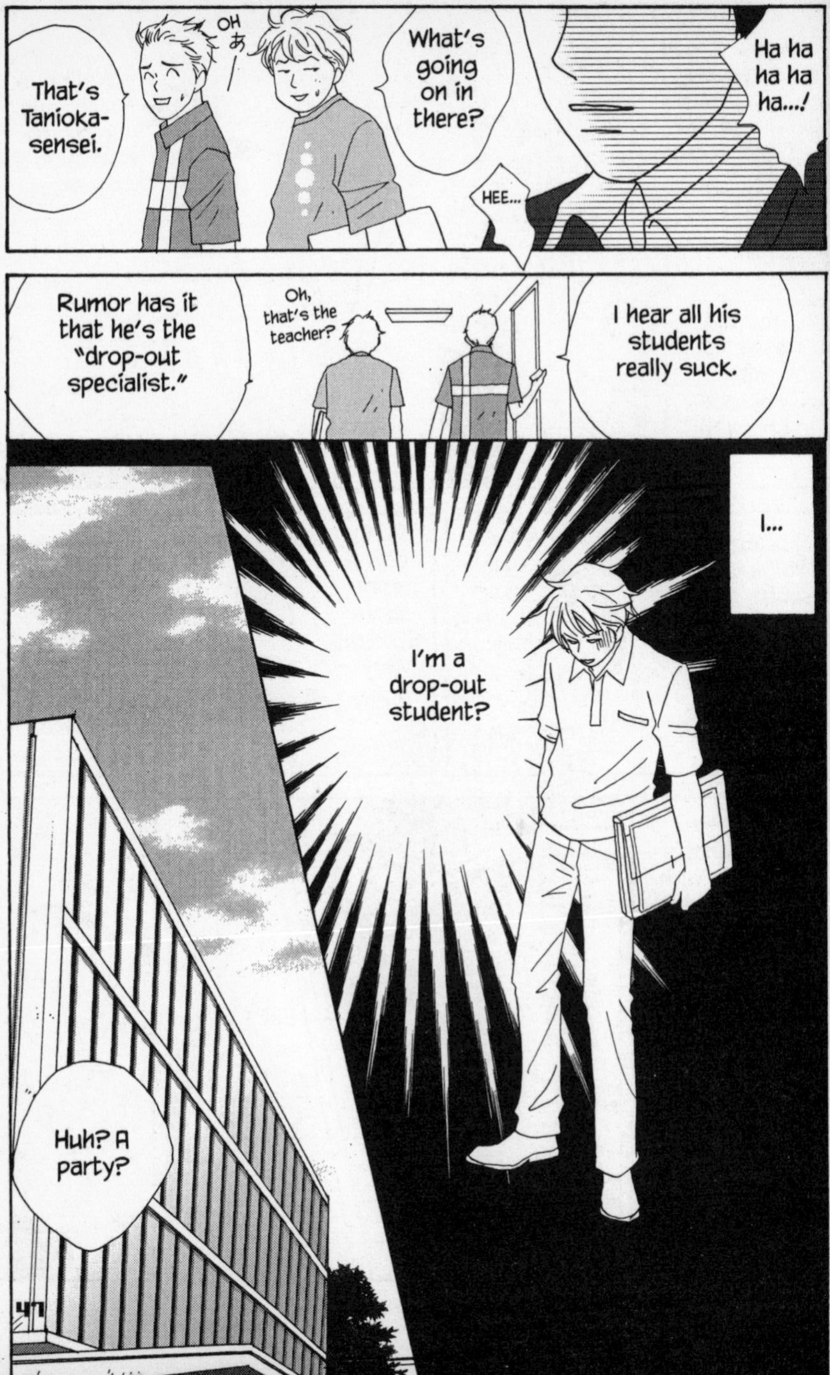
Ha ha ha ha ha...!
What's going on in there?
OH あ
HEE...
That's Tanioka-sensei.
I hear all his students really suck.
Oh, that's the teacher?
Rumor has it that he's the "drop-out specialist."
I...
I'm a drop-out student?
Huh? A party?

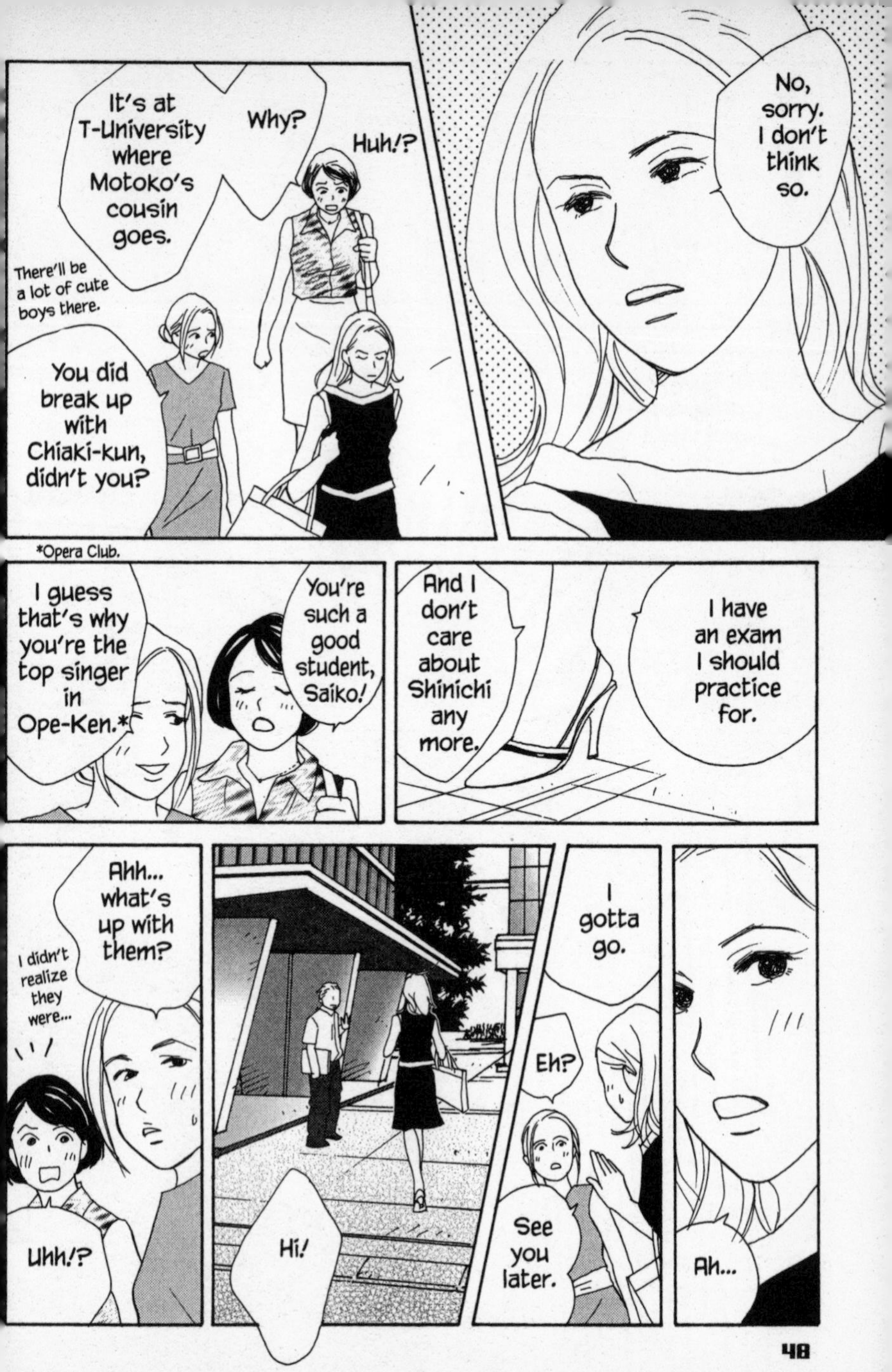
No, sorry. I don't think so.
Huh!?
Why?
It's at T-University where Motoko's cousin goes.
There'll be a lot of cute boys there.
You did break up with Chiaki-kun, didn't you?
I have an exam I should practice for.
And I don't care about Shinichi any more.
You're such a good student, Saiko!
I guess that's why you're the top singer in Ope-Ken.*
Ah...
I gotta go.
Eh?
See you later.
Hi!
Ahh... what's up with them?
I didn't realize they were...
Uhh!?

*Opera Club.

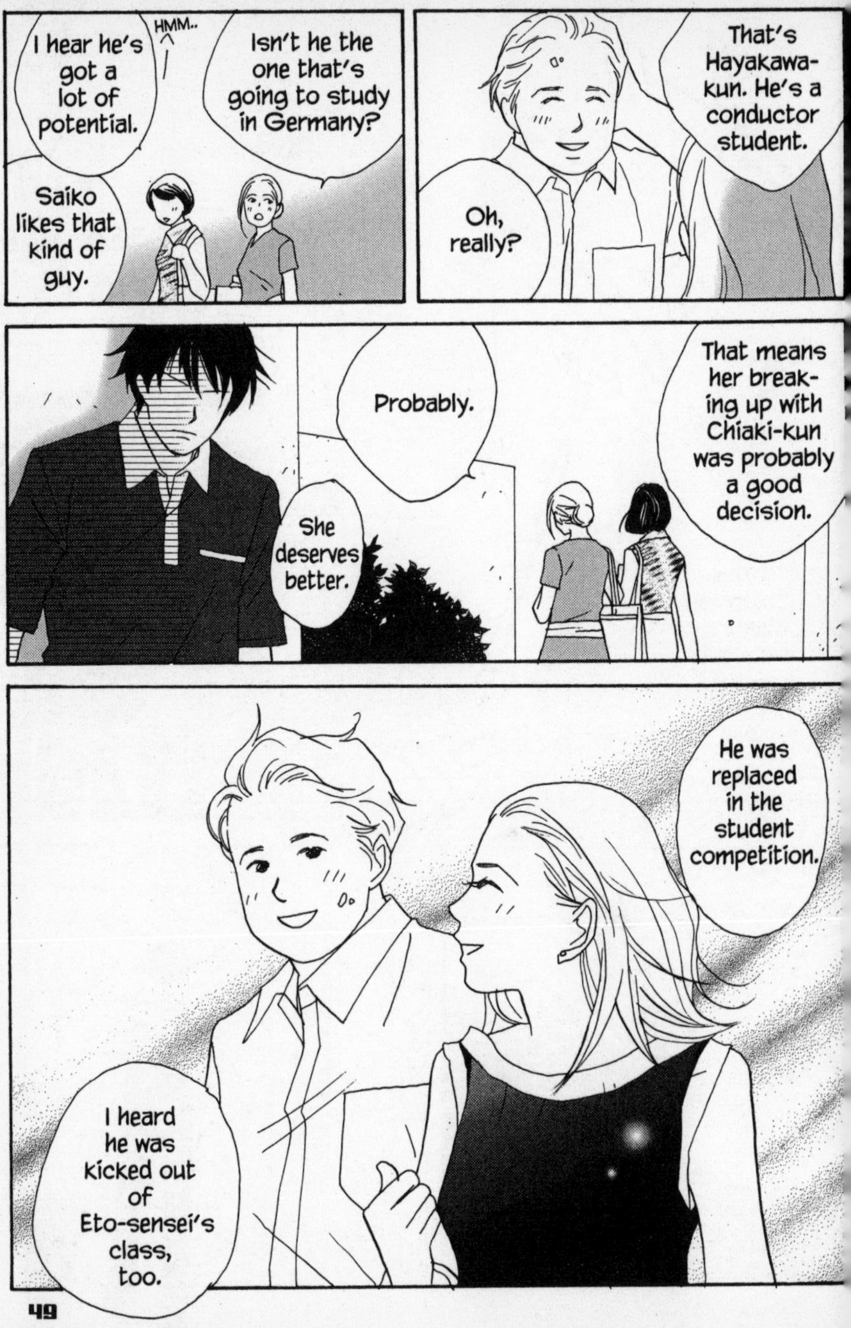

That's Hayakawa-kun. He's a conductor student.
Oh, really?
Isn't he the one that's going to study in Germany?
HMM..
I hear he's got a lot of potential.
Saiko likes that kind of guy.
That means her breaking up with Chiaki-kun was probably a good decision.
Probably.
She deserves better.
He was replaced in the student competition.
I heard he was kicked out of Eto-sensei's class, too.

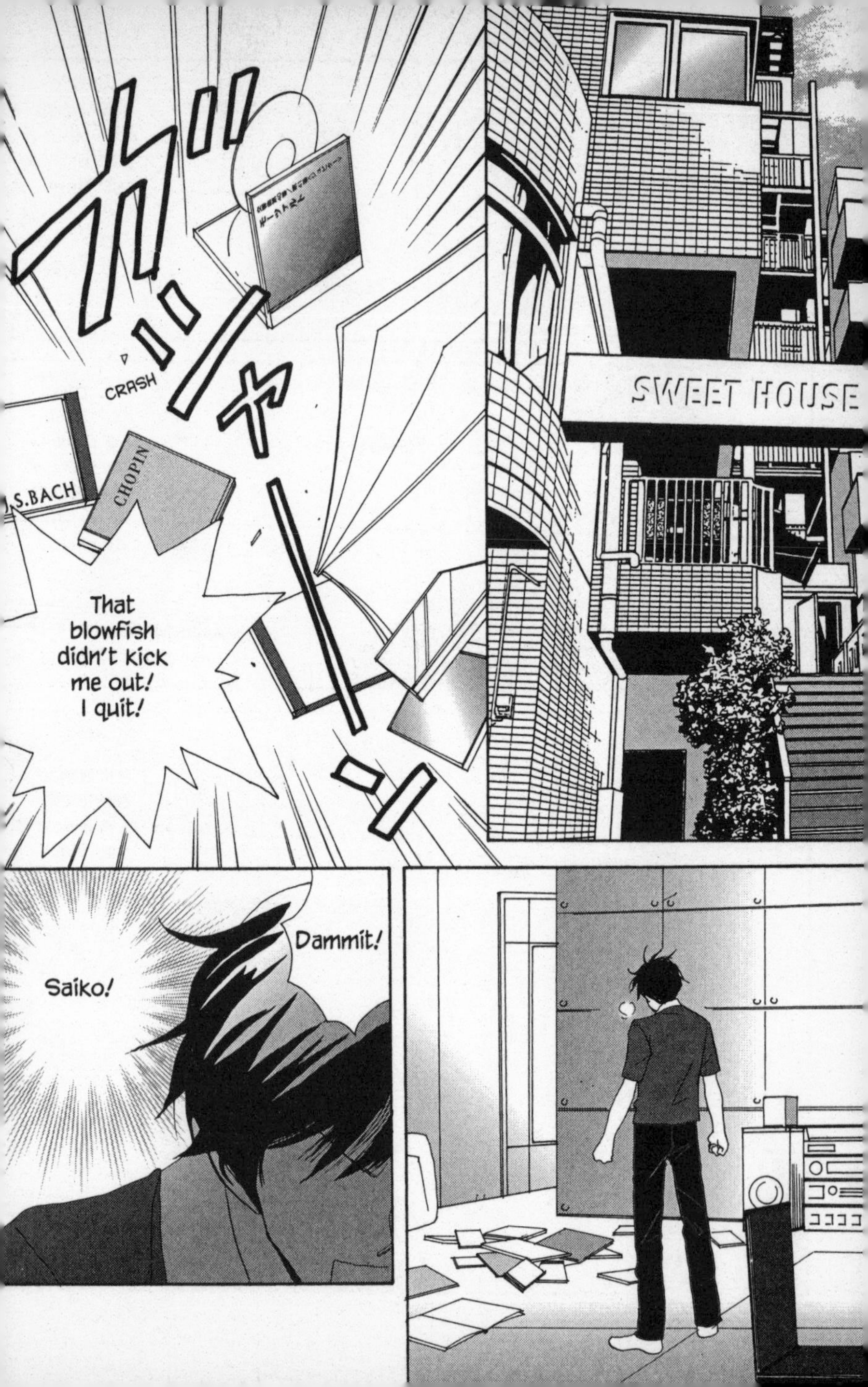
SWEET HOUSE
CRASH
S.BACH
CHOPIN
That blowfish didn't kick me out! I quit!
Dammit!
Saiko!

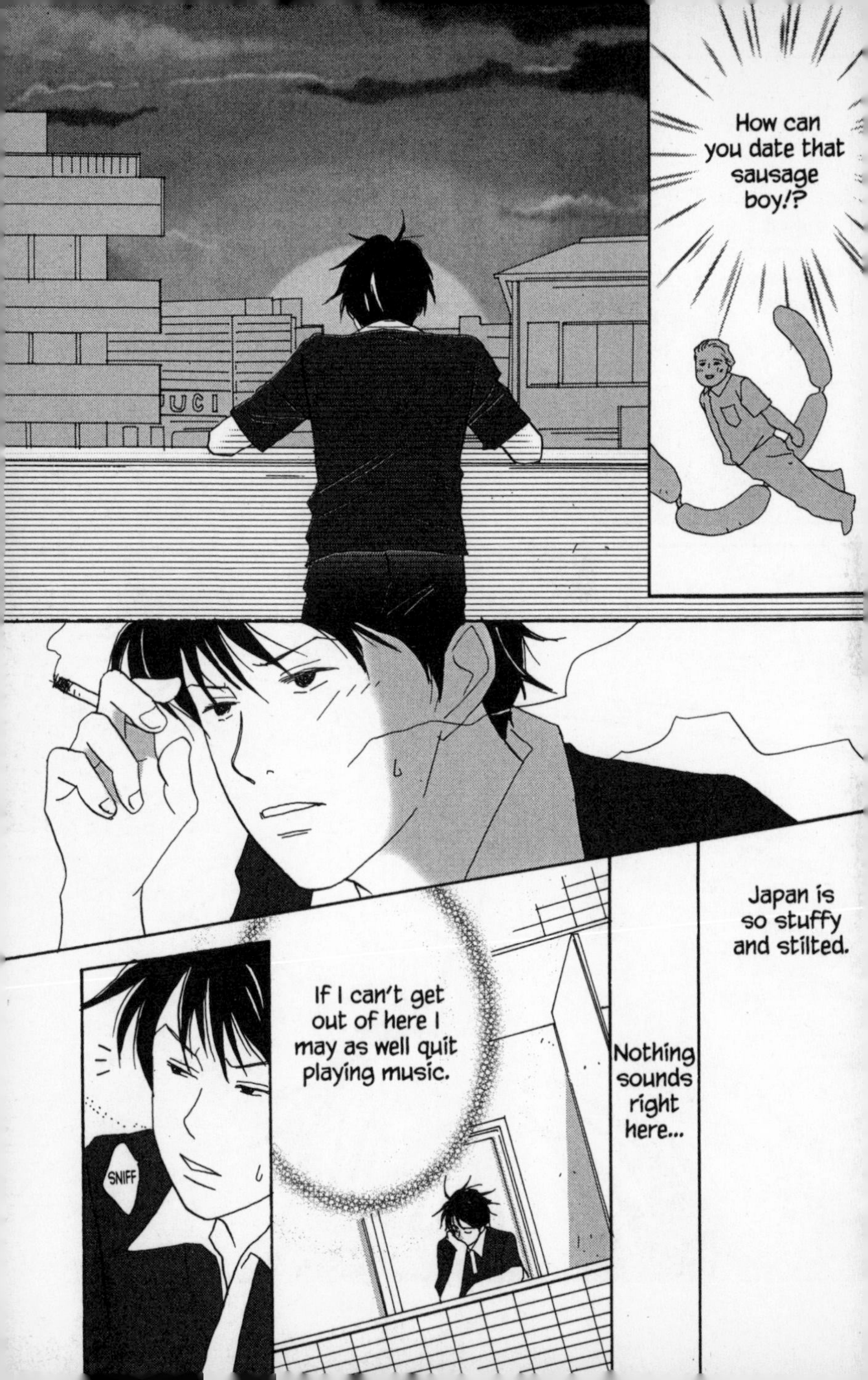
How can you date that sausage boy!?
Japan is so stuffy and stilted.
Nothing sounds right here...
If I can't get out of here I may as well quit playing music.
SNIFF

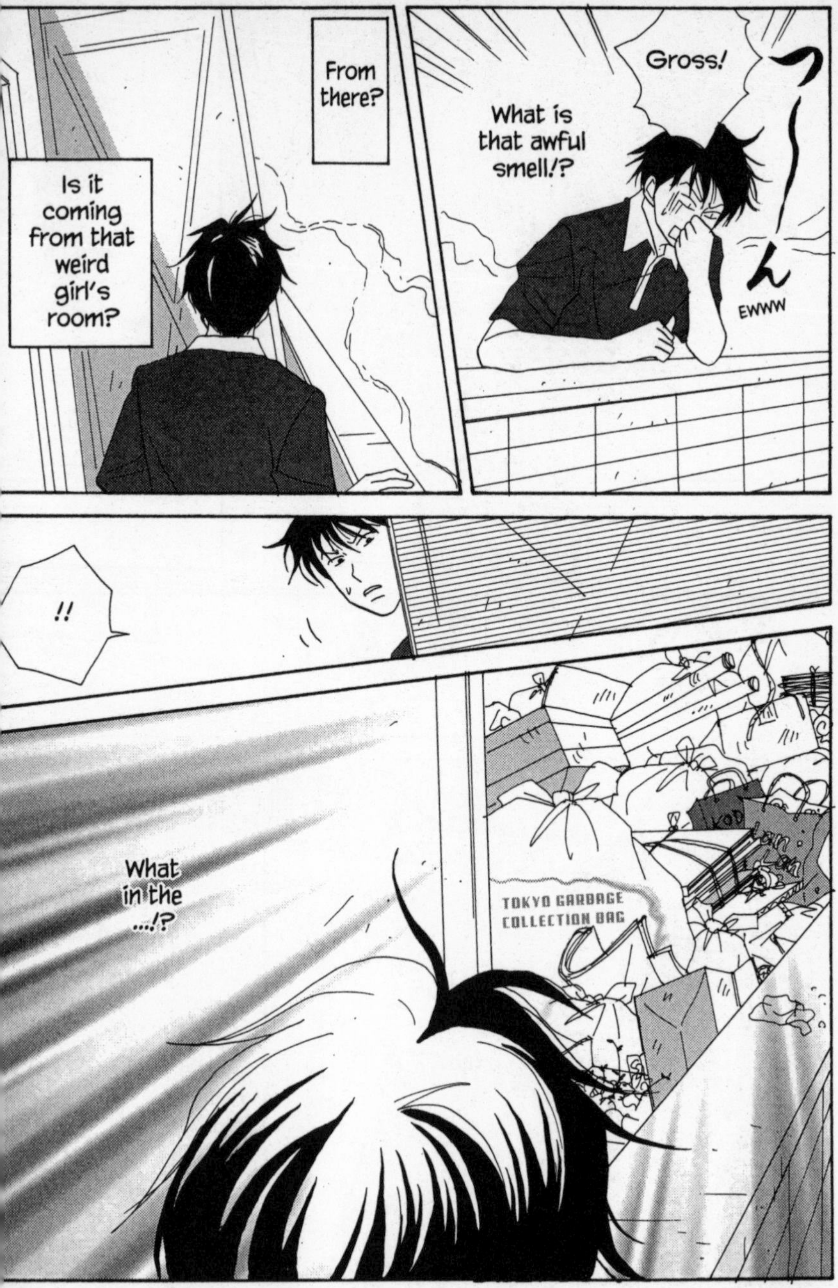
Gross!
What is that awful smell!?
つーん
EWWW
From there?
Is it coming from that weird girl's room?
!!
TOKYO GARBAGE COLLECTION BAG
What in the ...!?

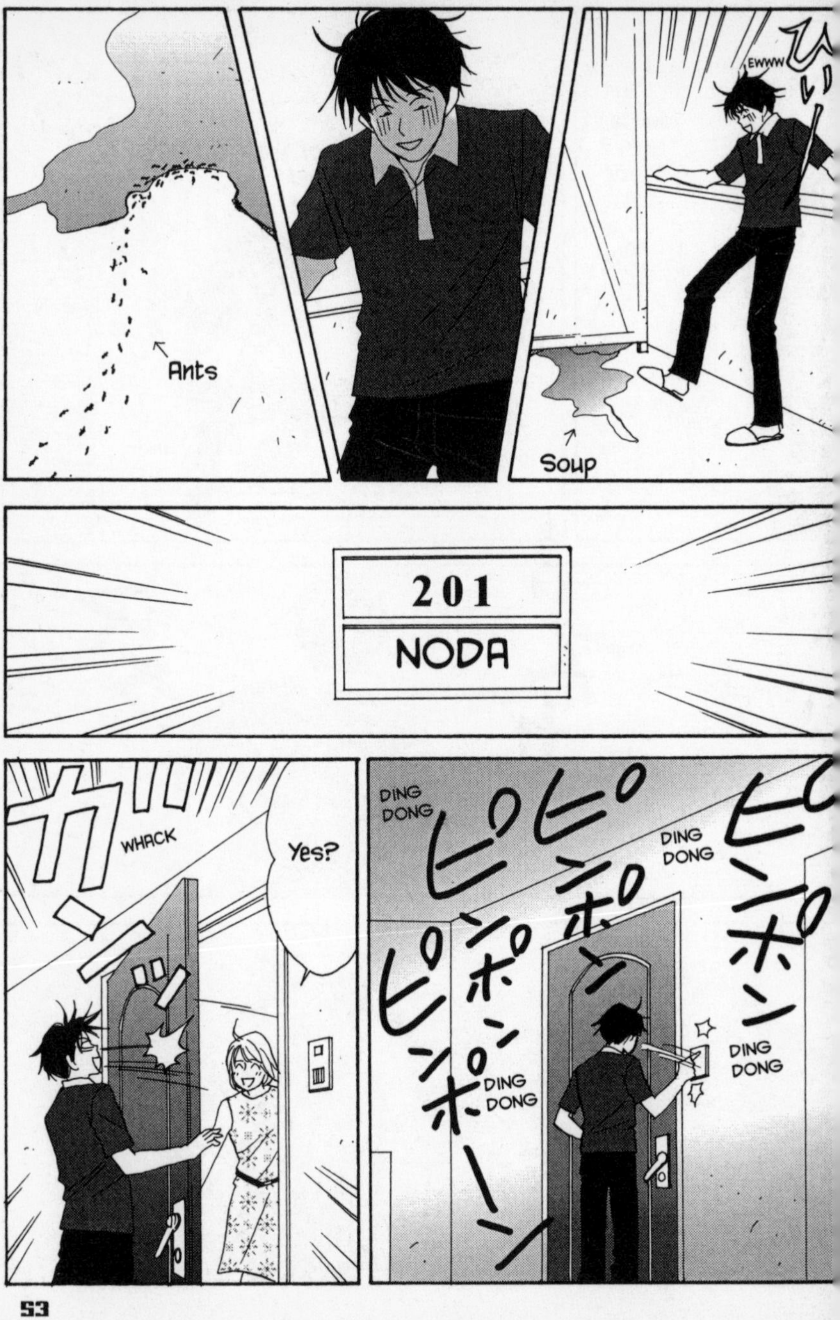
ひぃ
EWWW
Soup
Ants
201
NODA
ピンポン
DING DONG
ピンポン
DING DONG
ピンポン
DING DONG
ピンポンピンポーン
DING DONG
Yes?
カーン
WHACK

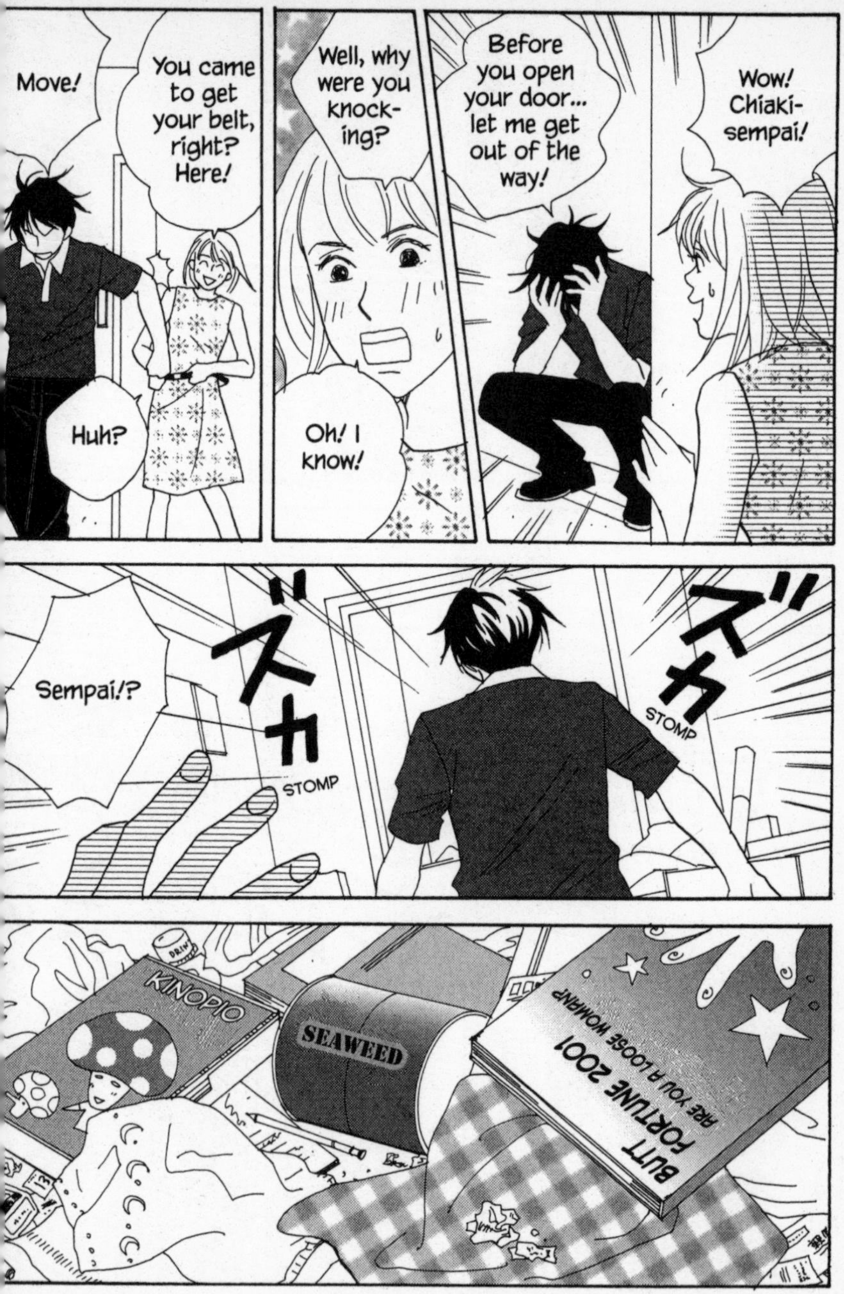
Wow! Chiaki-sempai!
Before you open your door... let me get out of the way!
Well, why were you knocking?
Oh! I know!
You came to get your belt, right? Here!
Move!
Huh?
ズカ
STOMP
Sempai!?
ズカ
STOMP
BUTT FORTUNE 2001
ARE YOU A LOOSE WOMAN?
SEAWEED
KINOPIO

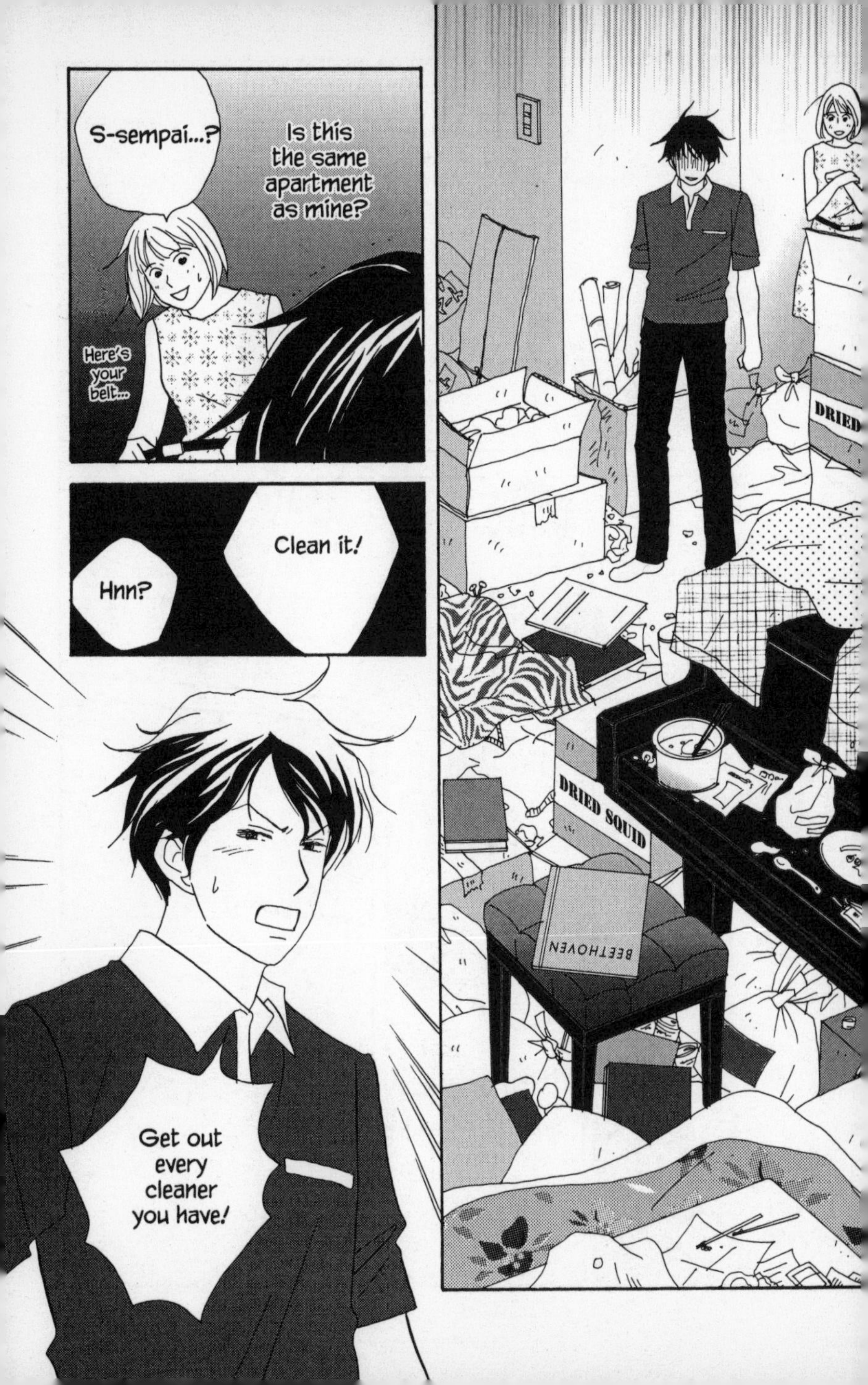
DRIED
DRIED SQUID
BEETHOVEN
S-sempai...?
Is this the same apartment as mine?
Here's your belt...
Clean it!
Hnn?
Get out every cleaner you have!

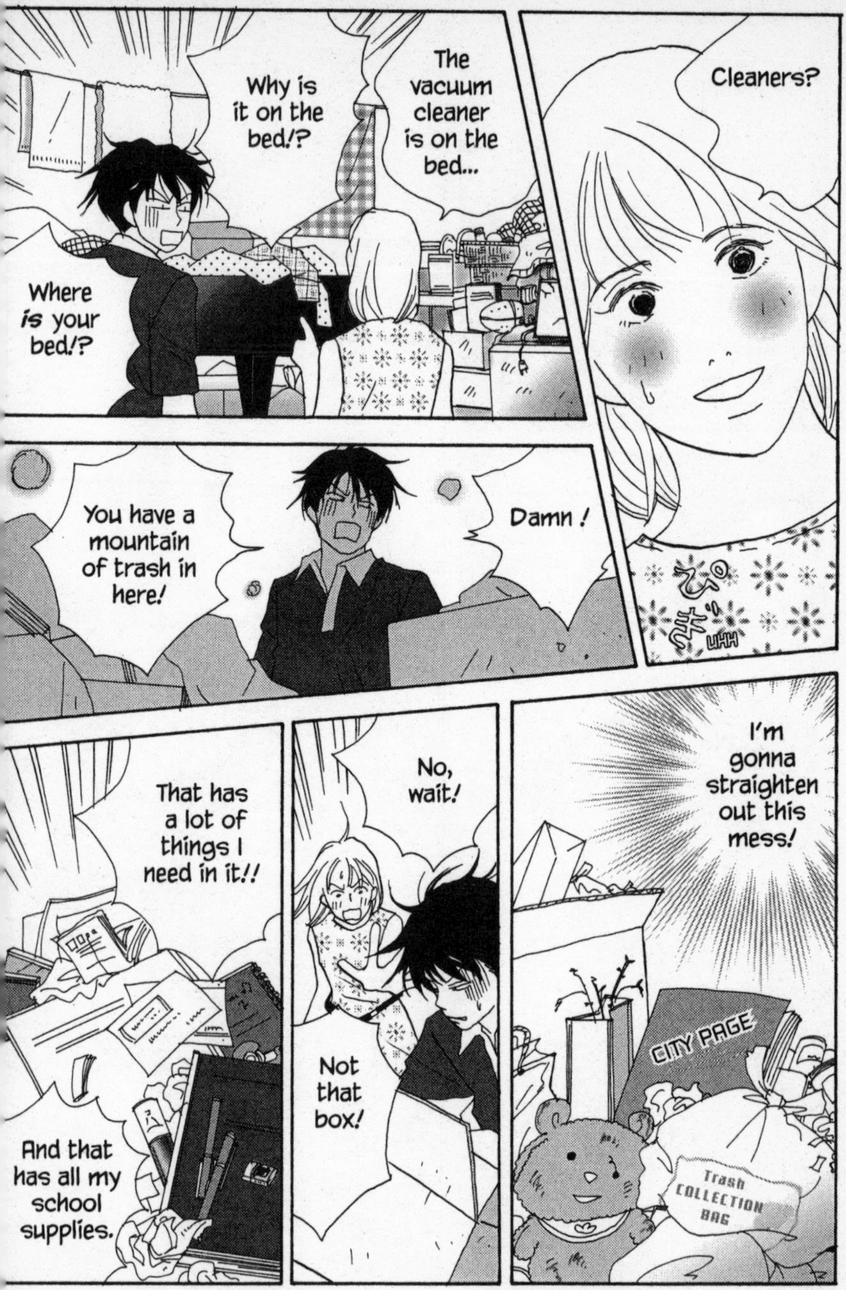
Cleaners?
UHH
The vacuum cleaner is on the bed...
Why is it on the bed!?
Where *is* your bed!?
Damn!
You have a mountain of trash in here!
I'm gonna straighten out this mess!
CITY PAGE
Trash COLLECTION BAG
No, wait!
Not that box!
That has a lot of things I need in it!!
And that has all my school supplies.

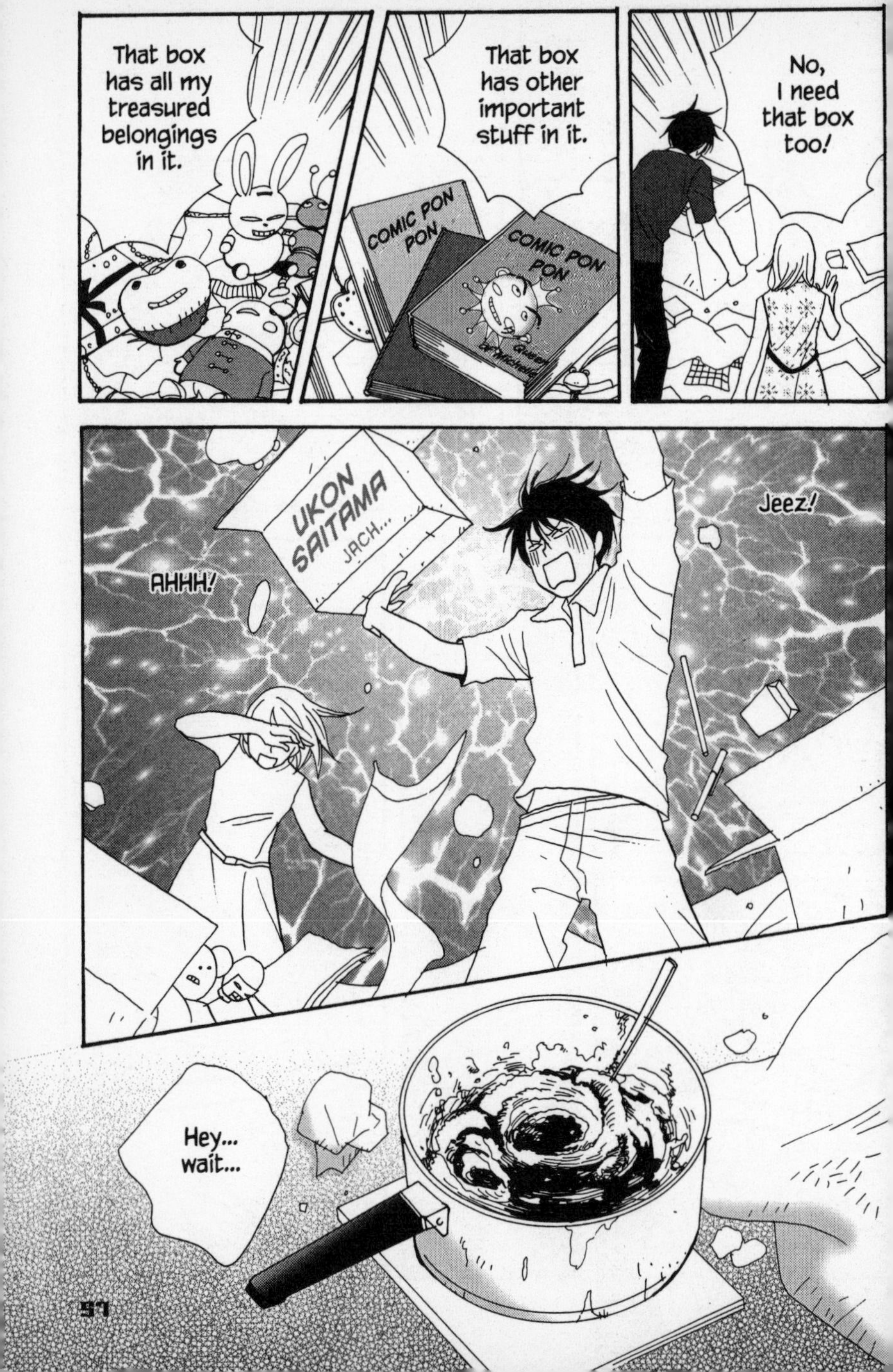
No, I need that box too!
That box has other important stuff in it.
COMIC PON PON
COMIC PON PON
That box has all my treasured belongings in it.
Jeez!
UKON SAITAMA JACH...
AHHH!
Hey... wait...

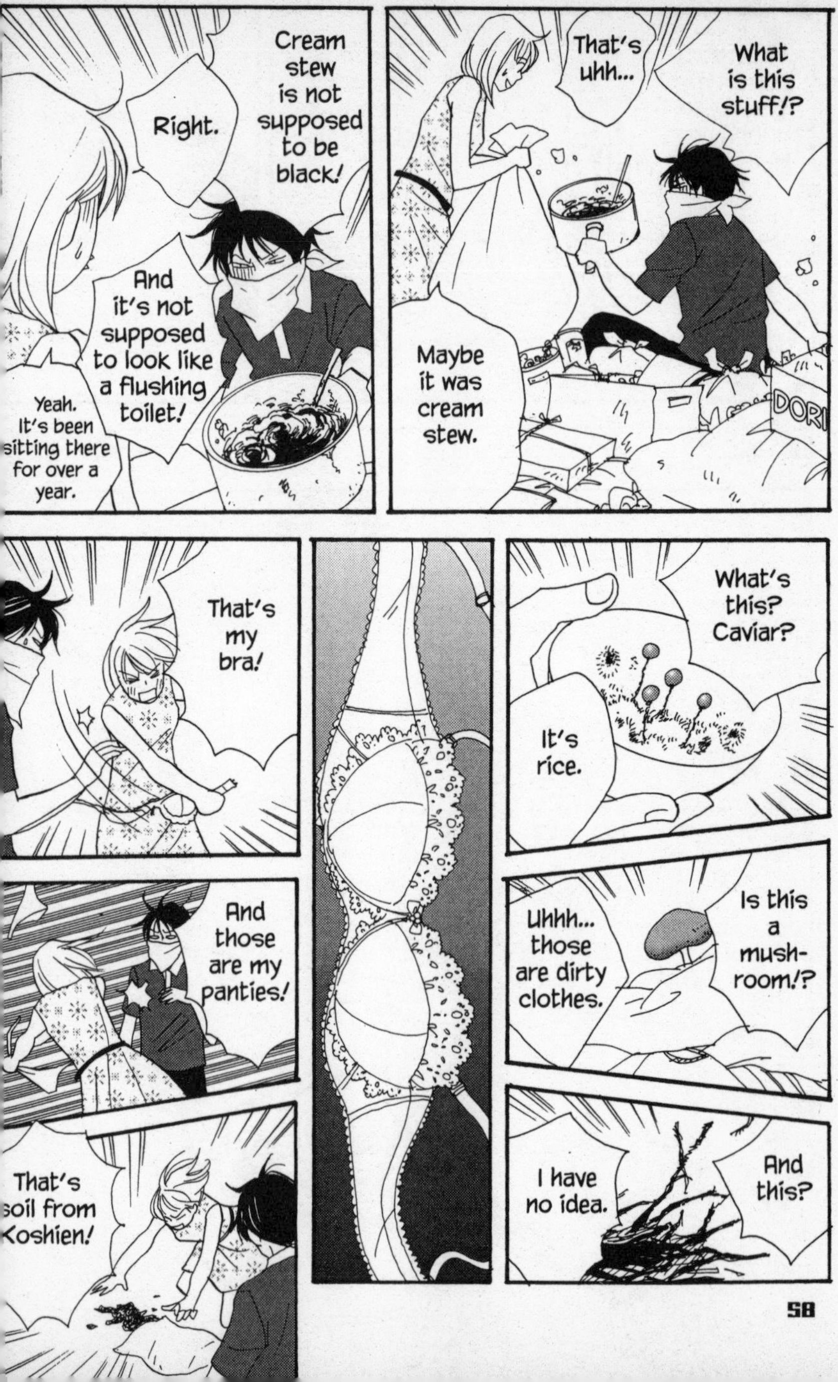

What is this stuff!?
That's uhh...
Maybe it was cream stew.
Cream stew is not supposed to be black!
Right.
And it's not supposed to look like a flushing toilet!
Yeah. It's been sitting there for over a year.
What's this? Caviar?
It's rice.
Is this a mushroom!?
Uhhh... those are dirty clothes.
And this?
I have no idea.
That's my bra!
And those are my panties!
That's soil from Koshien!

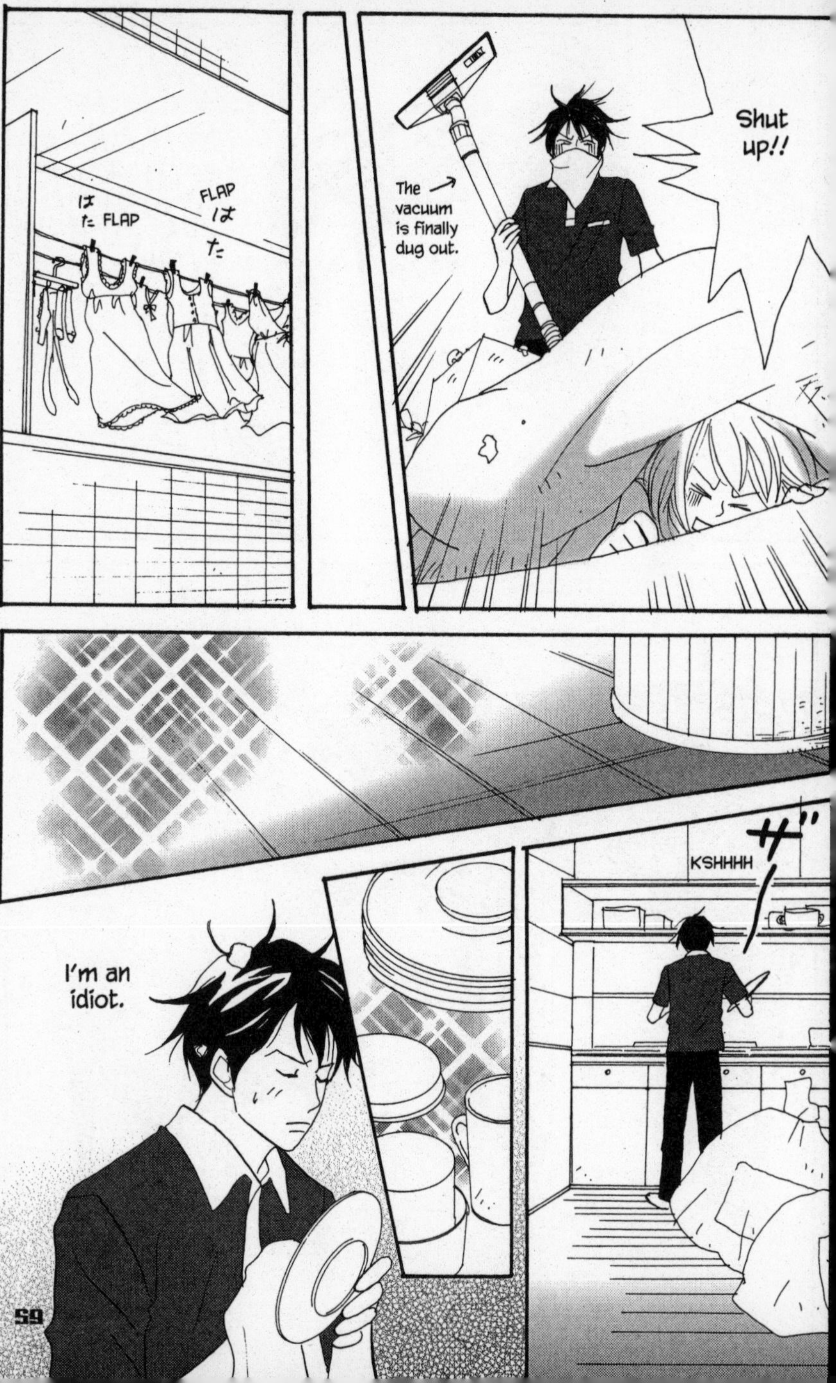
Shut up!!
The vacuum is finally dug out.
FLAP はた
はた FLAP
ザー
KSHHHH
I'm an idiot.

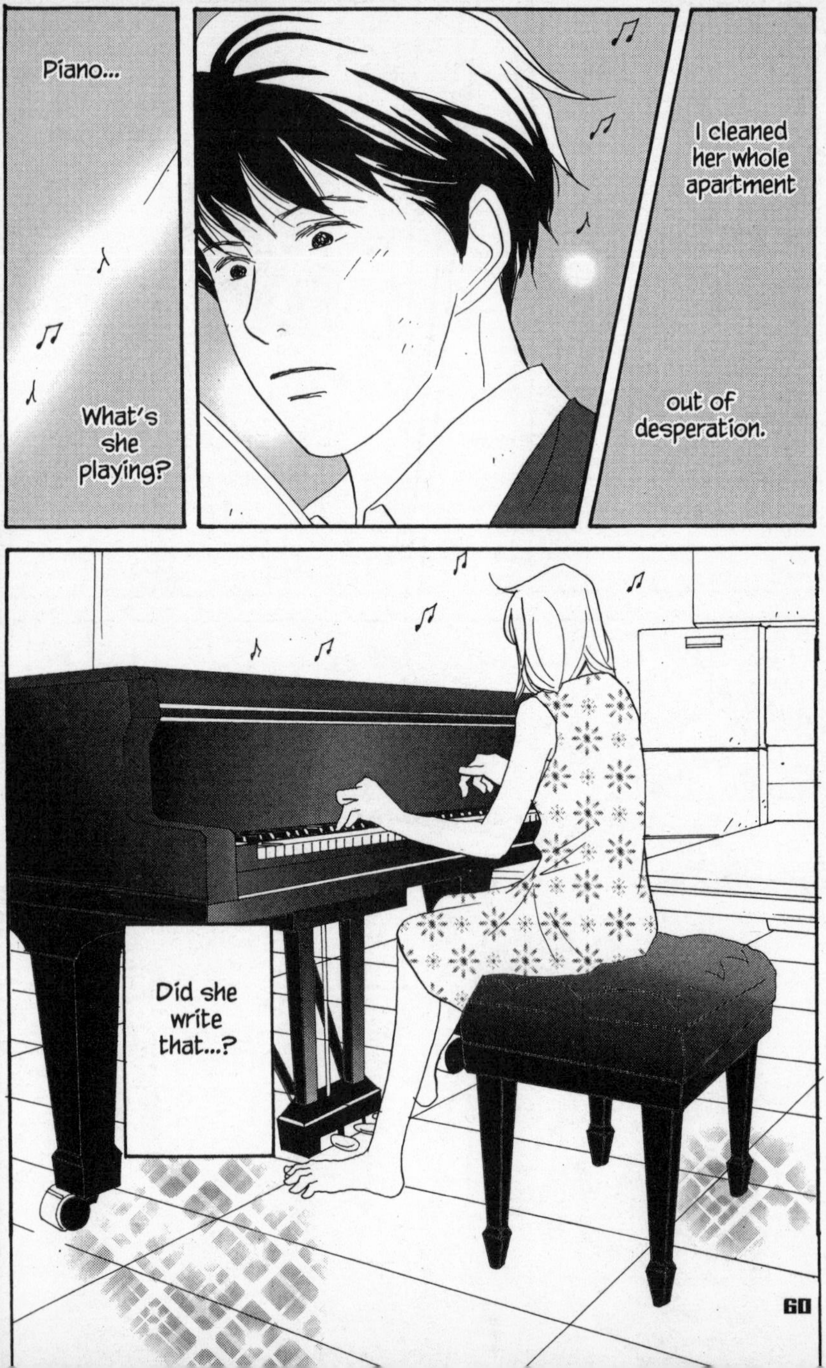
I cleaned her whole apartment
out of desperation.
Piano...
What's she playing?
Did she write that...?

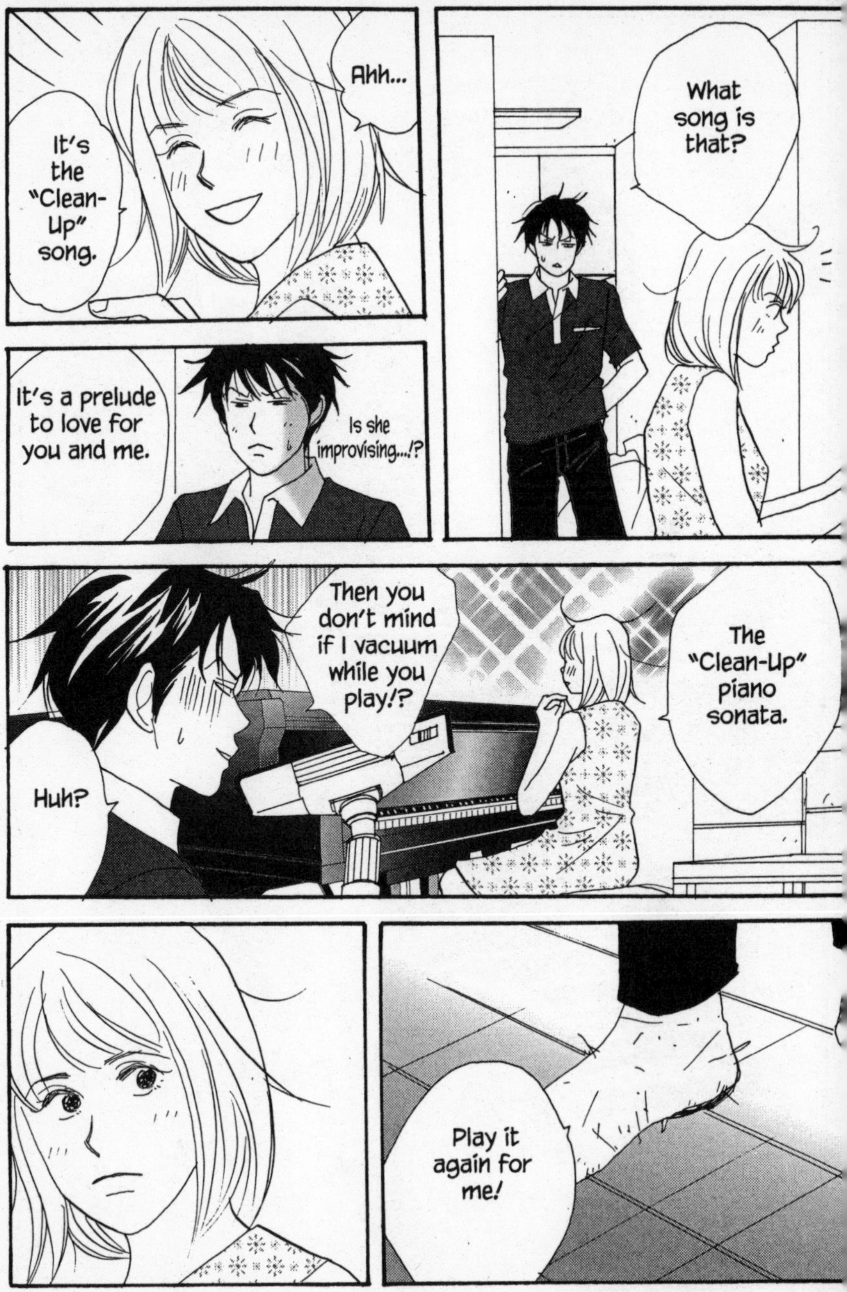
What song is that?
Ahh...
It's the "Clean-Up" song.
It's a prelude to love for you and me.
Is she improvising...!?
The "Clean-Up" piano sonata.
Then you don't mind if I vacuum while you play!?
Huh?
Play it again for me!

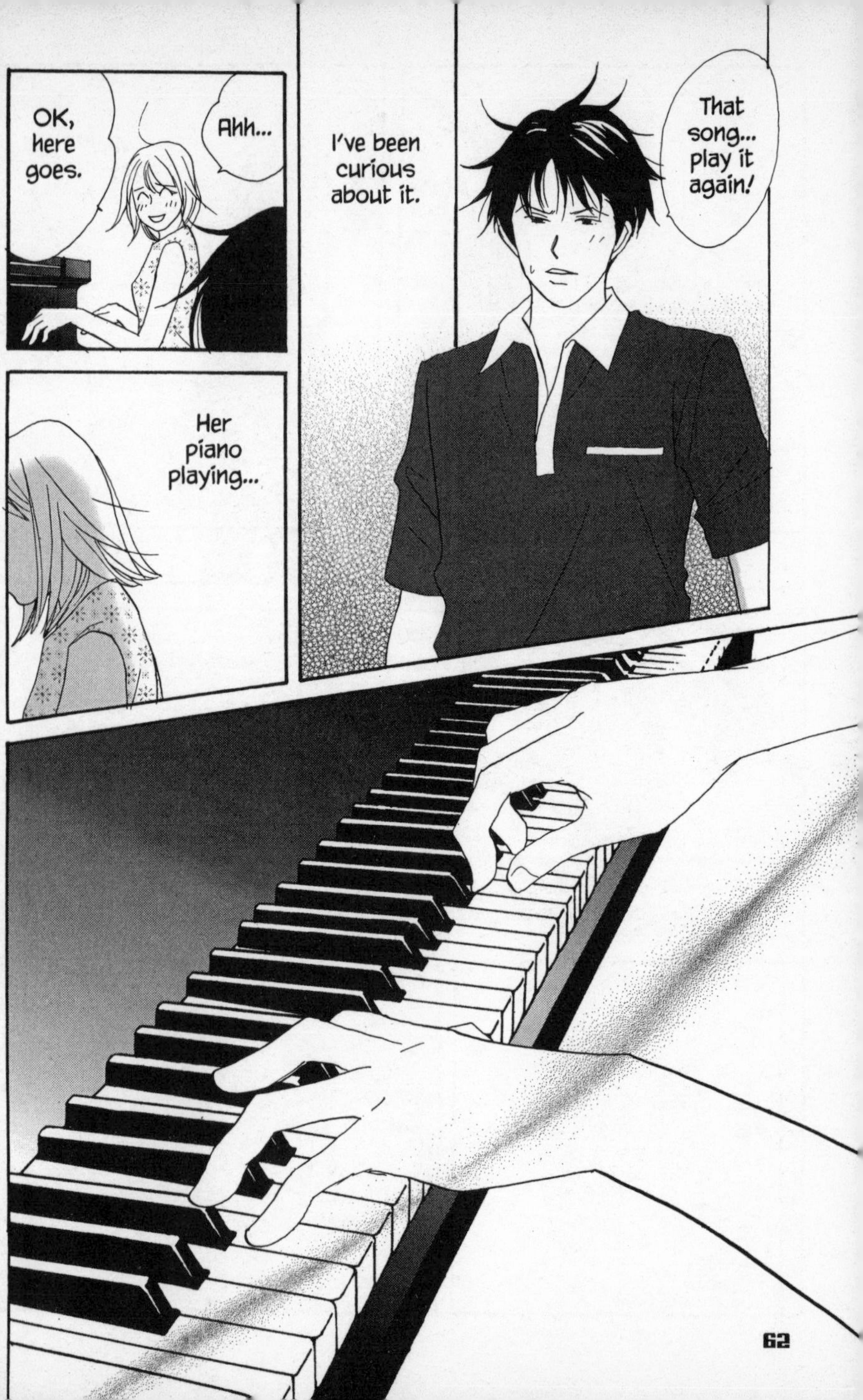
That song... play it again!
I've been curious about it.
Ahh...
OK, here goes.
Her piano playing...

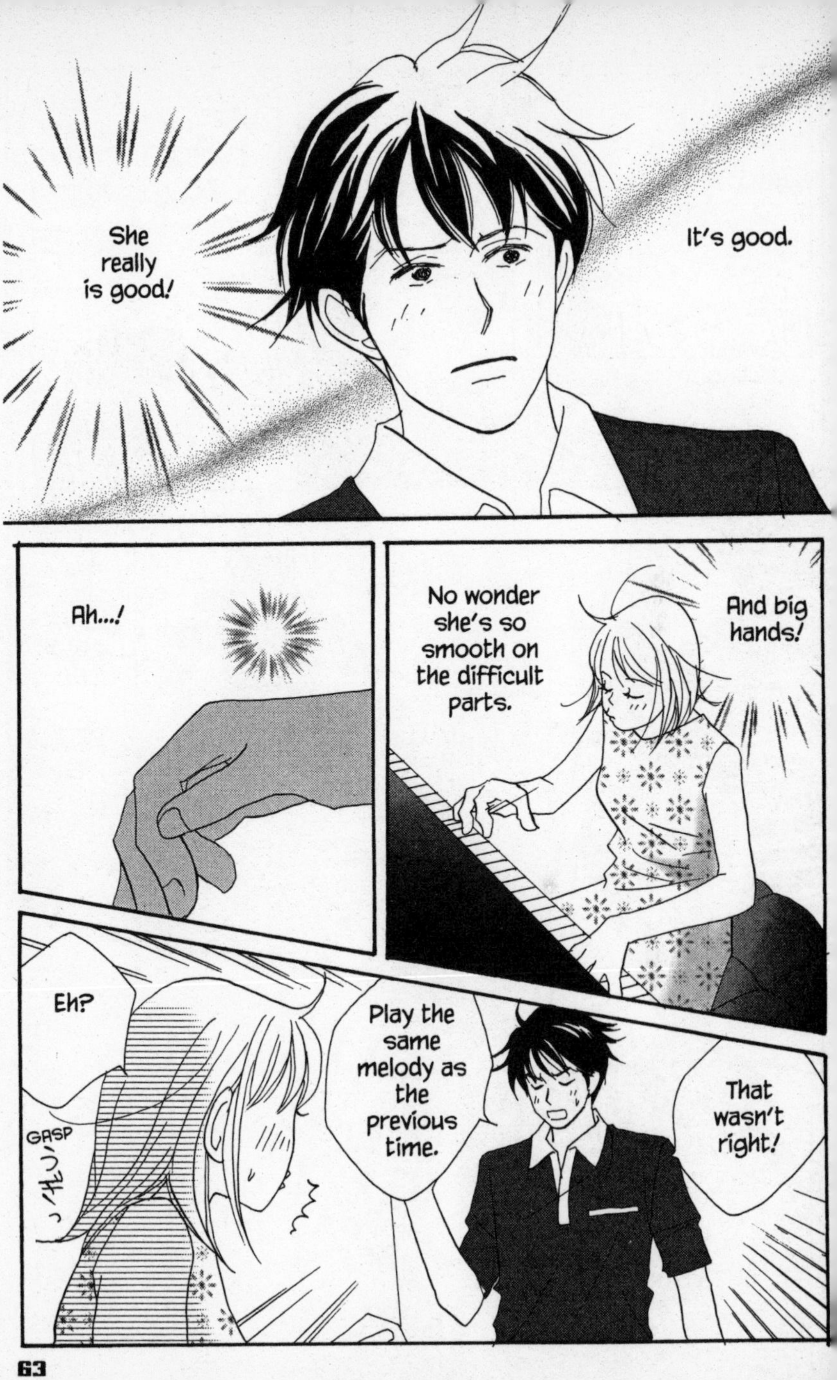
It's good.
She really is good!
And big hands!
No wonder she's so smooth on the difficult parts.
Ah...!
That wasn't right!
Play the same melody as the previous time.
Eh?
GASP

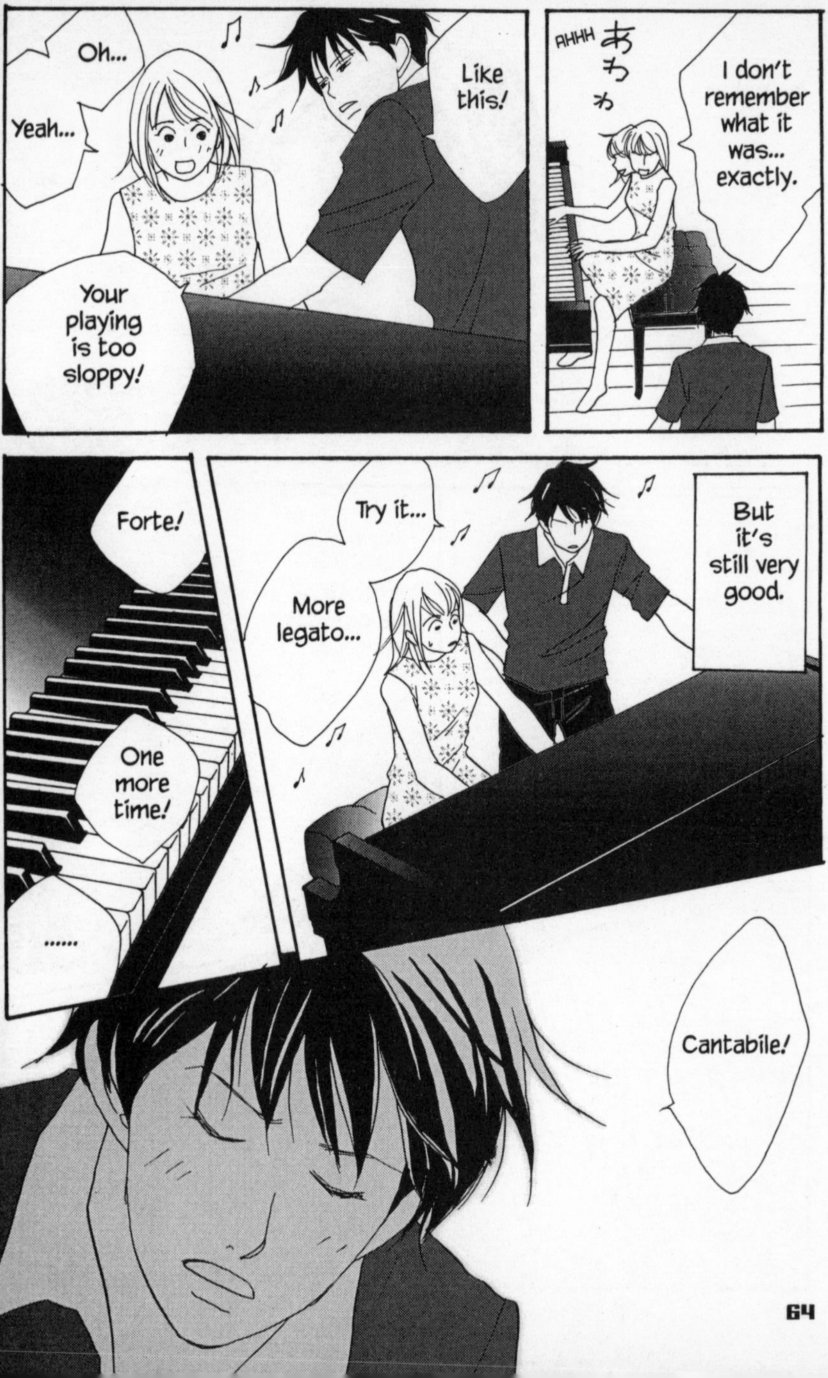
AHHH
あわわ
I don't remember what it was... exactly.
Like this!
Oh...
Yeah...
Your playing is too sloppy!
But it's still very good.
Try it...
More legato...
Forte!
One more time!
......
Cantabile!

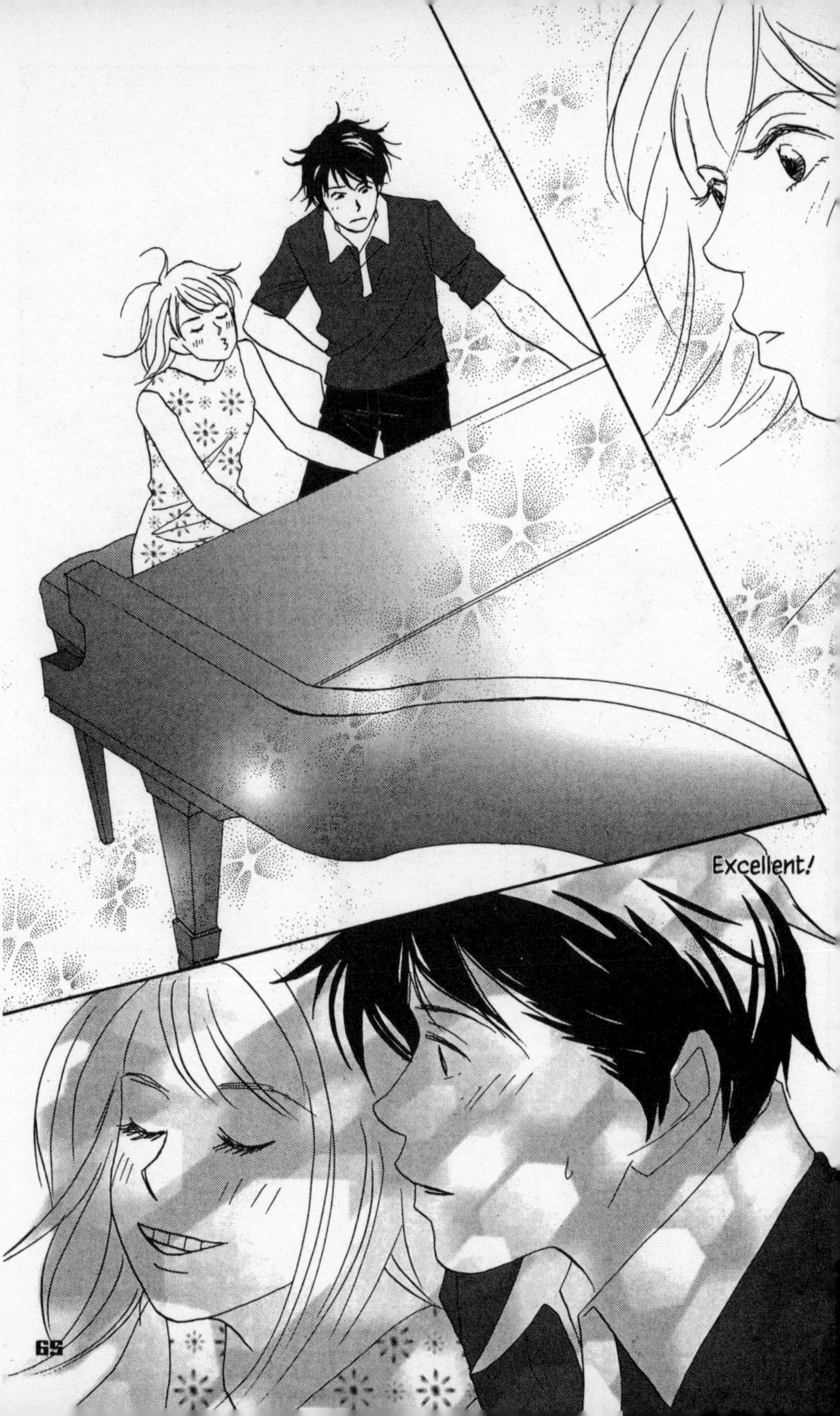
Excellent!

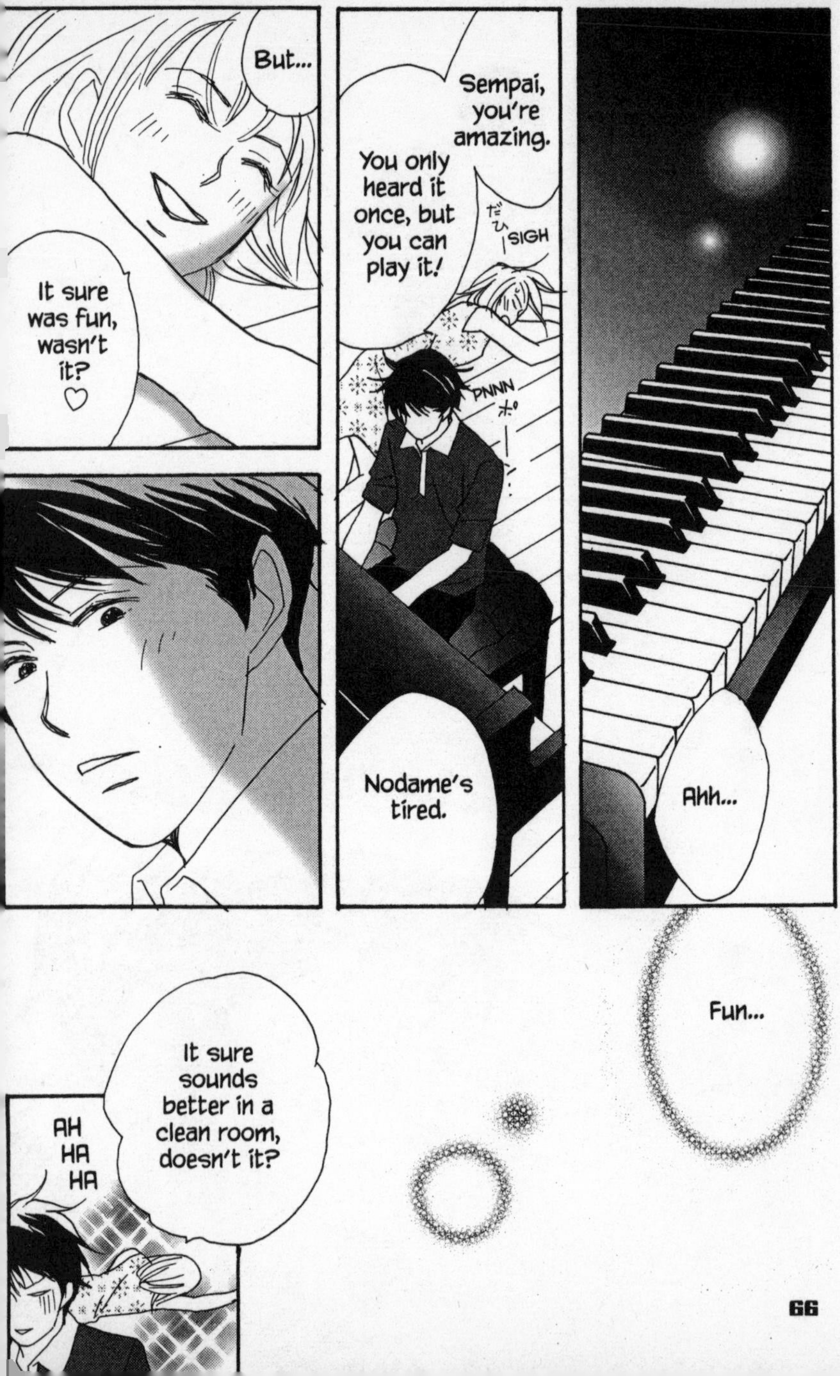
Ahh...
Sempai, you're amazing.
You only heard it once, but you can play it!
SIGH
PNNN
Nodame's tired.
But...
It sure was fun, wasn't it? ♡
Fun...
It sure sounds better in a clean room, doesn't it?
AH HA HA

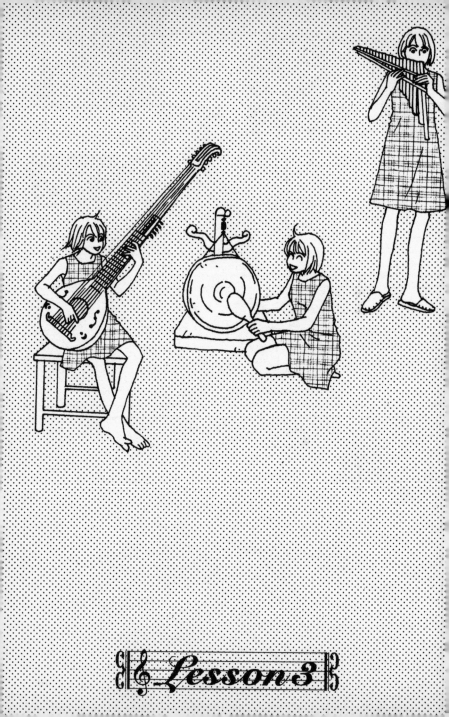

Lesson 3

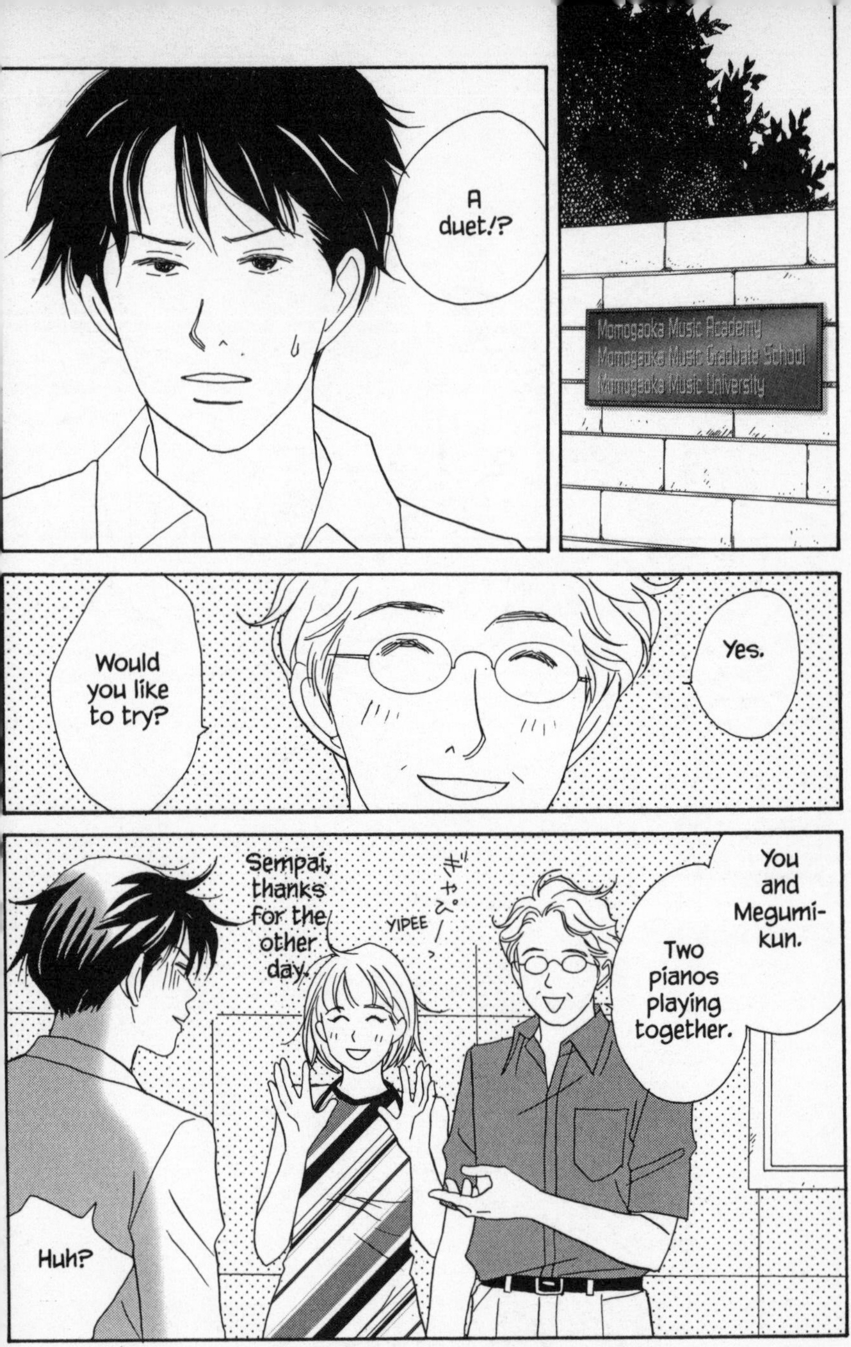
Momogaoka Music Academy
Momogaoka Music Graduate School
Momogaoka Music University
A duet!?
Yes.
Would you like to try?
You and Megumi-kun.
Two pianos playing together.
YIPEE
Sempai, thanks for the other day.
Huh?

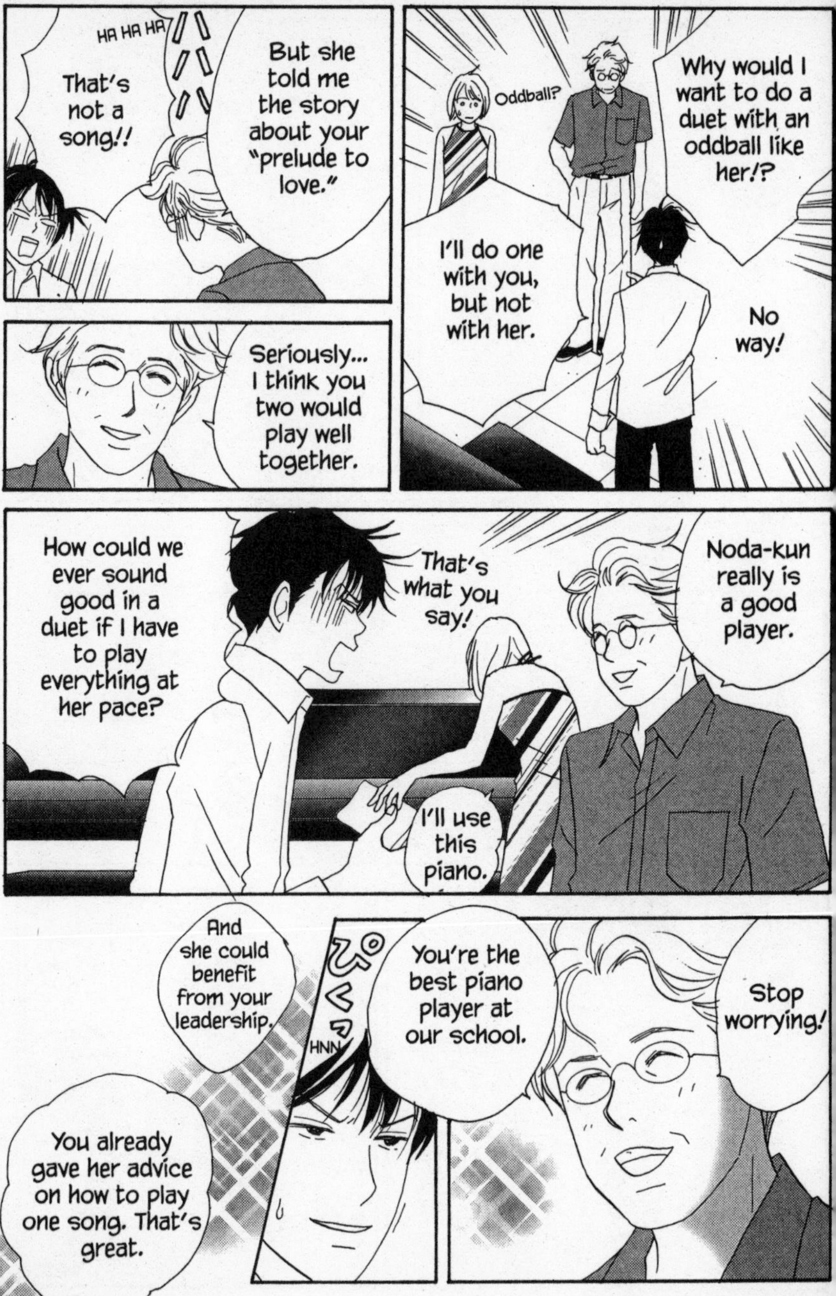
No way!
Why would I want to do a duet with an oddball like her!?
Oddball?
I'll do one with you, but not with her.
But she told me the story about your "prelude to love."
HA HA HA
That's not a song!!
Seriously... I think you two would play well together.
Noda-kun really is a good player.
That's what you say!
How could we ever sound good in a duet if I have to play everything at her pace?
I'll use this piano.
Stop worrying!
You're the best piano player at our school.
HNN
And she could benefit from your leadership.
You already gave her advice on how to play one song. That's great.

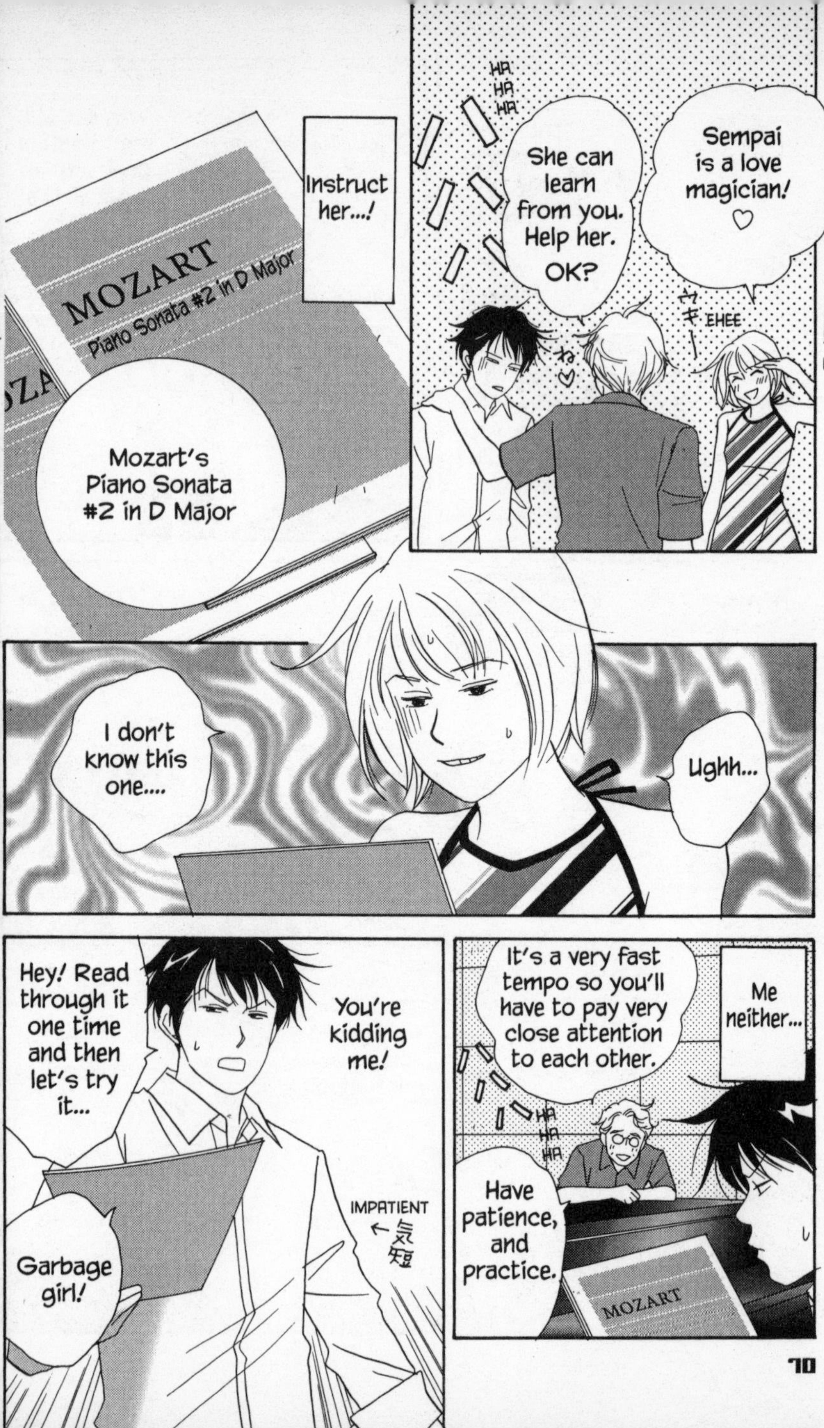
Sempai is a love magician! ♡
SALUTE
EHEE
ね
She can learn from you. Help her. OK?
HA HA HA
Instruct her...!
MOZART
Piano Sonata #2 in D Major
Mozart's Piano Sonata #2 in D Major
Ughh...
I don't know this one....
Me neither...
It's a very fast tempo so you'll have to pay very close attention to each other.
HA HA HA
Have patience, and practice.
MOZART
You're kidding me!
Hey! Read through it one time and then let's try it...
IMPATIENT
気短
Garbage girl!

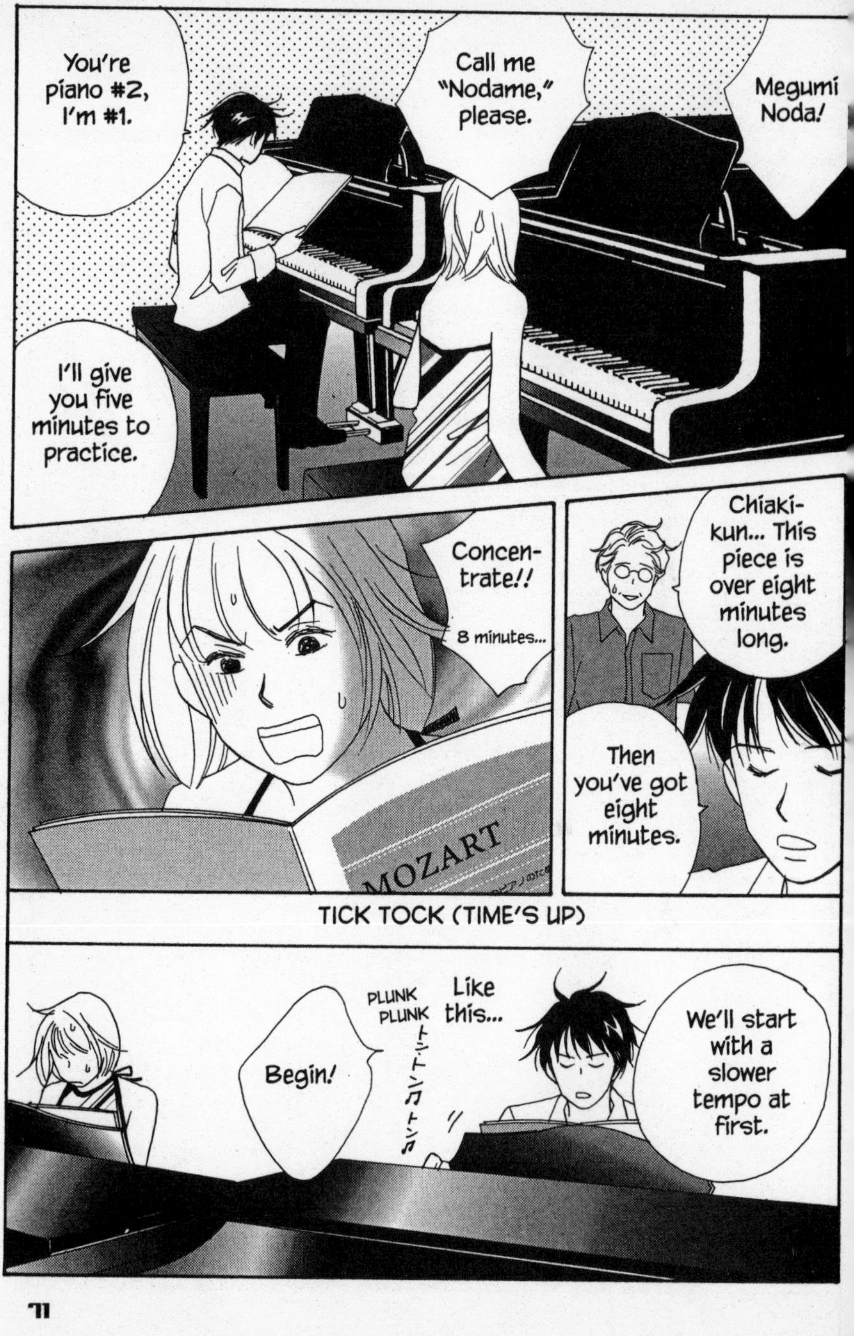
Megumi Noda!
Call me "Nodame," please.
You're piano #2, I'm #1.
I'll give you five minutes to practice.
Chiaki-kun... This piece is over eight minutes long.
Then you've got eight minutes.
Concentrate!!
8 minutes...
MOZART
TICK TOCK (TIME'S UP)
We'll start with a slower tempo at first.
Like this...
PLUNK PLUNK
Begin!

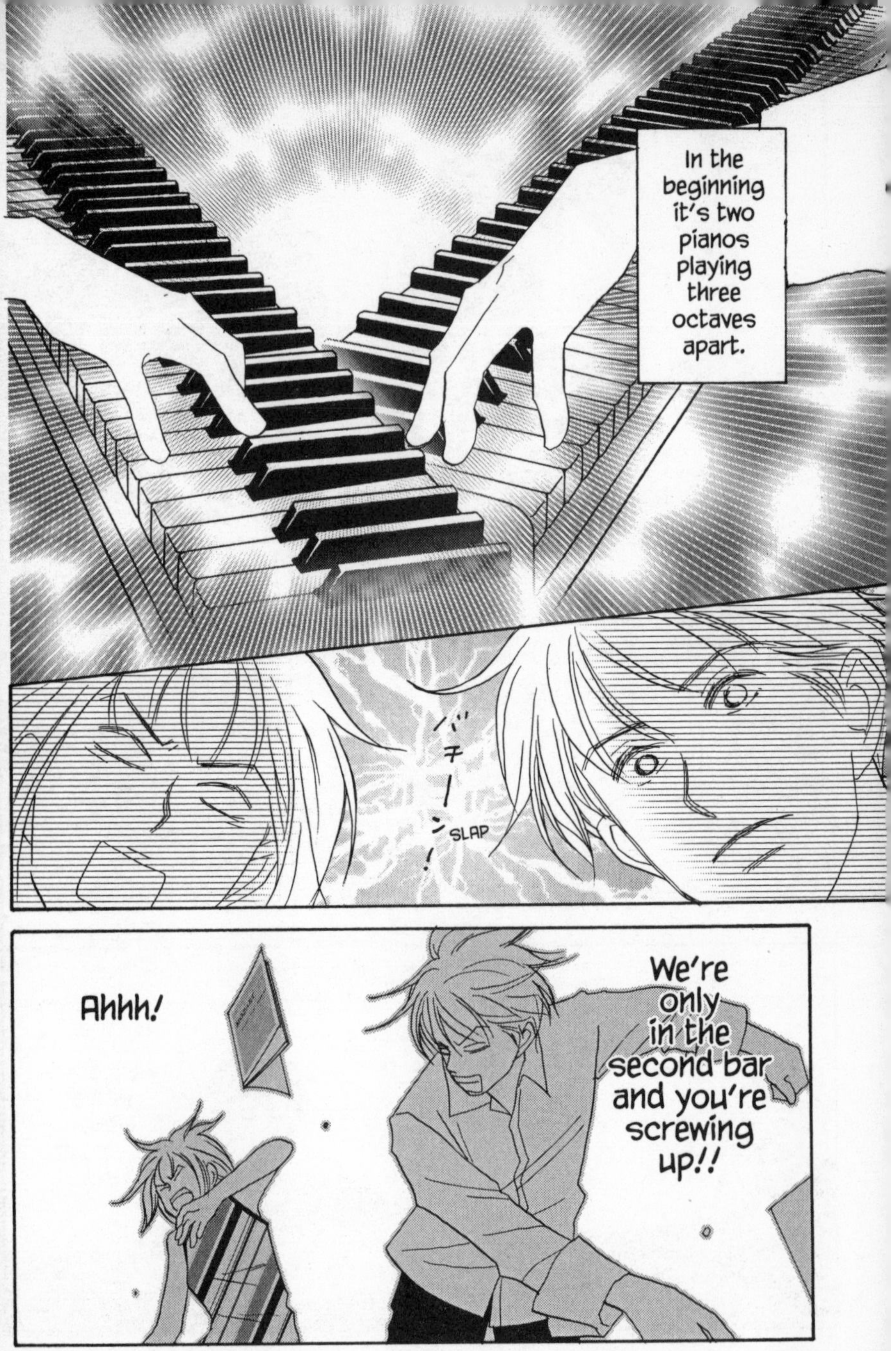
In the beginning it's two pianos playing three octaves apart.
バチーン!
SLAP
We're only in the second bar and you're screwing up!!
Ahhh!

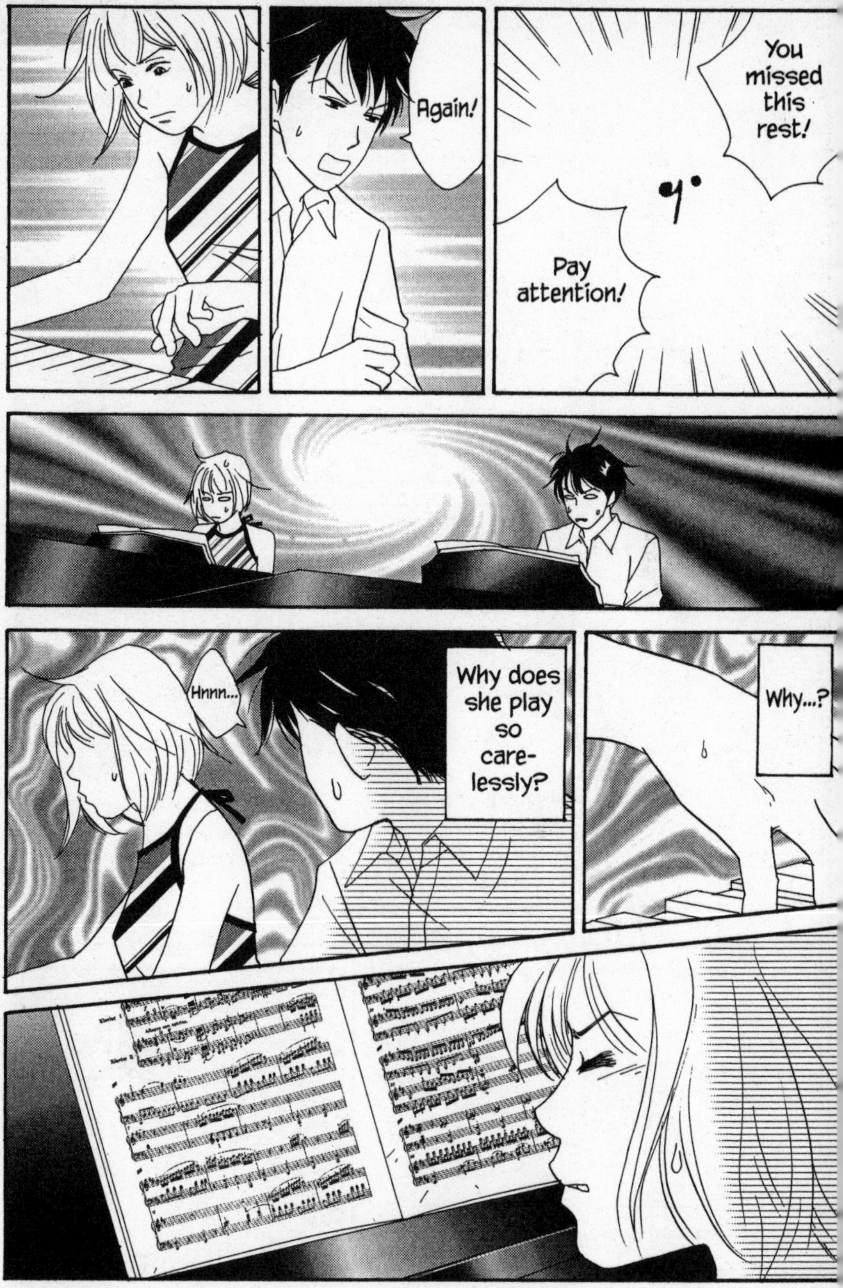
You missed this rest!
Pay attention!
Again!
Why...?
Why does she play so care-lessly?
Hnnn...

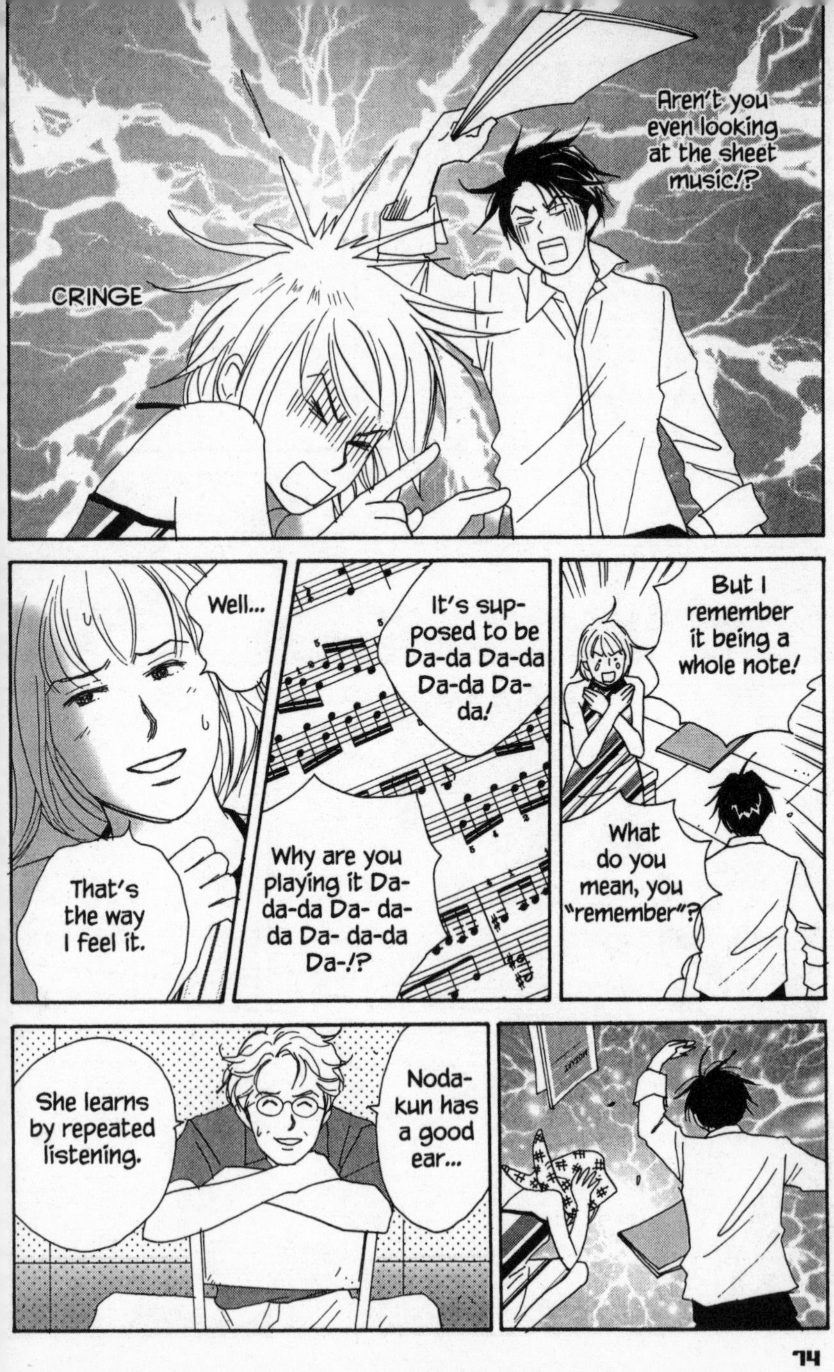
Aren't you even looking at the sheet music!?
CRINGE
But I remember it being a whole note!
What do you mean, you "remember"?
It's supposed to be Da-da Da-da Da-da Da-da!
Why are you playing it Da-da-da Da- da-da Da- da-da Da-!?
Well...
That's the way I feel it.
Noda-kun has a good ear...
She learns by repeated listening.

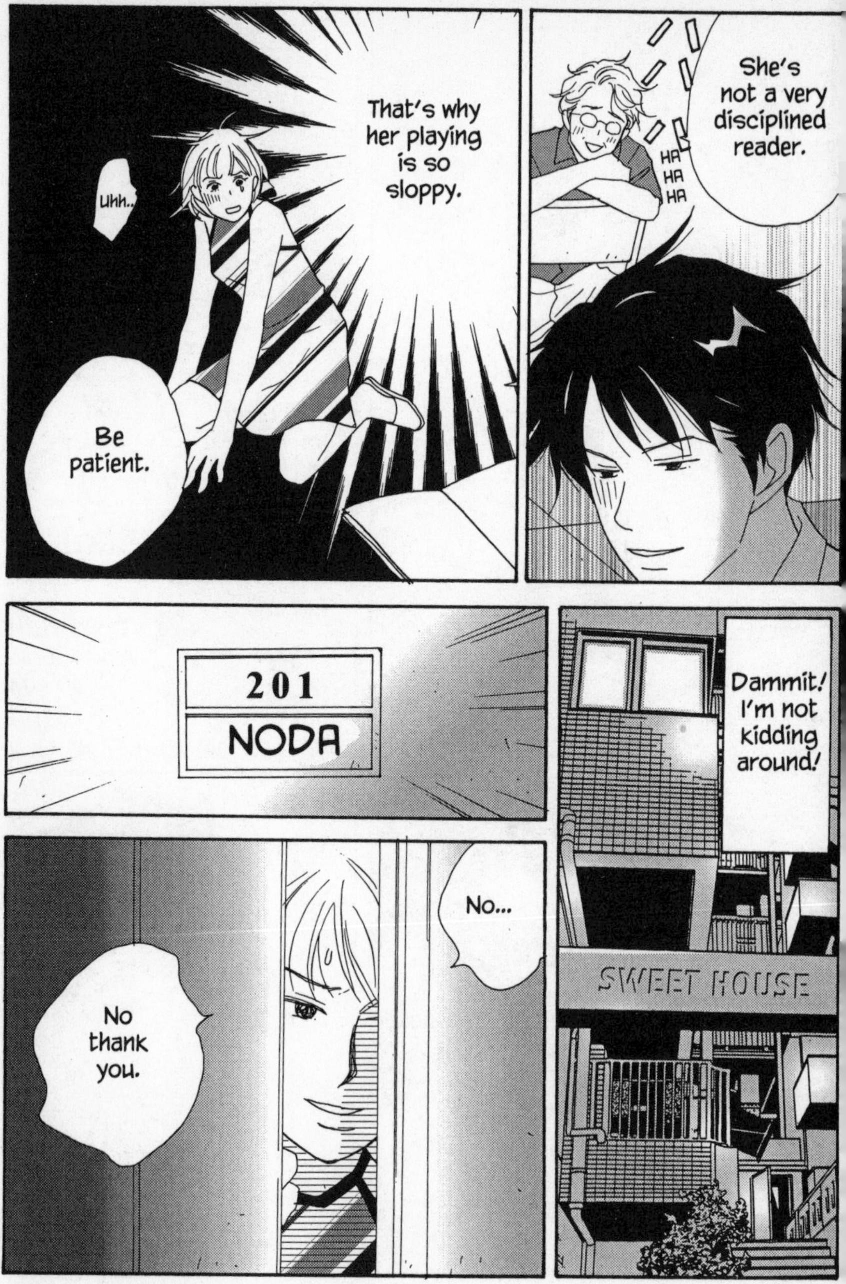
She's not a very disciplined reader.
HA HA HA
That's why her playing is so sloppy.
uhh..
Be patient.
Dammit! I'm not kidding around!
SWEET HOUSE
201
NODA
No...
No thank you.

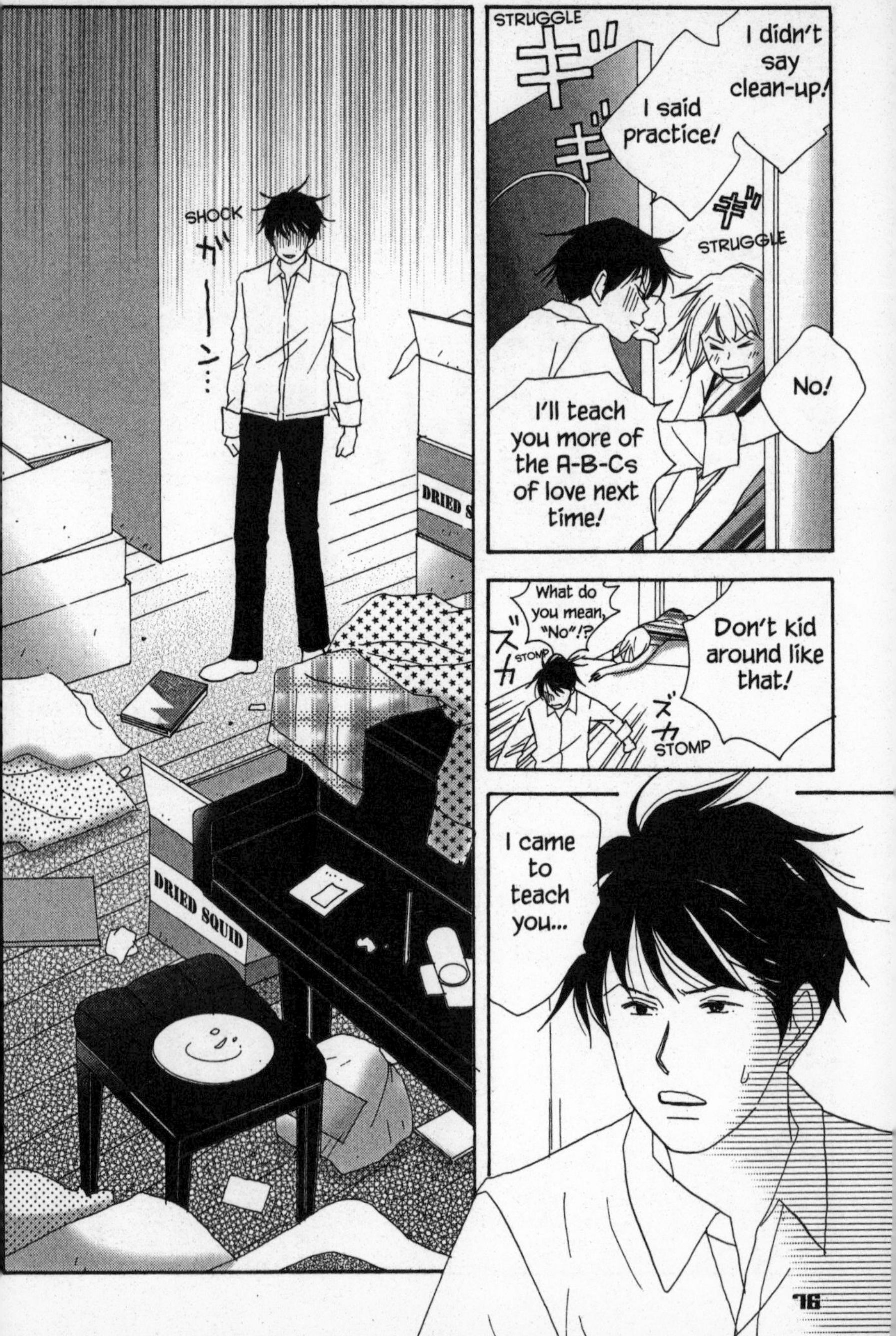
STRUGGLE
I didn't say clean-up!
I said practice!
STRUGGLE
No!
I'll teach you more of the A-B-Cs of love next time!
Don't kid around like that!
What do you mean, "No"!?
STOMP
STOMP
I came to teach you...
SHOCK

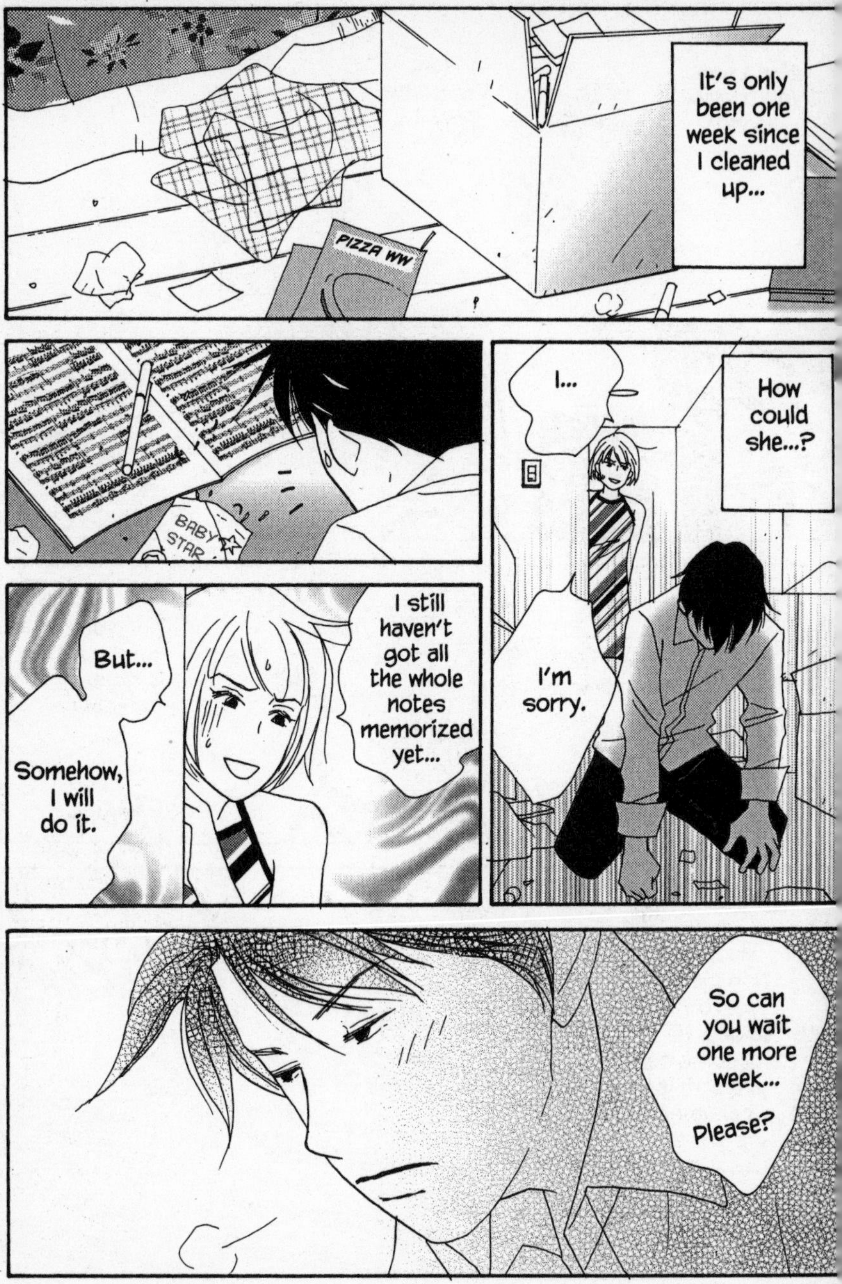
It's only been one week since I cleaned up...
PIZZA WW
How could she...?
I...
I'm sorry.
BABY STAR
I still haven't got all the whole notes memorized yet...
But...
Somehow, I will do it.
So can you wait one more week...
Please?

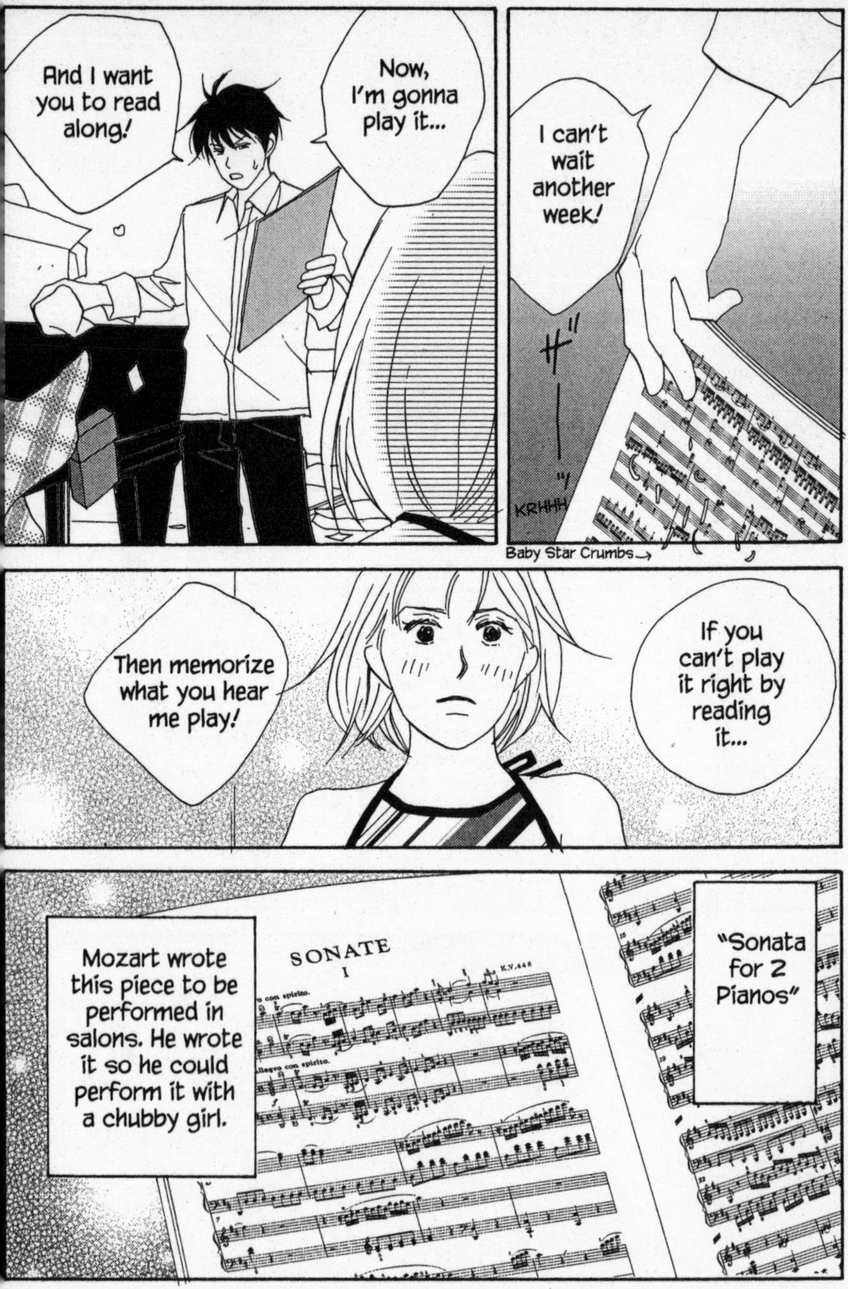
I can't wait another week!
KRHHH
Baby Star Crumbs
Now, I'm gonna play it...
And I want you to read along!
If you can't play it right by reading it...
Then memorize what you hear me play!
"Sonata for 2 Pianos"
Mozart wrote this piece to be performed in salons. He wrote it so he could perform it with a chubby girl.
SONATE
I

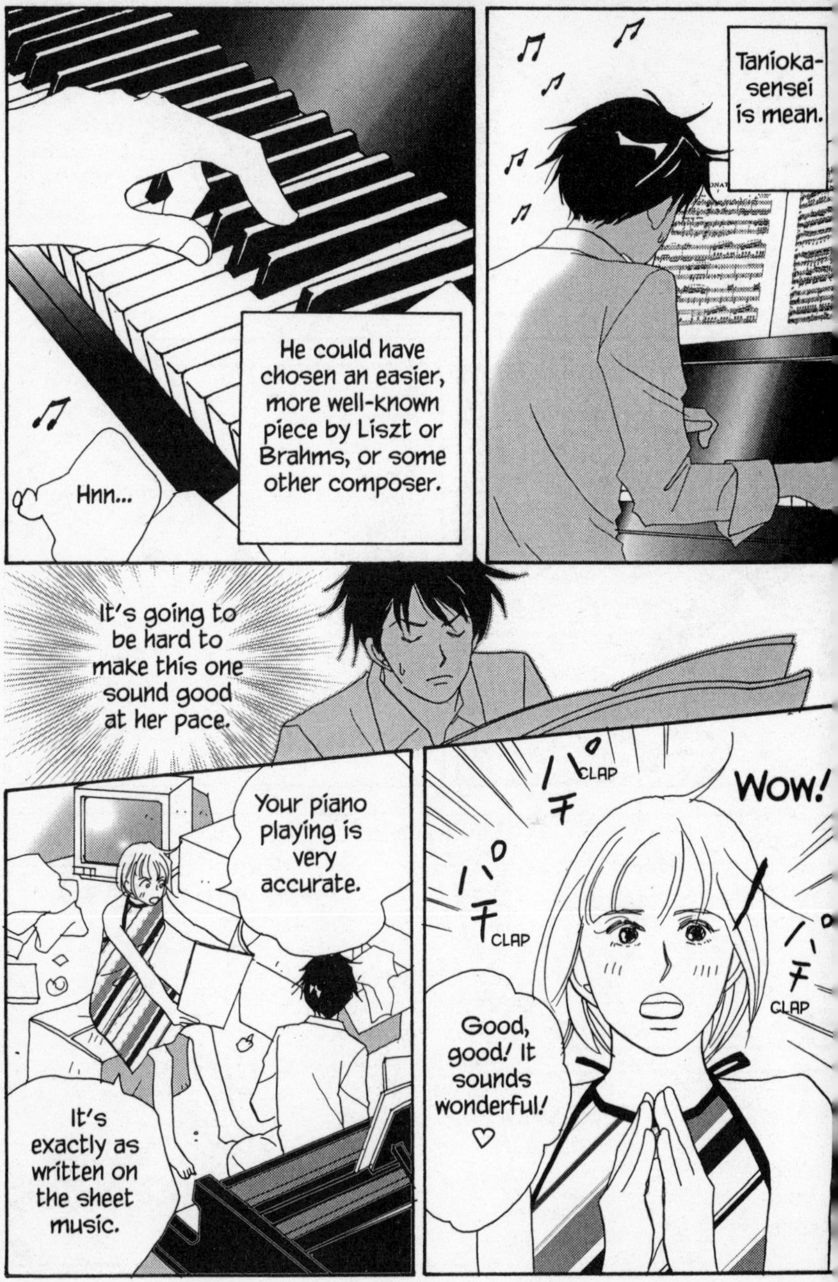
Tanioka-sensei is mean.
He could have chosen an easier, more well-known piece by Liszt or Brahms, or some other composer.
Hnn...
It's going to be hard to make this one sound good at her pace.
パチ CLAP
WOW!
パチ CLAP
パチ CLAP
Good, good! It sounds wonderful! ♡
Your piano playing is very accurate.
It's exactly as written on the sheet music.

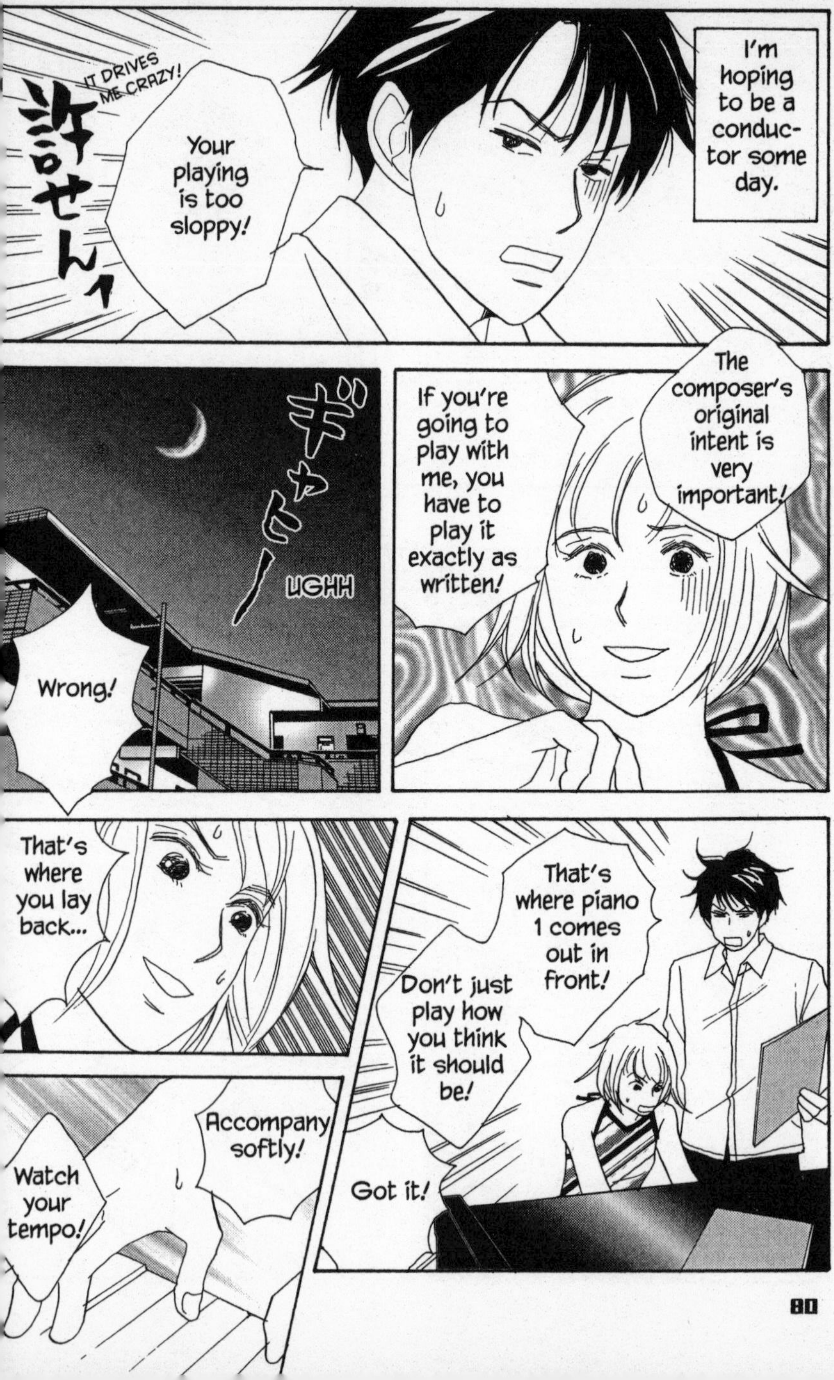
I'm hoping to be a conductor some day.
Your playing is too sloppy!
IT DRIVES ME CRAZY!
許せん
The composer's original intent is very important!
If you're going to play with me, you have to play it exactly as written!
ギャヒー
UGHH
Wrong!
That's where piano 1 comes out in front!
Don't just play how you think it should be!
Got it!
That's where you lay back...
Accompany softly!
Watch your tempo!

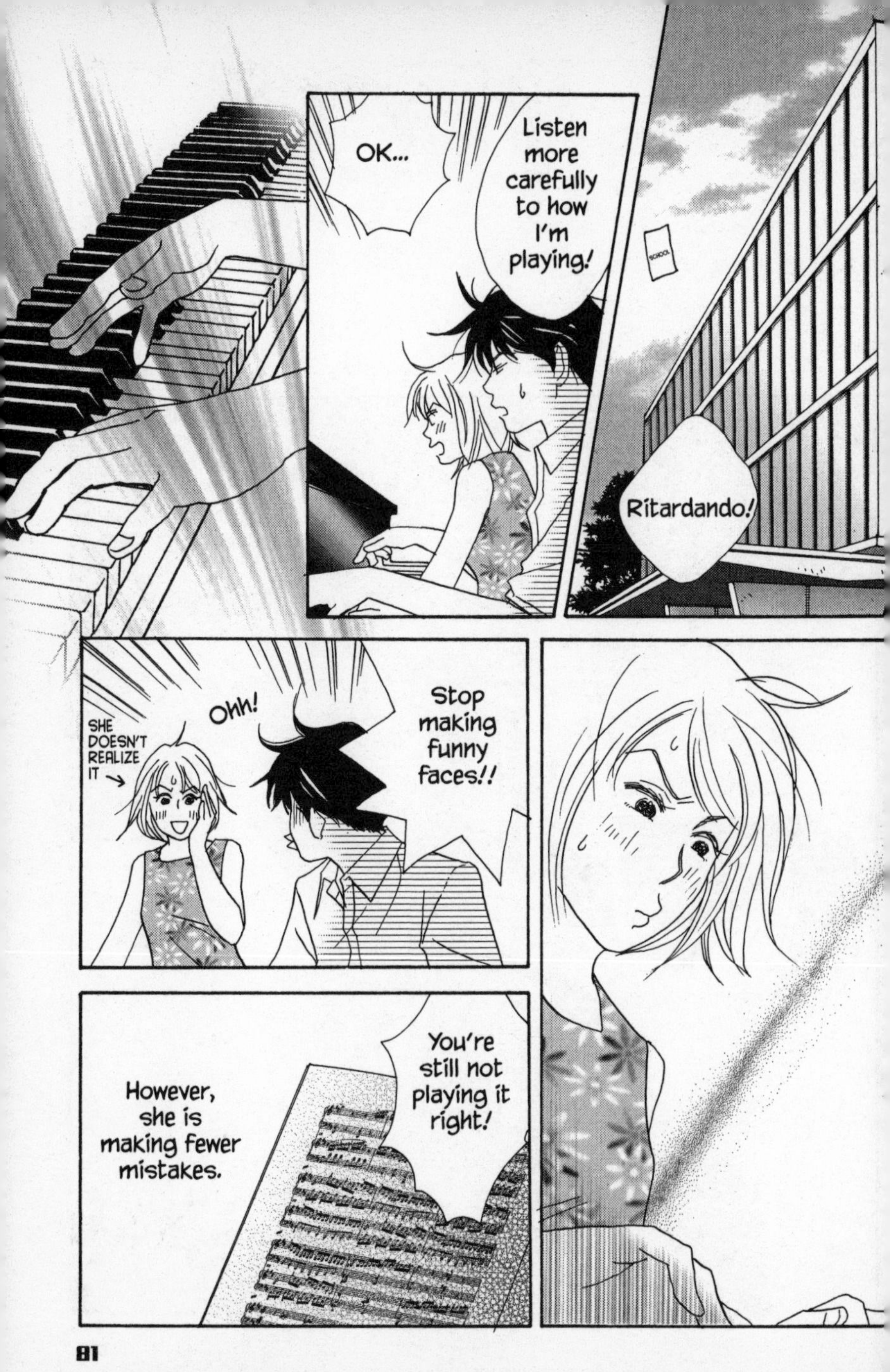
SCHOOL
Ritardando!
Listen more carefully to how I'm playing!
OK...
Stop making funny faces!!
Ohh!
SHE DOESN'T REALIZE IT
You're still not playing it right!
However, she is making fewer mistakes.

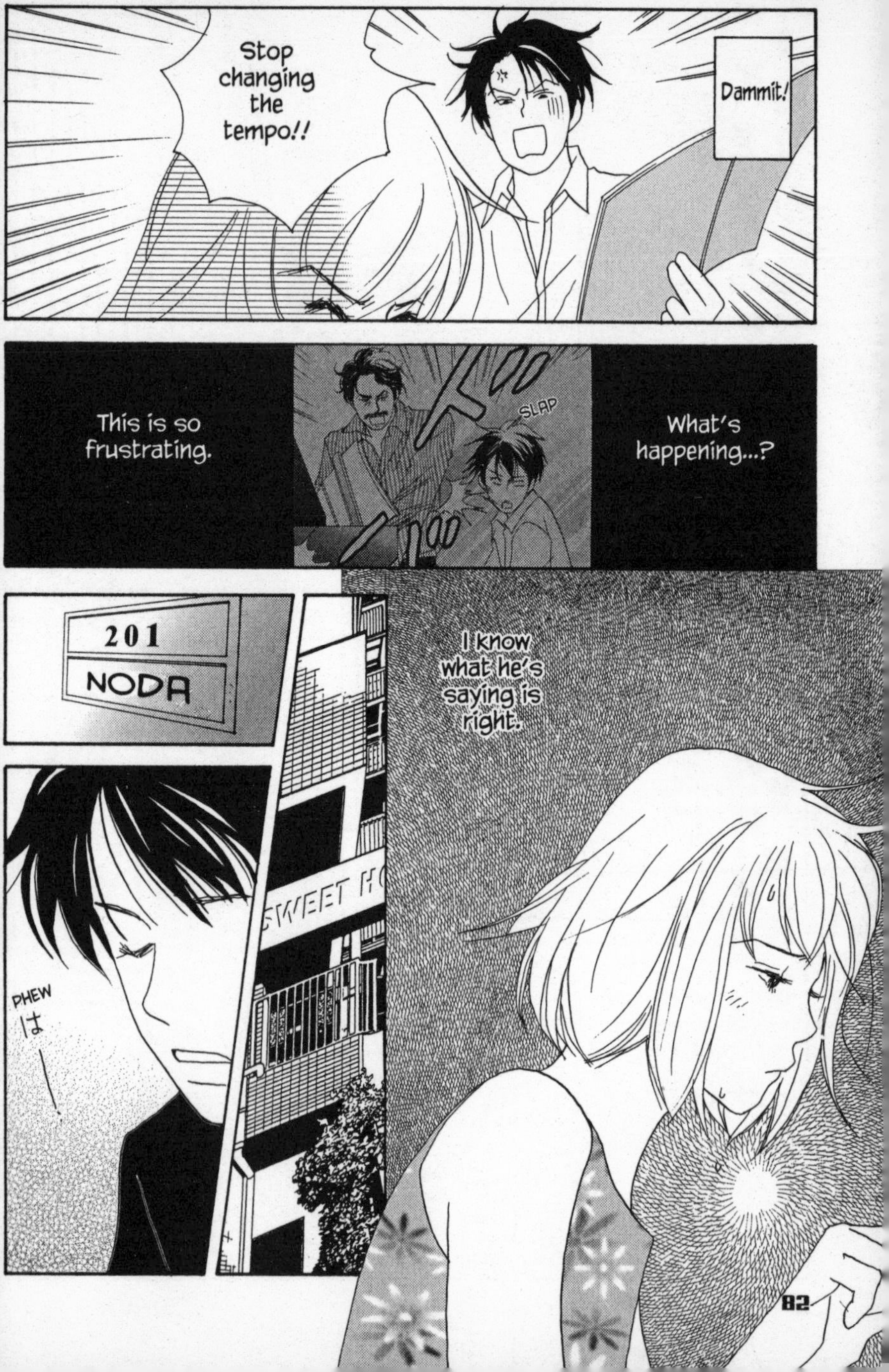

Dammit!
Stop changing the tempo!!
What's happening...?
SLAP
This is so frustrating.
I know what he's saying is right.
201
NODA
SWEET H
PHEW
は一

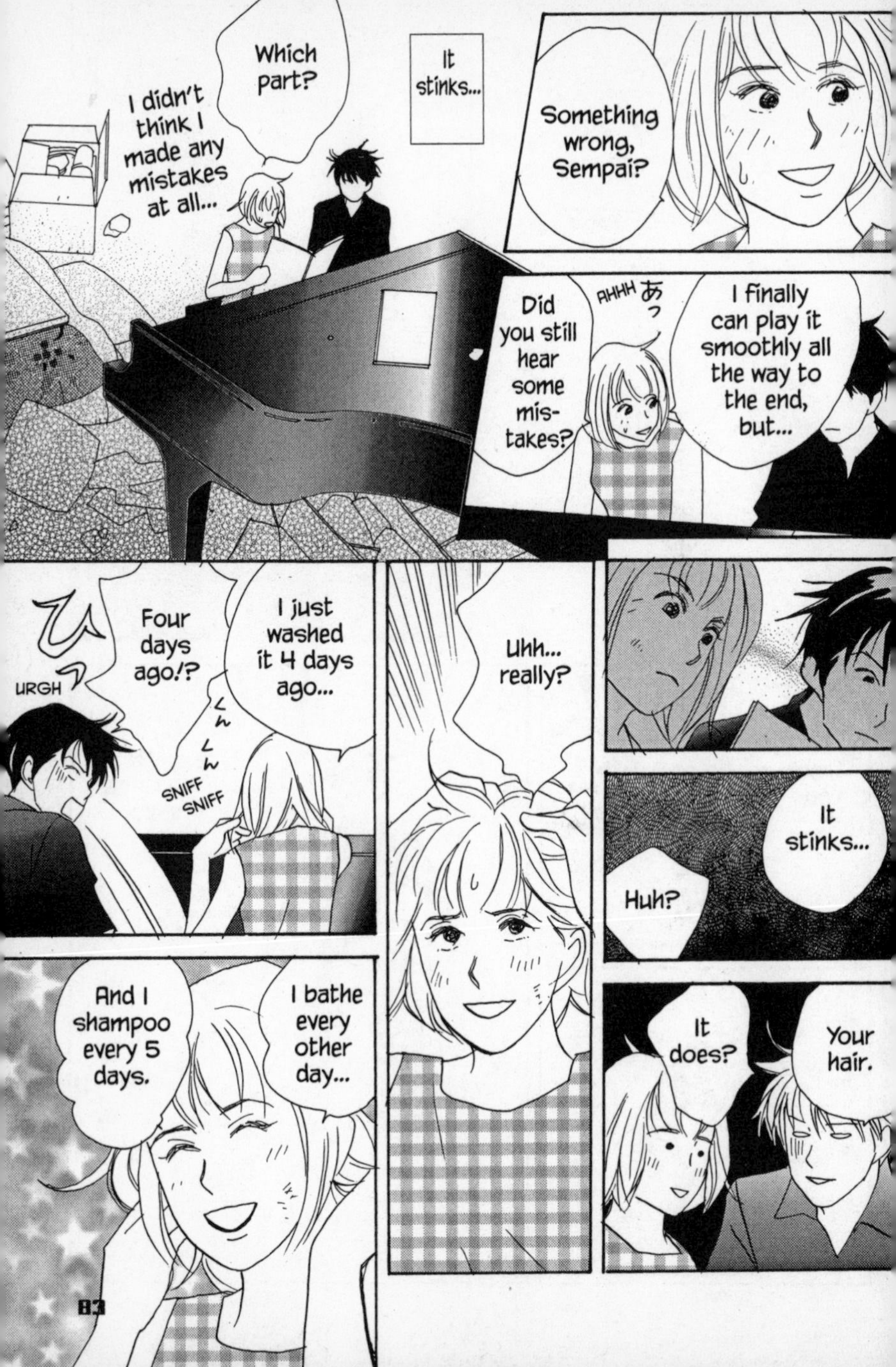
Something wrong, Sempai?
I finally can play it smoothly all the way to the end, but...
AHHH あっ
Did you still hear some mistakes?
It stinks...
Which part?
I didn't think I made any mistakes at all...
It stinks...
Huh?
Your hair.
It does?
Uhh... really?
I just washed it 4 days ago...
Four days ago!?
URGH ひ
SNIFF SNIFF くんくん
I bathe every other day...
And I shampoo every 5 days.

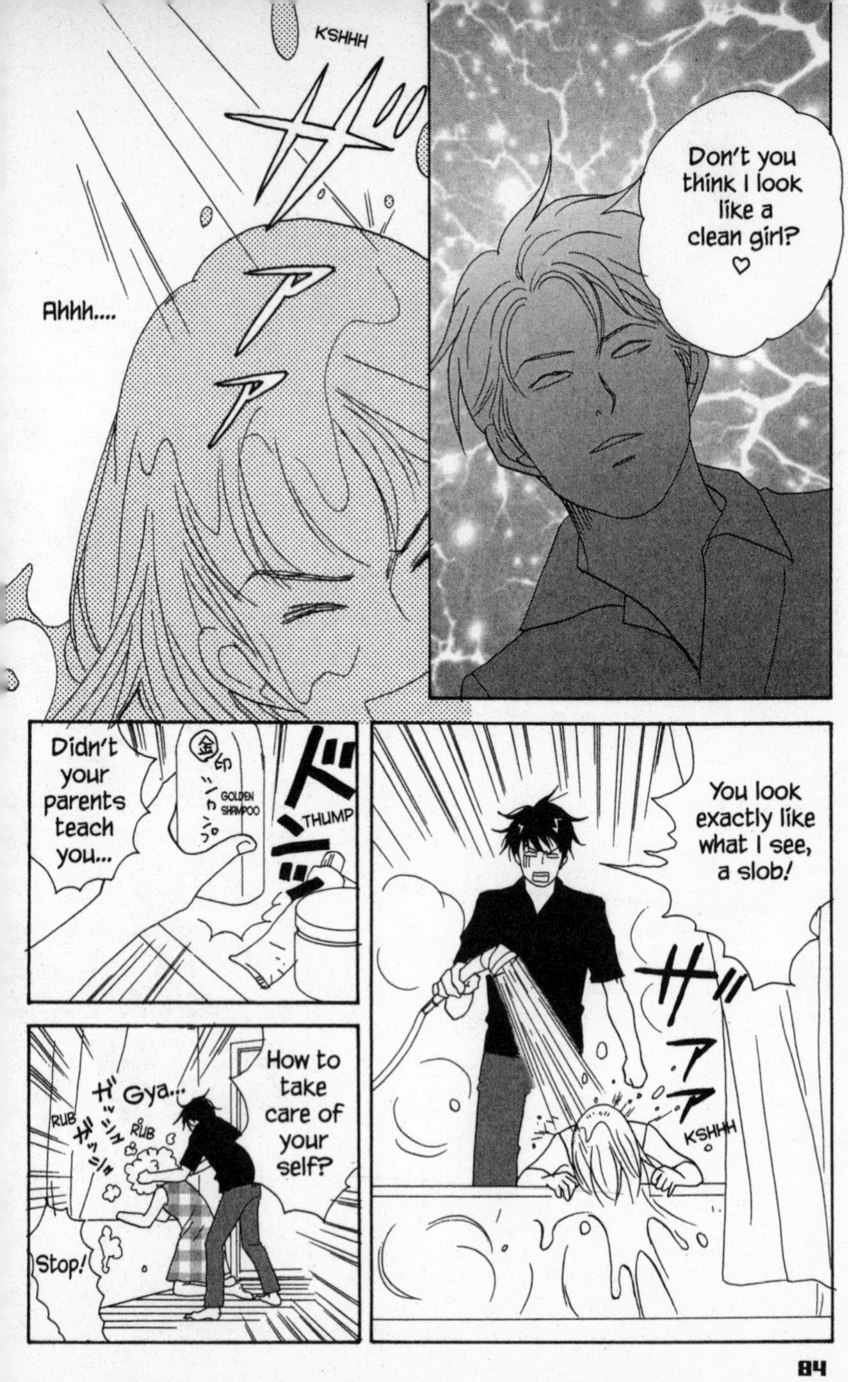
Don't you think I look like a clean girl? ♡
KSHHH
Ahhh....
You look exactly like what I see, a slob!
KSHHH
Didn't your parents teach you...
GOLDEN SHAMPOO
THUMP
How to take care of your self?
Gya...
RUB
RUB
Stop!

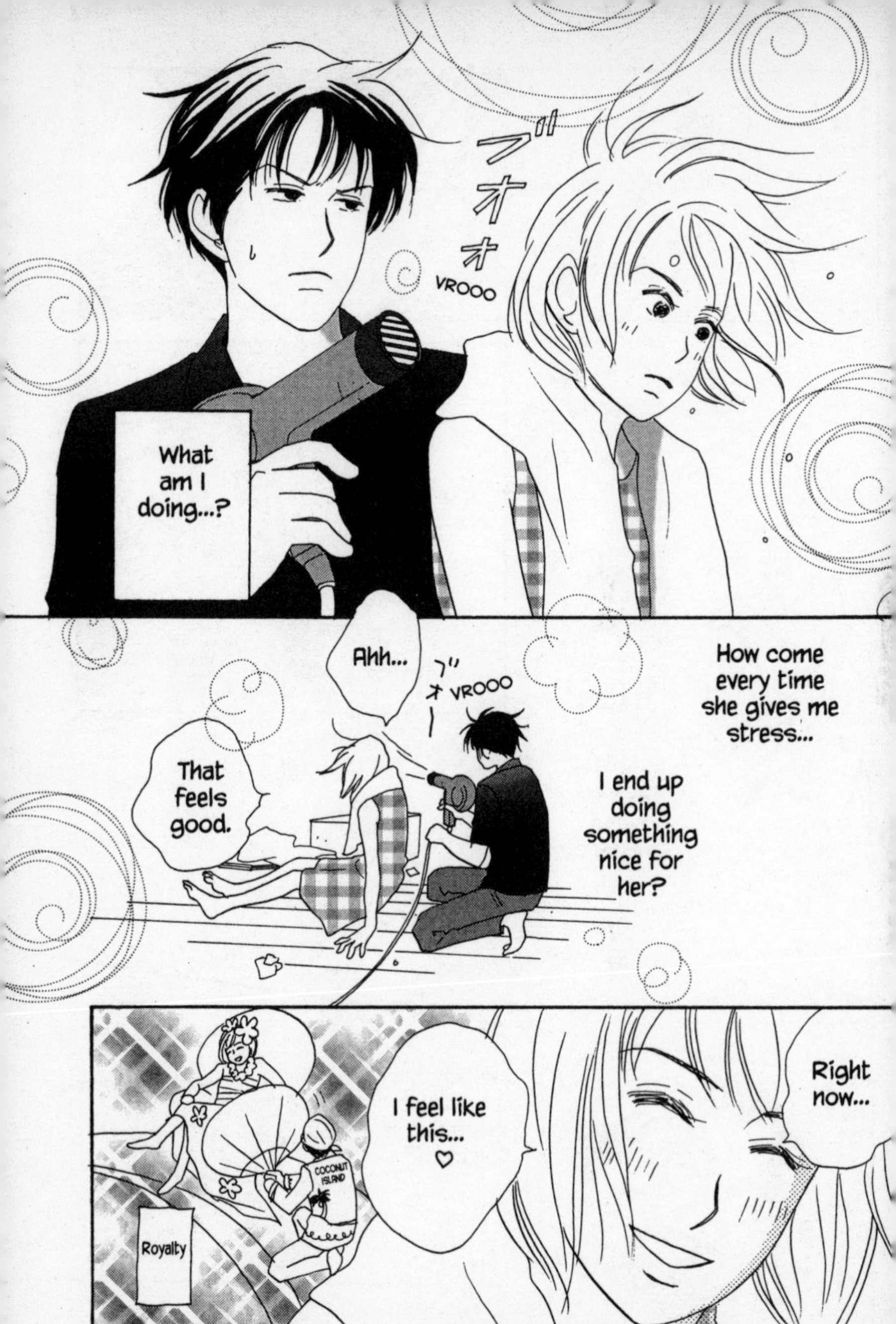
ブオオ
VROOO
What am I doing...?
How come every time she gives me stress...
I end up doing something nice for her?
ブオー
VROOO
Ahh...
That feels good.
Right now...
I feel like this... ♡
COCONUT ISLAND
Royalty

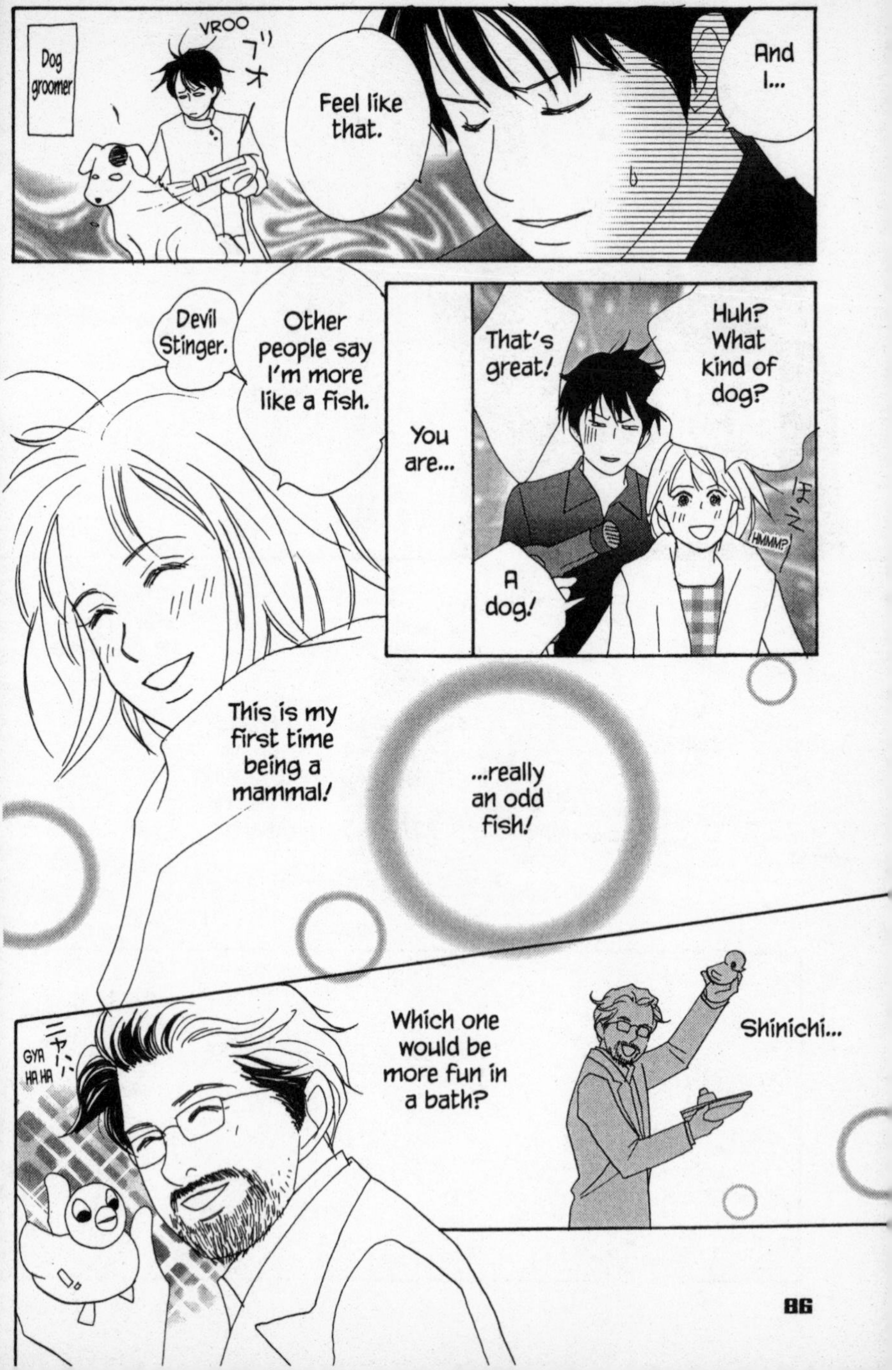
And I...
Feel like that.
Dog groomer
VROO
ブオ
Huh? What kind of dog?
ほえ
HMMM?
That's great!
A dog!
You are...
Other people say I'm more like a fish.
Devil Stinger.
...really an odd fish!
This is my first time being a mammal!
Shinichi...
Which one would be more fun in a bath?
ニャハハ
GYA HA HA

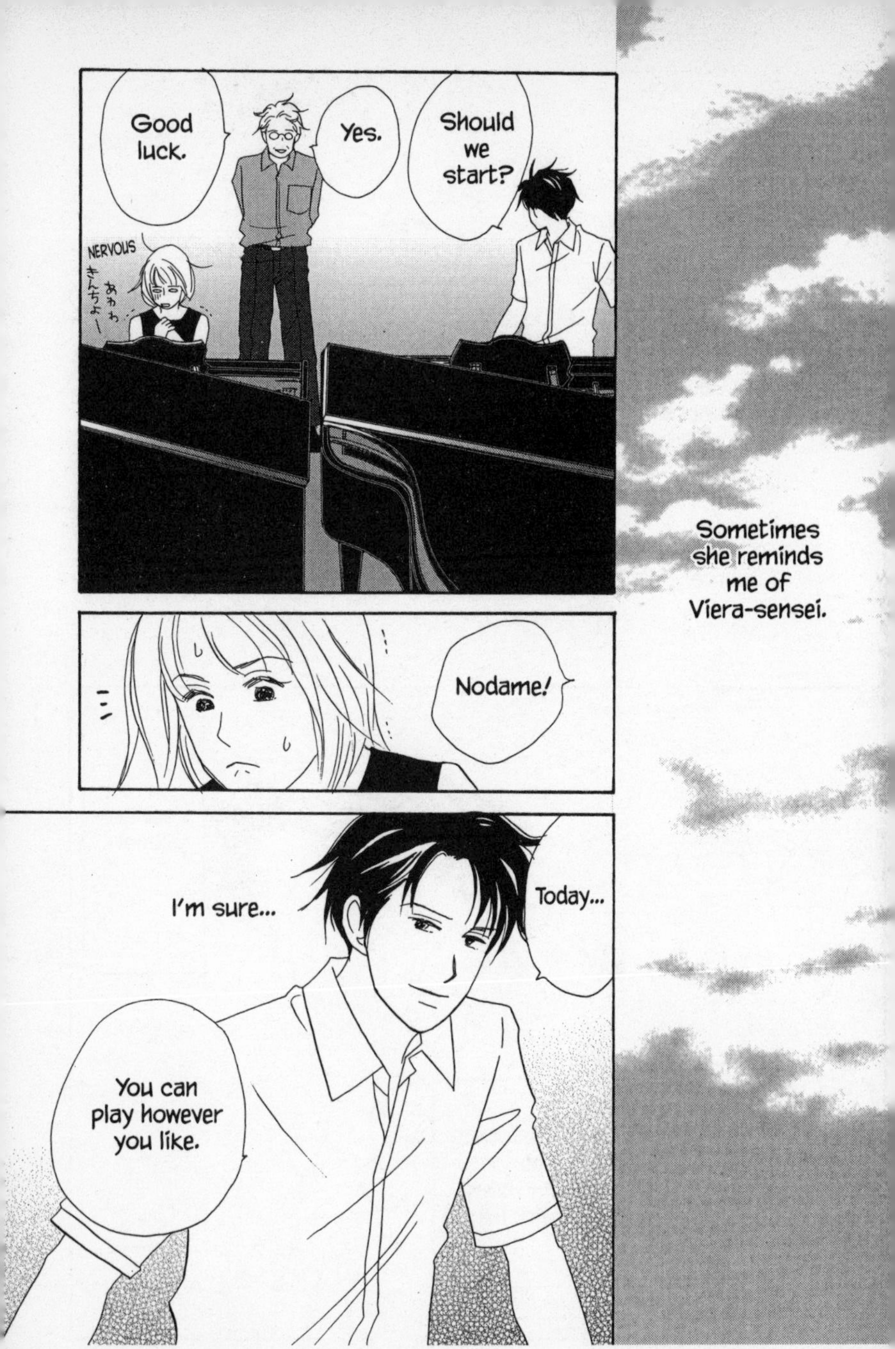
Sometimes she reminds me of Viera-sensei.
Should we start?
Yes.
Good luck.
NERVOUS
あゎゎ
きんちょー
Nodame!
Today...
I'm sure...
You can play however you like.

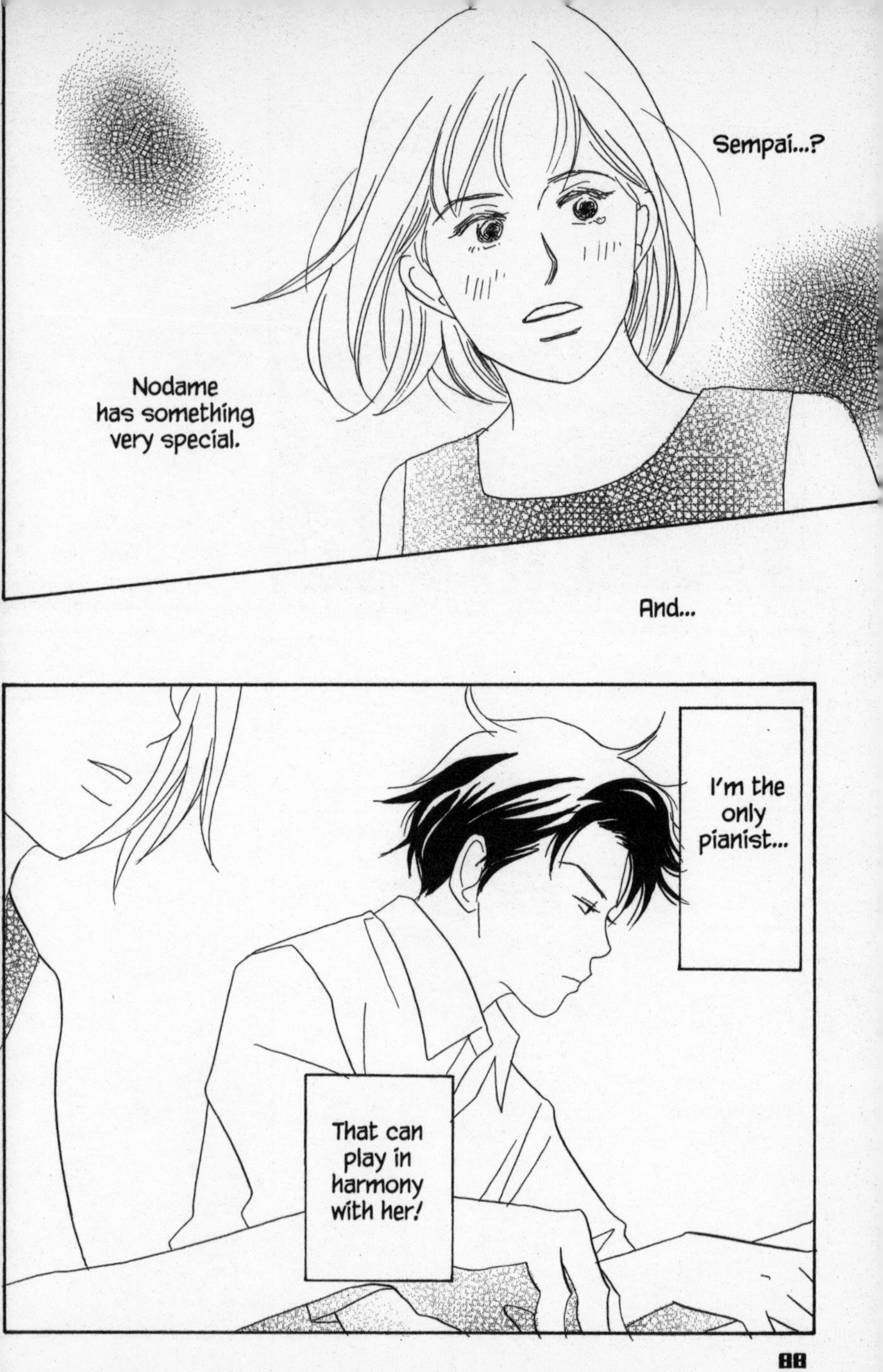
Sempai...?
Nodame has something very special.
And...
I'm the only pianist...
That can play in harmony with her!

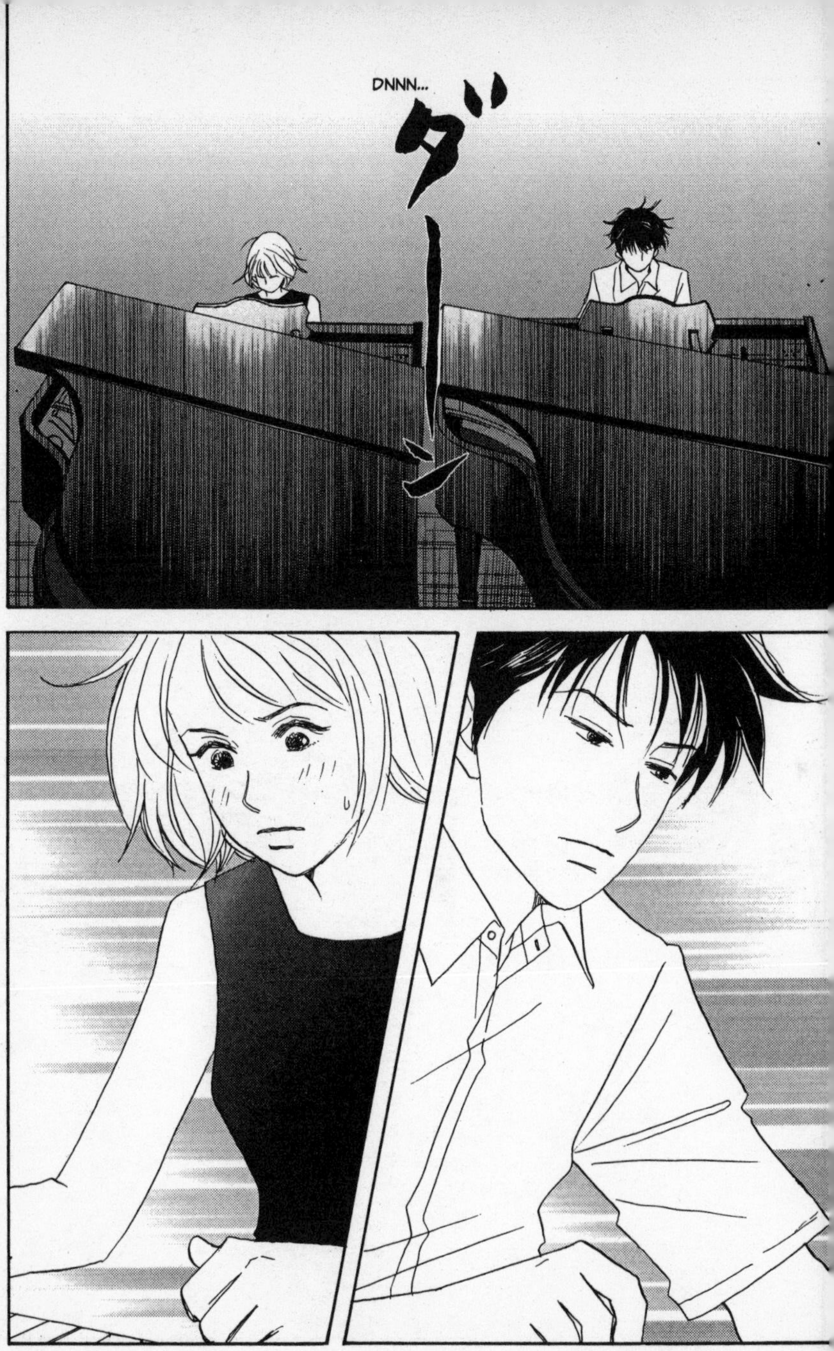
DNNN...
ダーン

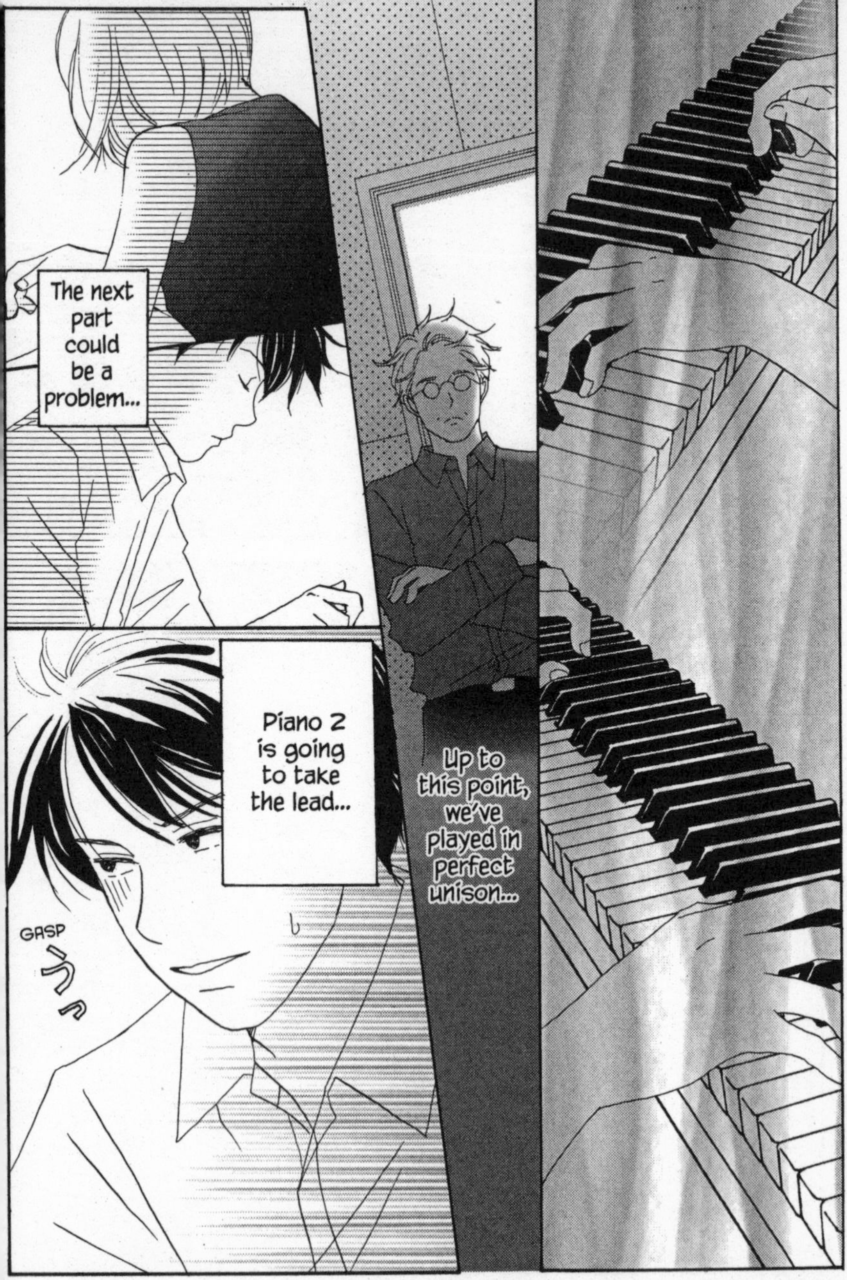
Up to this point, we've played in perfect unison...
The next part could be a problem...
Piano 2 is going to take the lead...
GASP

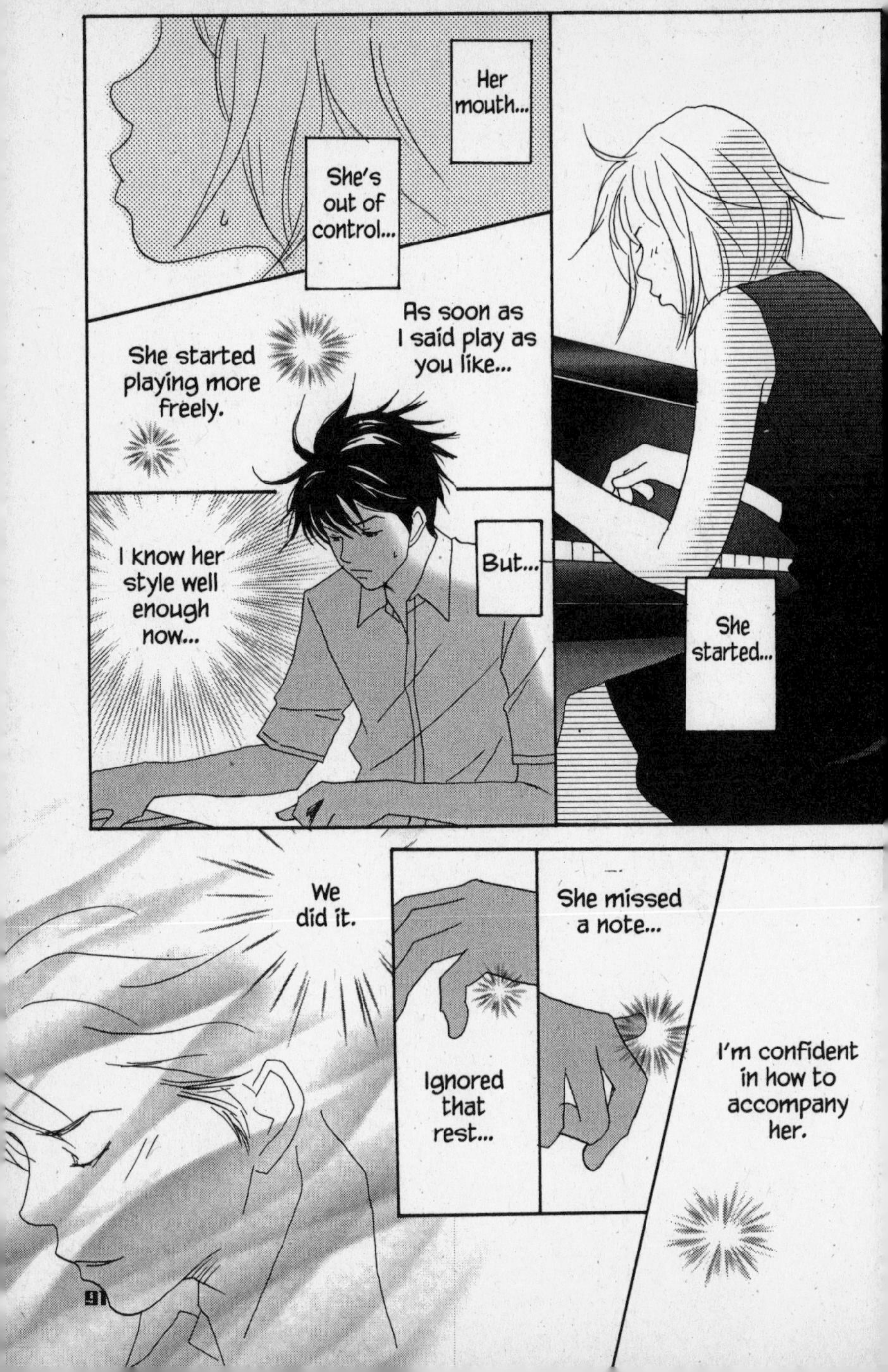

She started...
Her mouth...
She's out of control...
As soon as I said play as you like...
She started playing more freely.
But...
I know her style well enough now...
I'm confident in how to accompany her.
She missed a note...
Ignored that rest...
We did it.

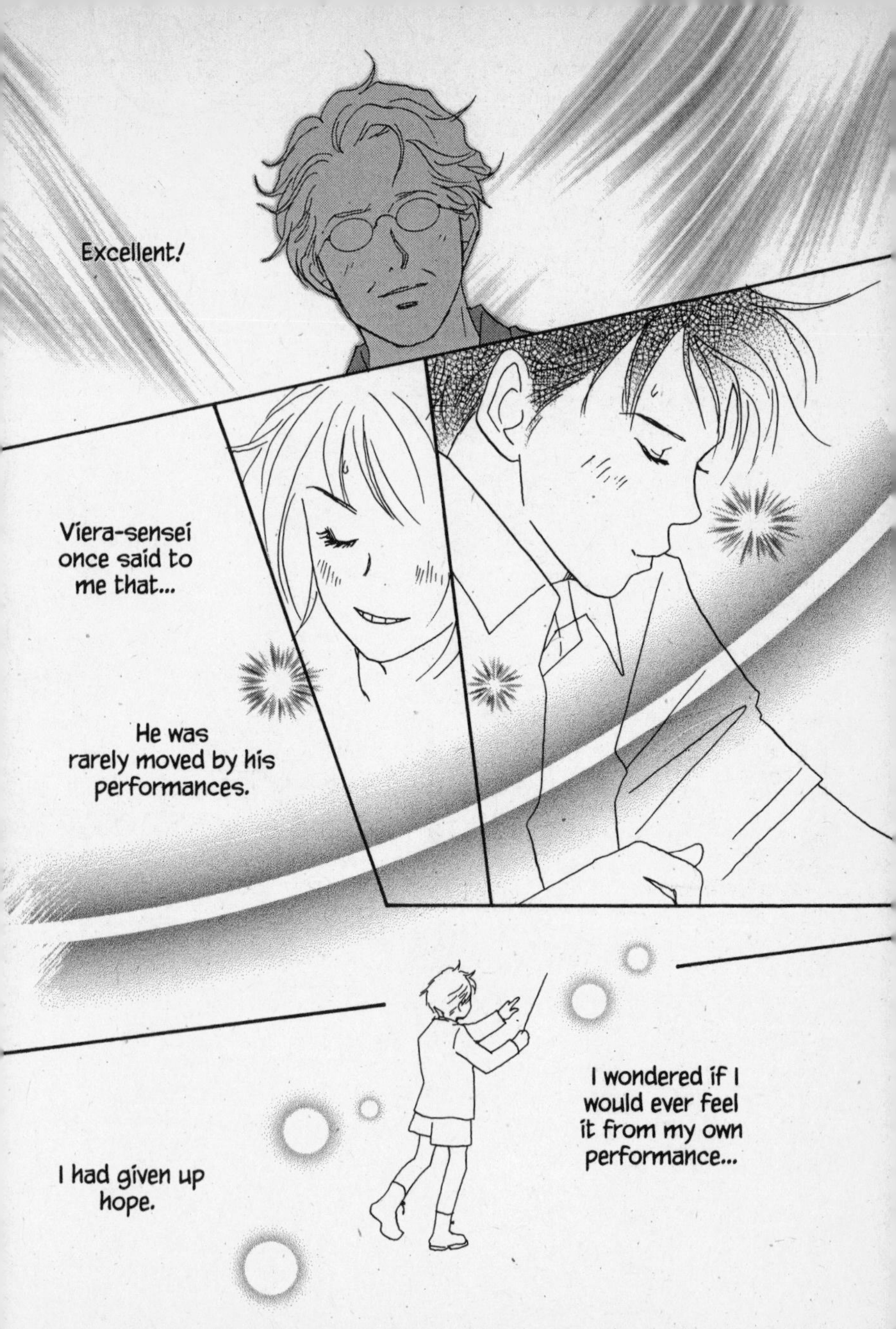
Excellent!
Viera-sensei once said to me that...
He was rarely moved by his performances.
I wondered if I would ever feel it from my own performance...
I had given up hope.

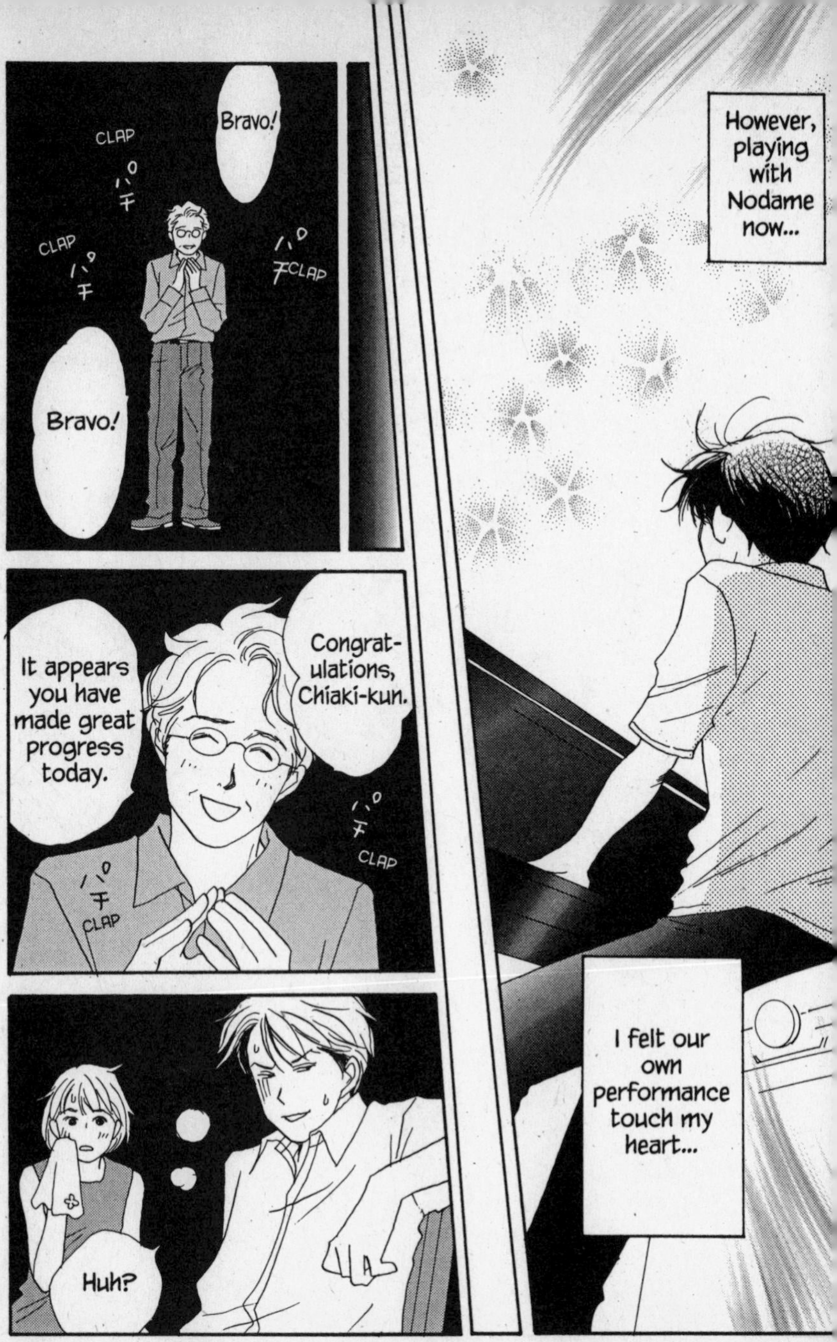
However, playing with Nodame now...
I felt our own performance touch my heart...
Bravo!
パチ CLAP
CLAP
パチ
CLAP
パチ
Bravo!
Congrat-ulations, Chiaki-kun.
It appears you have made great progress today.
パチ
CLAP
パチ
CLAP
Huh?

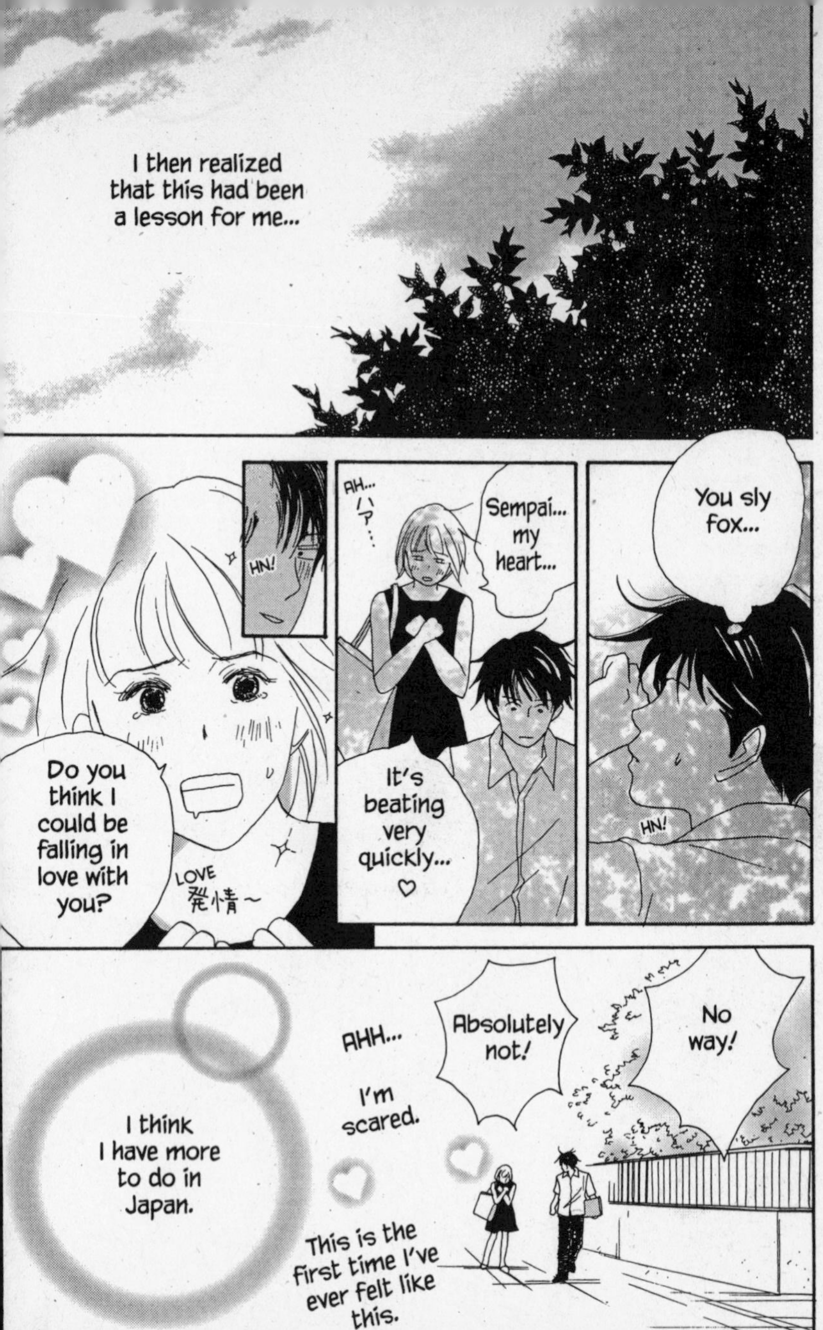
I then realized that this had been a lesson for me...
You sly fox...
HN!
AH... ハァ・・・
Sempai... my heart...
It's beating very quickly... ♡
HN!
Do you think I could be falling in love with you?
LOVE 発情～
No way!
Absolutely not!
AHH...
I'm scared.
This is the first time I've ever felt like this.
I think I have more to do in Japan.

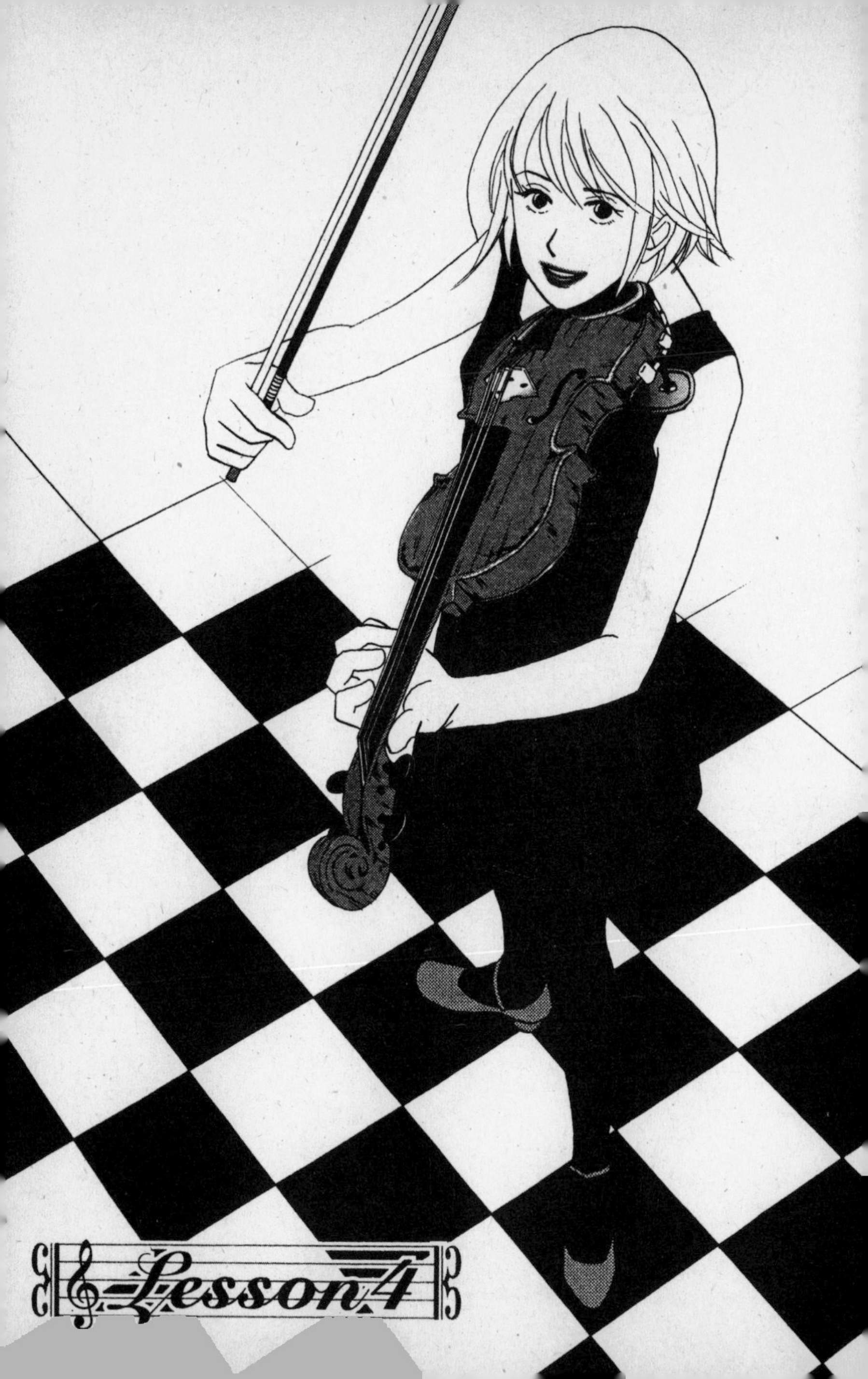
Lesson 4

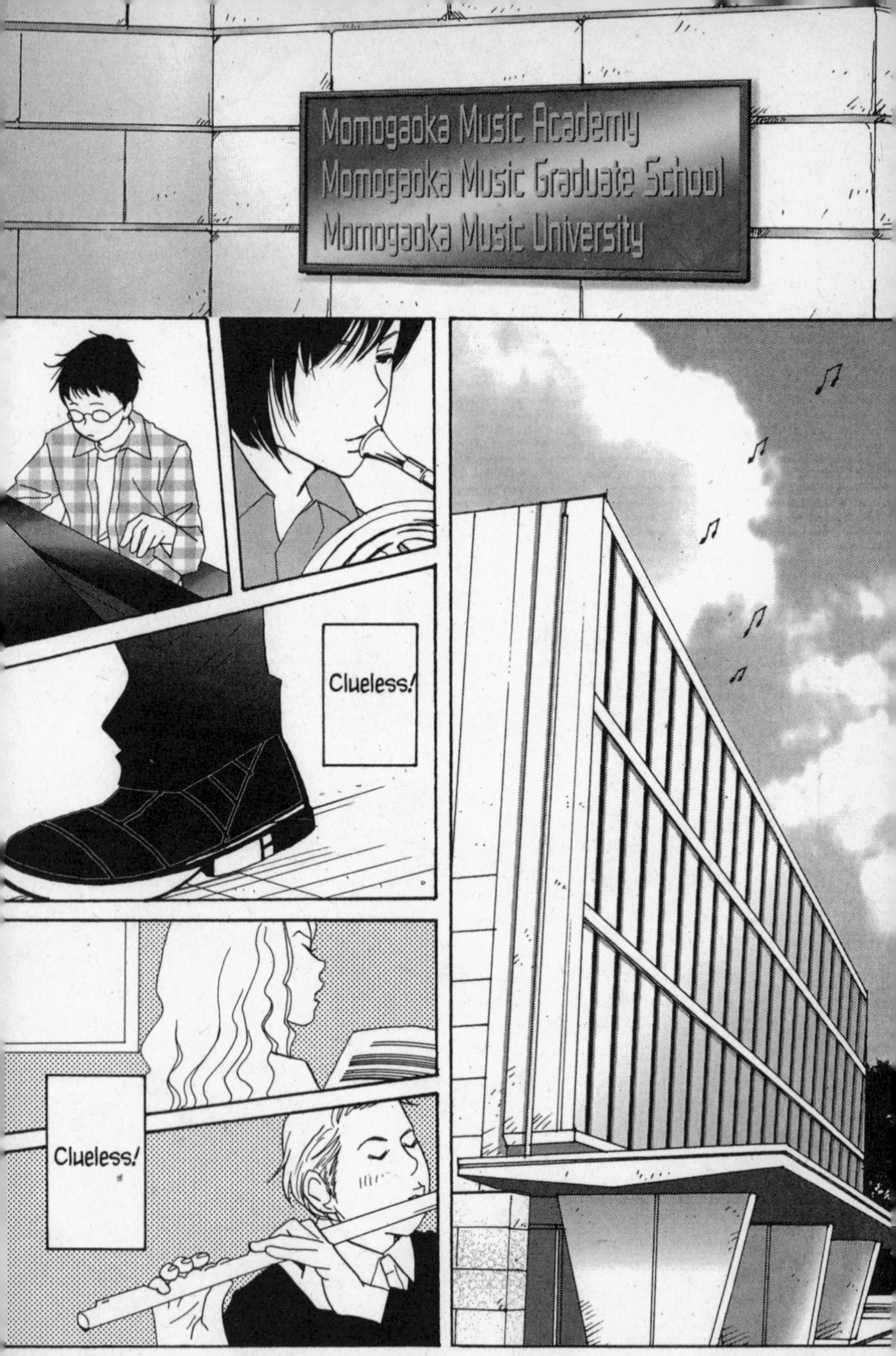
Momogaoka Music Academy
Momogaoka Music Graduate School
Momogaoka Music University
Clueless!
Clueless!

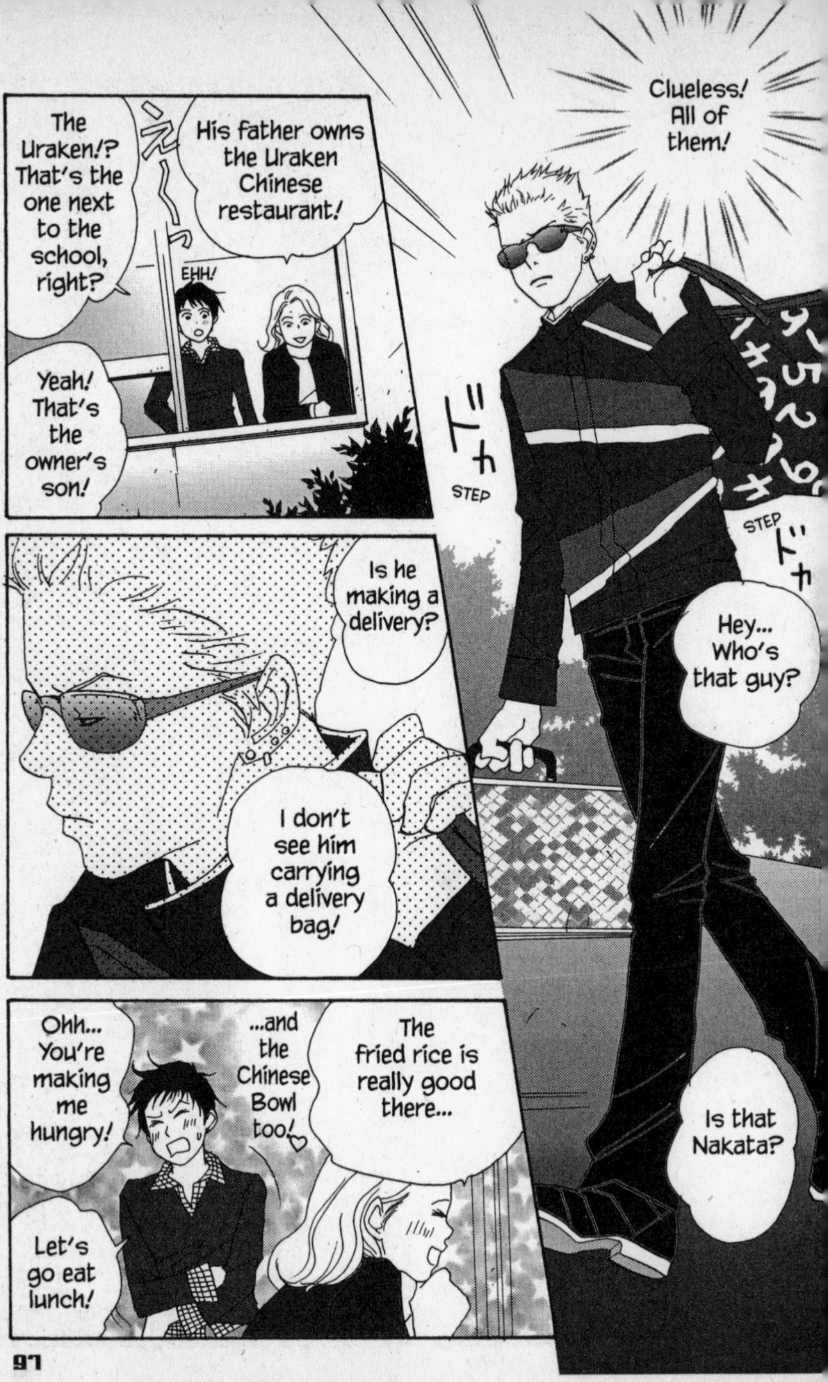
Clueless! All of them!
ドカ STEP
STEP ドカ
Hey... Who's that guy?
Is that Nakata?
His father owns the Uraken Chinese restaurant!
え〜っ
EHH!
The Uraken!? That's the one next to the school, right?
Yeah! That's the owner's son!
Is he making a delivery?
I don't see him carrying a delivery bag!
The fried rice is really good there...
...and the Chinese Bowl too!♡
Ohh... You're making me hungry!
Let's go eat lunch!

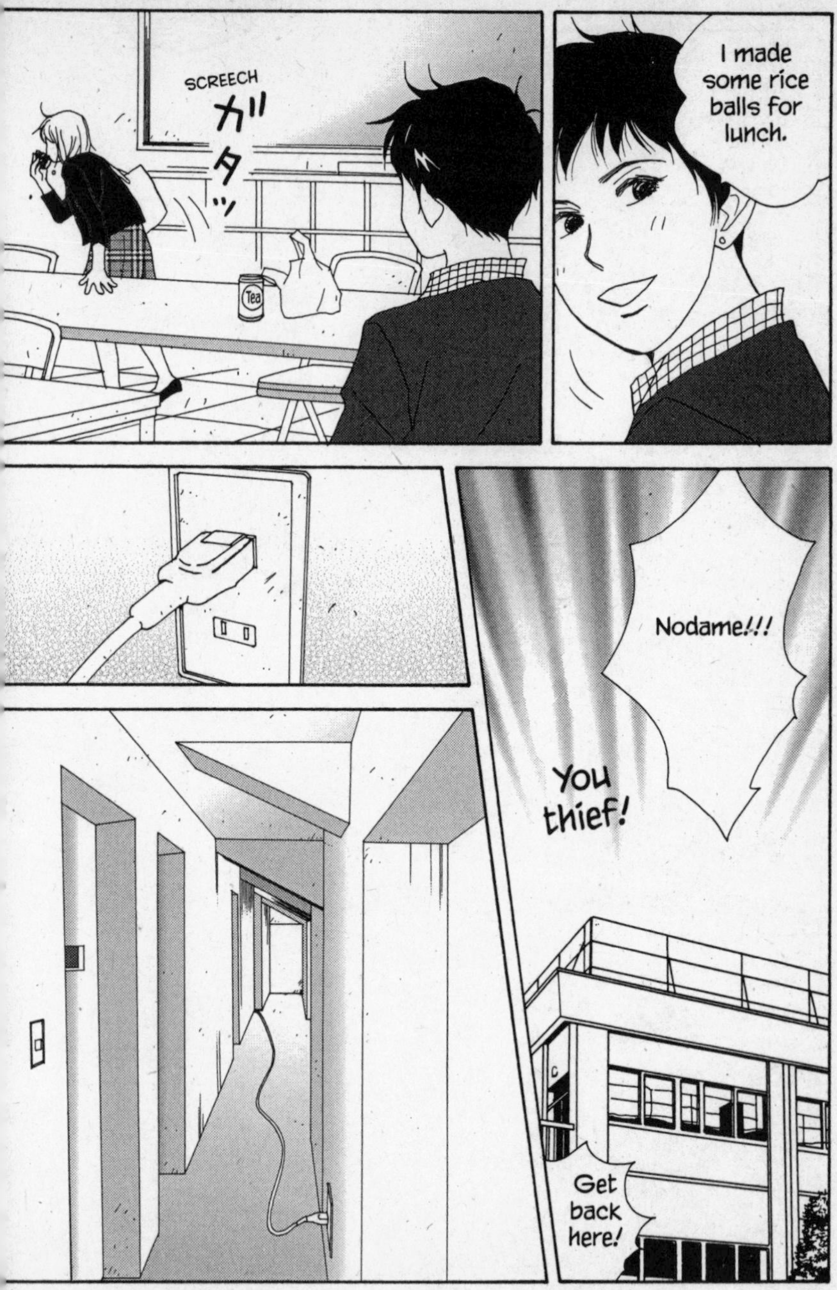
I made some rice balls for lunch.
SCREECH
ガタッ
Tea
Nodame!!!
You thief!
Get back here!

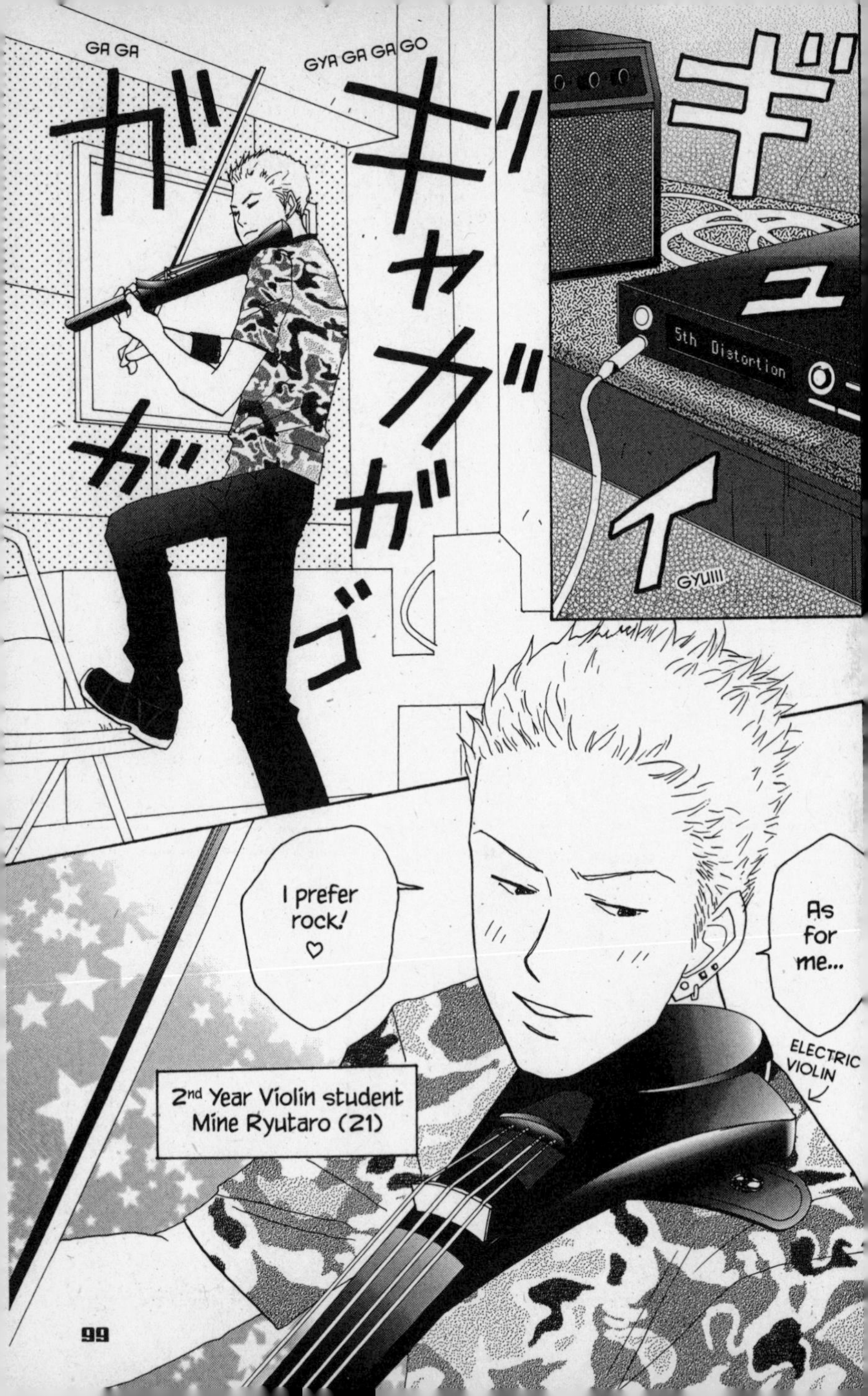

5th Distortion
ギュイ
GYUIII
ガガ
GA GA
ギャガガゴ
GYA GA GA GO
As for me...
I prefer rock! ♡
2nd Year Violin student
Mine Ryutaro (21)
ELECTRIC VIOLIN

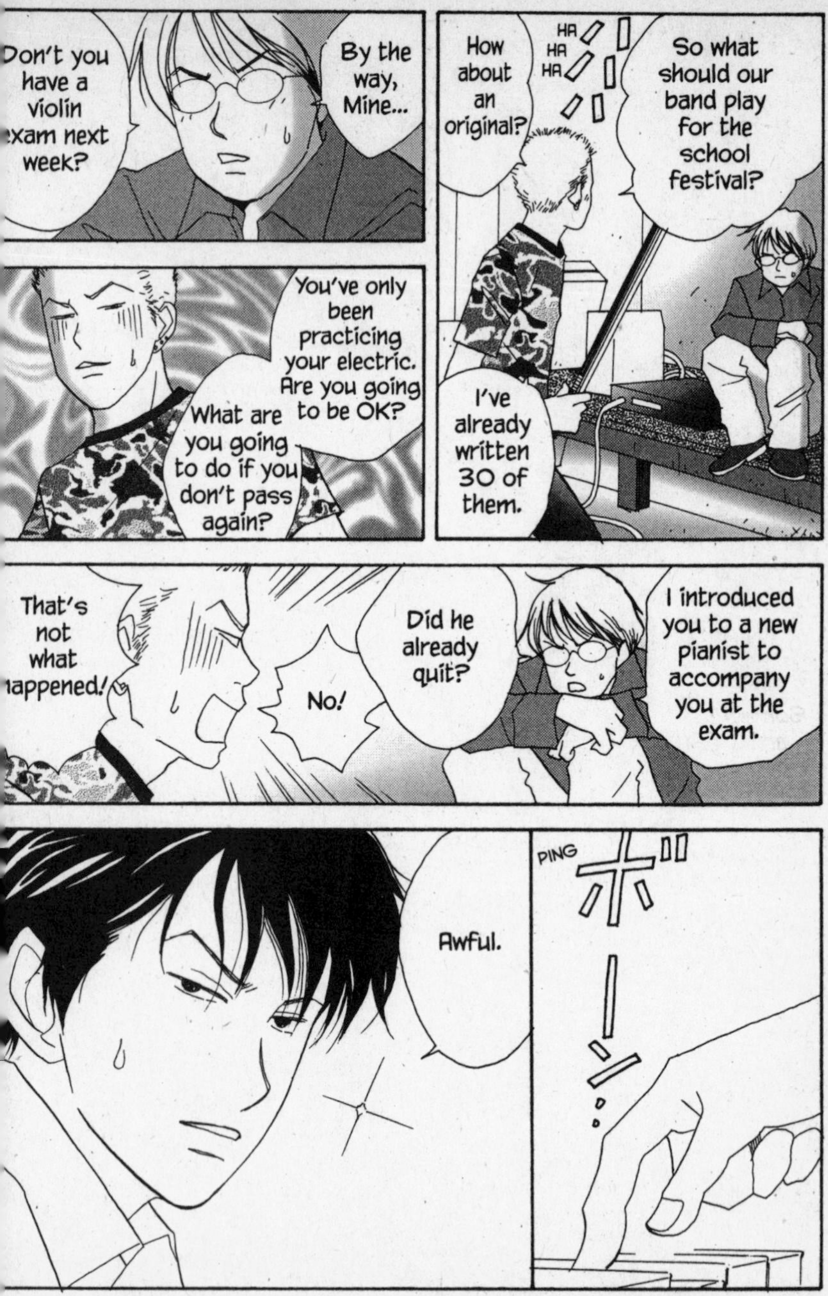
So what should our band play for the school festival?
HA HA HA
How about an original?
I've already written 30 of them.
By the way, Mine...
Don't you have a violin exam next week?
You've only been practicing your electric. Are you going to be OK?
What are you going to do if you don't pass again?
I introduced you to a new pianist to accompany you at the exam.
Did he already quit?
No!
That's not what happened!
PING
Awful.

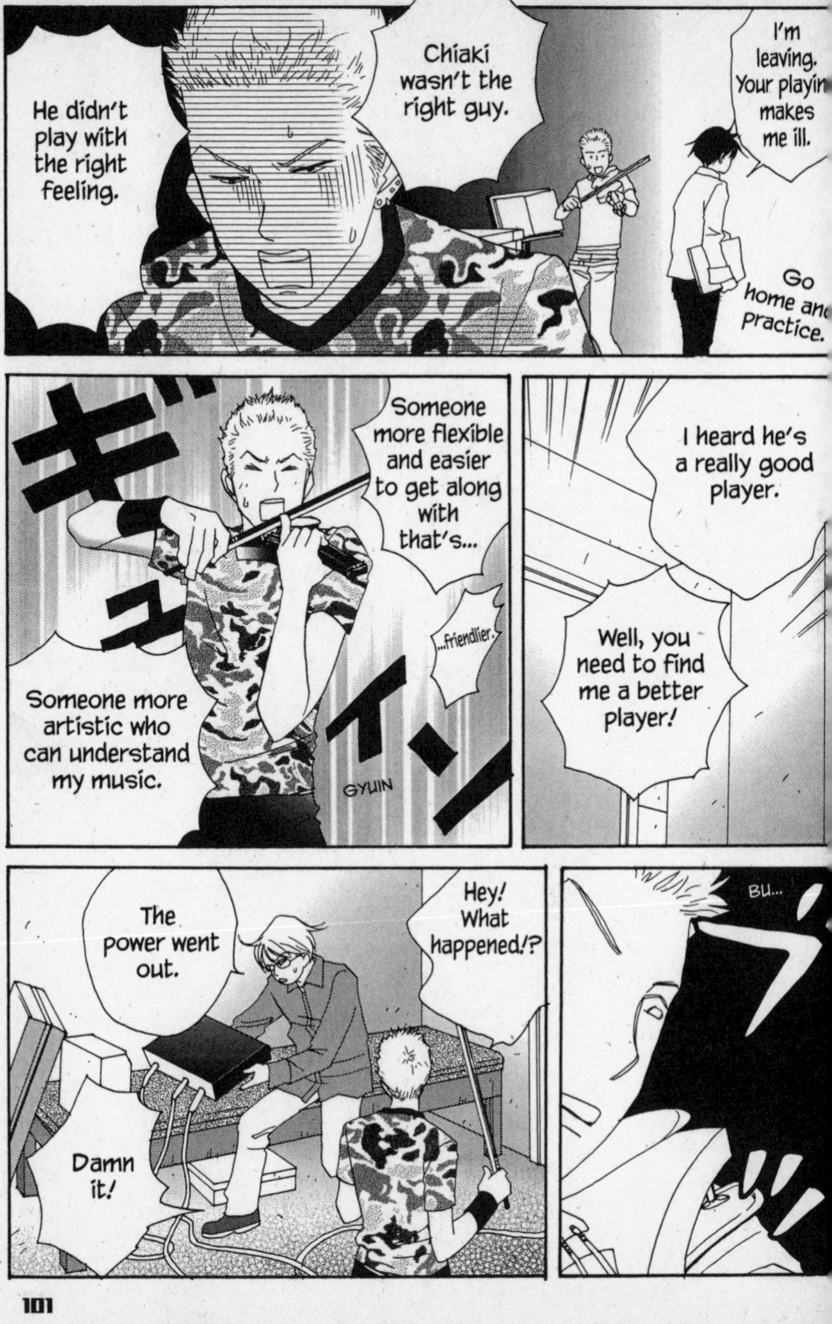
I'm leaving. Your playin makes me ill.
Go home an Practice.
Chiaki wasn't the right guy.
He didn't play with the right feeling.
I heard he's a really good player.
Well, you need to find me a better player!
Someone more flexible and easier to get along with that's...
...friendlier.
Someone more artistic who can understand my music.
GYUIN
BU...
Hey! What happened!?
The power went out.
Damn it!

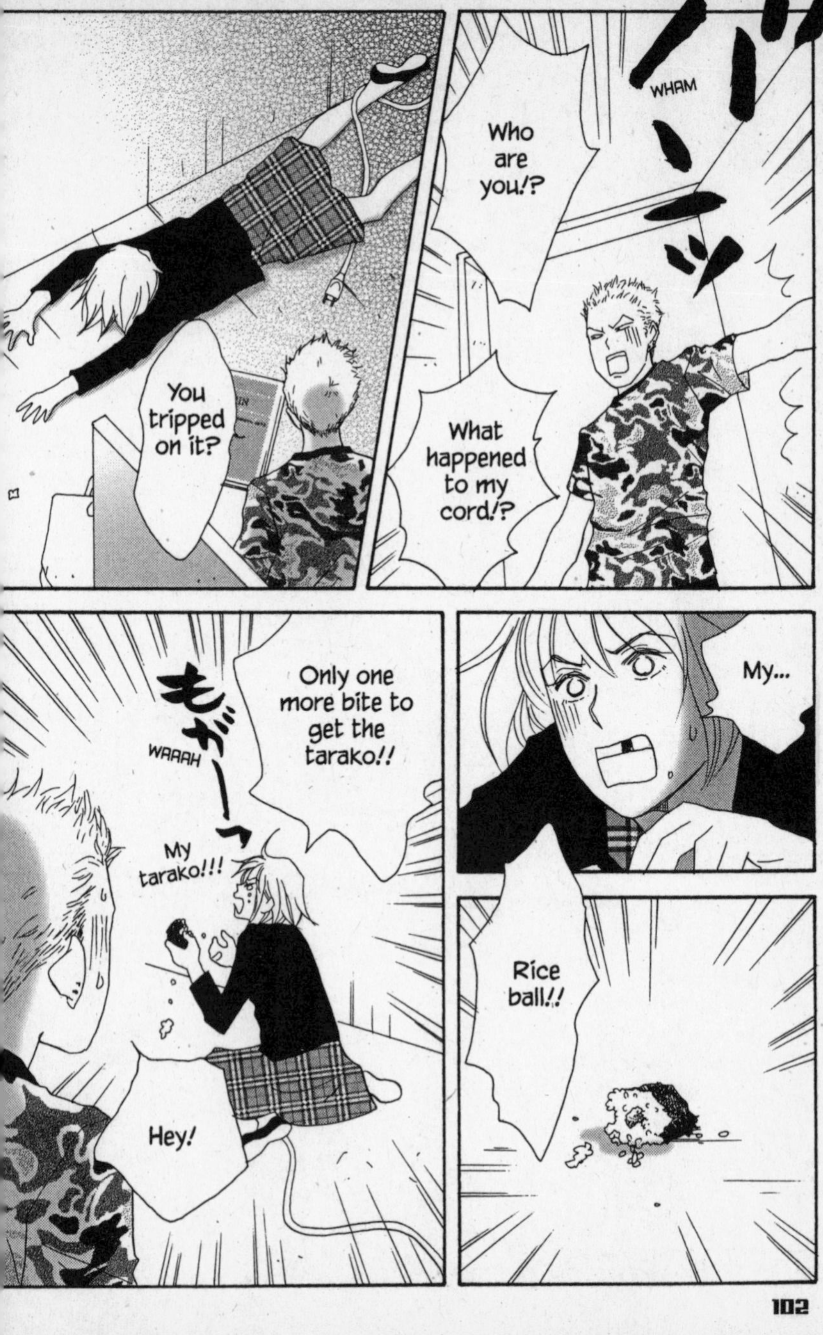
WHAM
Who are you!?
What happened to my cord!?
You tripped on it?
My...
Rice ball!!
Only one more bite to get the tarako!!
もがーっ
WAAAH
My tarako!!!
Hey!

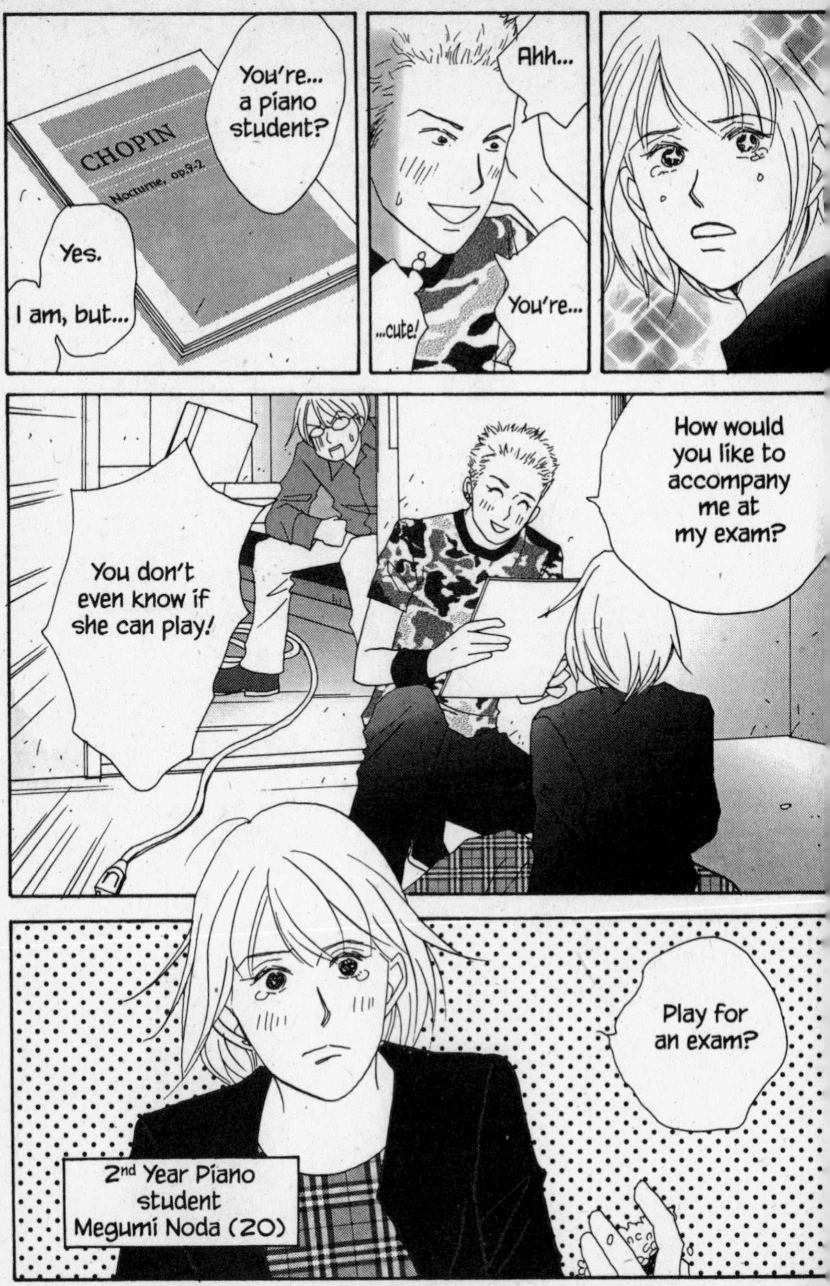

Ahh...
You're...
...cute!
You're... a piano student?
CHOPIN
Nocturne, op.9-2
Yes.
I am, but...
How would you like to accompany me at my exam?
You don't even know if she can play!
Play for an exam?
2nd Year Piano student Megumi Noda (20)

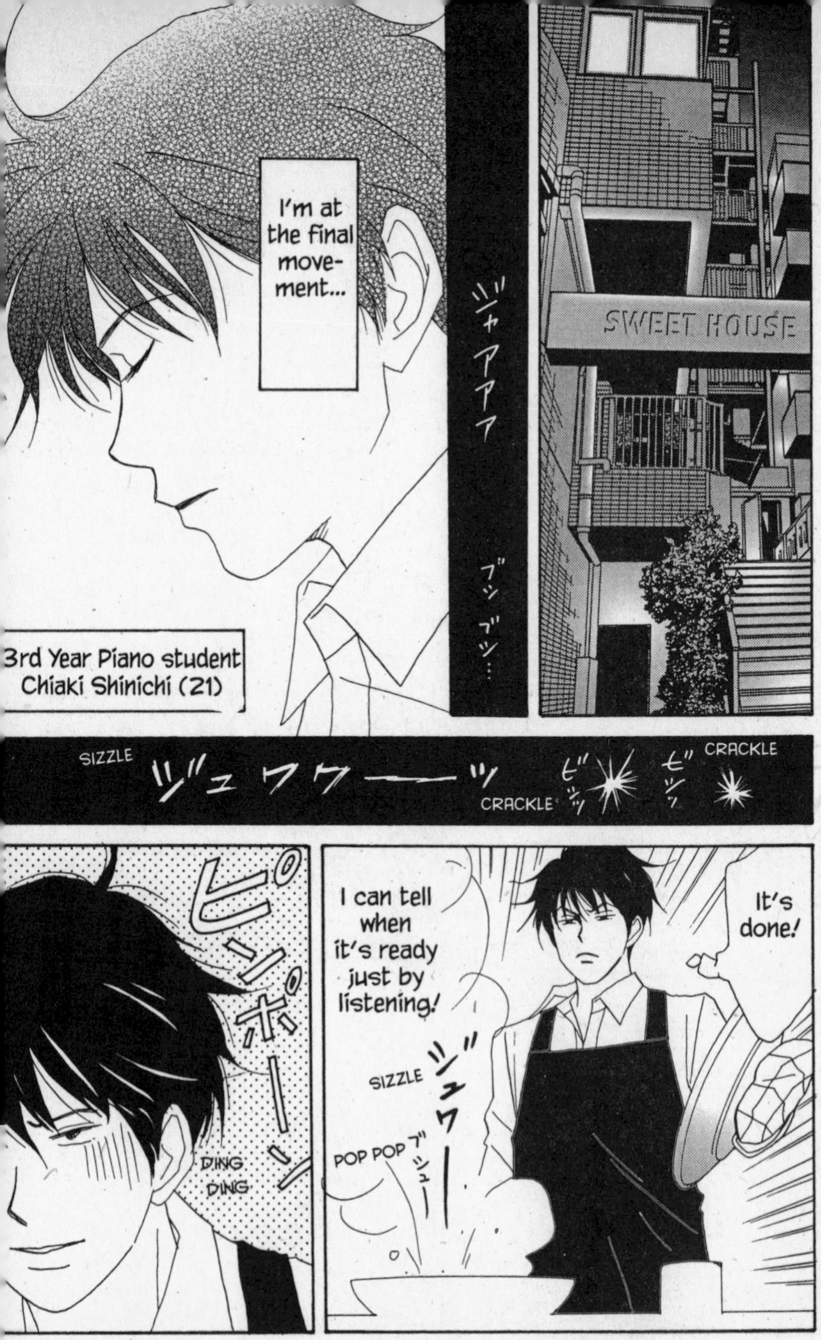
SWEET HOUSE
ジャアアア
ブツブツ…
I'm at the final movement...
3rd Year Piano student Chiaki Shinichi (21)
CRACKLE
ビッ
CRACKLE
ビッ
SIZZLE
ジュワーーッ
It's done!
I can tell when it's ready just by listening!
SIZZLE
ジュワー
POP POP
ブシュー
ピンポーン
DING DING

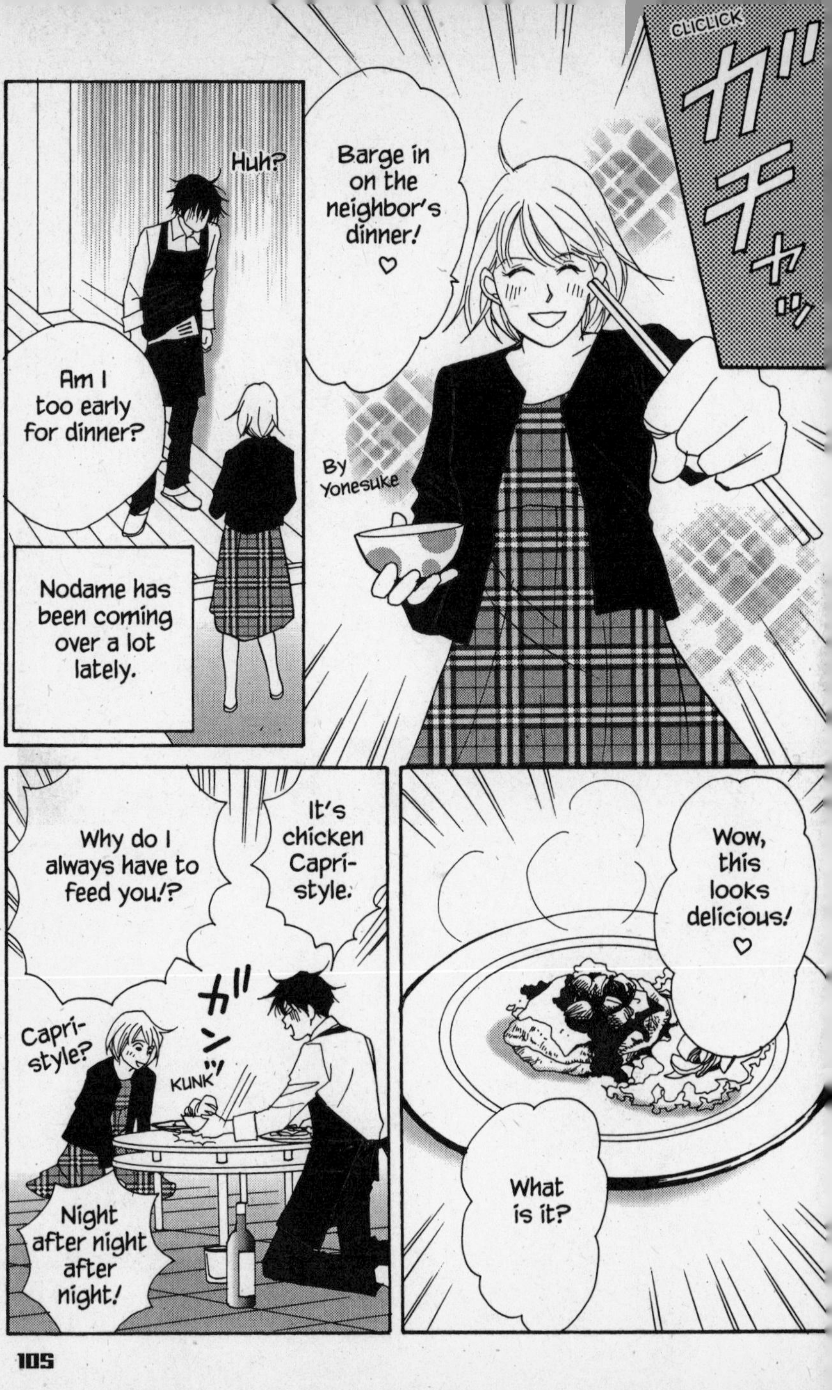
CLICLICK
ガチャッ
Barge in on the neighbor's dinner! ♡
By Yonesuke
Huh?
Am I too early for dinner?
Nodame has been coming over a lot lately.
Wow, this looks delicious! ♡
What is it?
It's chicken Capri-style.
Why do I always have to feed you!?
Capri-style?
ガンッ
KUNK
Night after night after night!

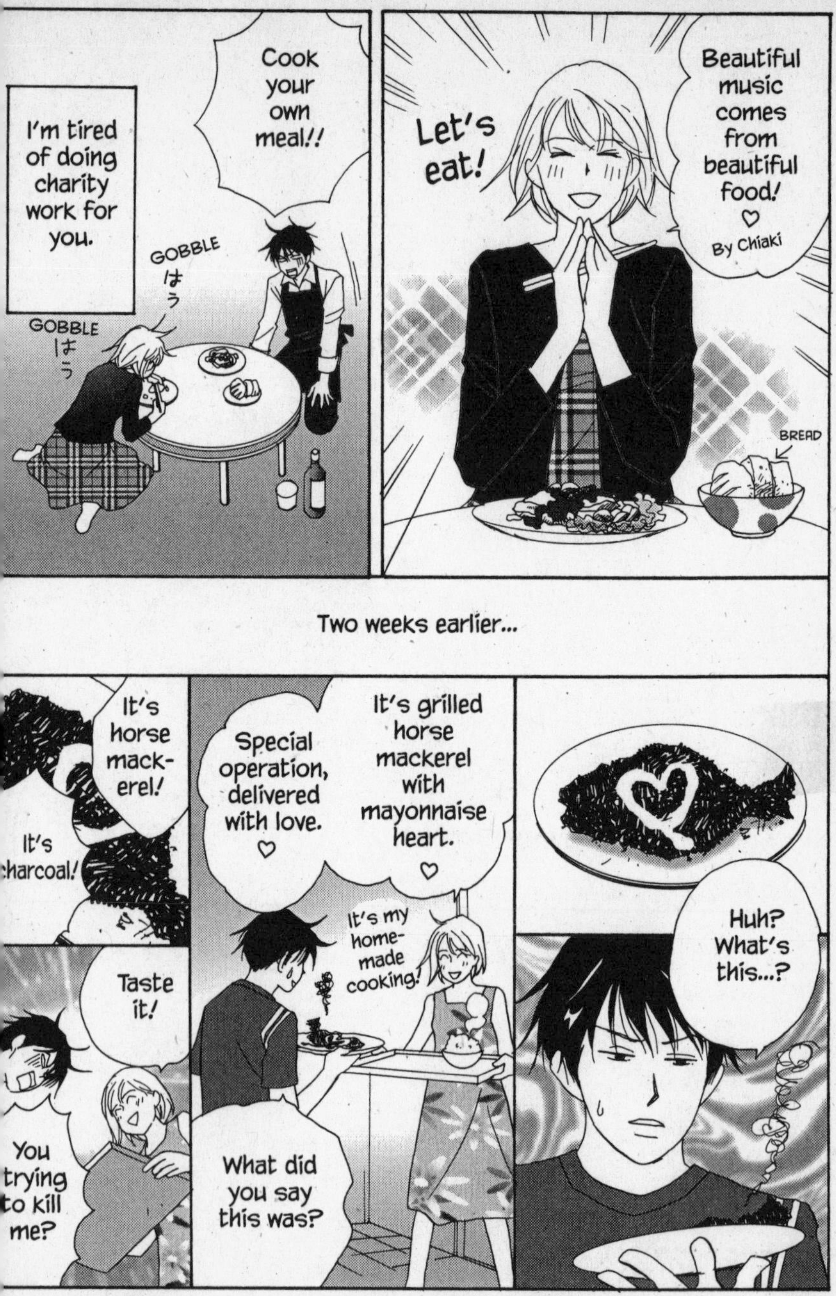
Let's eat!
Beautiful music comes from beautiful food! ♡ By Chiaki
BREAD
Cook your own meal!!
I'm tired of doing charity work for you.
GOBBLE はぅ
GOBBLE はぅ
Two weeks earlier...
Huh? What's this...?
It's grilled horse mackerel with mayonnaise heart. ♡
Special operation, delivered with love. ♡
It's my home-made cooking!
What did you say this was?
It's horse mack-erel!
It's charcoal!
Taste it!
You trying to kill me?

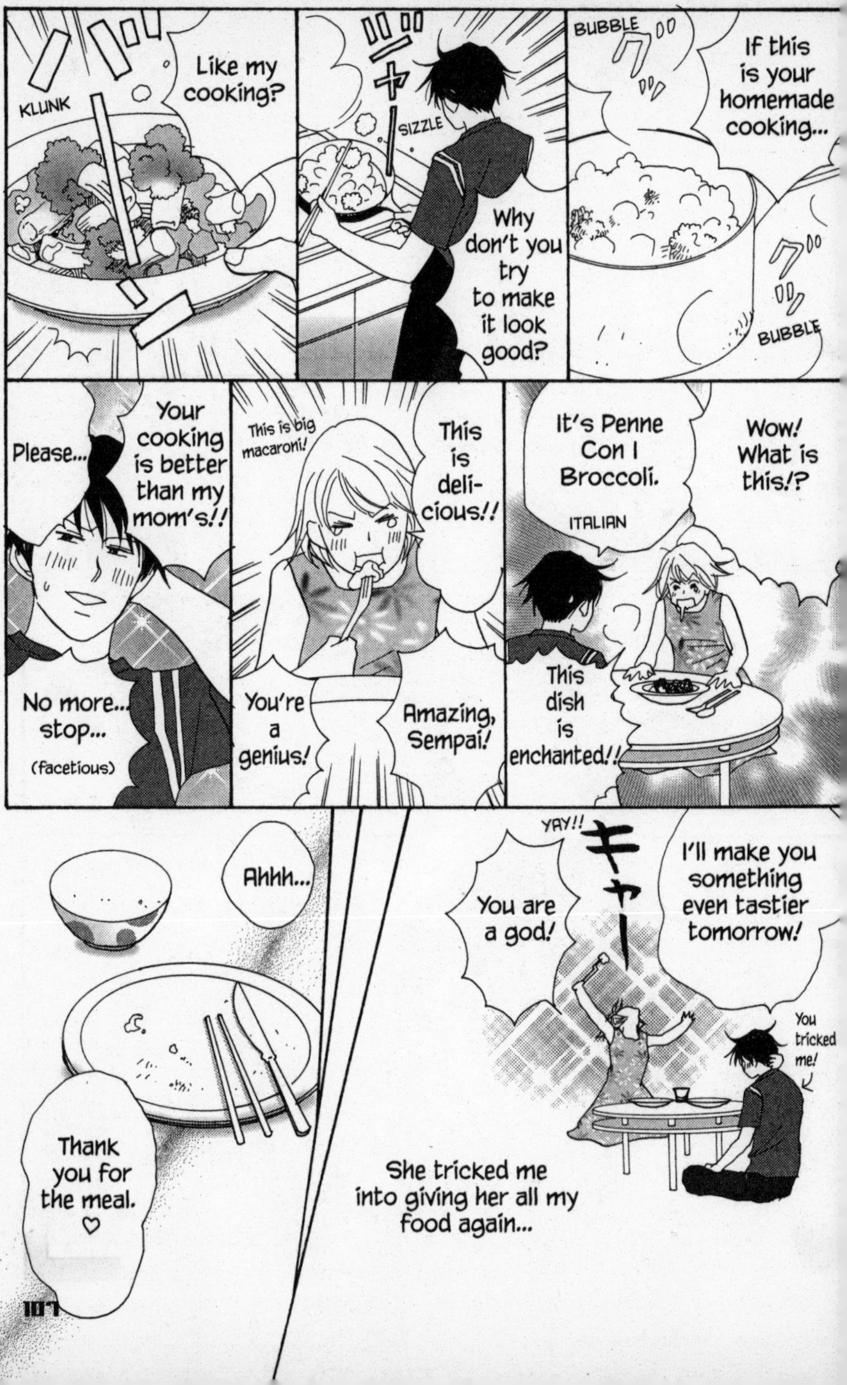
BUBBLE
If this is your homemade cooking...
BUBBLE
SIZZLE
Why don't you try to make it look good?
Like my cooking?
KLUNK
Wow! What is this!?
It's Penne Con I Broccoli.
ITALIAN
This dish is enchanted!!
This is delicious!!
This is big macaroni!
Amazing, Sempai!
You're a genius!
Your cooking is better than my mom's!!
Please...
No more... stop...
(facetious)
I'll make you something even tastier tomorrow!
YAY!!
You are a god!
You tricked me!
She tricked me into giving her all my food again...
Ahhh...
Thank you for the meal. ♡

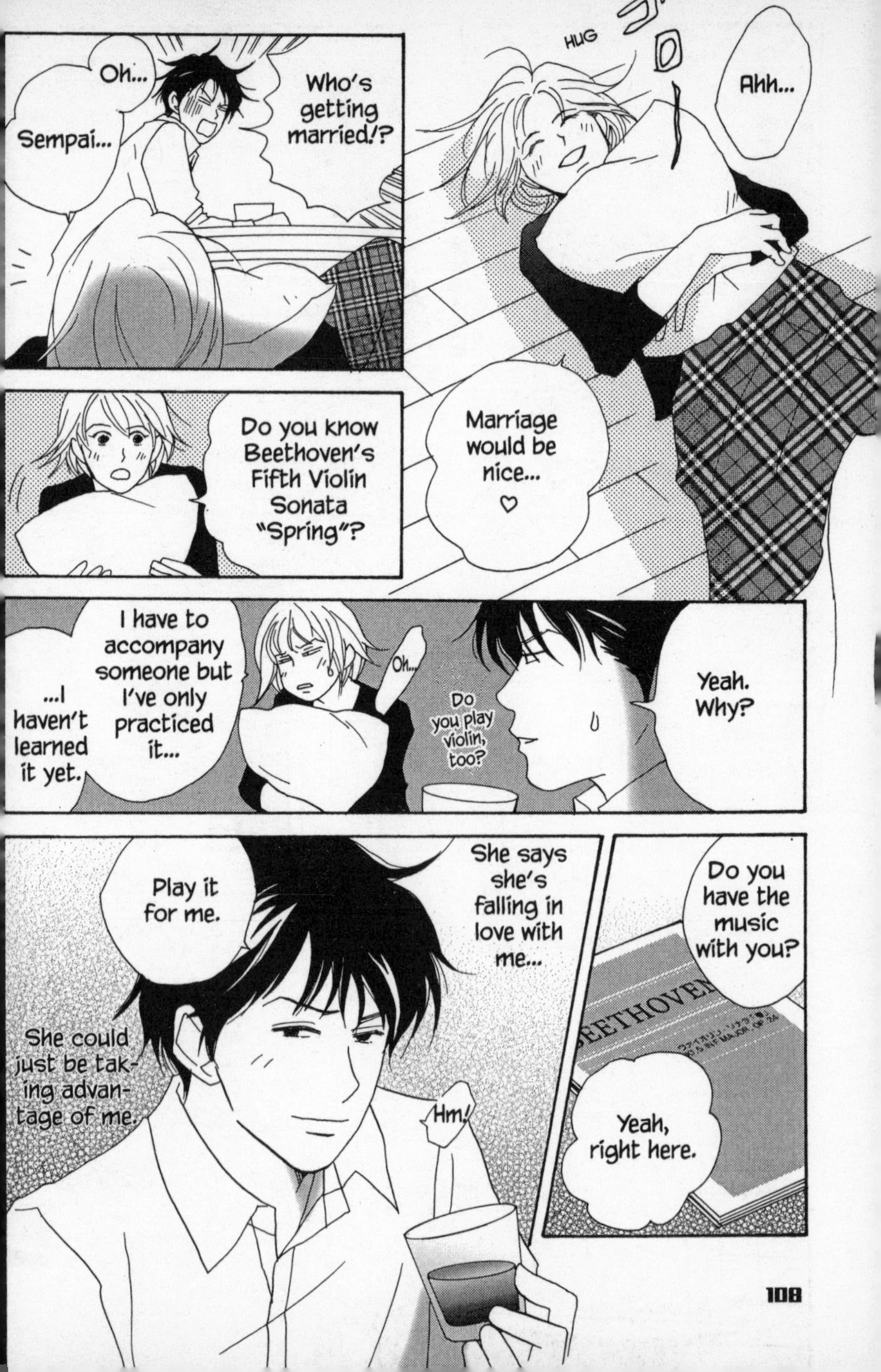
HUG
Ahh...
Marriage would be nice... ♡
Who's getting married!?
Oh...
Sempai...
Do you know Beethoven's Fifth Violin Sonata "Spring"?
Yeah. Why?
Do you play violin, too?
Oh...
I have to accompany someone but I've only practiced it...
...I haven't learned it yet.
Do you have the music with you?
BEETHOVEN
Yeah, right here.
She says she's falling in love with me...
Play it for me.
Hm!
She could just be tak-ing advan-tage of me.

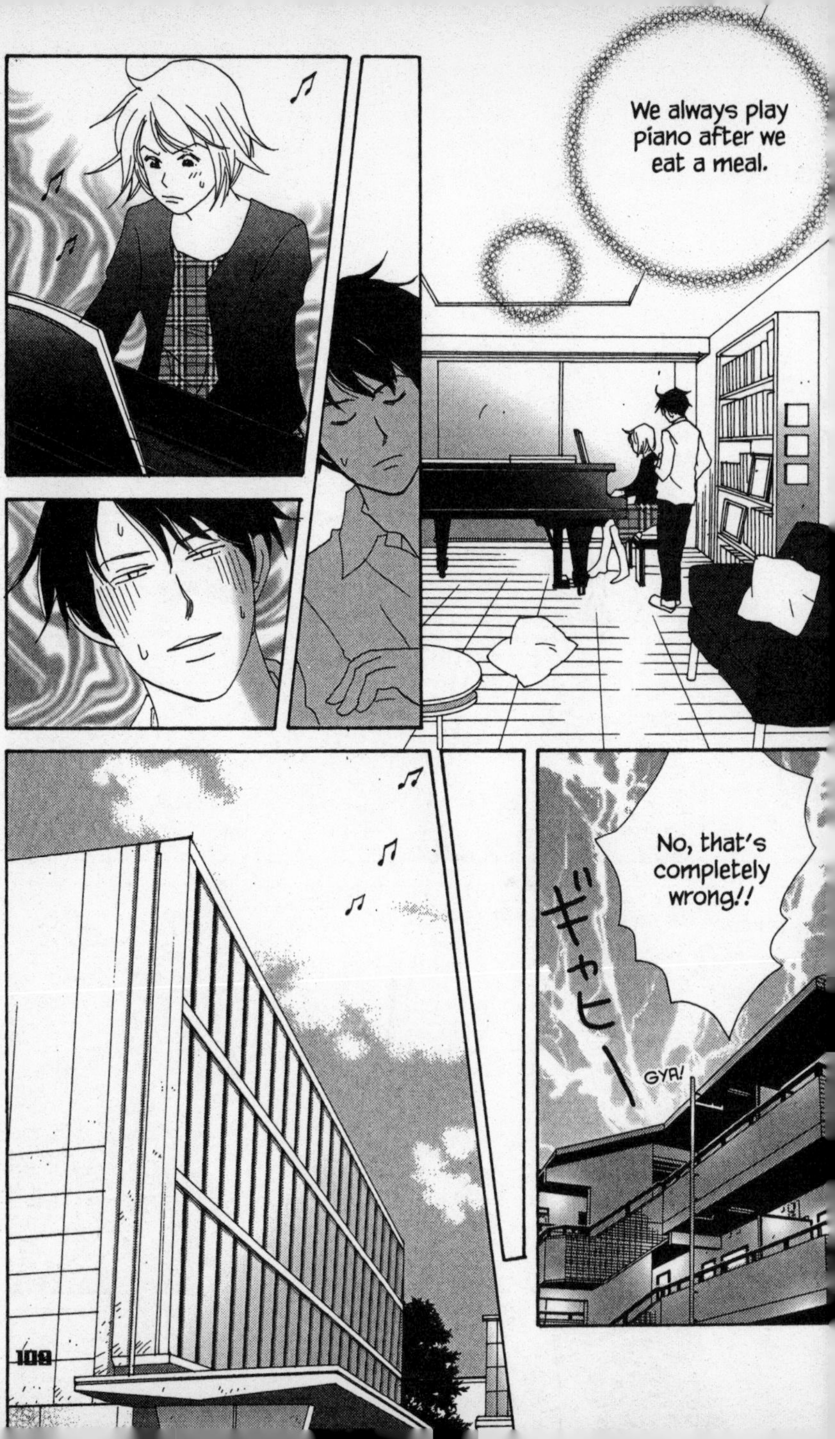
We always play piano after we eat a meal.
No, that's completely wrong!!
ギャヒー
GYA!

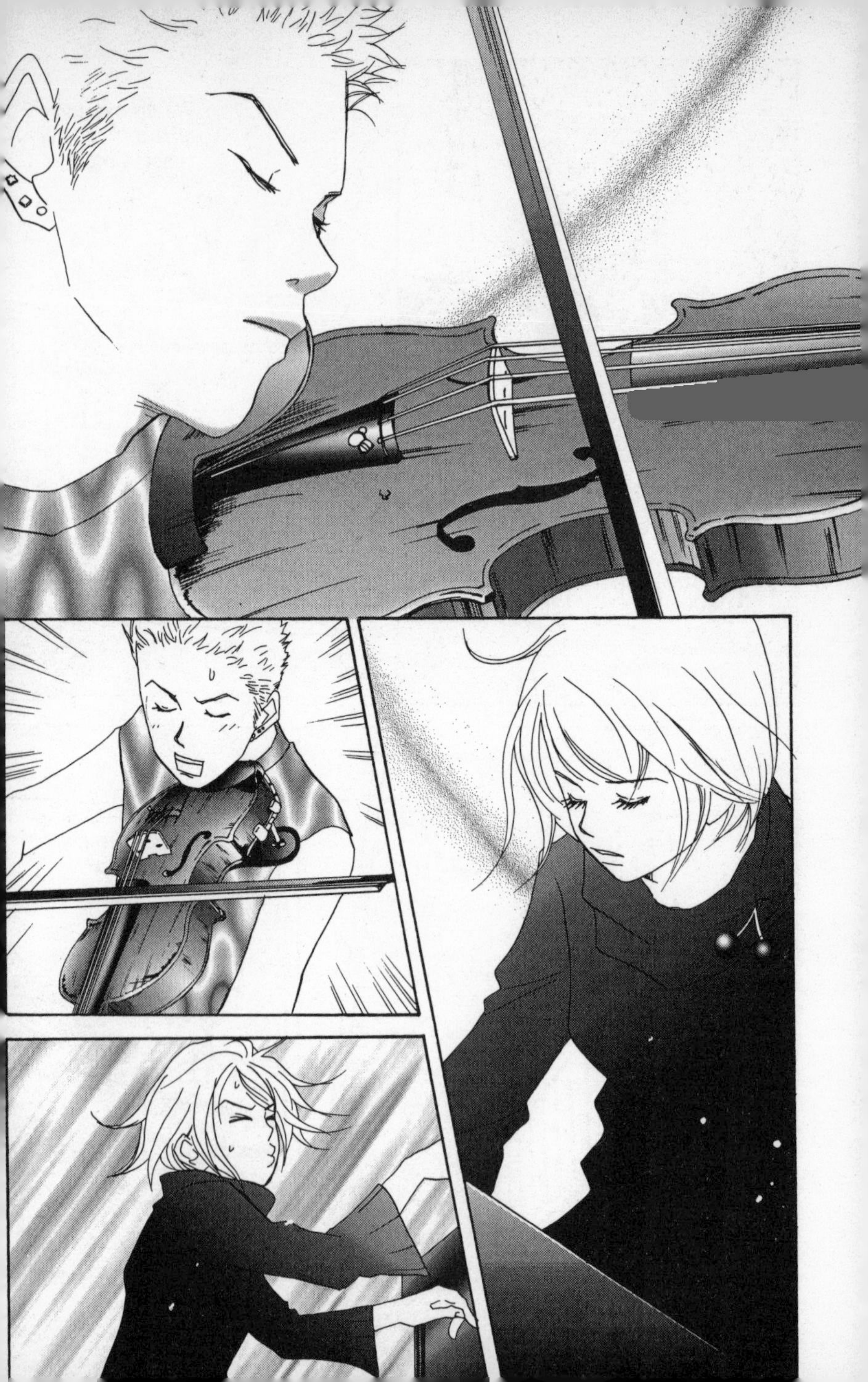

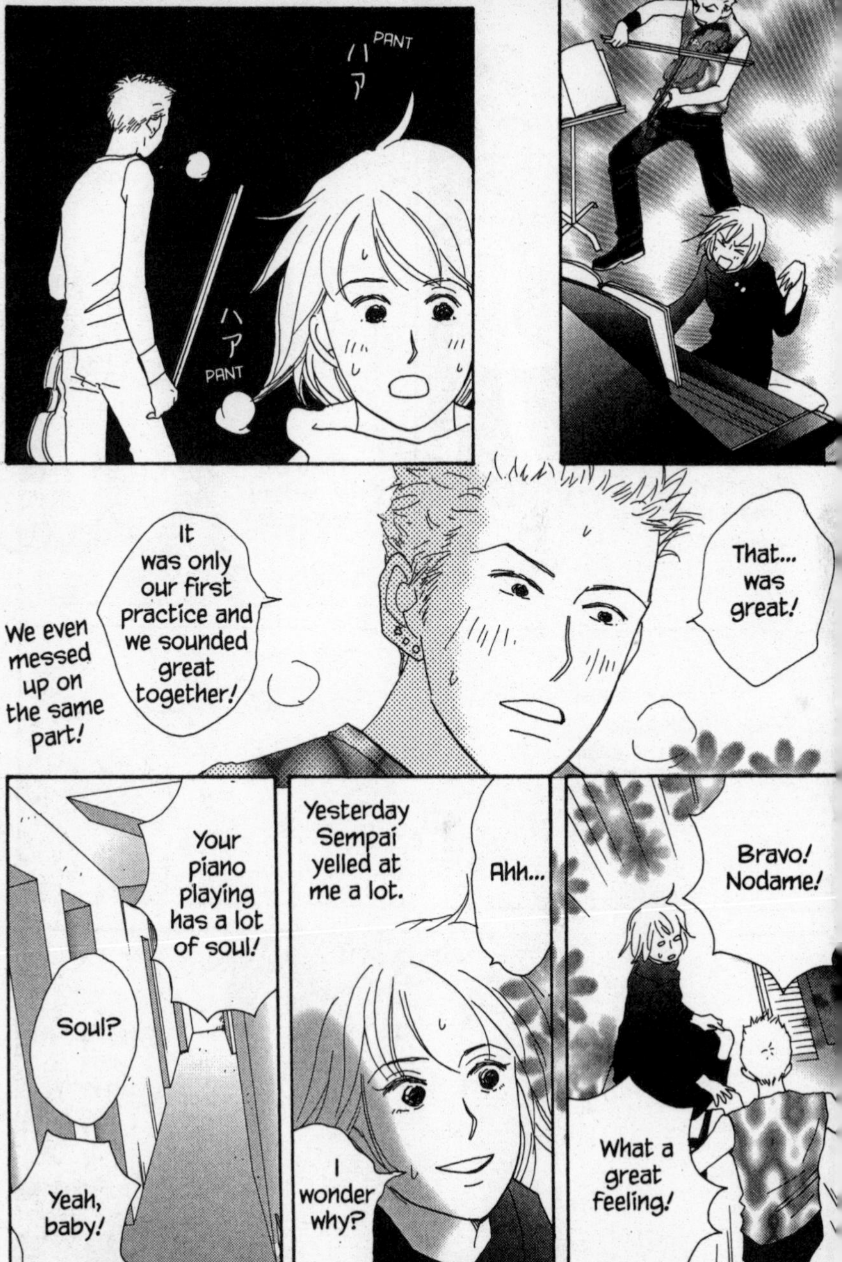
ハァ PANT
ハァ PANT
That... was great!
It was only our first practice and we sounded great together!
We even messed up on the same part!
Bravo! Nodame!
What a great feeling!
Ahh...
Yesterday Sempai yelled at me a lot.
I wonder why?
Your piano playing has a lot of soul!
Soul?
Yeah, baby!

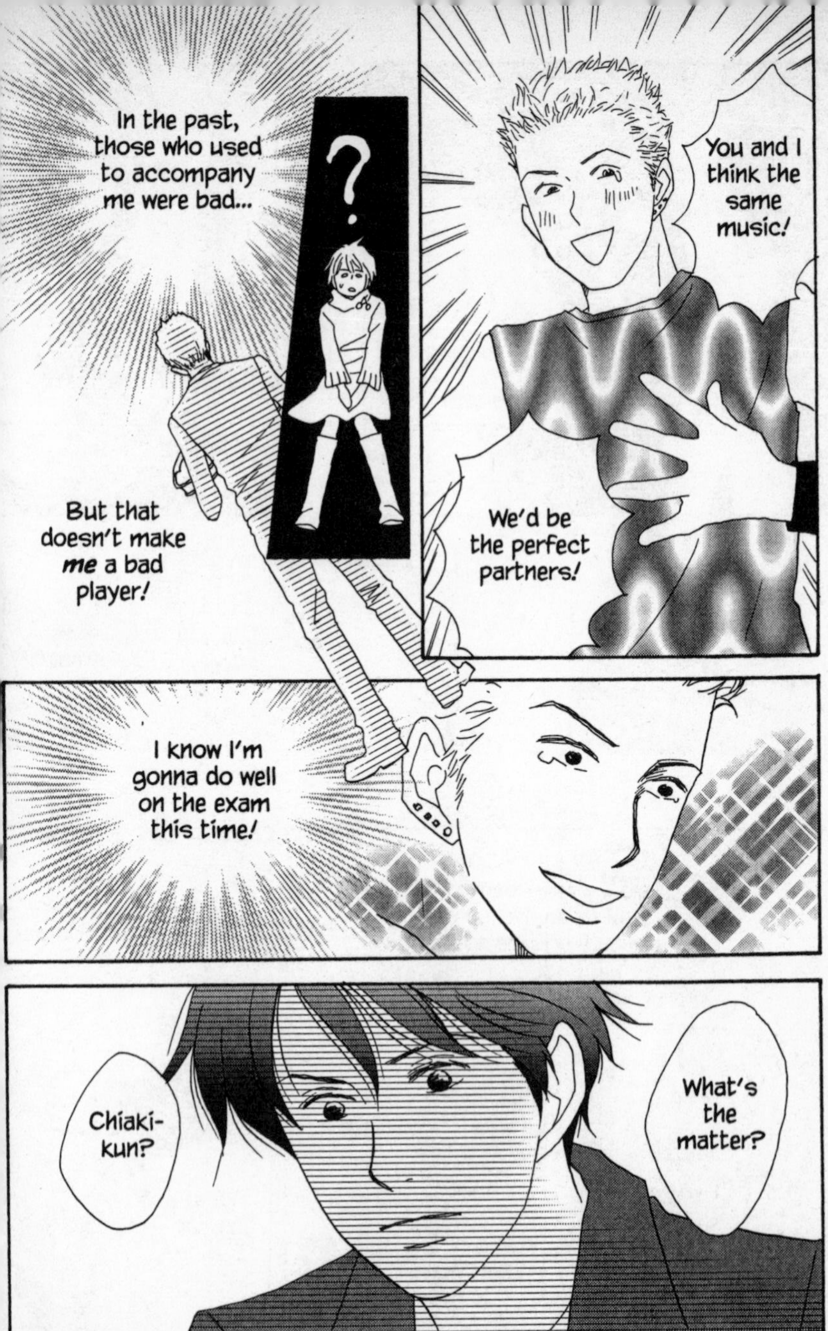
You and I think the same music!
We'd be the perfect partners!
In the past, those who used to accompany me were bad...
?
But that doesn't make *me* a bad player!
I know I'm gonna do well on the exam this time!
What's the matter?
Chiaki-kun?

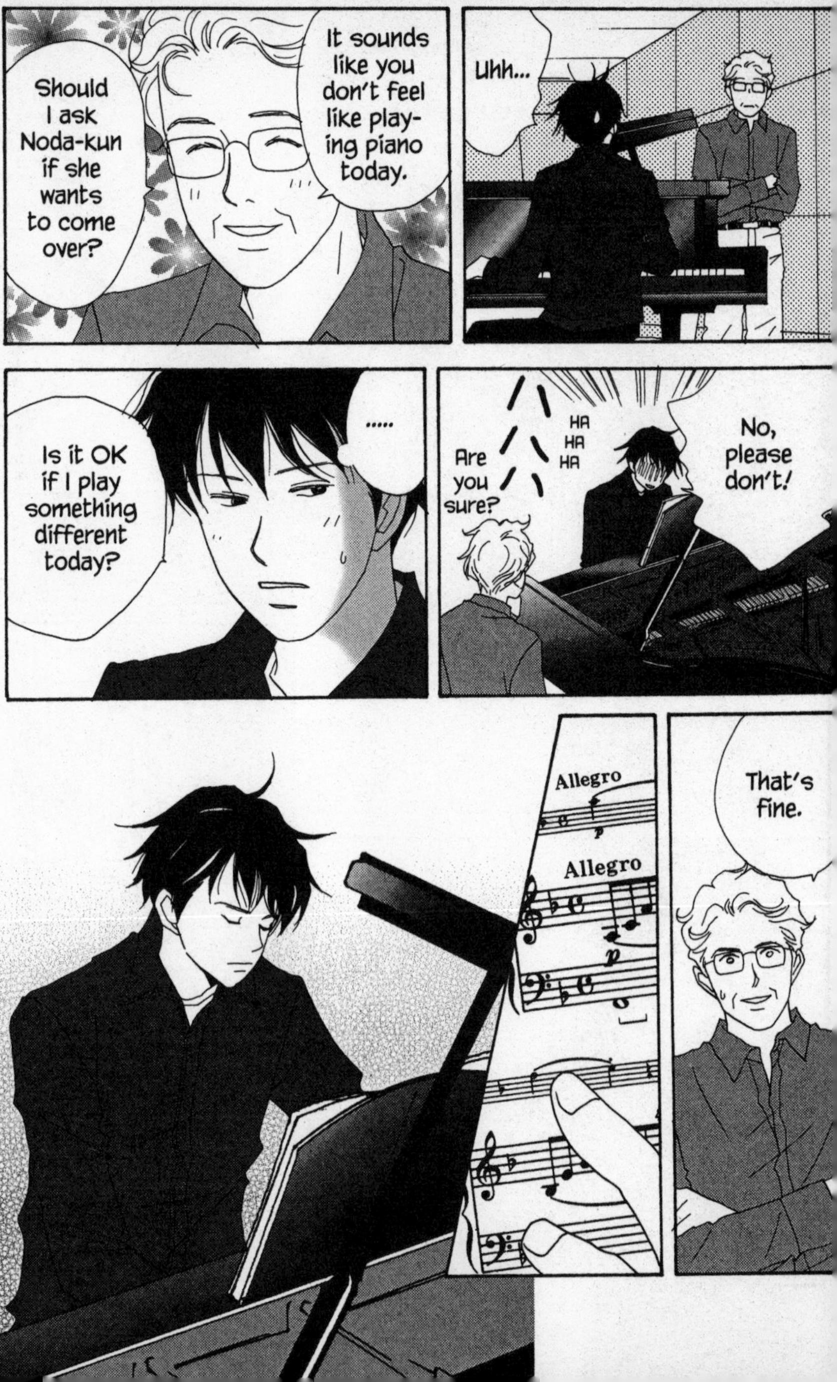
Uhh...
It sounds like you don't feel like play-ing piano today.
Should I ask Noda-kun if she wants to come over?
No, please don't!
HA HA HA
Are you sure?
.....
Is it OK if I play something different today?
That's fine.
Allegro
Allegro

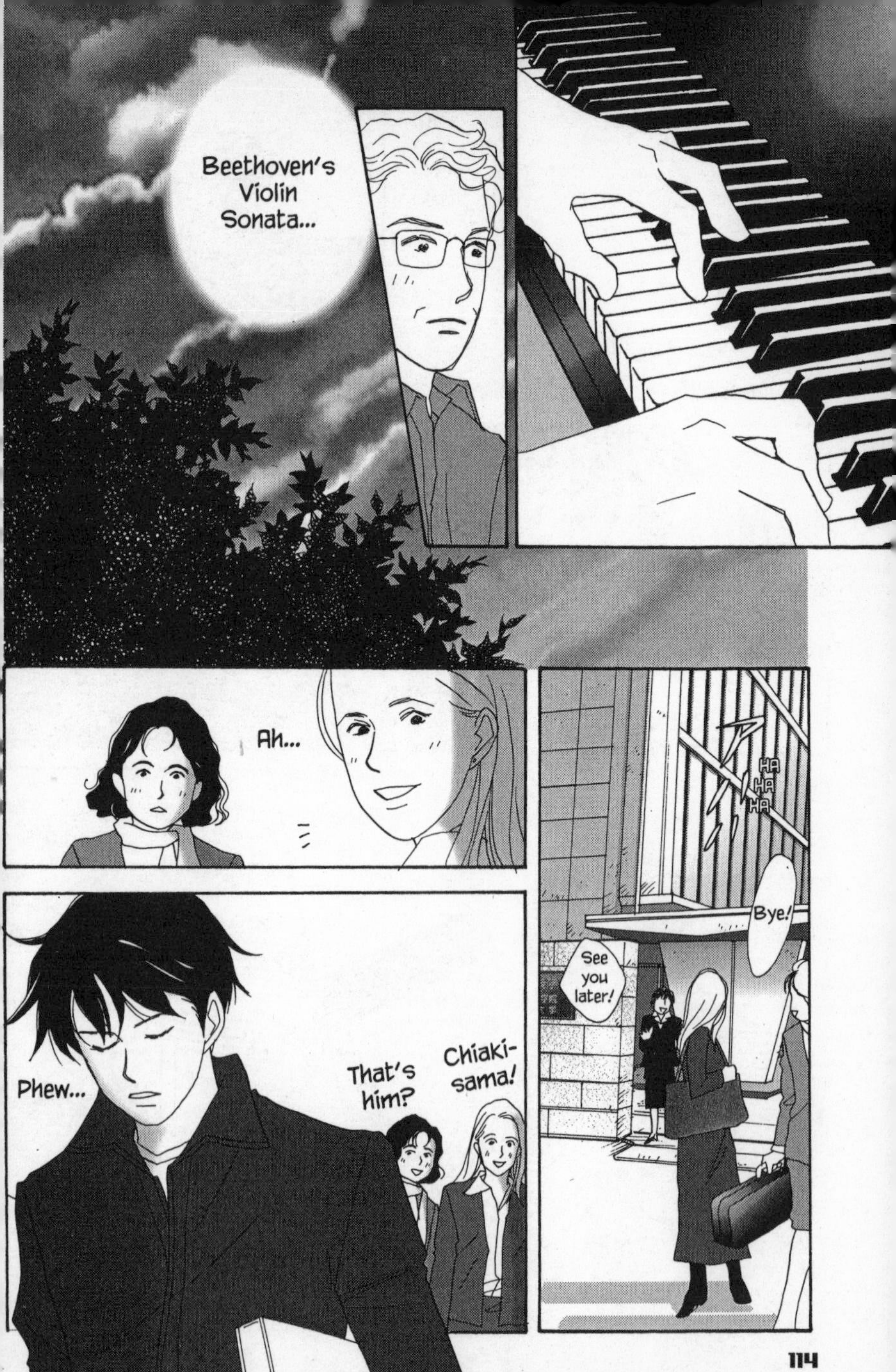
Beethoven's Violin Sonata...
HA HA HA
Bye!
See you later!
Ah...
Chiaki-sama!
That's him?
Phew...

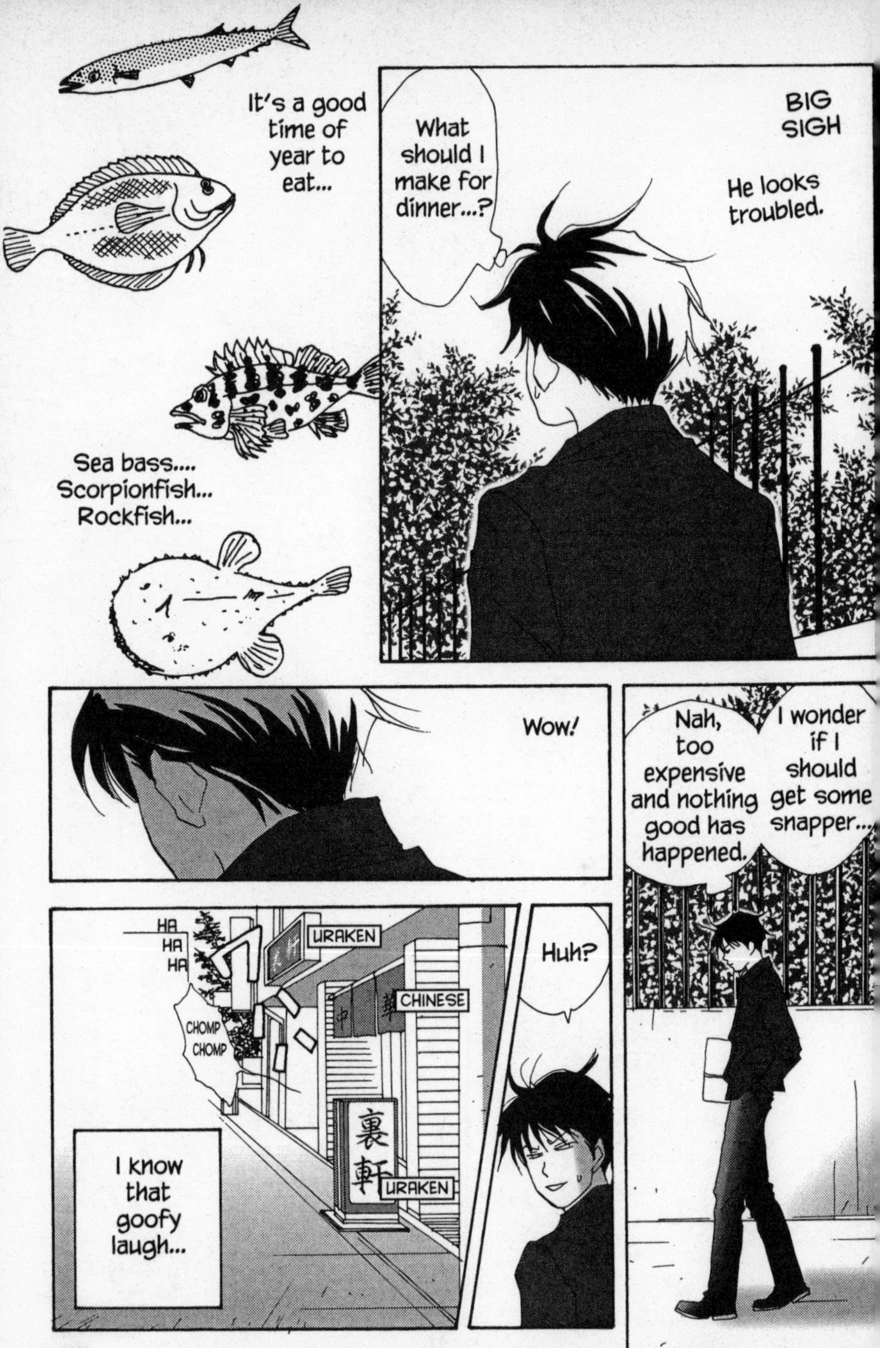
BIG SIGH
He looks troubled.
What should I make for dinner...?
It's a good time of year to eat...
Sea bass.... Scorpionfish... Rockfish...
I wonder if I should get some snapper...
Nah, too expensive and nothing good has happened.
Wow!
Huh?
HA HA HA
URAKEN
CHINESE
CHOMP CHOMP
裏軒
URAKEN
I know that goofy laugh...

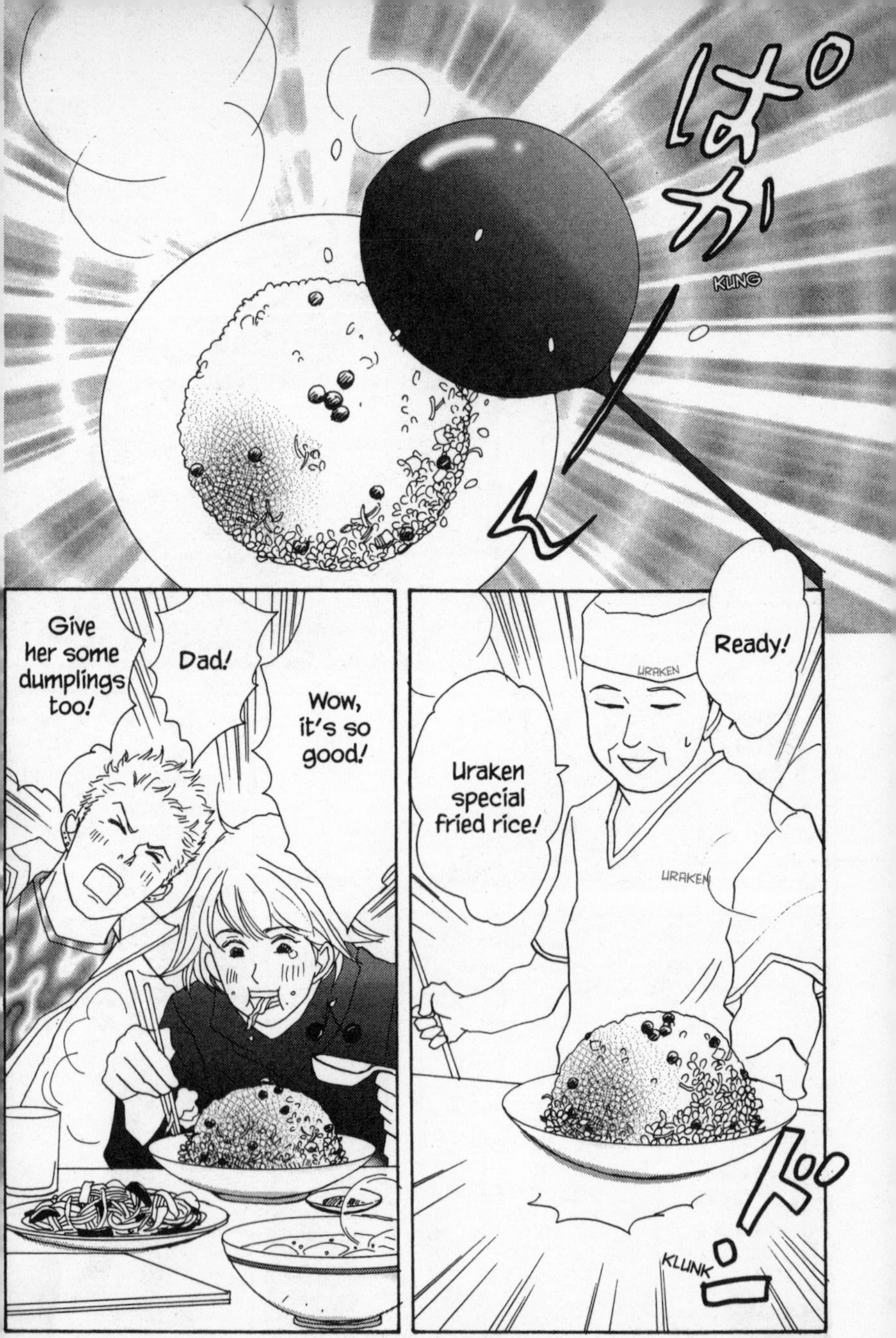
ぱかーん
KUNG
Ready!
URAKEN
Uraken special fried rice!
URAKEN
ドン
KLUNK
Wow, it's so good!
Dad!
Give her some dumplings too!

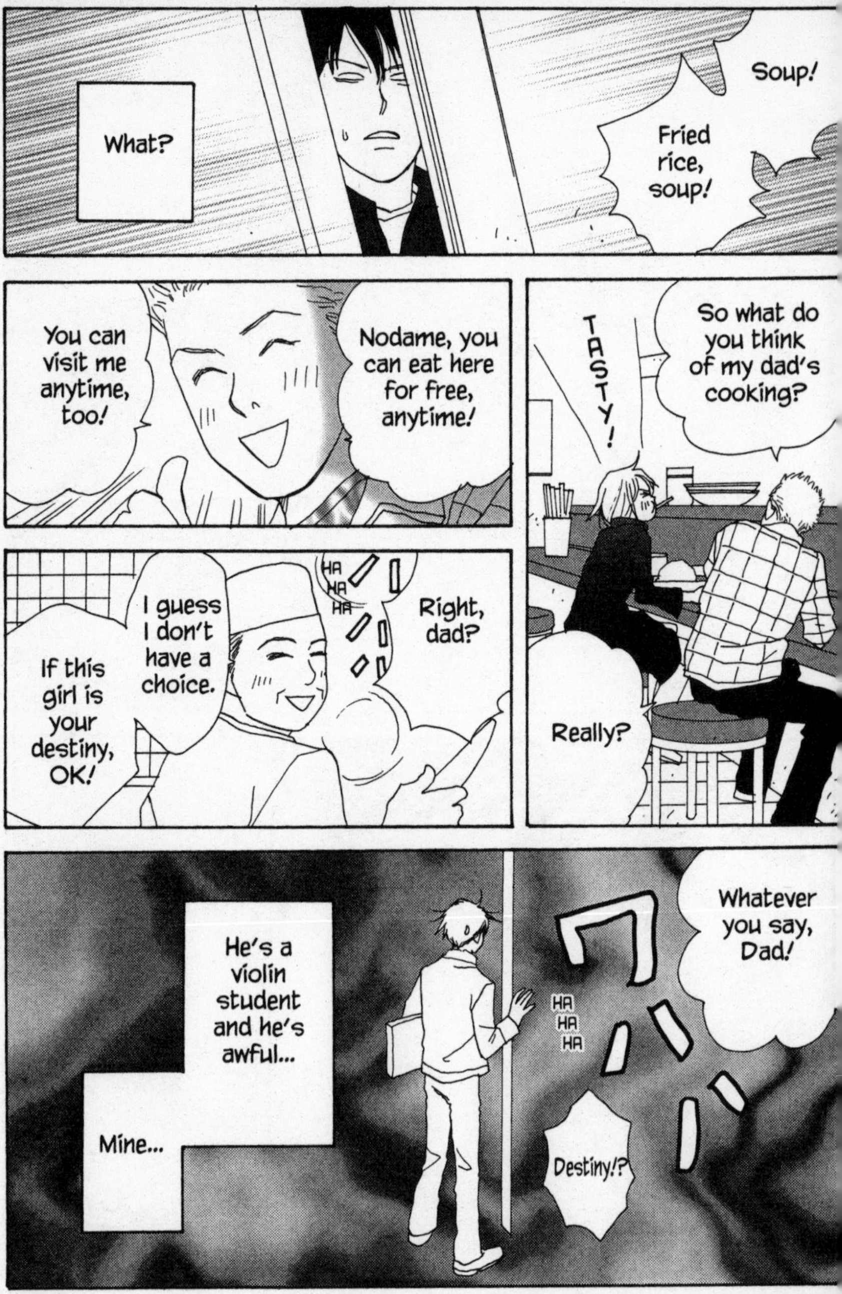
Soup!
Fried rice, soup!
What?
So what do you think of my dad's cooking?
TASTY!
Really?
Nodame, you can eat here for free, anytime!
You can visit me anytime, too!
Right, dad?
HA HA HA
I guess I don't have a choice.
If this girl is your destiny, OK!
Whatever you say, Dad!
HA HA HA
Destiny!?
He's a violin student and he's awful...
Mine...

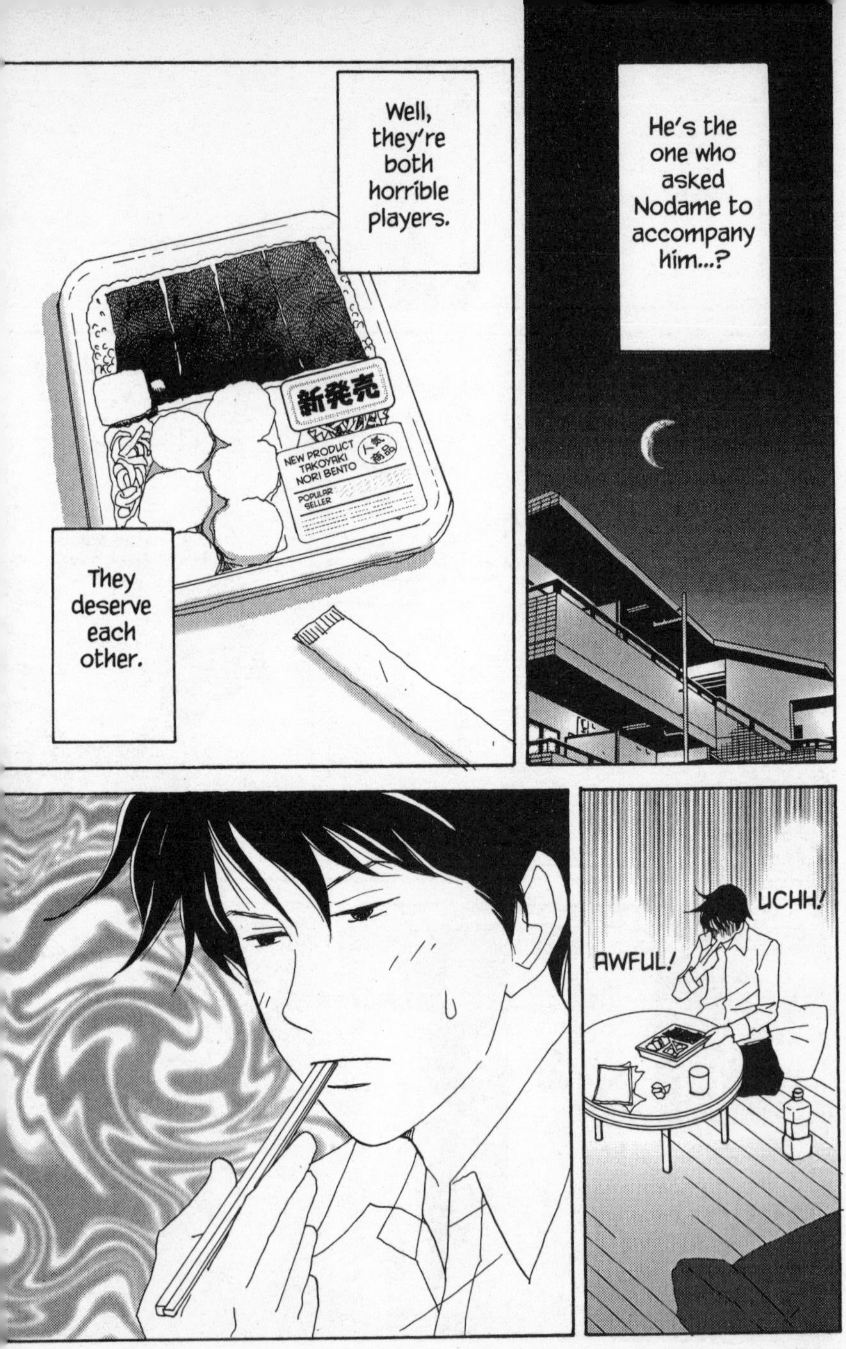
He's the one who asked Nodame to accompany him...?
Well, they're both horrible players.
新発売
NEW PRODUCT TAKOYAKI NORI BENTO
人気商品
POPULAR SELLER
They deserve each other.
UCHH!
AWFUL!

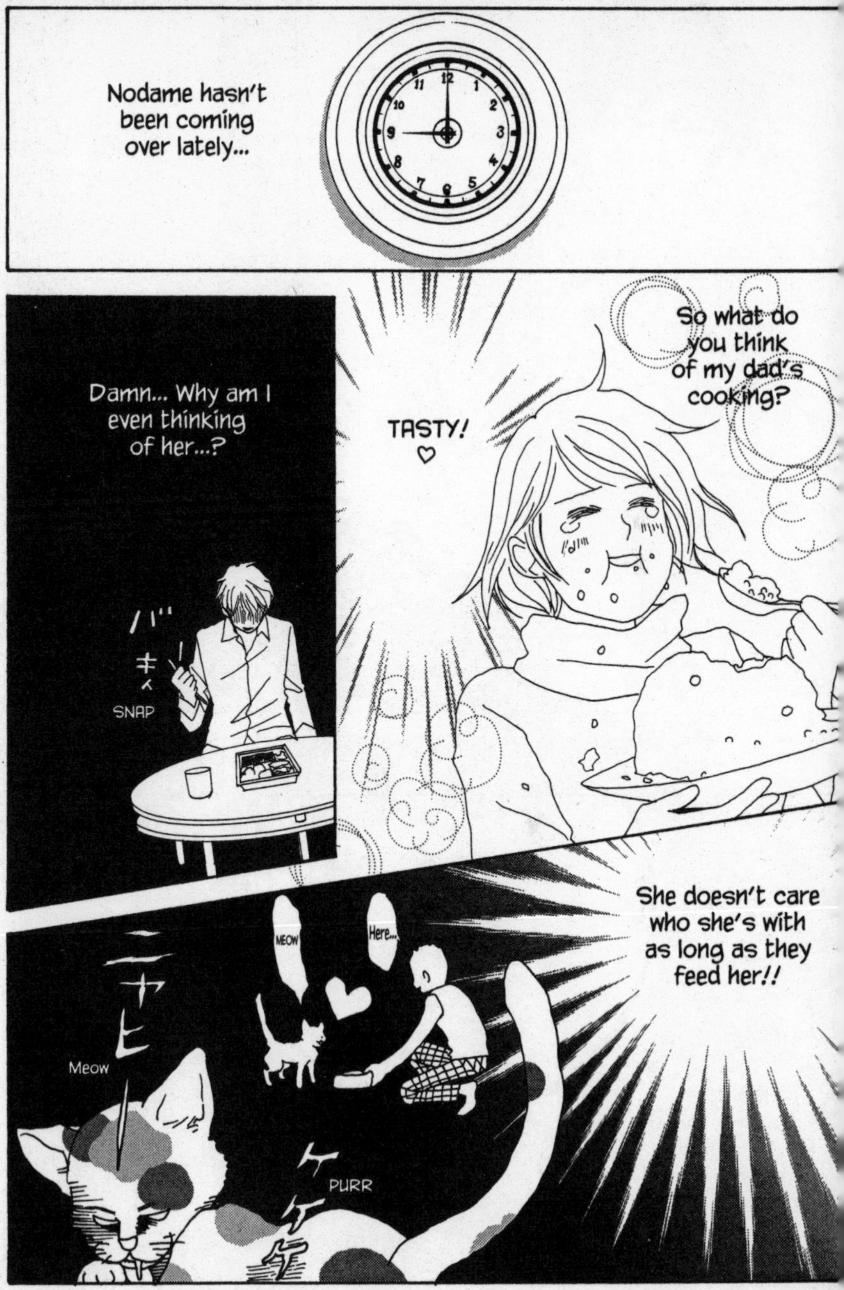
Nodame hasn't been coming over lately...
So what do you think of my dad's cooking?
TASTY! ♡
Damn... Why am I even thinking of her...?
SNAP
She doesn't care who she's with as long as they feed her!!
Here...
MEOW
Meow
PURR

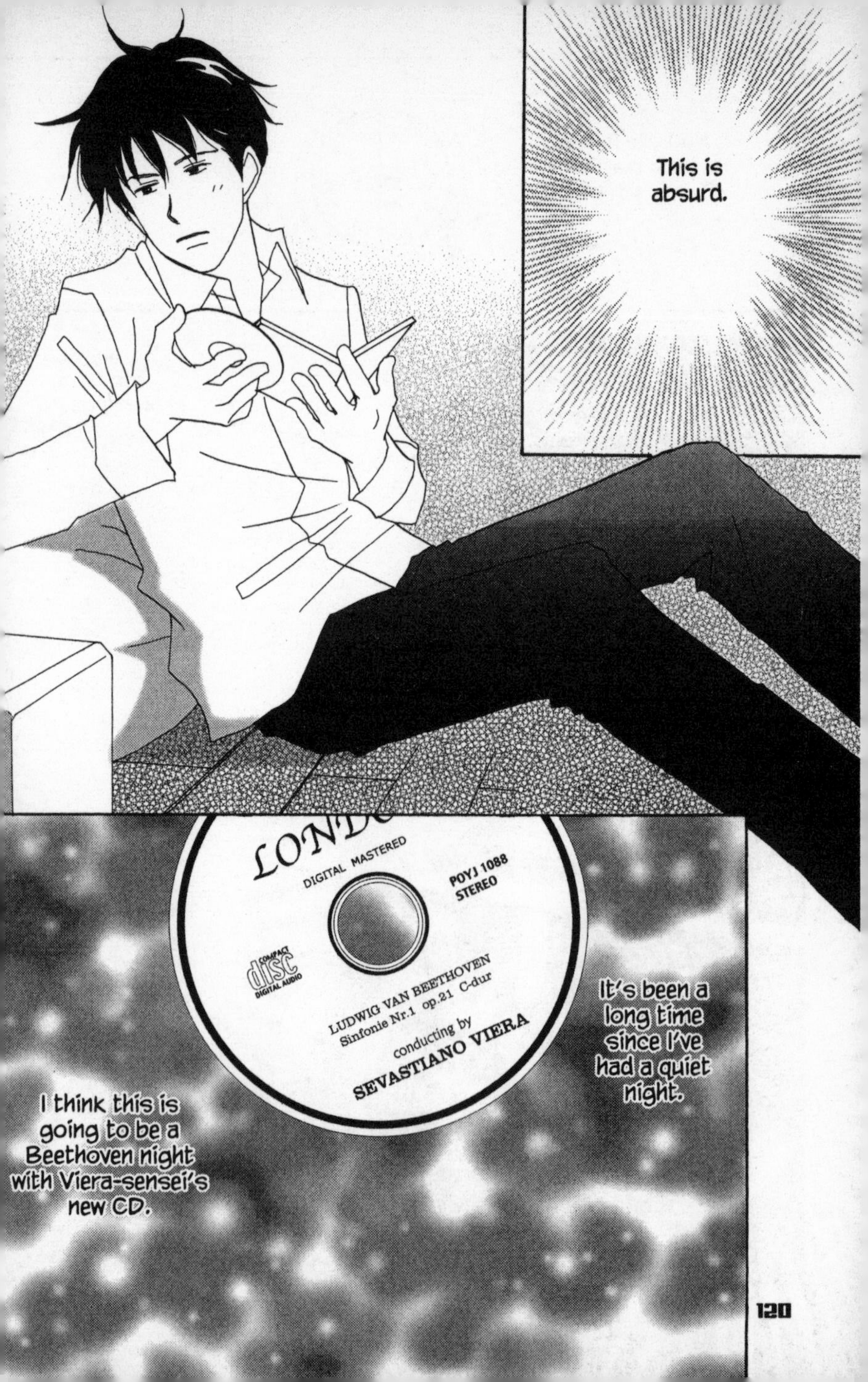
This is absurd.
It's been a long time since I've had a quiet night.
DIGITAL MASTERED
POYJ 1088
STEREO
COMPACT disc DIGITAL AUDIO
LUDWIG VAN BEETHOVEN
Sinfonie Nr.1 op.21 C-dur
conducting by
SEVASTIANO VIERA
I think this is going to be a Beethoven night with Viera-sensei's new CD.

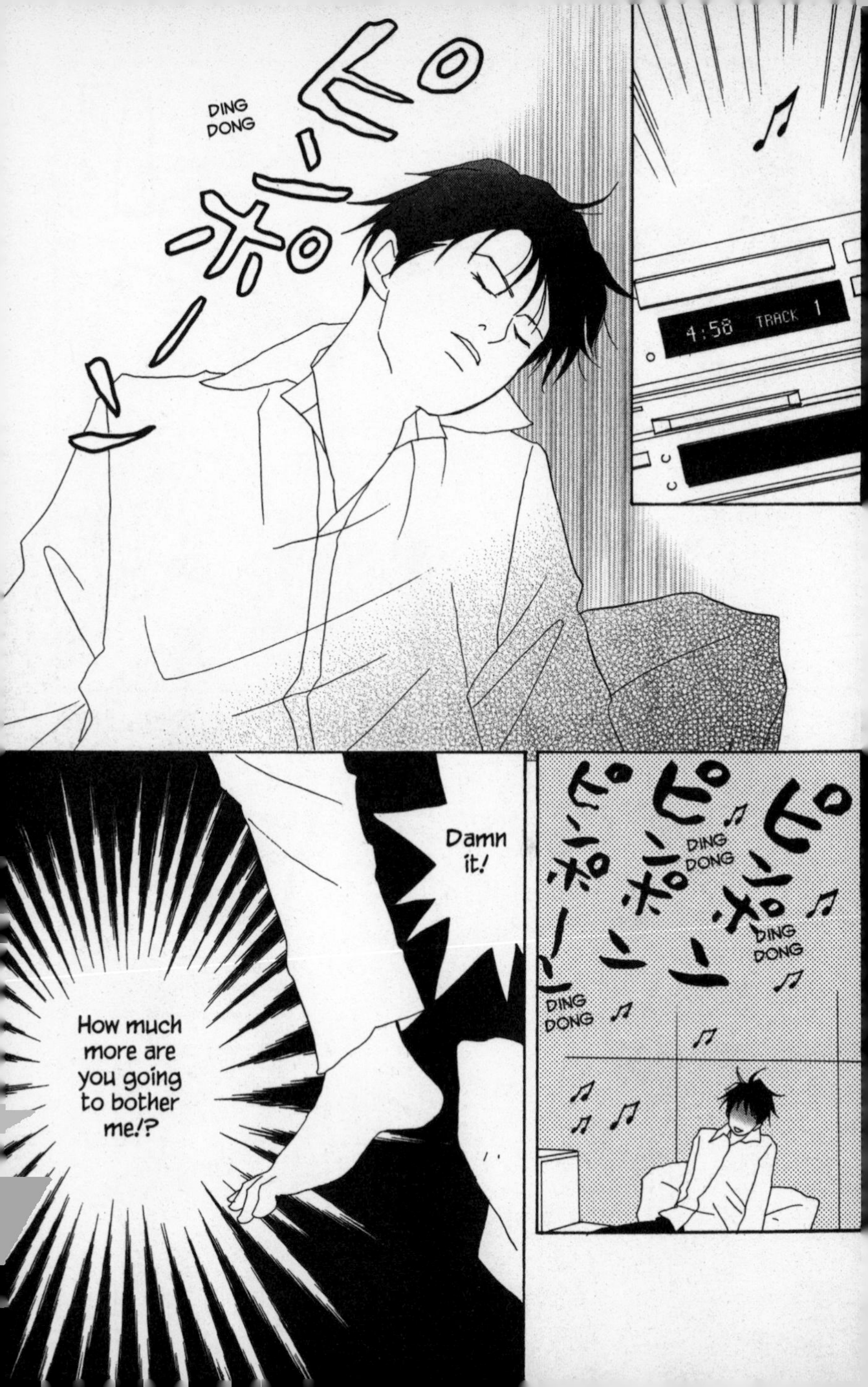
4:58 TRACK 1
DING DONG
DING DONG
DING DONG
DING DONG
Damn it!
How much more are you going to bother me!?

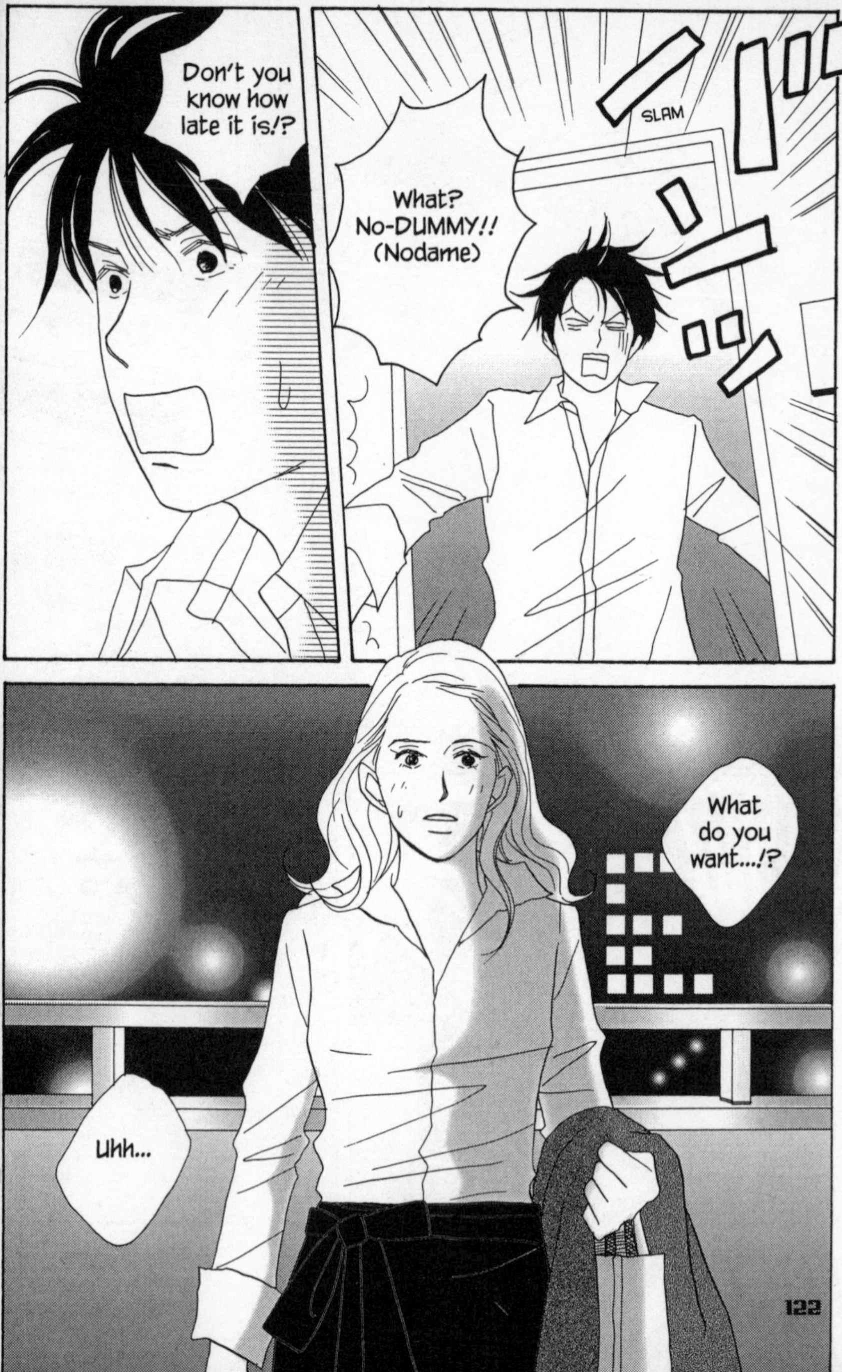
What? No-DUMMY!! (Nodame)
SLAM
Don't you know how late it is!?
What do you want...!?
Uhh...

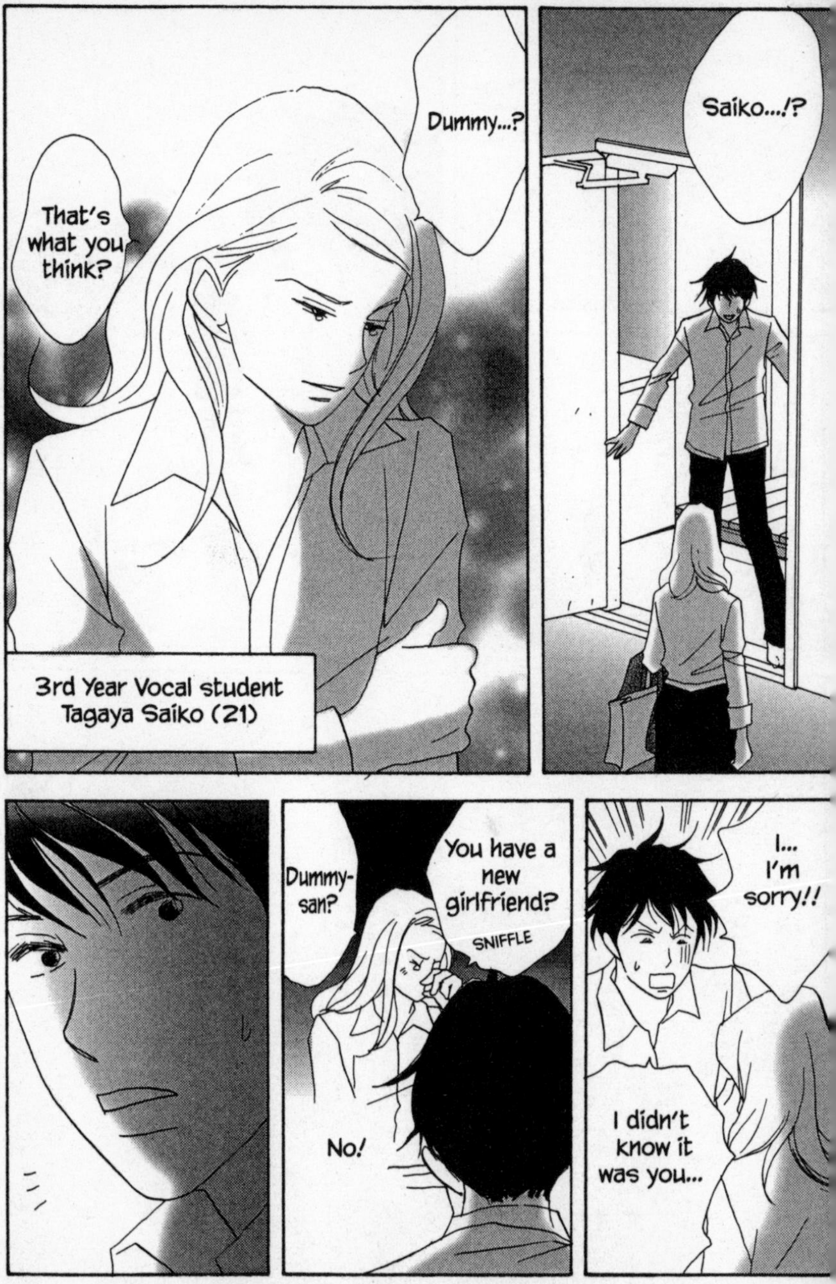
Saiko...!?
Dummy...?
That's what you think?
3rd Year Vocal student Tagaya Saiko (21)
I... I'm sorry!!
I didn't know it was you...
You have a new girlfriend?
Dummy-san?
SNIFFLE
No!

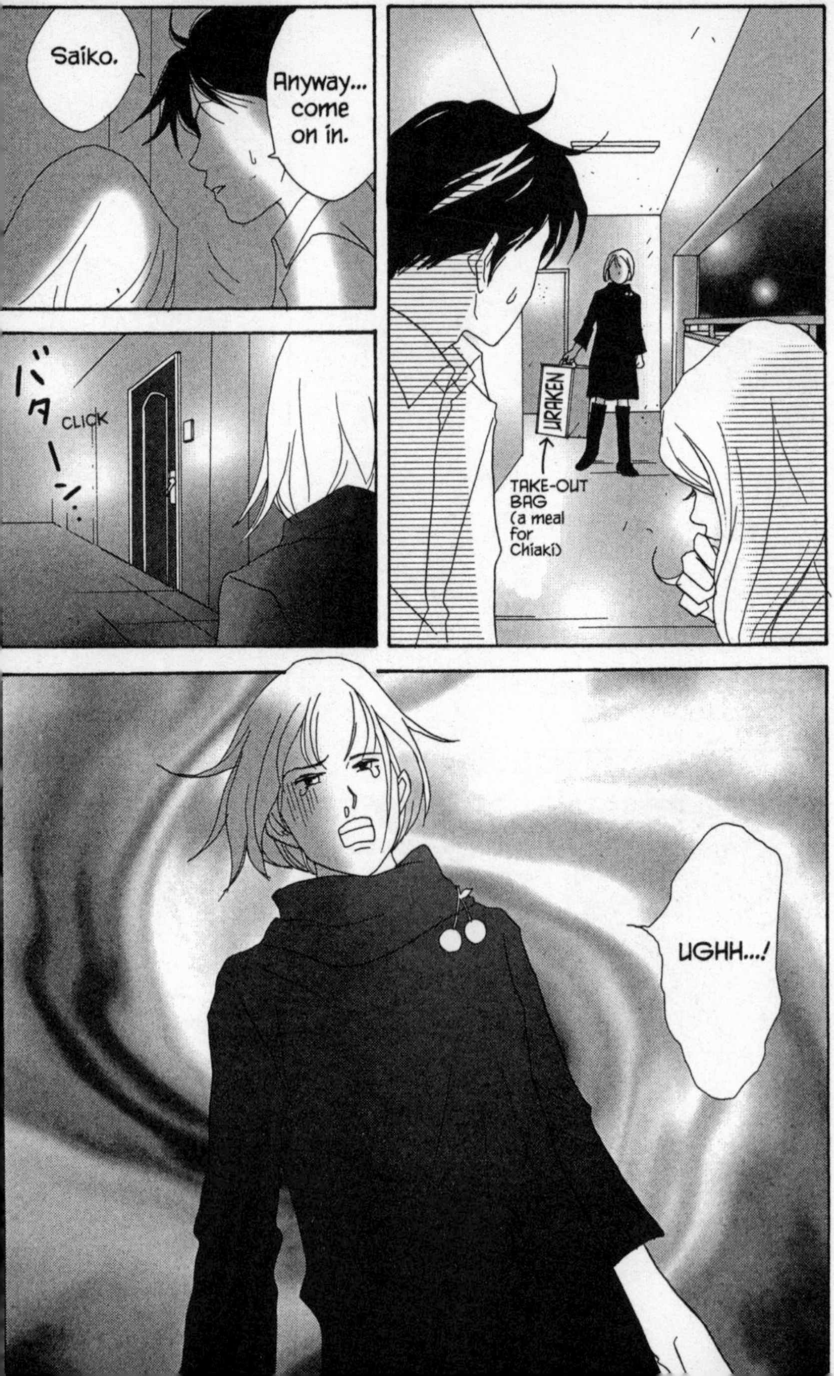
URAKEN
TAKE-OUT BAG (a meal for Chiaki)
Saiko.
Anyway... come on in.
バターン
CLICK
UGHH...!

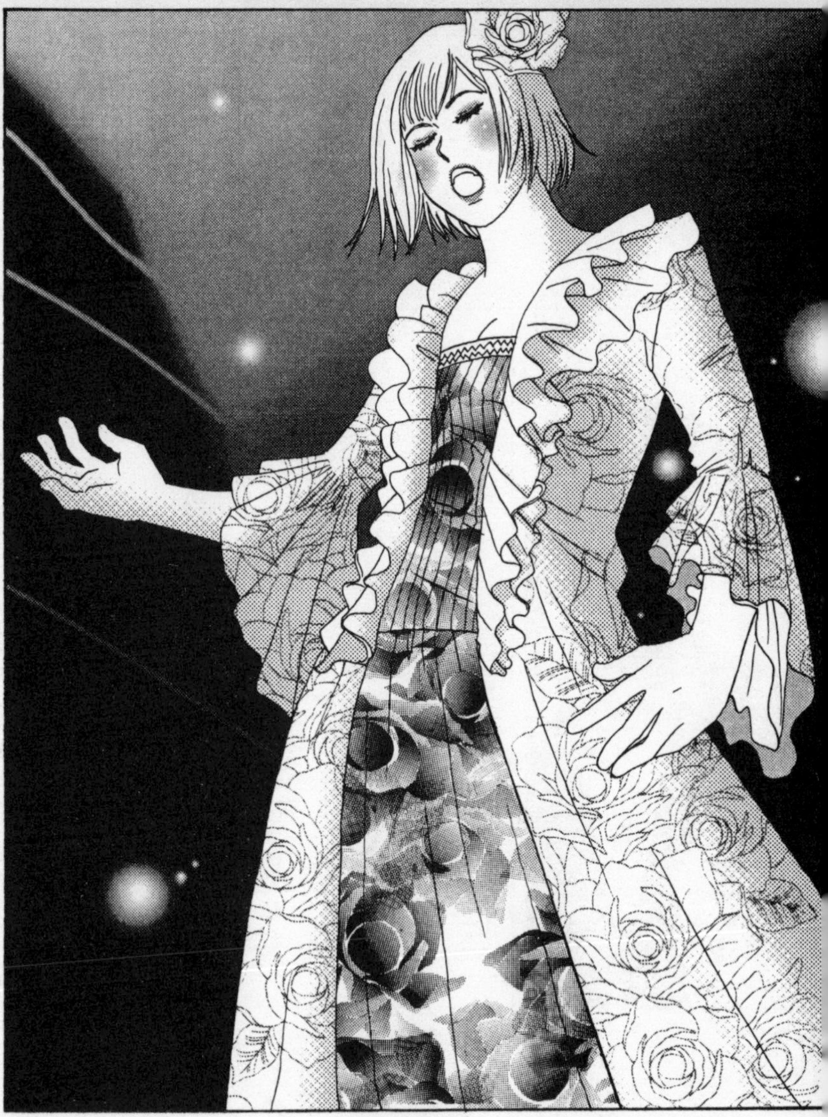

Lesson 5

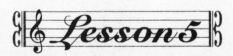

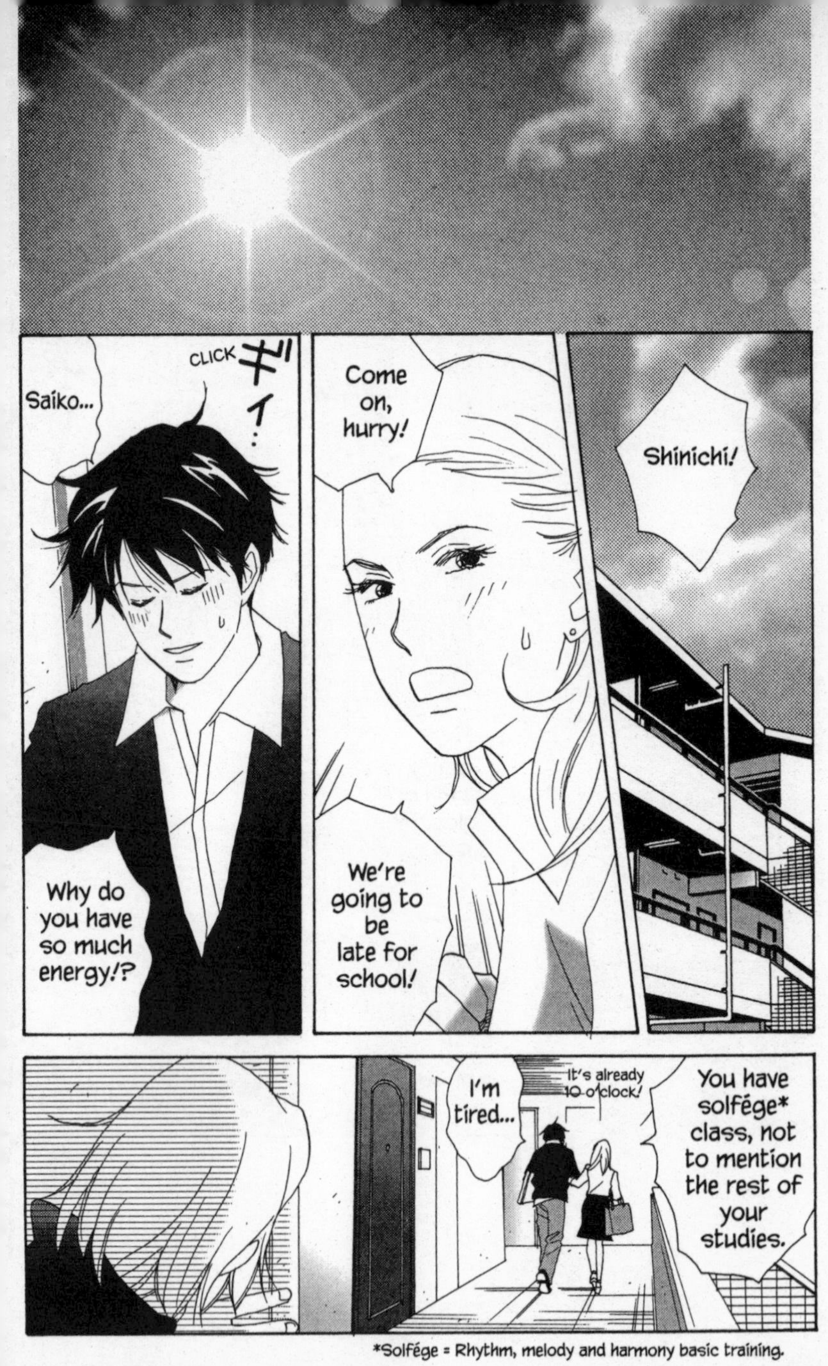
Shinichi!
Come on, hurry!
We're going to be late for school!
CLICK
ギイ…
Saiko...
Why do you have so much energy!?
You have solfége* class, not to mention the rest of your studies.
It's already 10 o'clock!
I'm tired...

*Solfége = Rhythm, melody and harmony basic training.

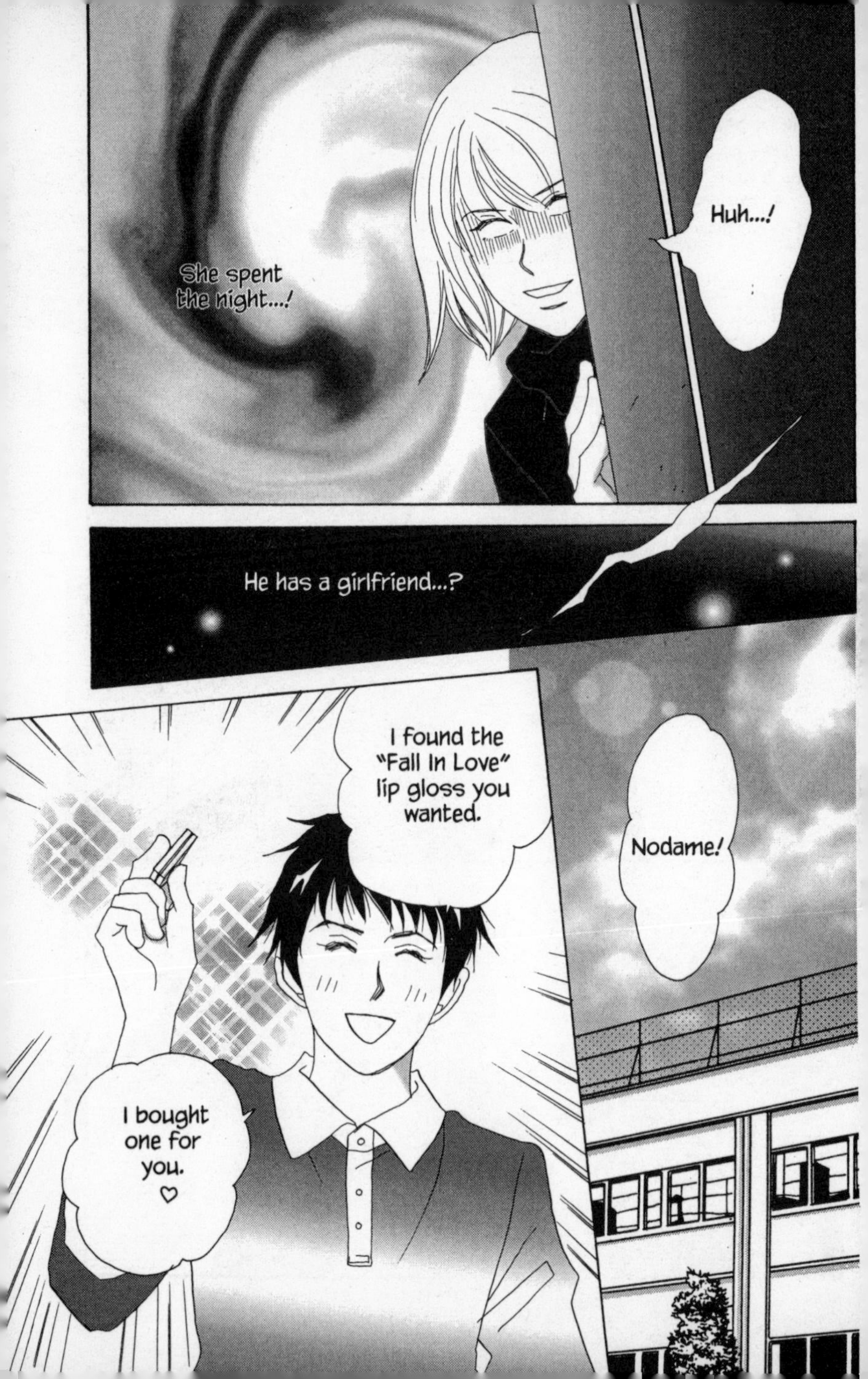
Huh...!
She spent the night...!
He has a girlfriend...?
Nodame!
I found the "Fall In Love" lip gloss you wanted.
I bought one for you. ♡

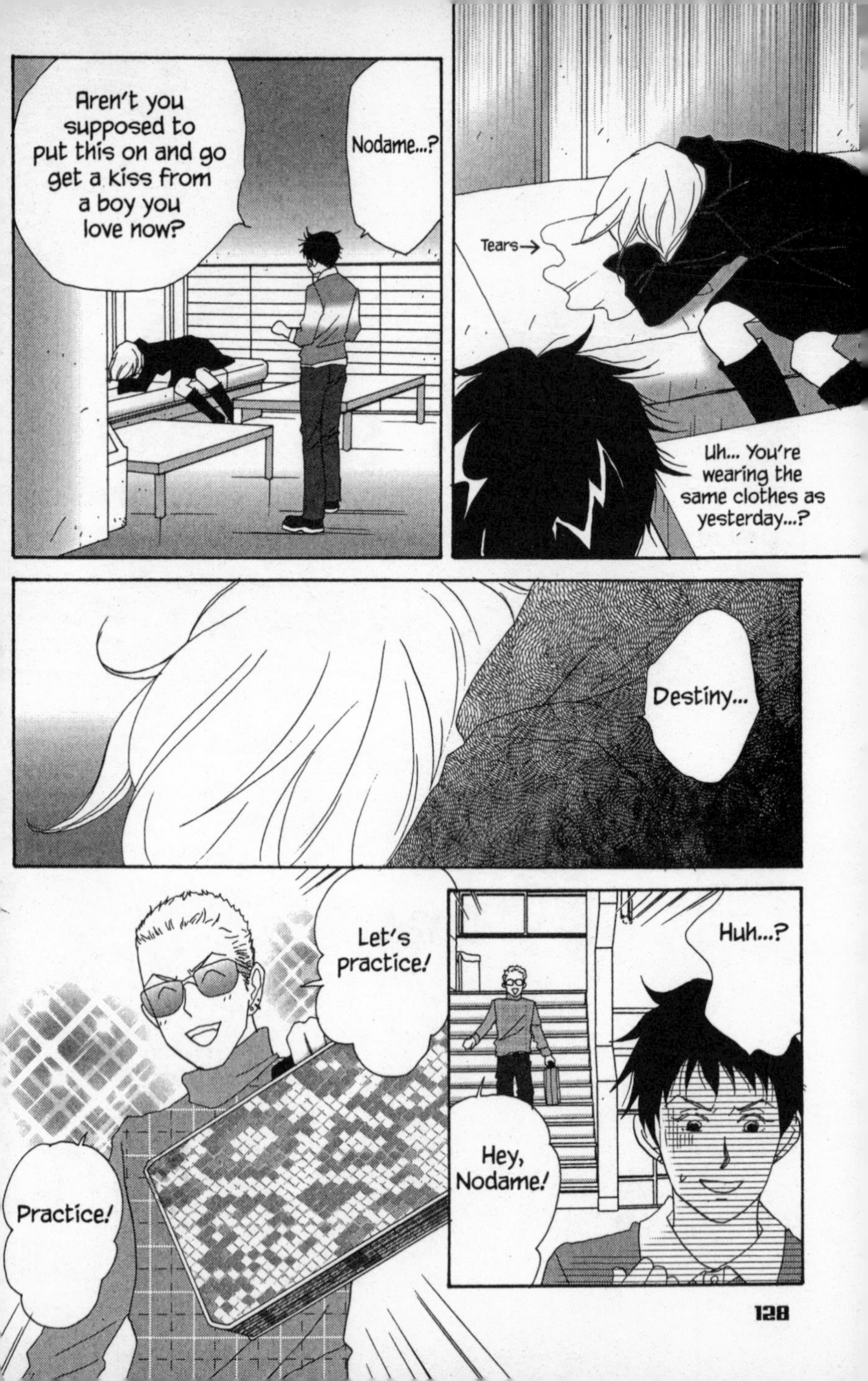
Tears→
Uh... You're wearing the same clothes as yesterday...?
Nodame...?
Aren't you supposed to put this on and go get a kiss from a boy you love now?
Destiny...
Huh...?
Hey, Nodame!
Let's practice!
Practice!

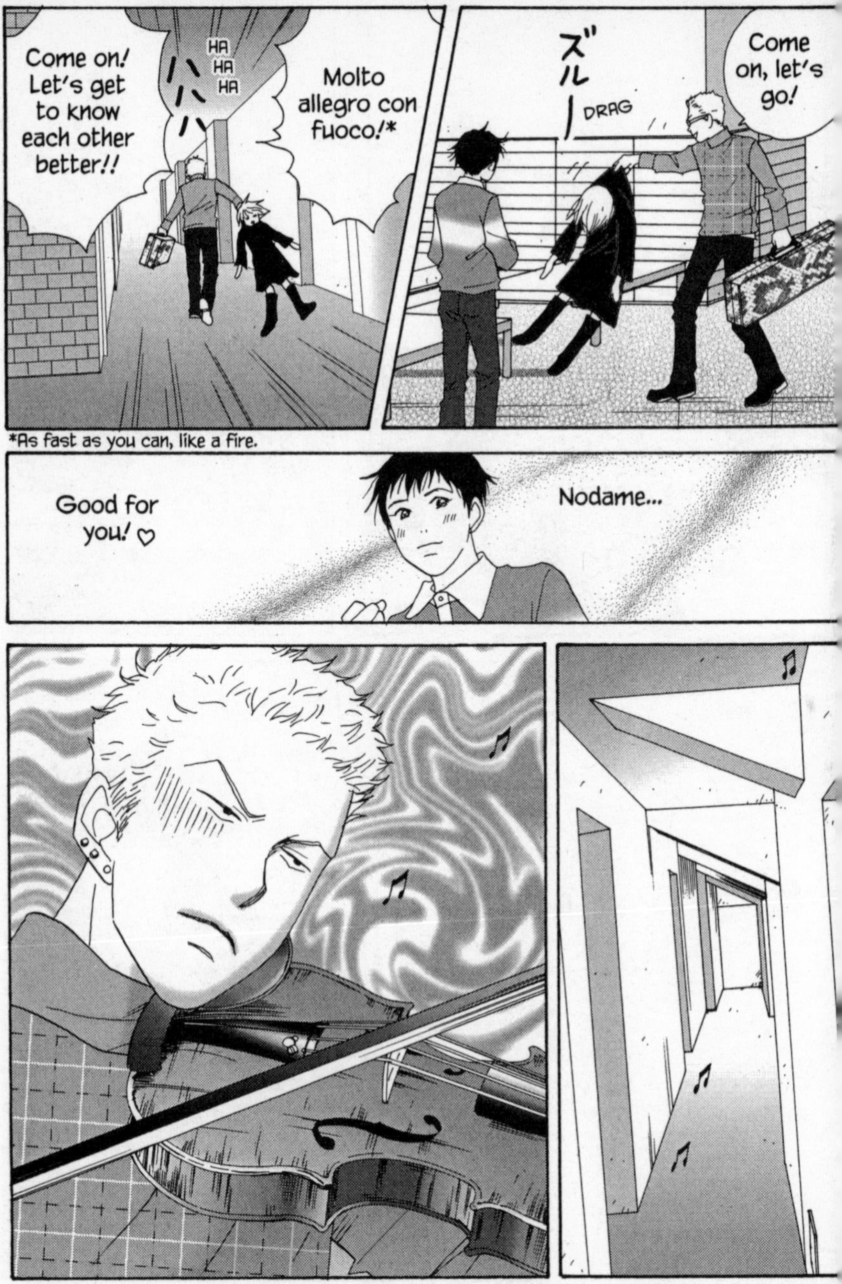
ズルー
DRAG
Come on, let's go!
Molto allegro con fuoco!*
ハハハ
HA HA HA
Come on! Let's get to know each other better!!
Nodame...
Good for you! ♡

*As fast as you can, like a fire.

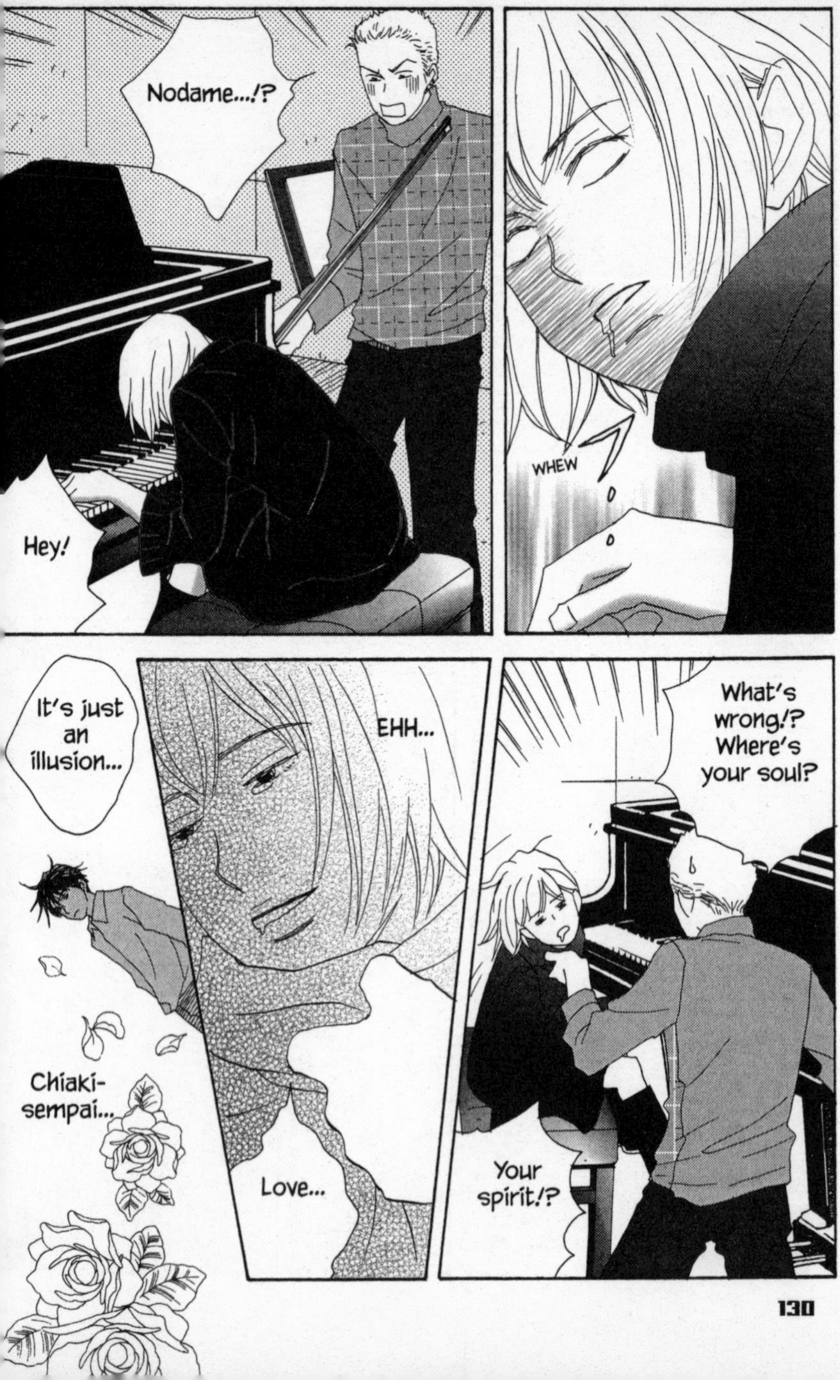
WHEW
Nodame...!?
Hey!
What's wrong!? Where's your soul?
Your spirit!?
EHH...
It's just an illusion...
Chiaki-sempai...
Love...

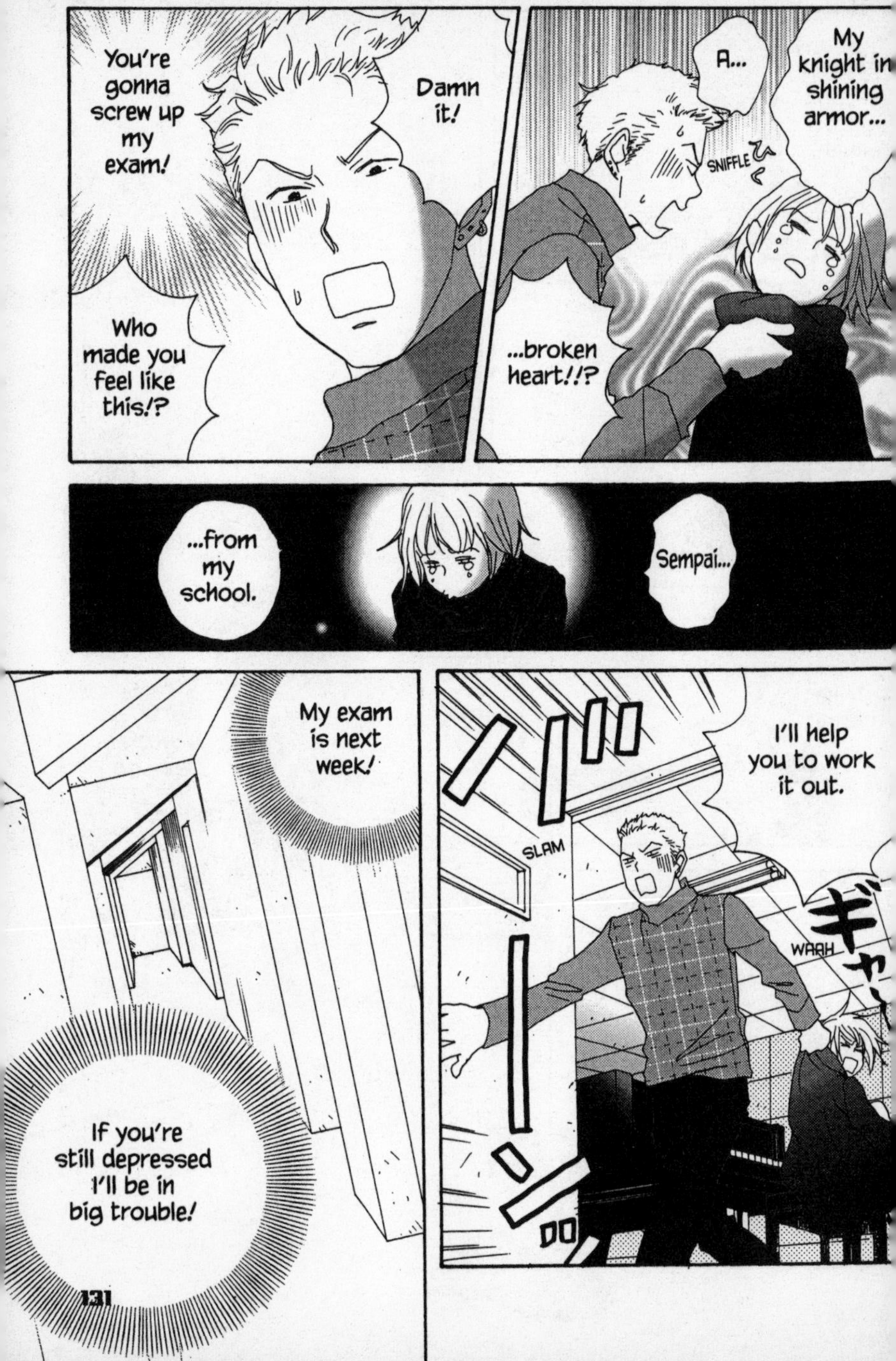

My knight in shining armor...
A...
SNIFFLE
...broken heart!!?
Damn it!
You're gonna screw up my exam!
Who made you feel like this!?
Sempai...
...from my school.
I'll help you to work it out.
ギャー
WAAH
SLAM
DO
My exam is next week!
If you're still depressed I'll be in big trouble!

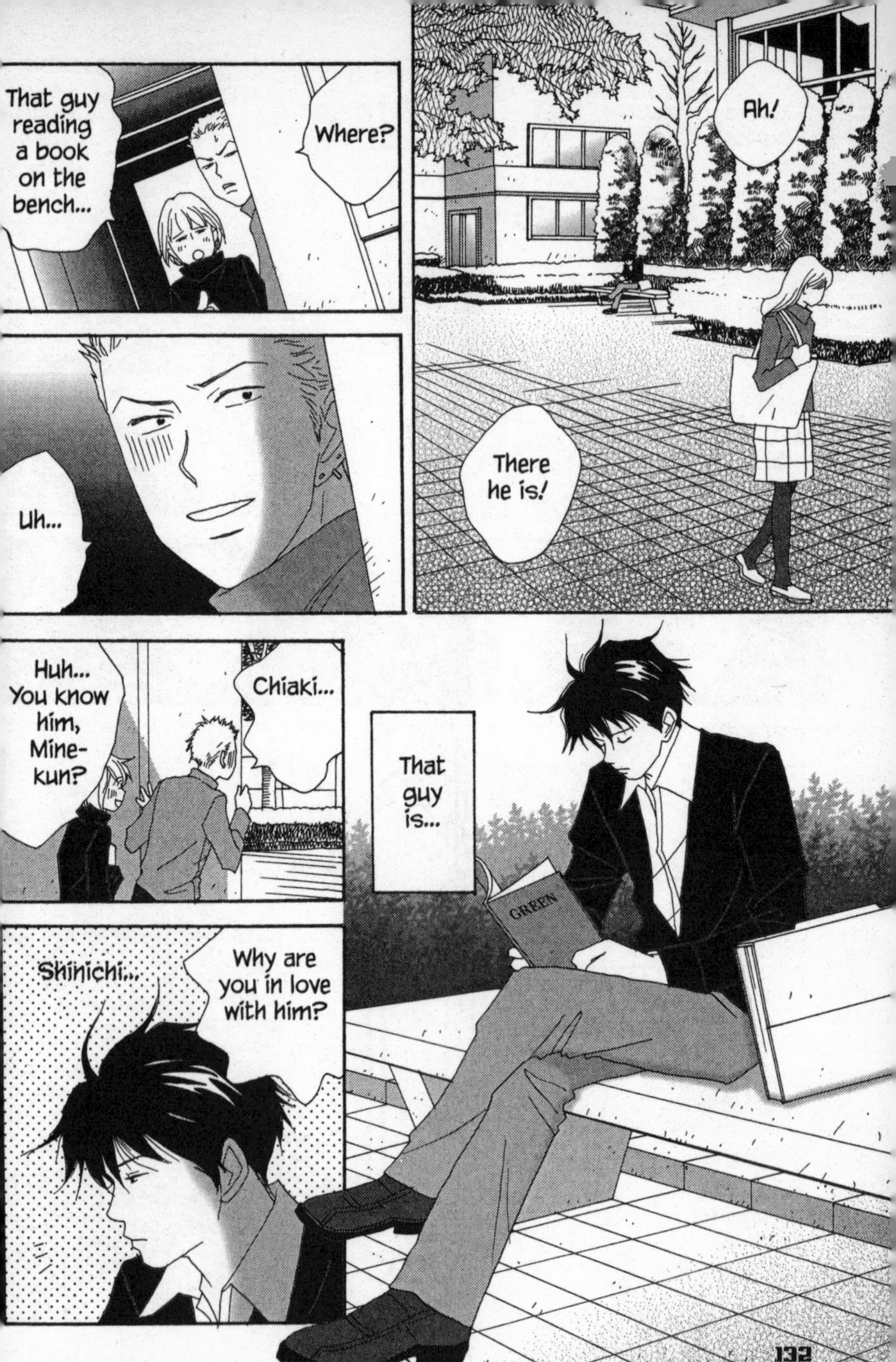
Ah!
There he is!
Where?
That guy reading a book on the bench...
Uh...
That guy is...
Chiaki...
Huh... You know him, Mine-kun?
Why are you in love with him?
Shinichi...

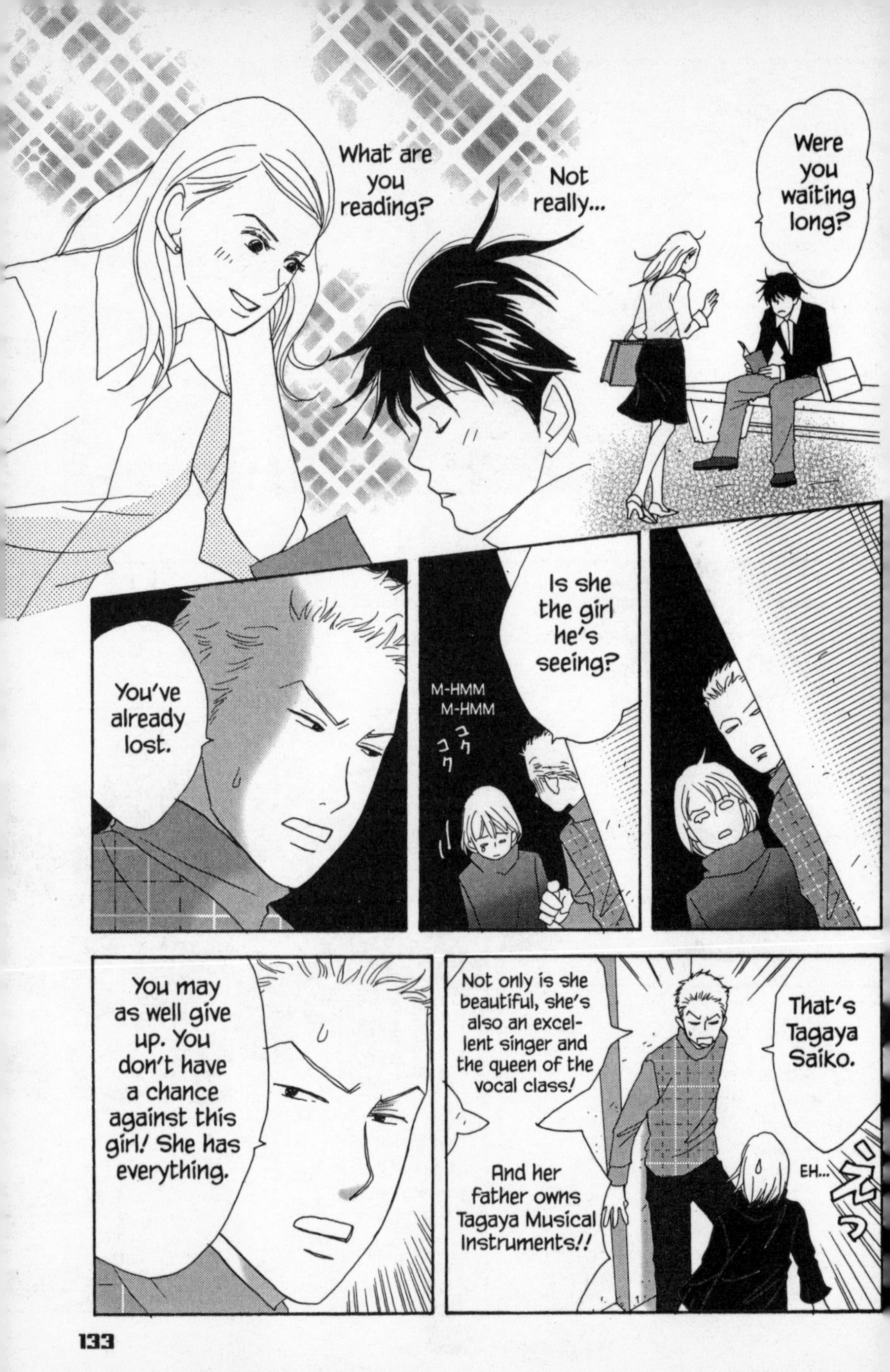
Were you waiting long?
Not really...
What are you reading?
Is she the girl he's seeing?
M-HMM M-HMM
You've already lost.
That's Tagaya Saiko.
EH...
Not only is she beautiful, she's also an excellent singer and the queen of the vocal class!
And her father owns Tagaya Musical Instruments!!
You may as well give up. You don't have a chance against this girl! She has everything.

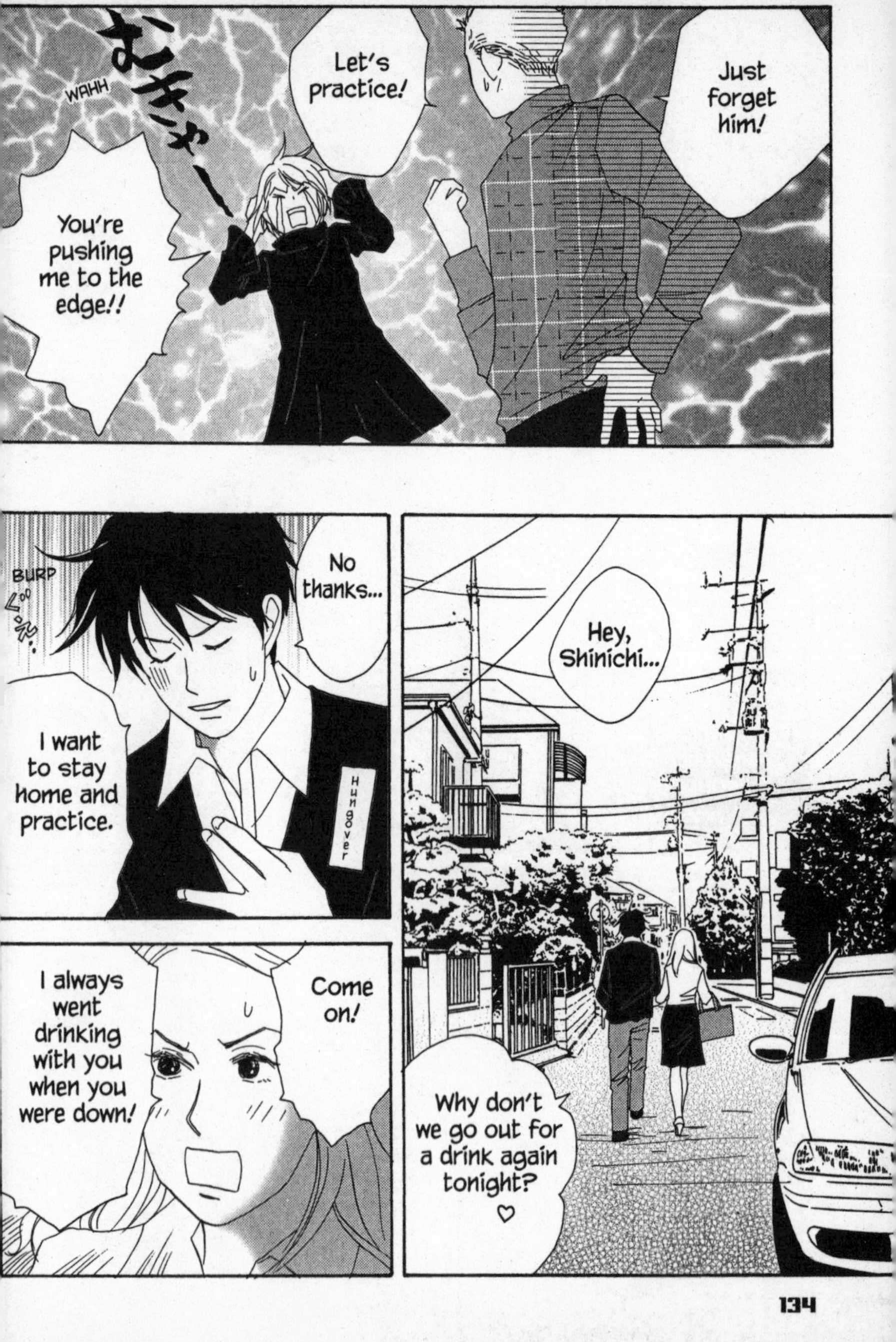
Just forget him!
Let's practice!
WAHH
You're pushing me to the edge!!
Hey, Shinichi...
Why don't we go out for a drink again tonight? ♡
No thanks...
BURP
Hungover
I want to stay home and practice.
Come on!
I always went drinking with you when you were down!

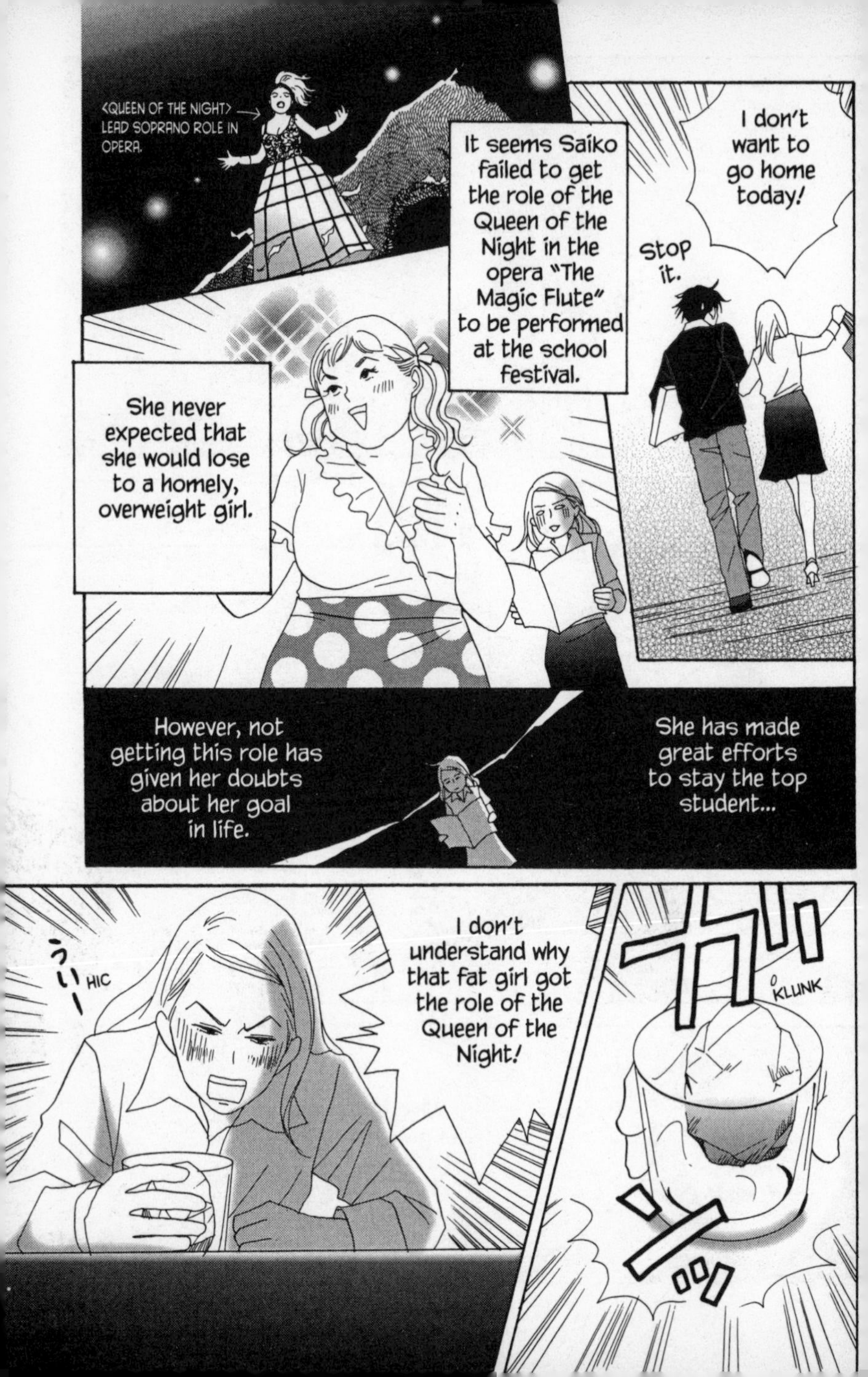
I don't want to go home today!
Stop it.
<QUEEN OF THE NIGHT> LEAD SOPRANO ROLE IN OPERA.
It seems Saiko failed to get the role of the Queen of the Night in the opera "The Magic Flute" to be performed at the school festival.
She never expected that she would lose to a homely, overweight girl.
She has made great efforts to stay the top student...
However, not getting this role has given her doubts about her goal in life.
KLUNK
I don't understand why that fat girl got the role of the Queen of the Night!
うぃー
HIC

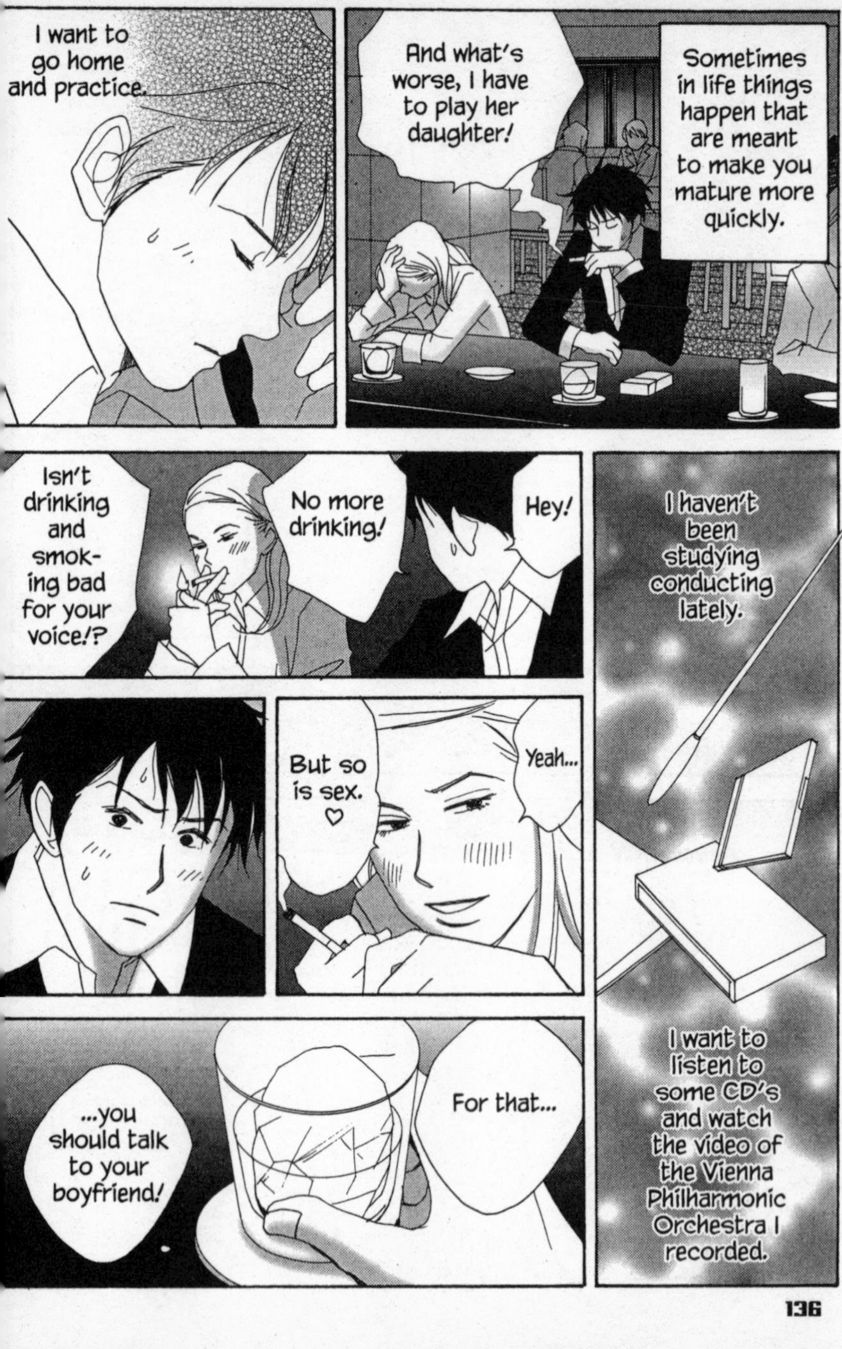
Sometimes in life things happen that are meant to make you mature more quickly.
And what's worse, I have to play her daughter!
I want to go home and practice.
I haven't been studying conducting lately.
I want to listen to some CD's and watch the video of the Vienna Philharmonic Orchestra I recorded.
Hey!
No more drinking!
Isn't drinking and smoking bad for your voice!?
Yeah...
But so is sex. ♡
For that...
...you should talk to your boyfriend!

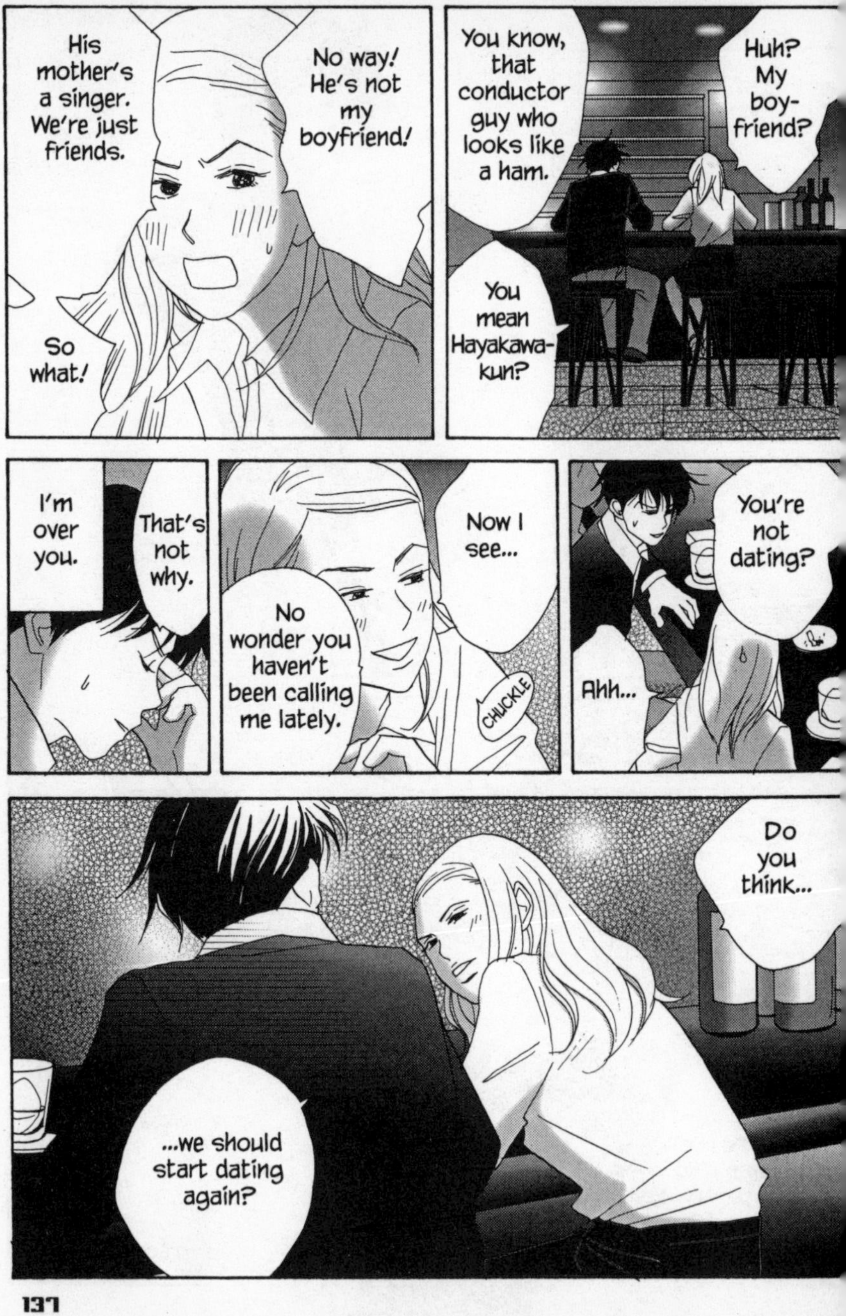
Huh? My boy-friend?
You know, that conductor guy who looks like a ham.
You mean Hayakawa-kun?
No way! He's not my boyfriend!
His mother's a singer. We're just friends.
So what!
You're not dating?
Ahh...
Now I see...
CHUCKLE
No wonder you haven't been calling me lately.
That's not why.
I'm over you.
Do you think...
...we should start dating again?

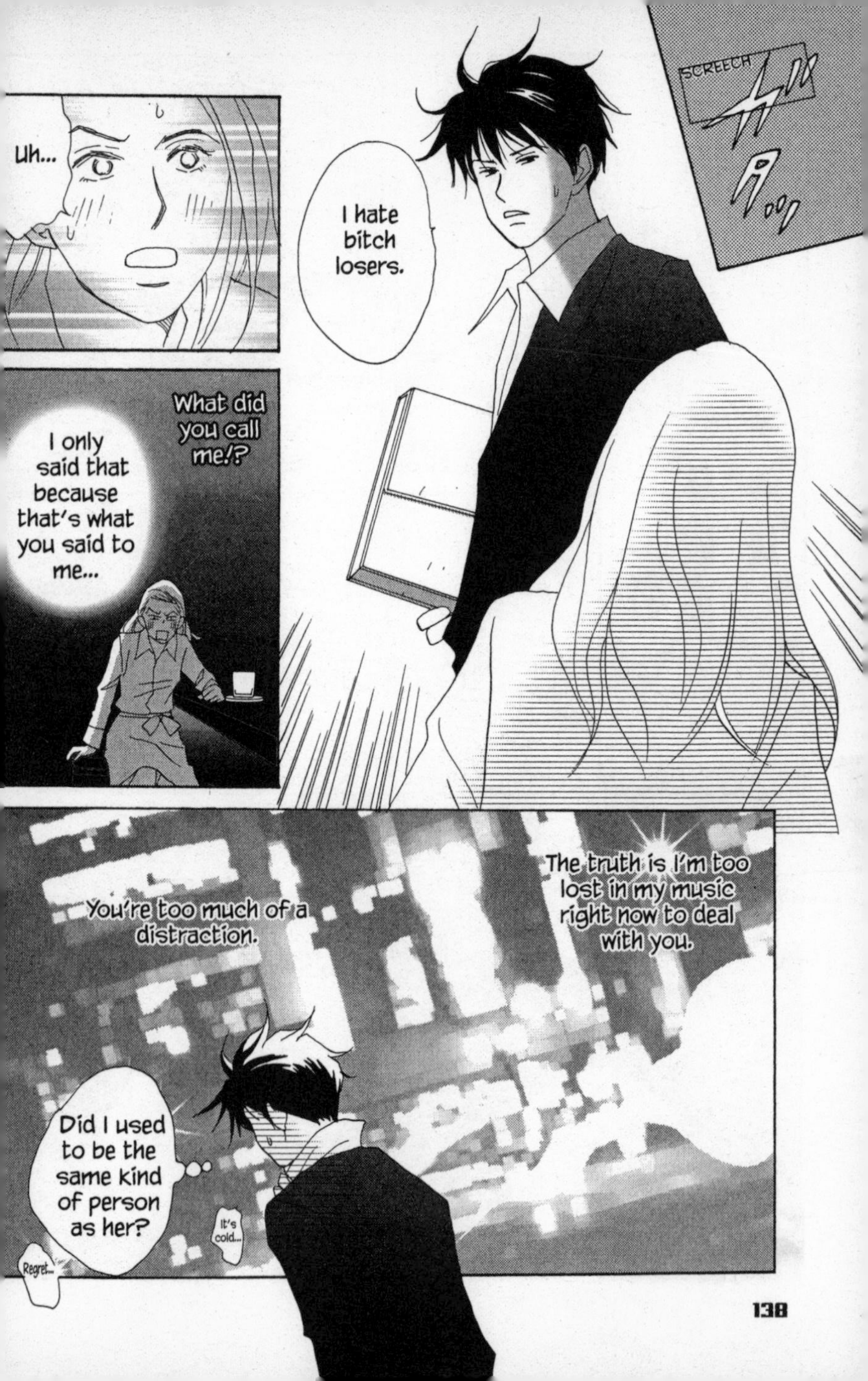
SCREECH
I hate bitch losers.
Uh...
What did you call me!?
I only said that because that's what you said to me...
The truth is I'm too lost in my music right now to deal with you.
You're too much of a distraction.
Did I used to be the same kind of person as her?
It's cold...
Regret...

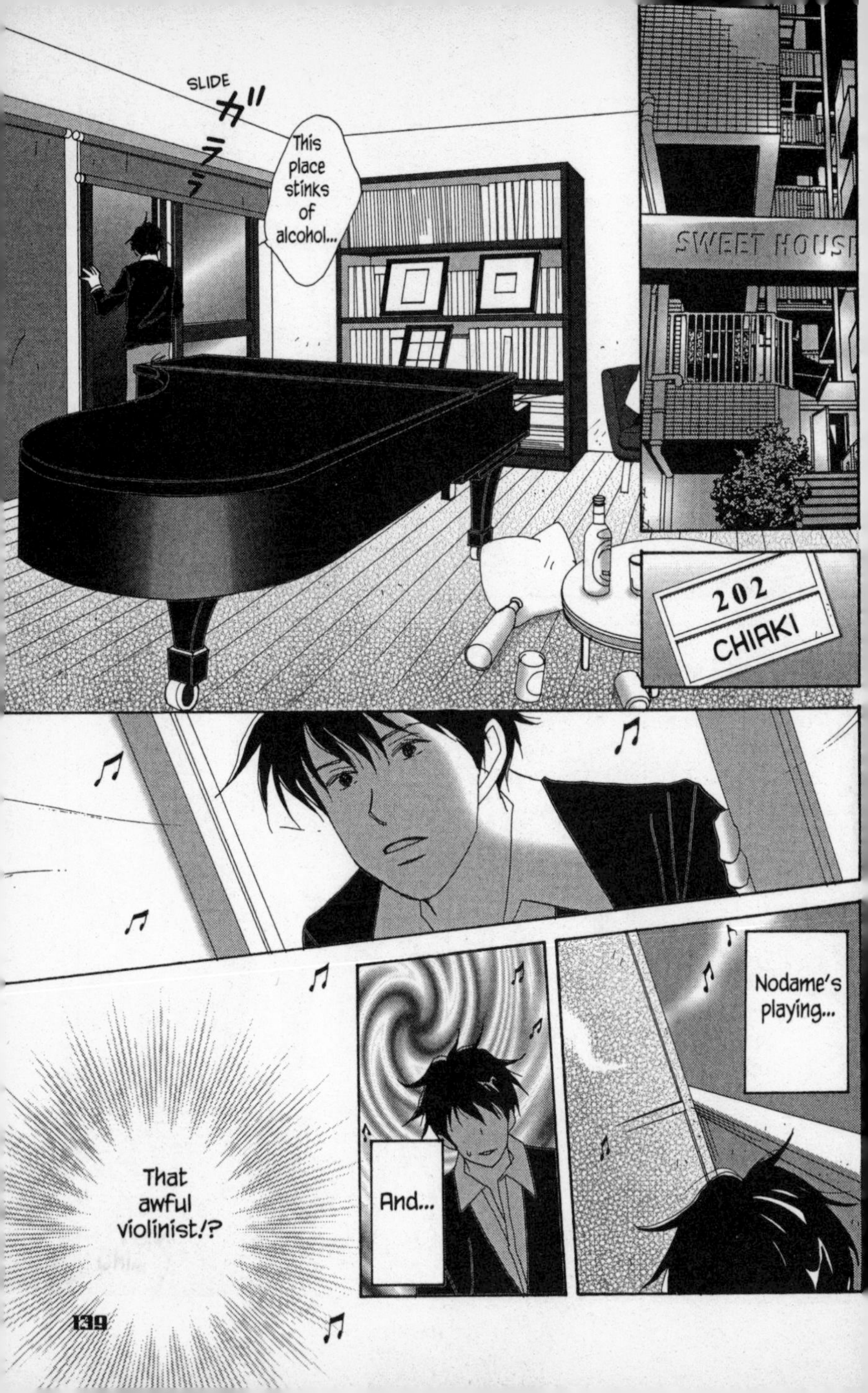
SWEET HOUS
202
CHIAKI
SLIDE
ガラ
This place stinks of alcohol...
Nodame's playing...
And...
That awful violinist!?

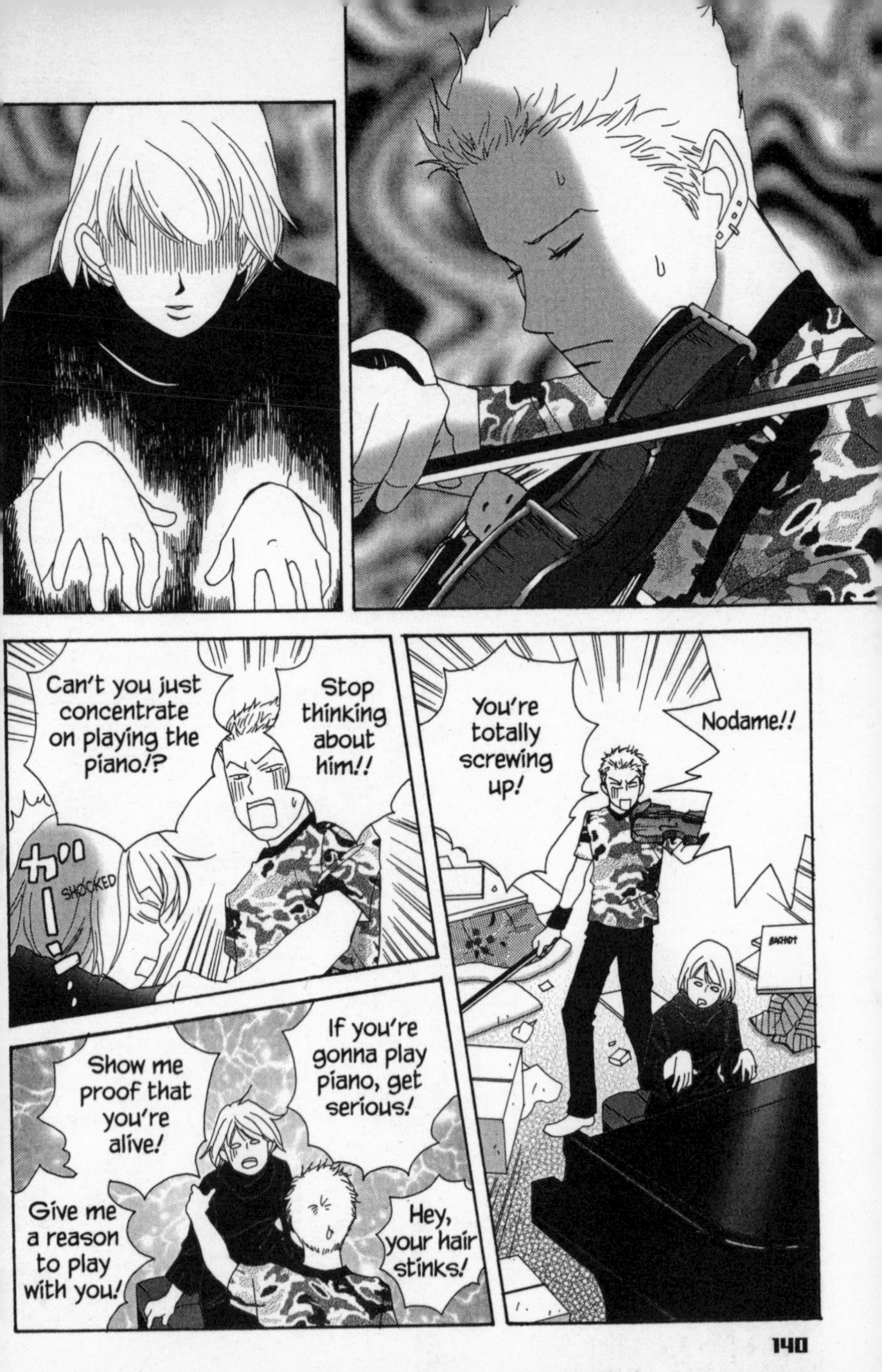
Nodame!!
You're totally screwing up!
Stop thinking about him!!
Can't you just concentrate on playing the piano!?
SHOCKED
If you're gonna play piano, get serious!
Show me proof that you're alive!
Hey, your hair stinks!
Give me a reason to play with you!

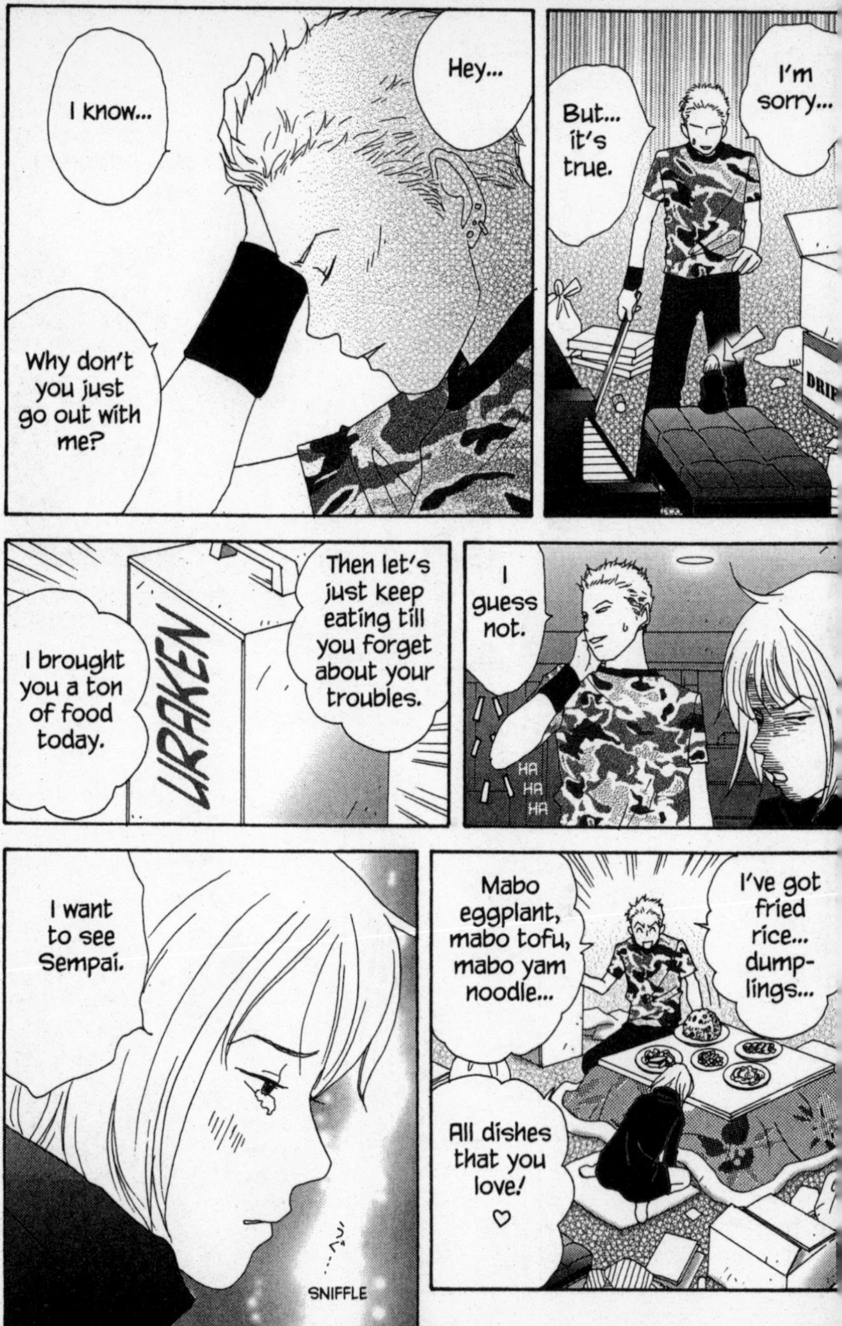
I'm sorry...
But... it's true.
Hey...
I know...
Why don't you just go out with me?
I guess not.
HA HA HA
Then let's just keep eating till you forget about your troubles.
I brought you a ton of food today.
URAKEN
I've got fried rice... dumplings...
Mabo eggplant, mabo tofu, mabo yam noodle...
All dishes that you love! ♡
I want to see Sempai.
SNIFFLE

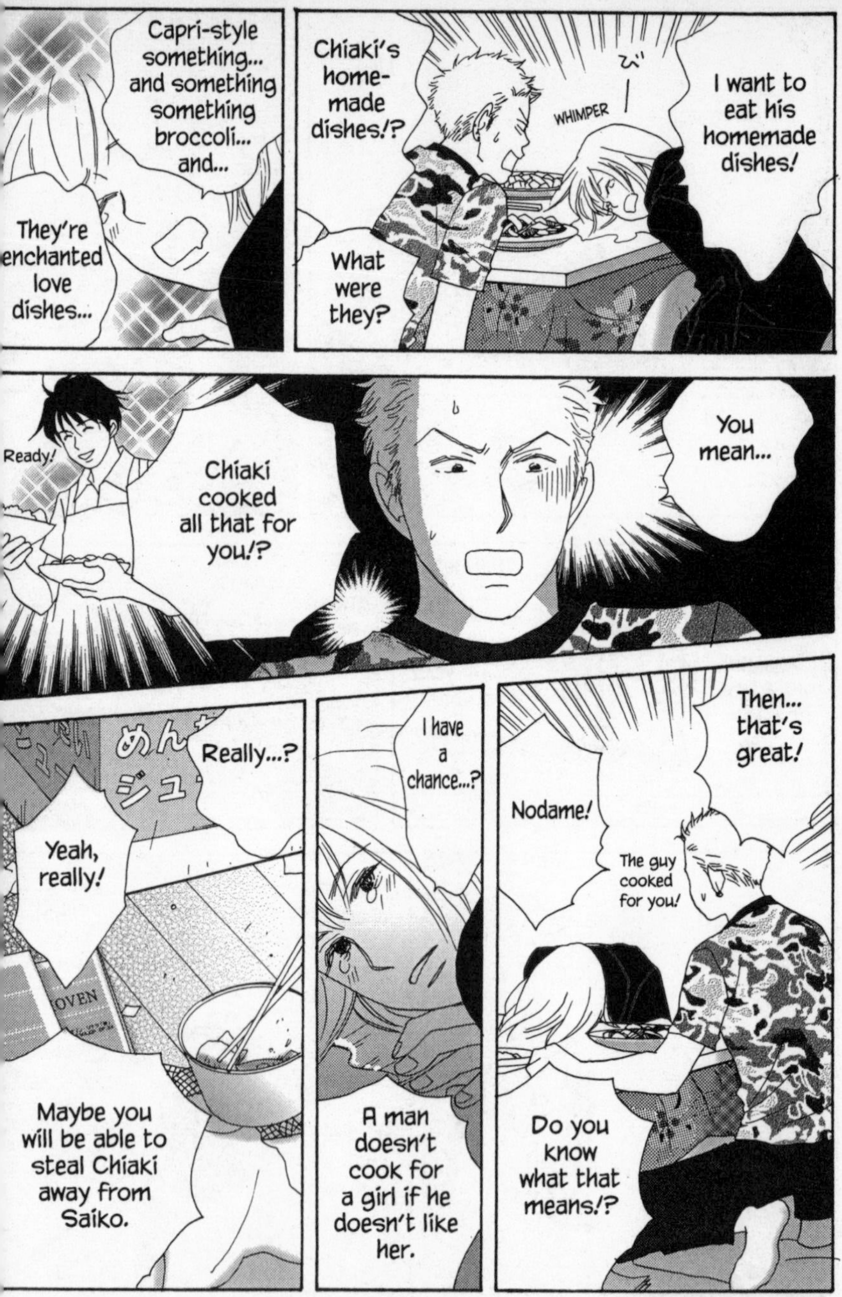
I want to eat his homemade dishes!
び
WHIMPER
Chiaki's home-made dishes!?
What were they?
Capri-style something... and something something broccoli... and...
They're enchanted love dishes...
You mean...
Chiaki cooked all that for you!?
Ready!
Then... that's great!
Nodame!
The guy cooked for you!
Do you know what that means!?
I have a chance...?
A man doesn't cook for a girl if he doesn't like her.
Really...?
Yeah, really!
OVEN
Maybe you will be able to steal Chiaki away from Saiko.

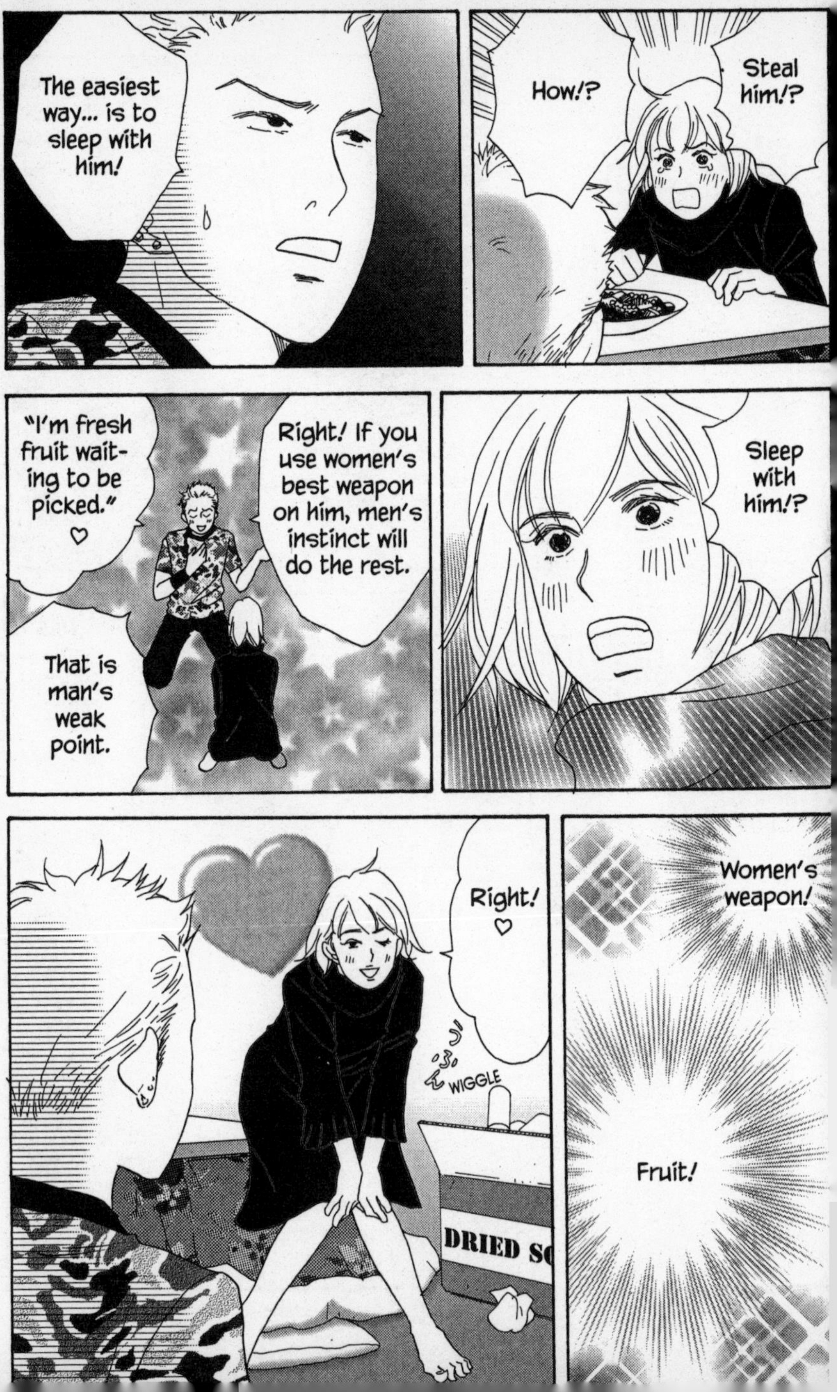
Steal him!?
How!?
The easiest way... is to sleep with him!
Sleep with him!?
Right! If you use women's best weapon on him, men's instinct will do the rest.
"I'm fresh fruit wait-ing to be picked." ♡
That is man's weak point.
Women's weapon!
Fruit!
Right! ♡
WIGGLE
DRIED SO

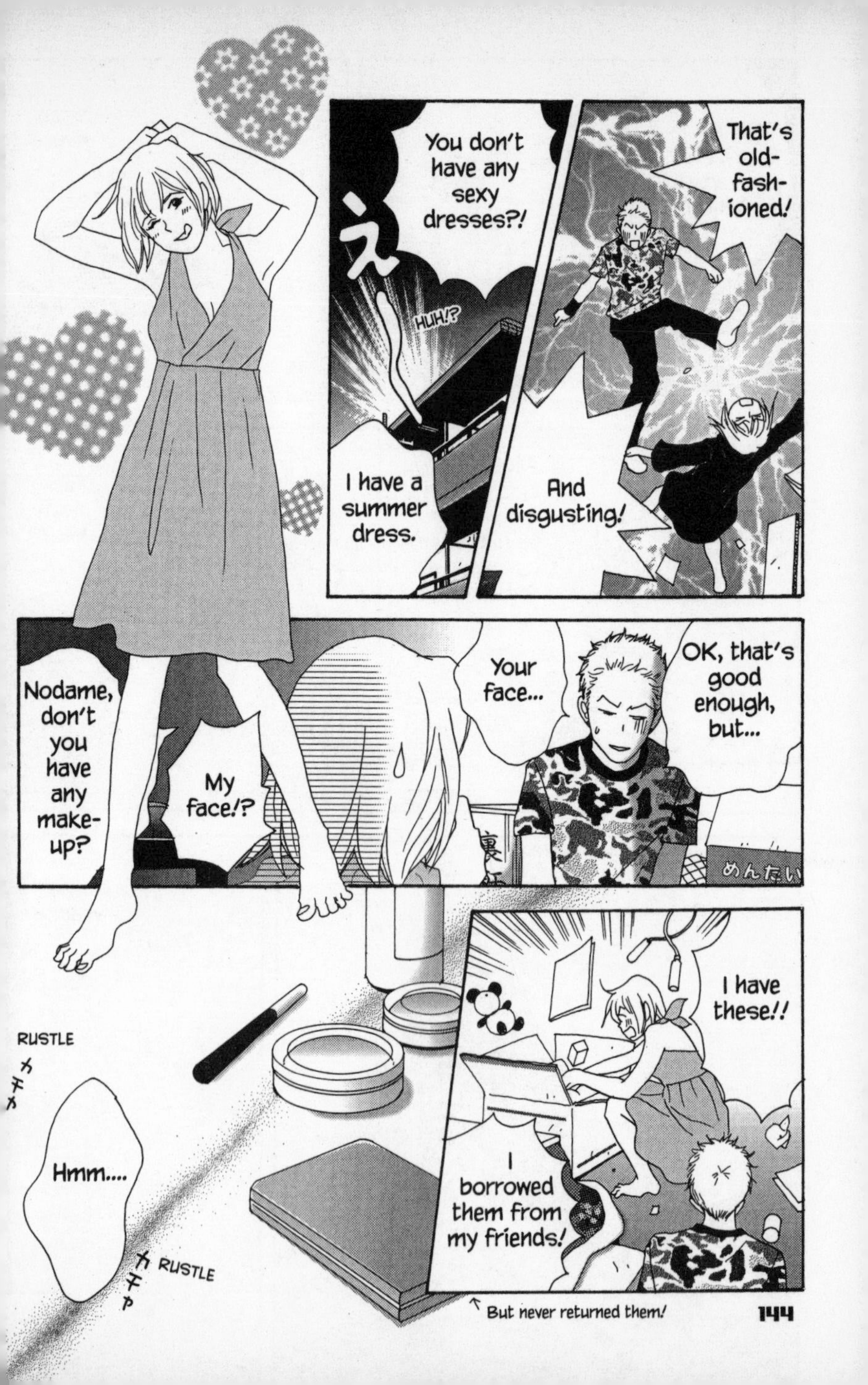
That's old-fashioned!
And disgusting!
You don't have any sexy dresses?!
え
HUH!?
I have a summer dress.
OK, that's good enough, but...
Your face...
My face!?
Nodame, don't you have any make-up?
めんたい
裏
I have these!!
I borrowed them from my friends!
But never returned them!
RUSTLE
カチャ
Hmm....
RUSTLE
カチャ

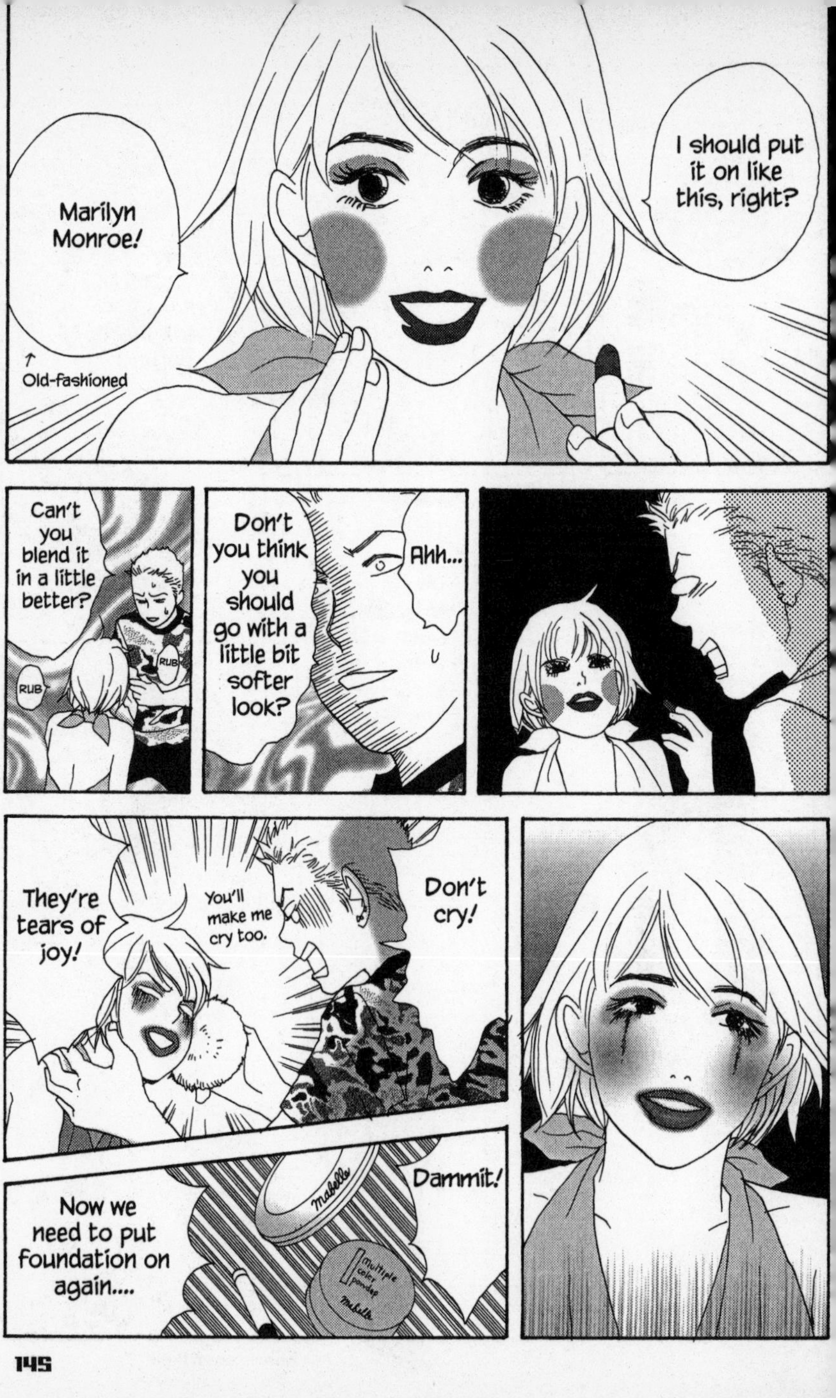
I should put it on like this, right?
Marilyn Monroe!
Old-fashioned
Ahh...
Don't you think you should go with a little bit softer look?
Can't you blend it in a little better?
RUB
RUB
Don't cry!
You'll make me cry too.
They're tears of joy!
Dammit!
mabelle
multiple color powder
mabelle
Now we need to put foundation on again....

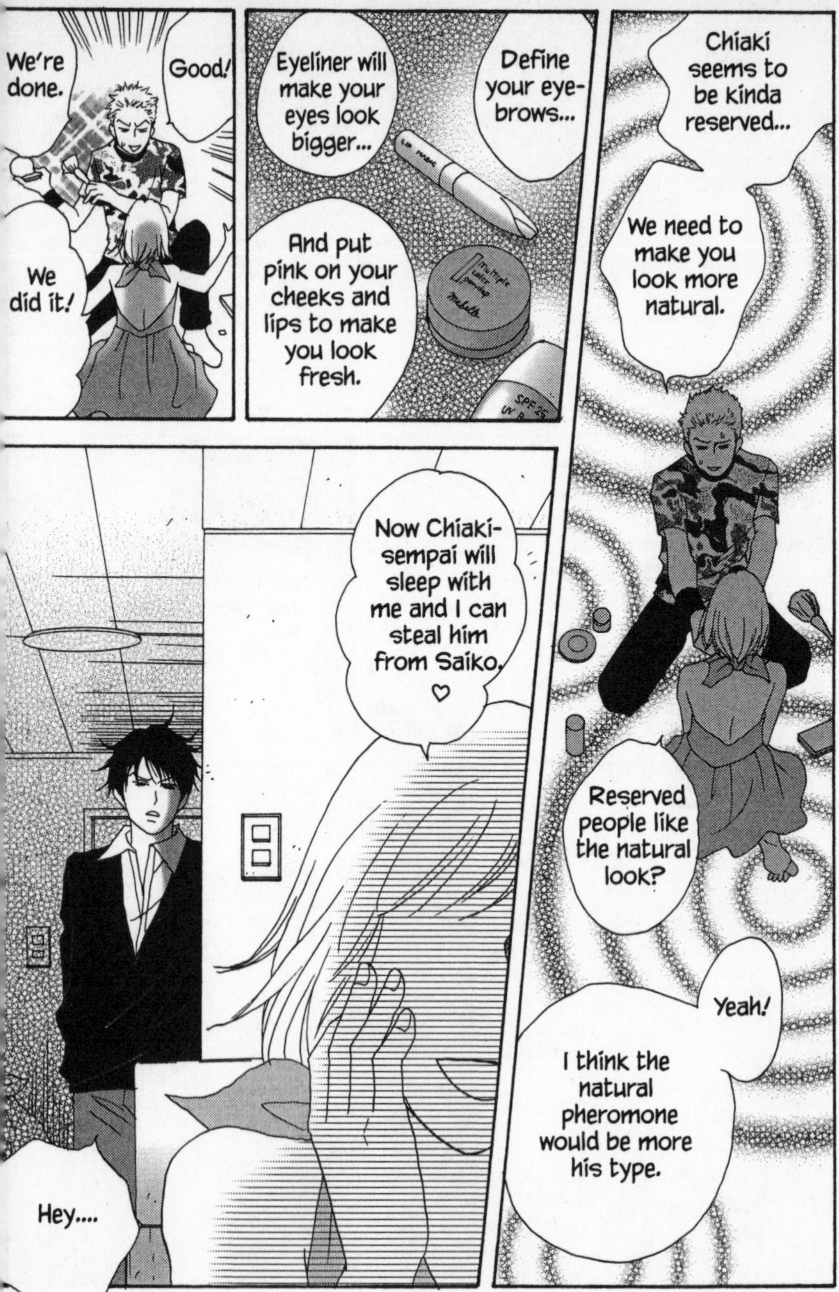
Chiaki seems to be kinda reserved...
We need to make you look more natural.
Reserved people like the natural look?
Yeah!
I think the natural pheromone would be more his type.
Define your eye-brows...
Eyeliner will make your eyes look bigger...
And put pink on your cheeks and lips to make you look fresh.
Good!
We're done.
We did it!
Now Chiaki-sempai will sleep with me and I can steal him from Saiko. ♡
Hey....

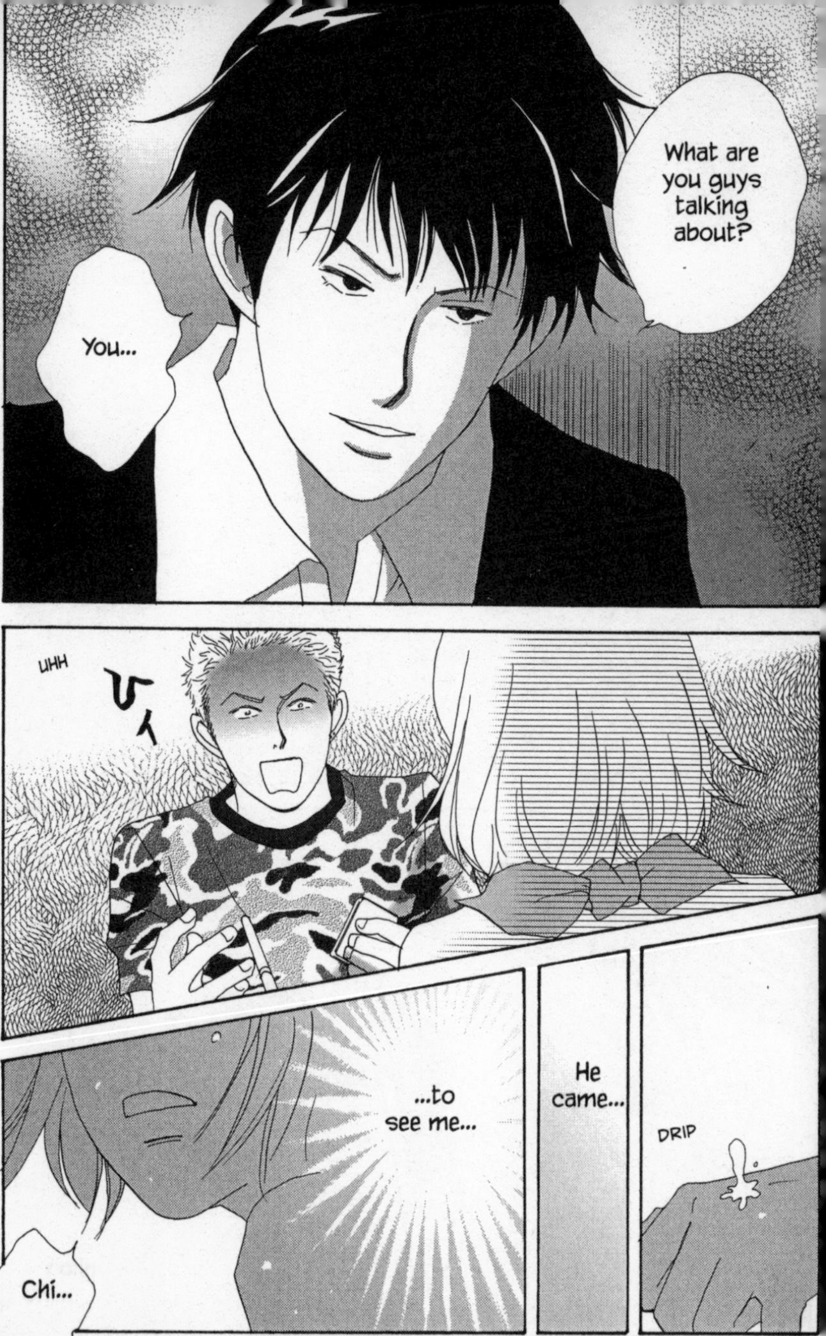
What are you guys talking about?
You...
UHH
ひィ
DRIP
He came...
...to see me...
Chi...

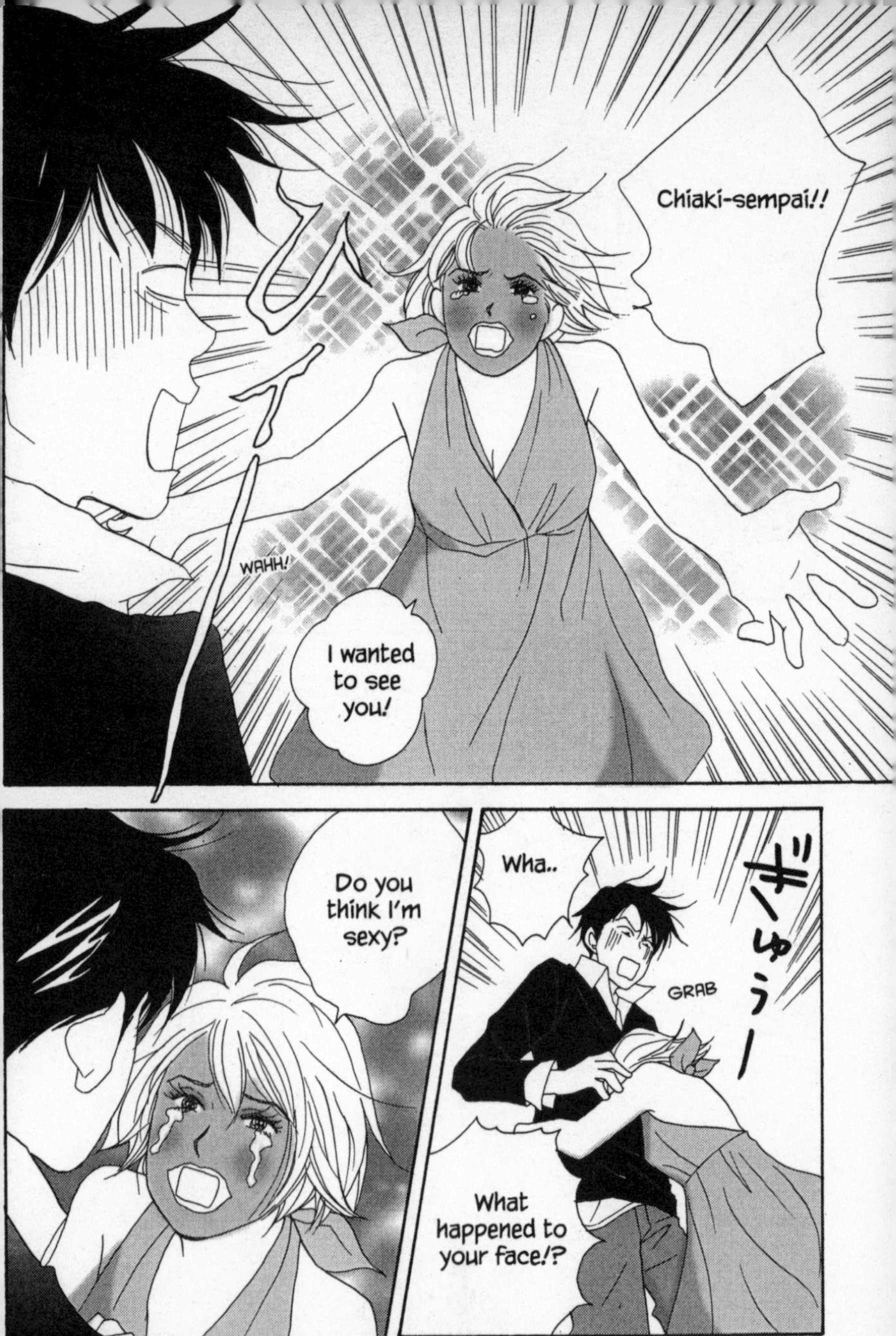
Chiaki-sempai!!
WAHH!
I wanted to see you!
Wha..
GRAB
What happened to your face!?
Do you think I'm sexy?

↖Too much make-up... Dutch-wife style

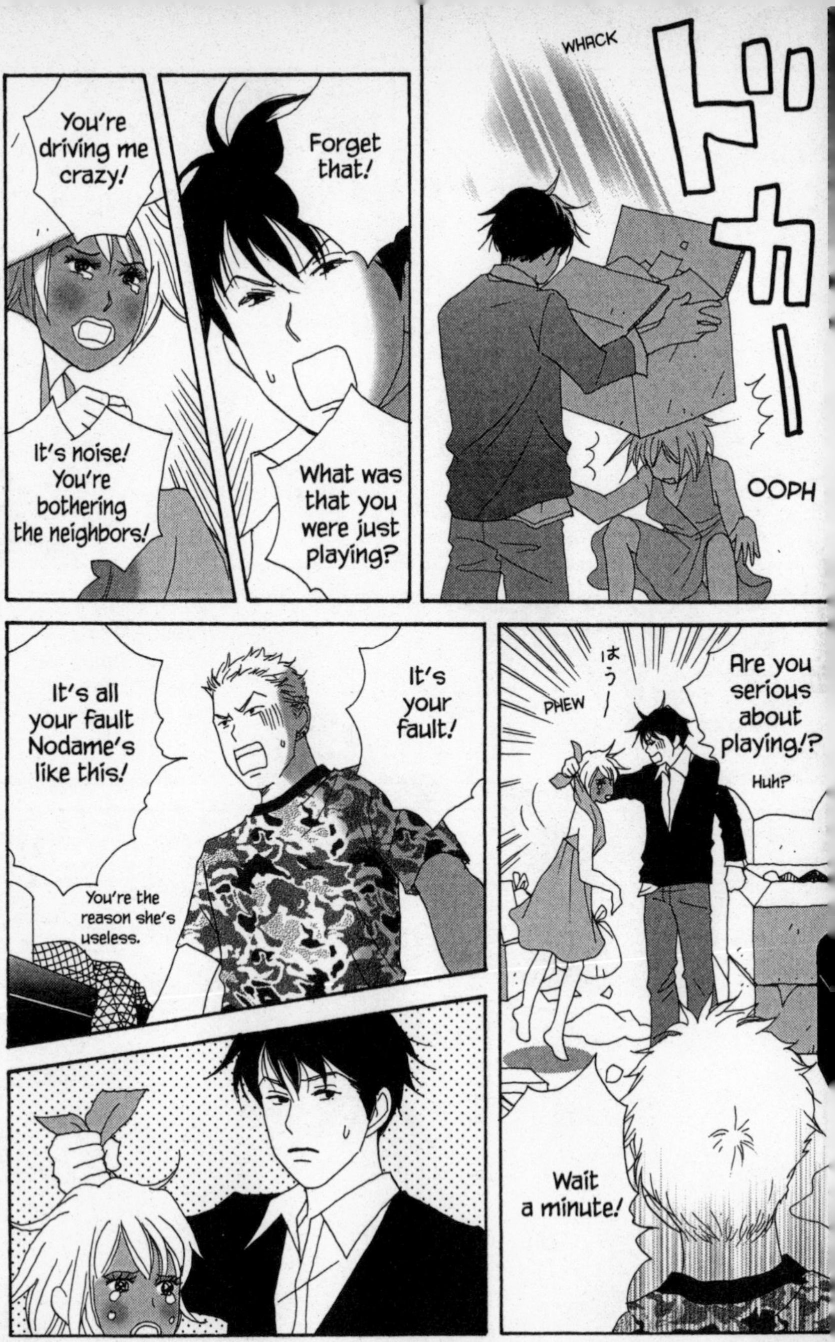
WHACK
ドカー
OOPH
Forget that!
What was that you were just playing?
You're driving me crazy!
It's noise! You're bothering the neighbors!
Are you serious about playing!?
Huh?
はう
PHEW
Wait a minute!
It's your fault!
It's all your fault Nodame's like this!
You're the reason she's useless.

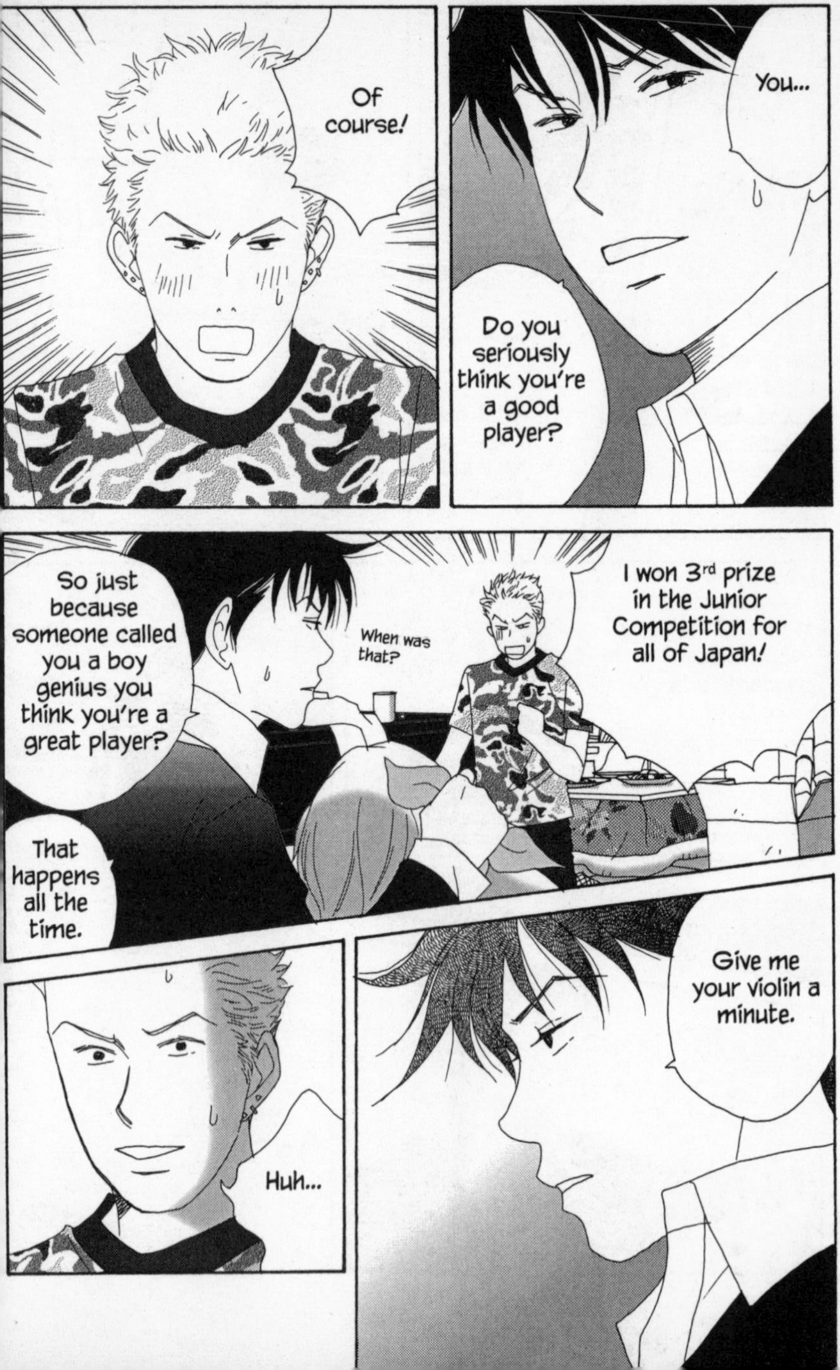
You...
Do you seriously think you're a good player?
Of course!
I won 3rd prize in the Junior Competition for all of Japan!
When was that?
So just because someone called you a boy genius you think you're a great player?
That happens all the time.
Give me your violin a minute.
Huh...

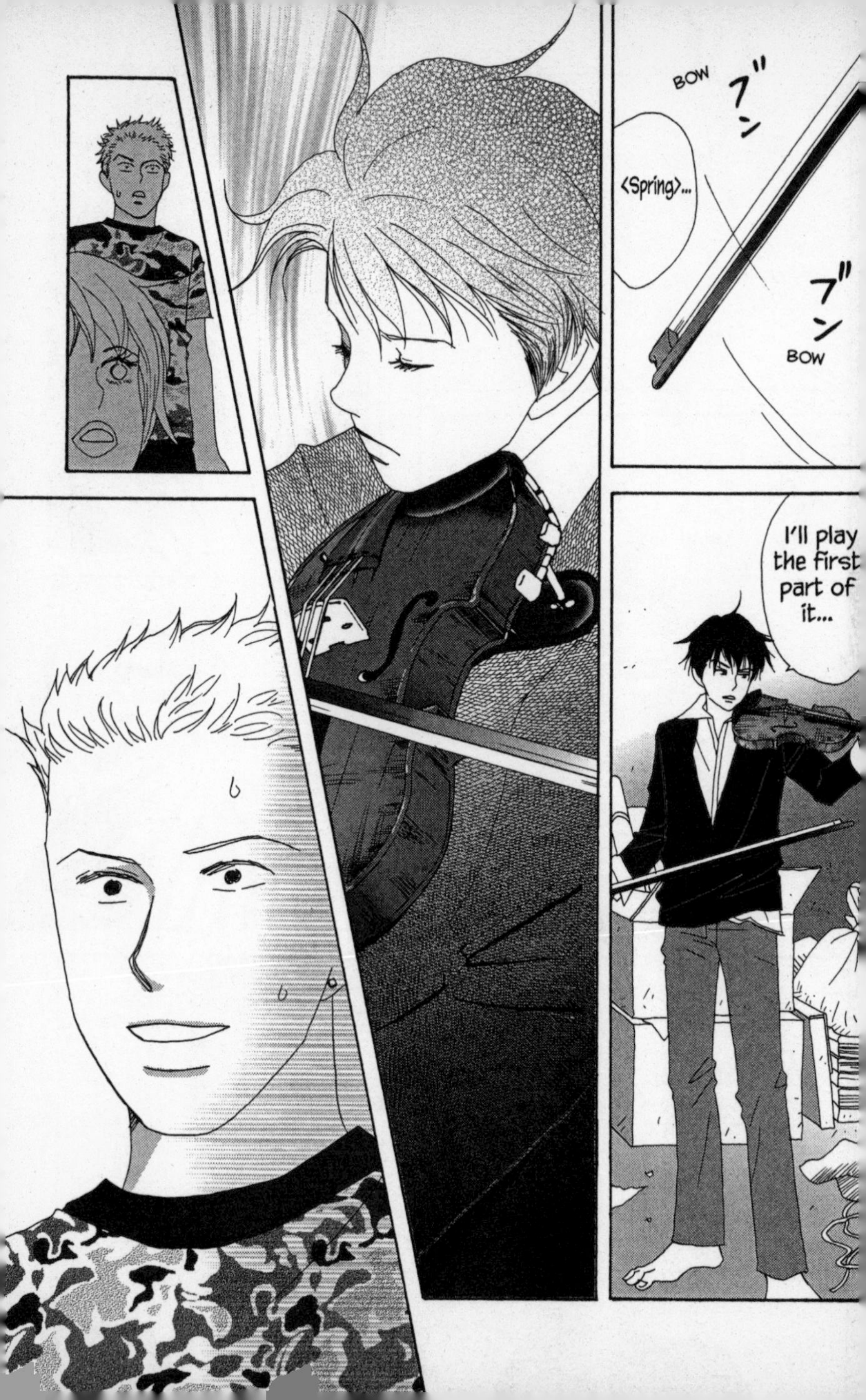
BOW
ブン
<Spring>...
ブン
BOW
I'll play the first part of it...
...

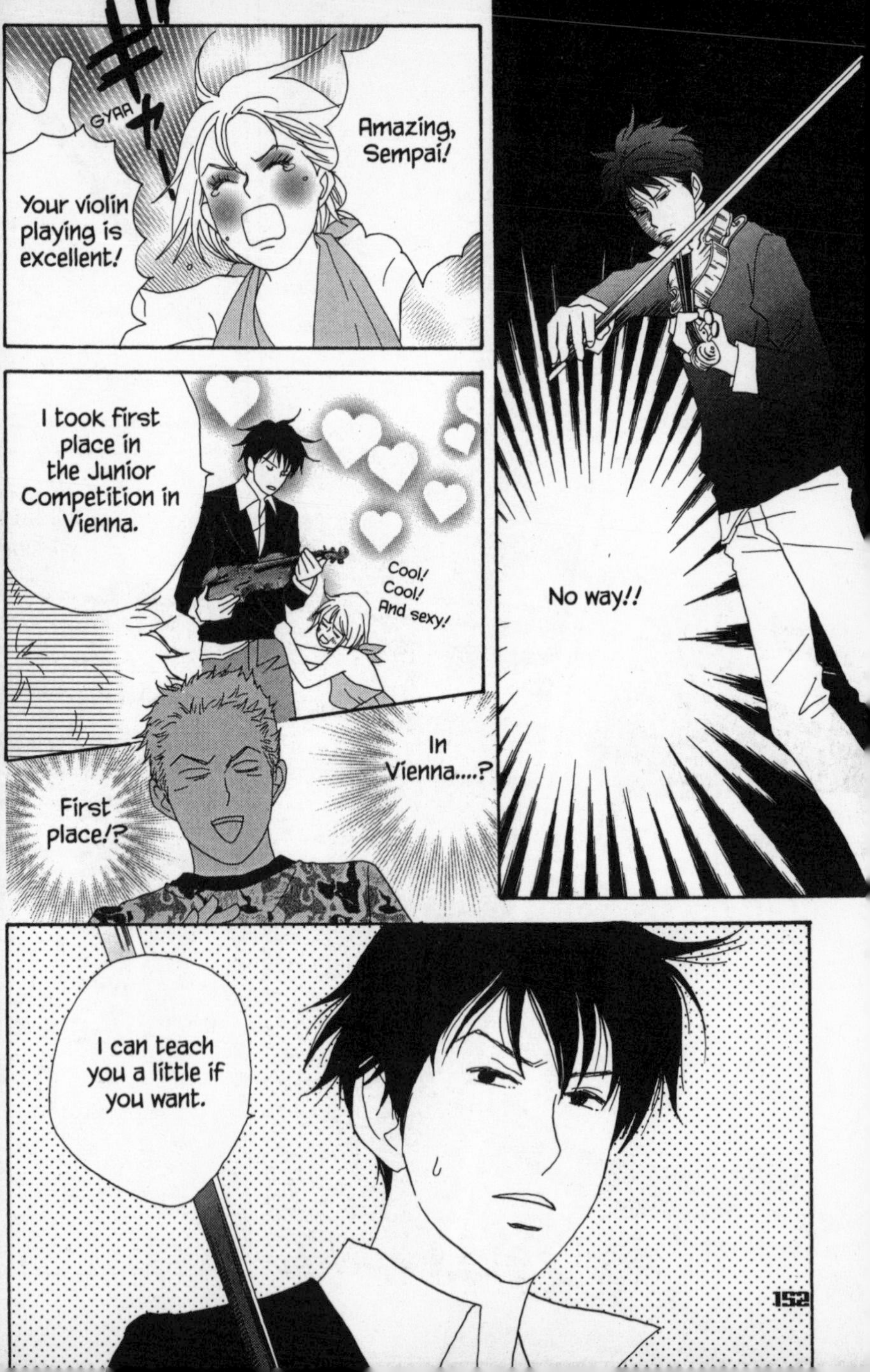
No way!!
GYAA
Amazing, Sempai!
Your violin playing is excellent!
I took first place in the Junior Competition in Vienna.
Cool! Cool! And sexy!
In Vienna....?
First place!?
I can teach you a little if you want.

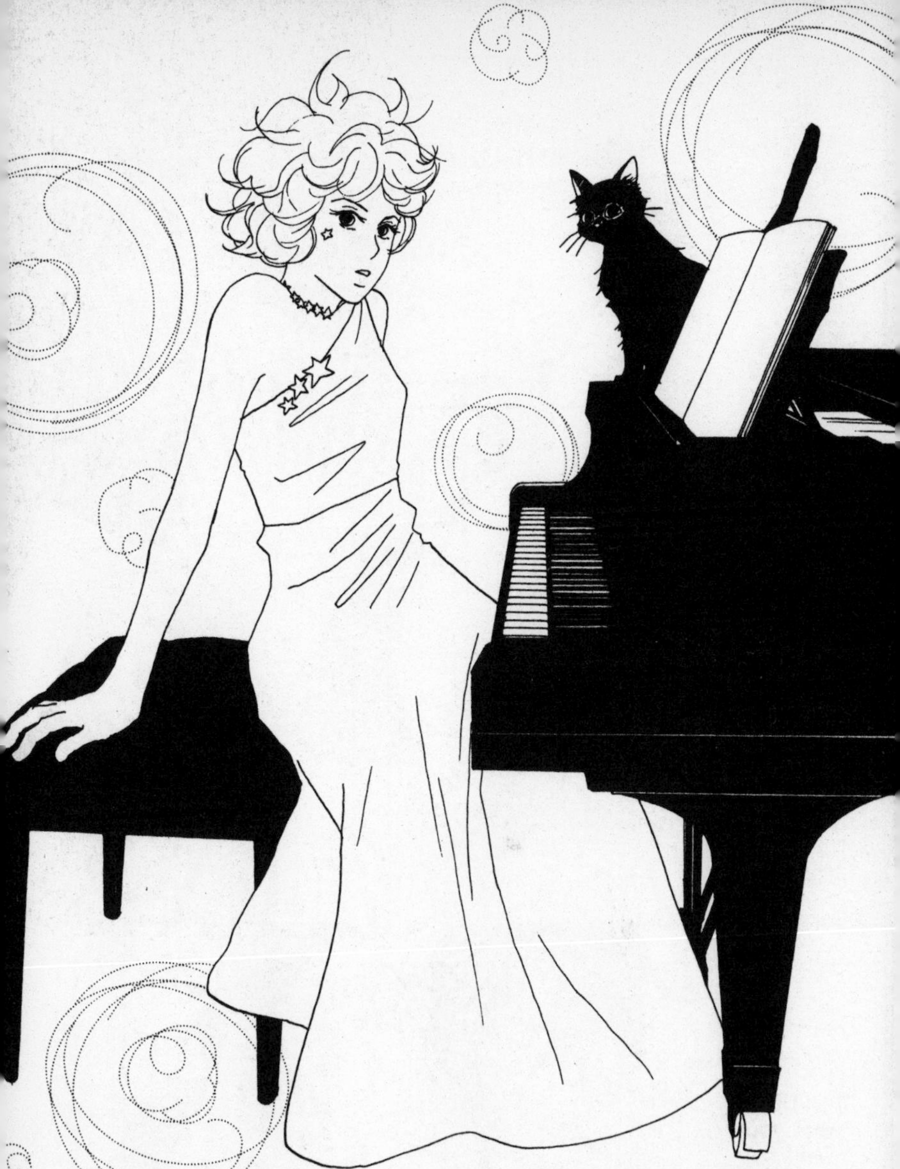

Lesson 6

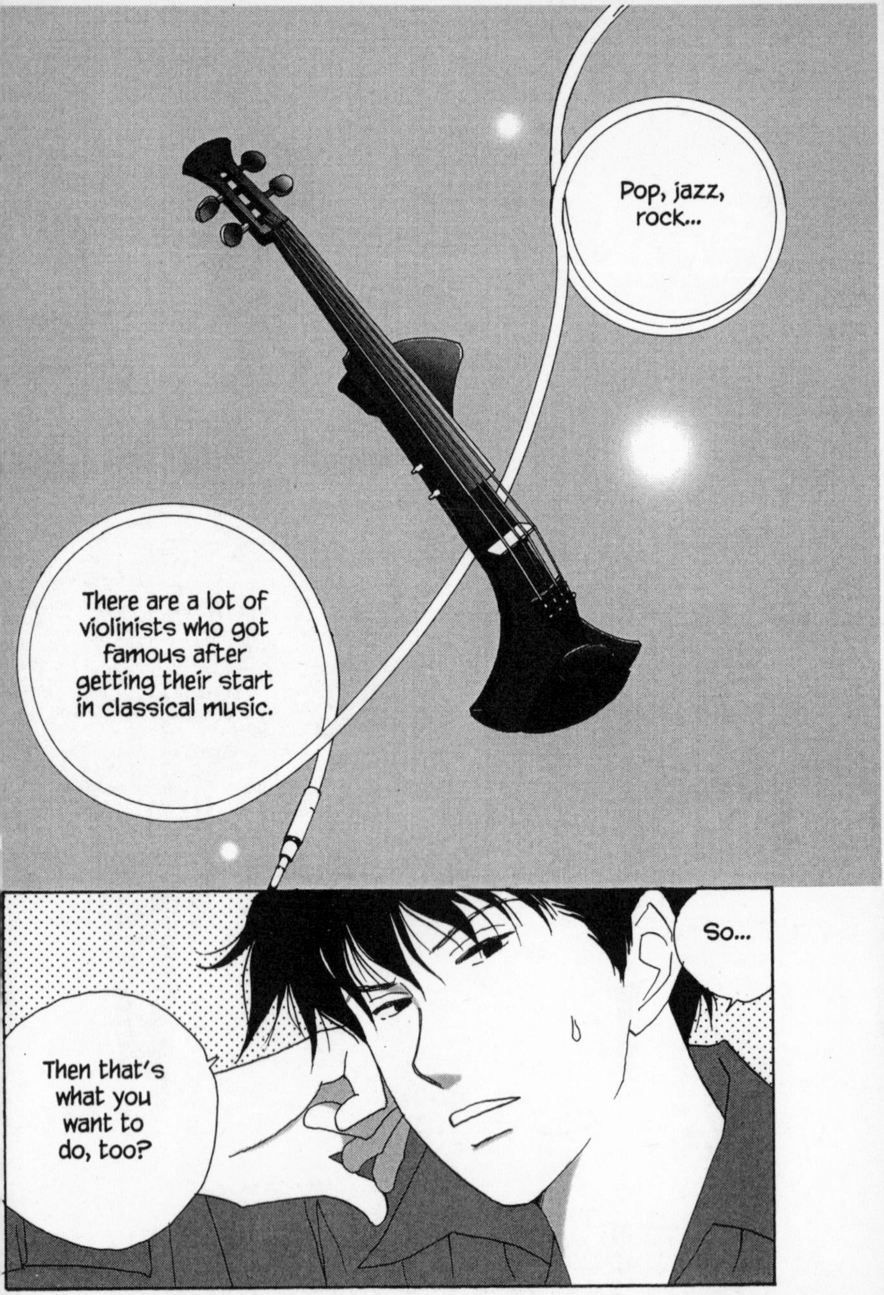
Pop, jazz, rock...
There are a lot of violinists who got famous after getting their start in classical music.
So...
Then that's what you want to do, too?

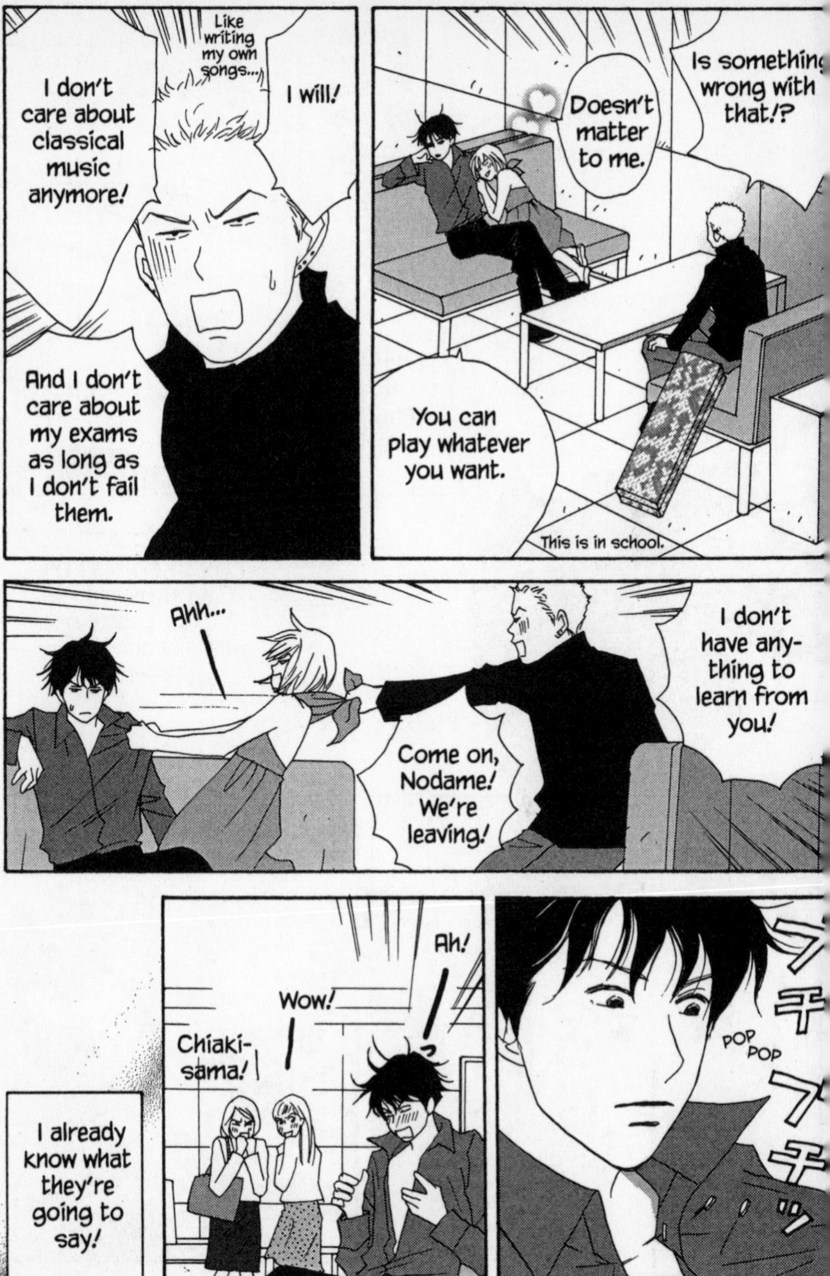

Is somethin
wrong with
that!?
Doesn't matter to me.
You can play whatever you want.
This is in school.
I will!
Like writing my own songs...
I don't care about classical music anymore!
And I don't care about my exams as long as I don't fail them.
I don't have any-thing to learn from you!
Come on, Nodame! We're leaving!
Ahh...
ブチブチッ
POP POP
Ah!
Wow!
Chiaki-sama!
I already know what they're going to say!

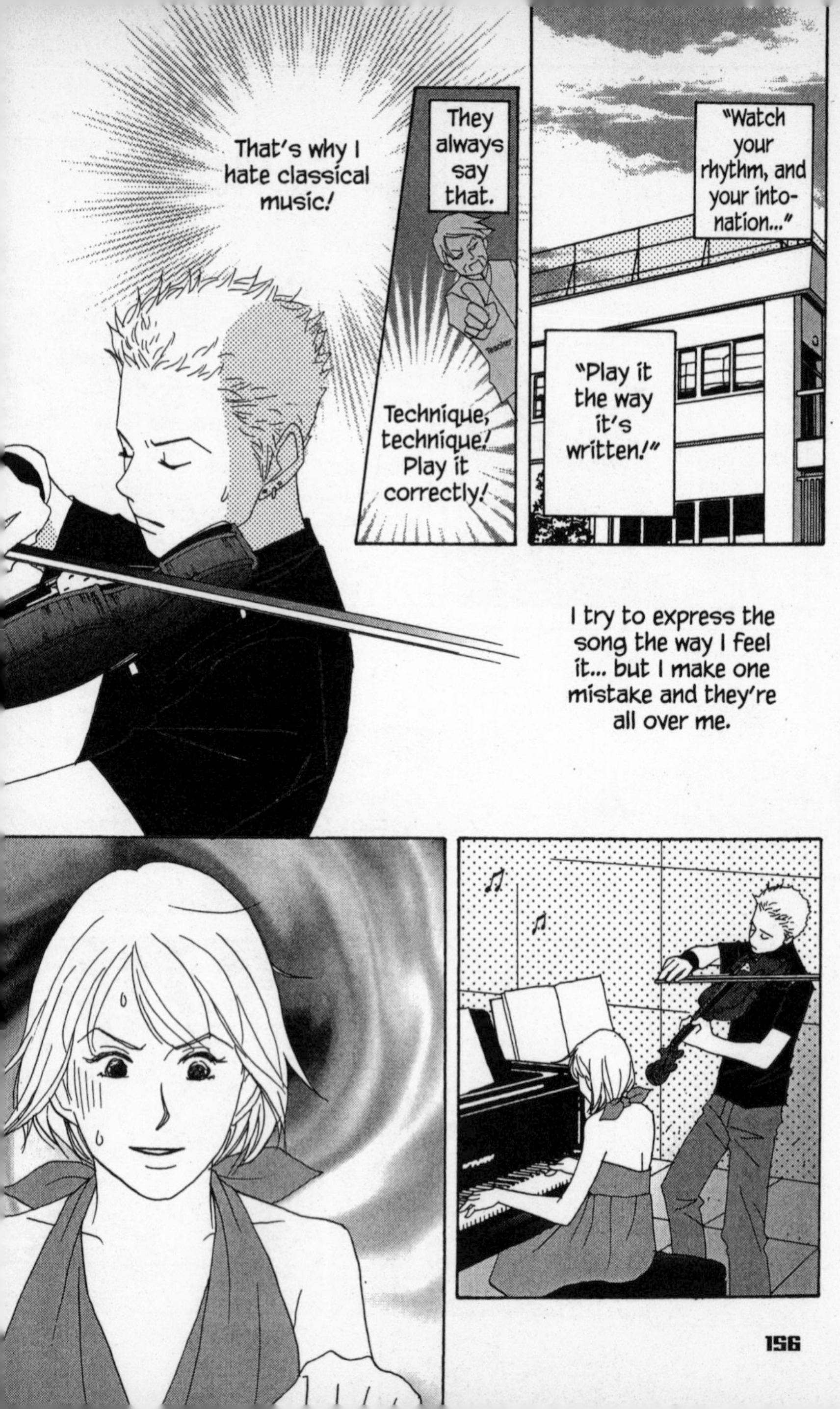
"Watch your rhythm, and your into-nation..."
"Play it the way it's written!"
They always say that.
Technique, technique! Play it correctly!
That's why I hate classical music!
I try to express the song the way I feel it... but I make one mistake and they're all over me.

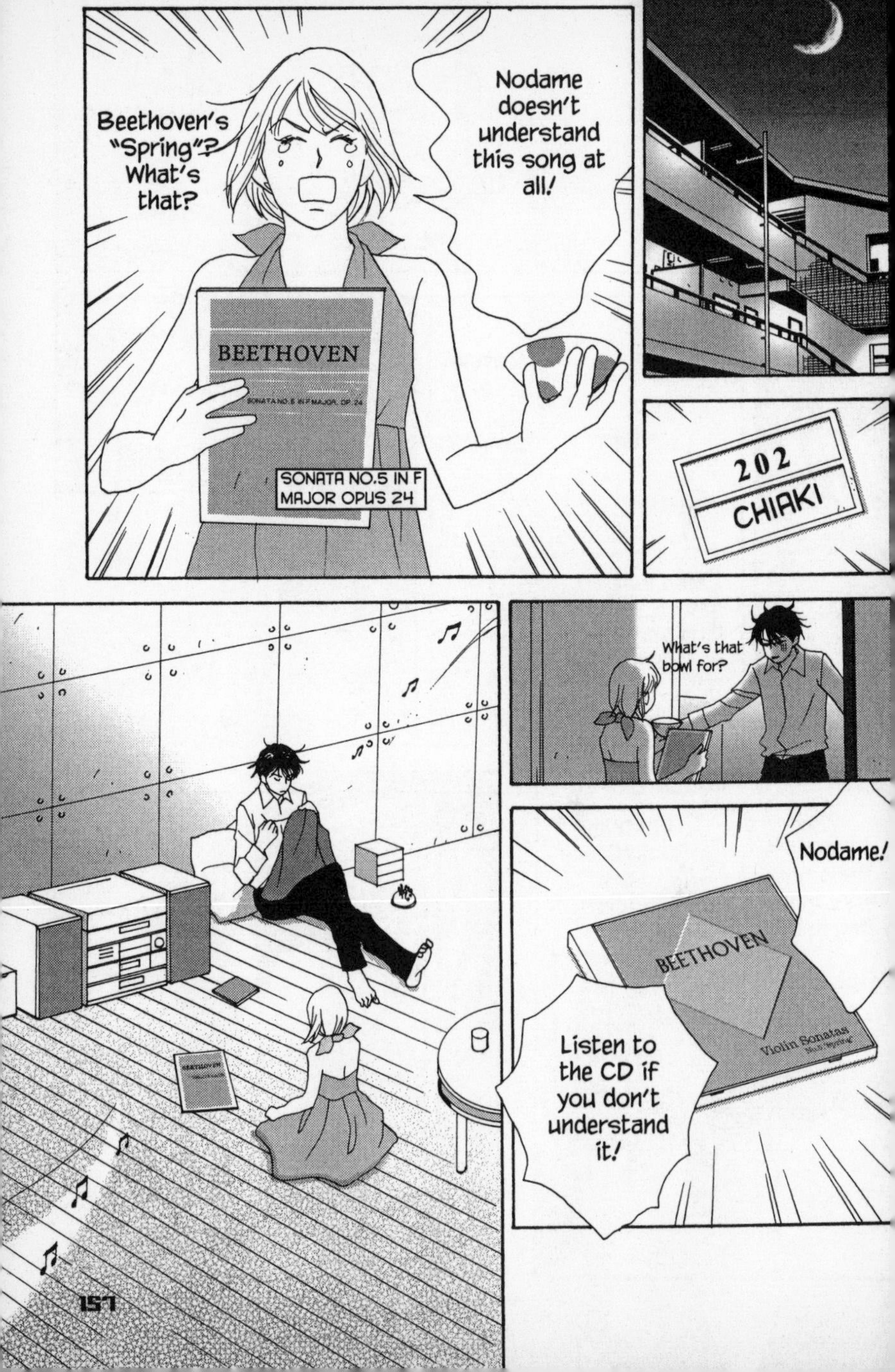

202
CHIAKI
Nodame doesn't understand this song at all!
Beethoven's "Spring"? What's that?
BEETHOVEN
SONATA NO.5 IN F MAJOR. OP. 24
SONATA NO.5 IN F MAJOR OPUS 24
What's that bowl for?
Nodame!
BEETHOVEN
Violin Sonatas
Listen to the CD if you don't understand it!
BEETHOVEN

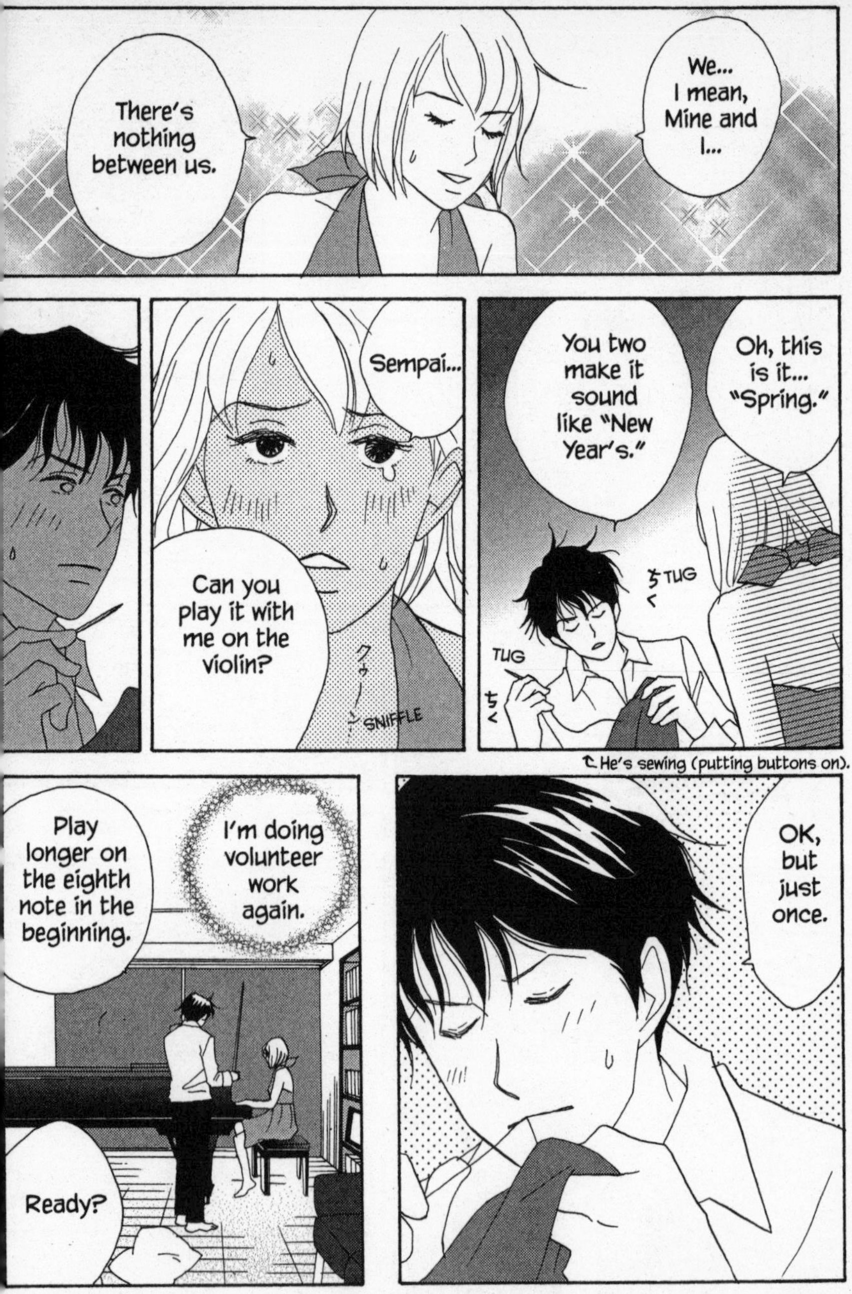
We... I mean, Mine and I...
There's nothing between us.
Oh, this is it... "Spring."
You two make it sound like "New Year's."
ちく TUG
TUG ちく
Sempai...
Can you play it with me on the violin?
クゥー SNIFFLE
He's sewing (putting buttons on).
OK, but just once.
I'm doing volunteer work again.
Play longer on the eighth note in the beginning.
Ready?

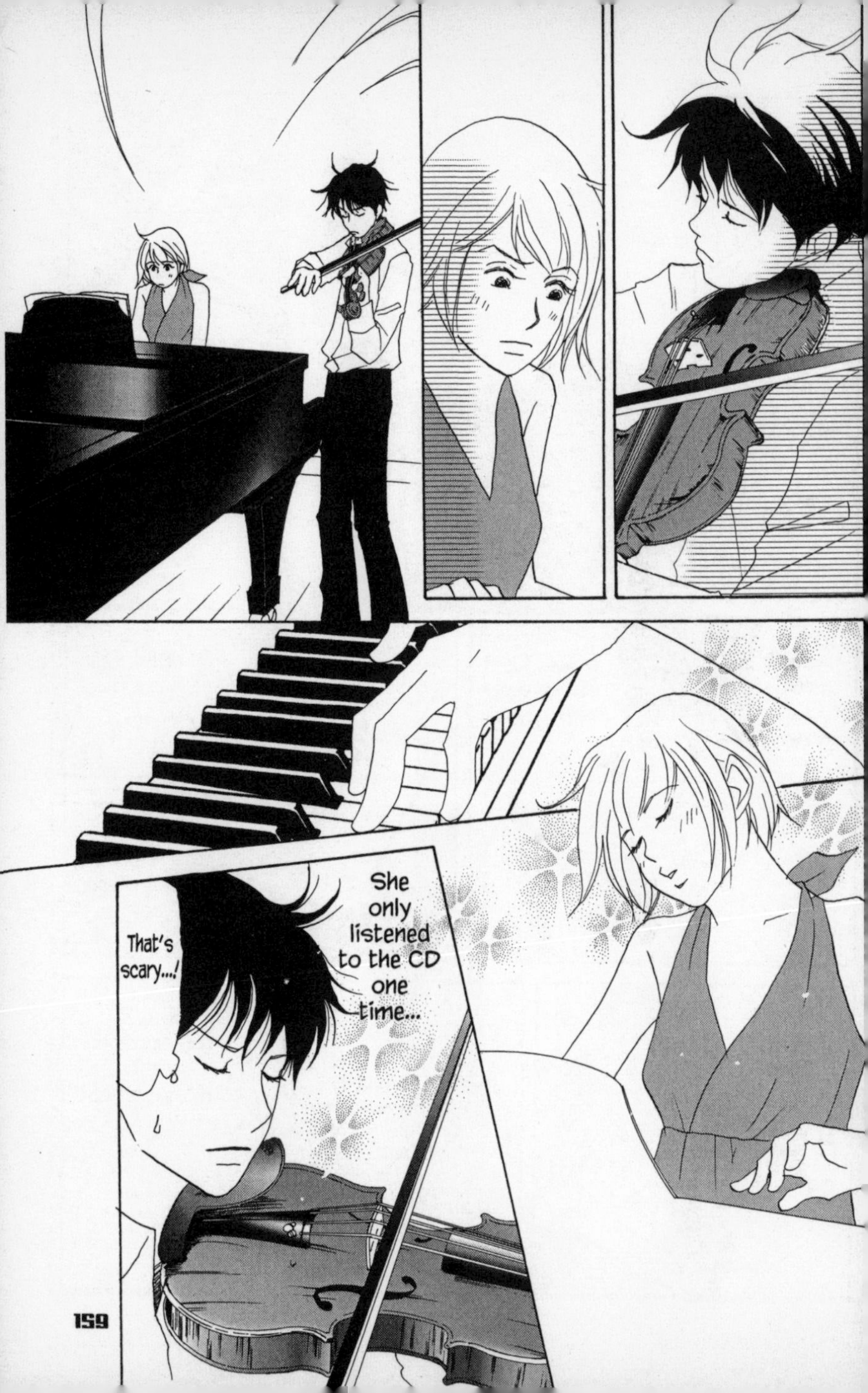
She only listened to the CD one time...
That's scary...!

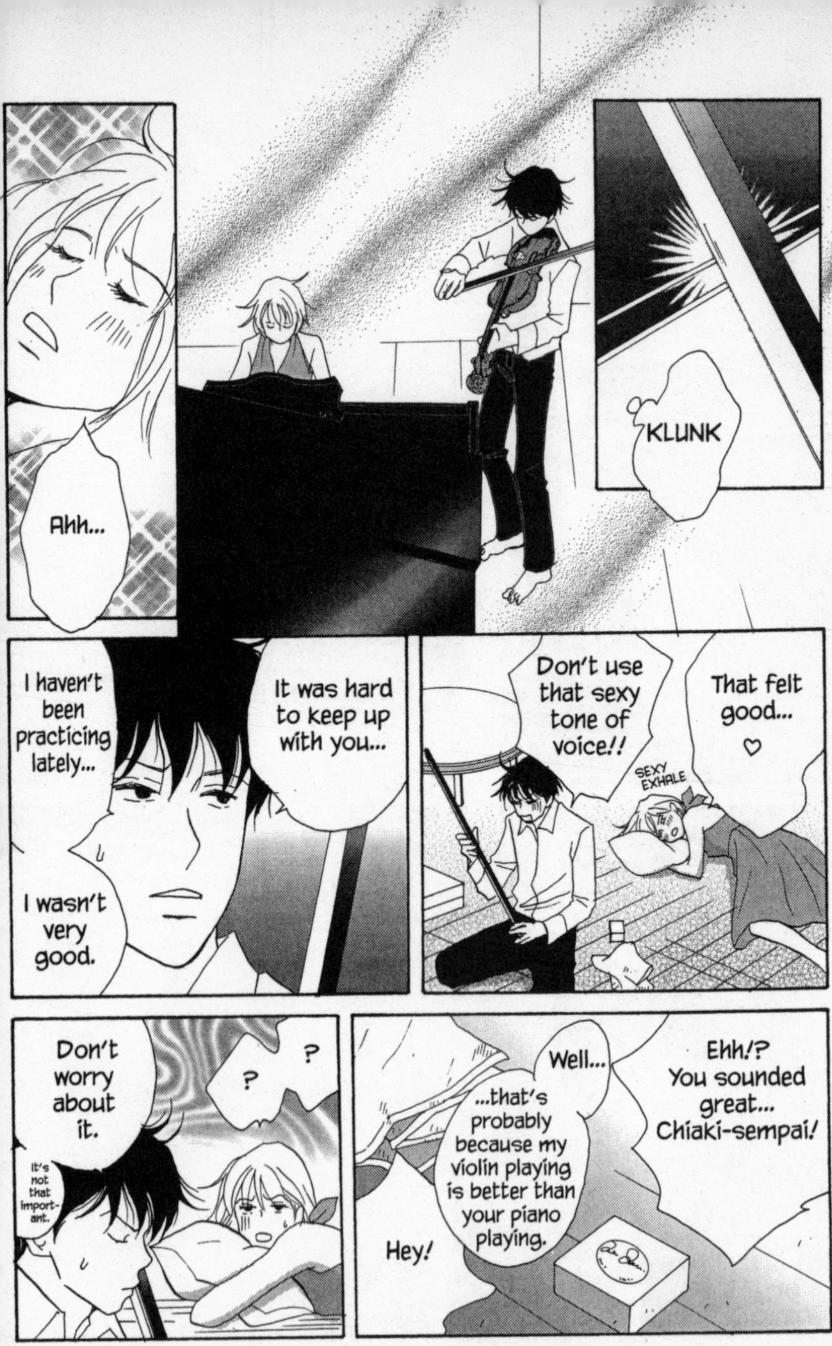

KLUNK
Ahh...
That felt good... ♡
SEXY EXHALE
Don't use that sexy tone of voice!!
It was hard to keep up with you...
I haven't been practicing lately...
I wasn't very good.
Ehh!? You sounded great... Chiaki-sempai!
Well...
...that's probably because my violin playing is better than your piano playing.
Hey!
?
?
Don't worry about it.
It's not that important.

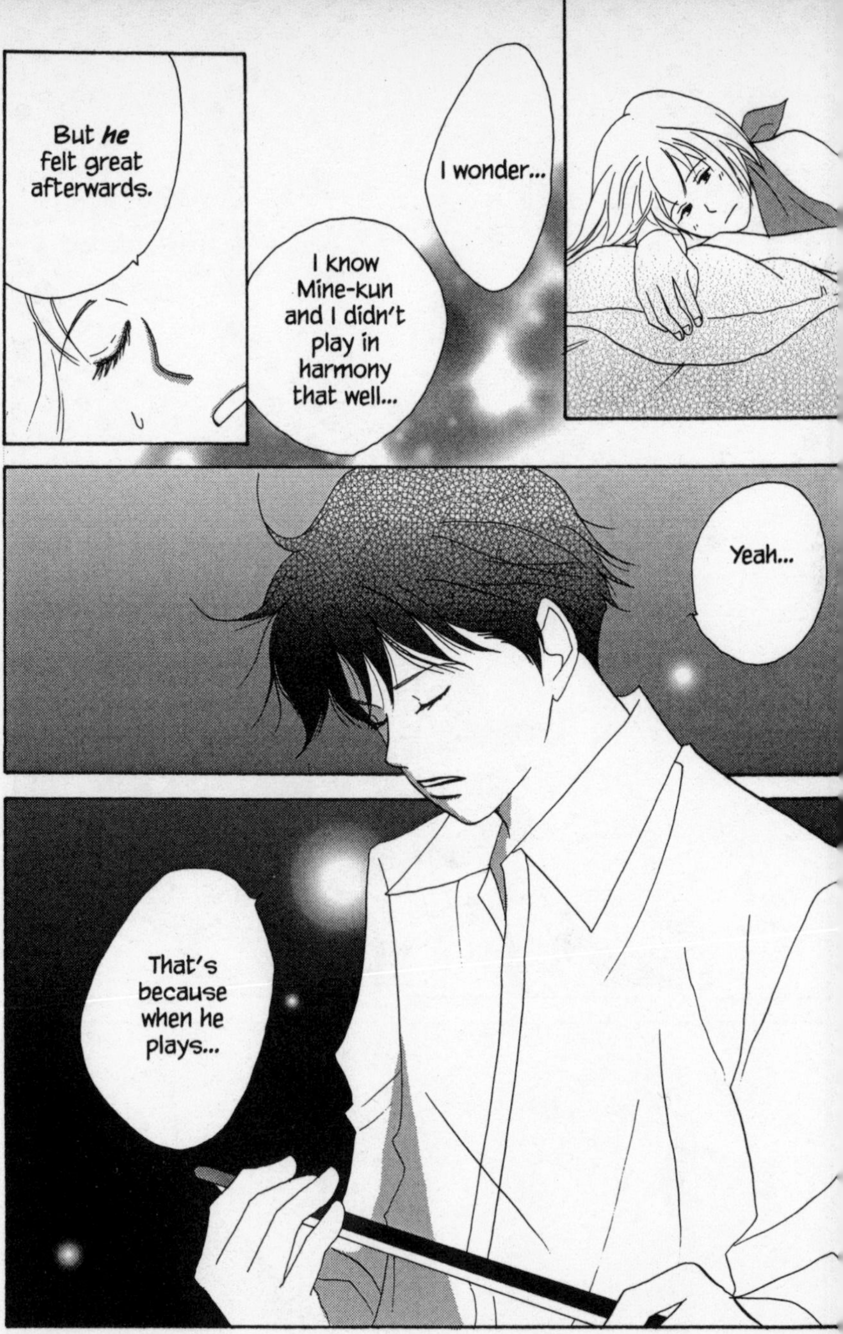
I wonder...
I know Mine-kun and I didn't play in harmony that well...
But *he* felt great afterwards.
Yeah...
That's because when he plays...

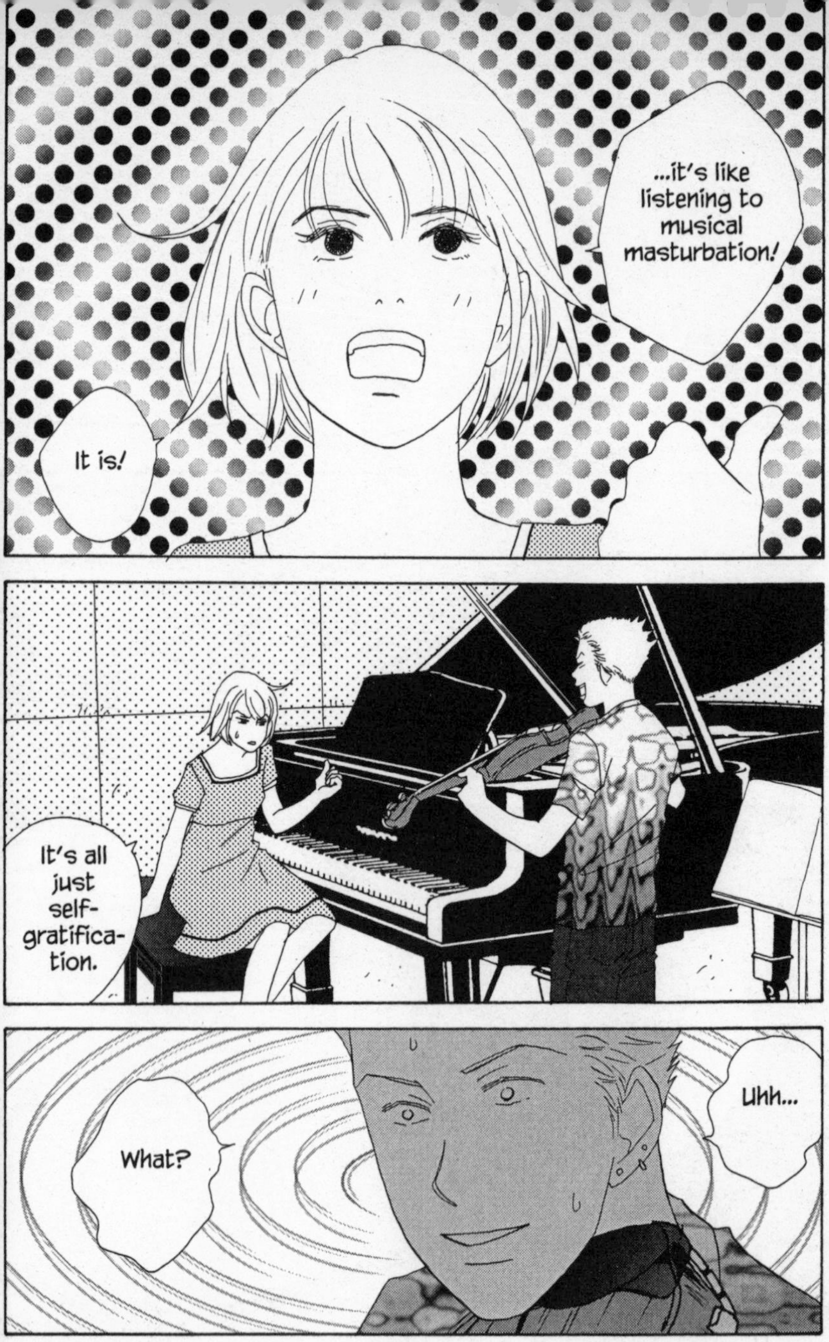
...it's like listening to musical masturbation!
It is!
It's all just self-gratifica-tion.
Uhh...
What?

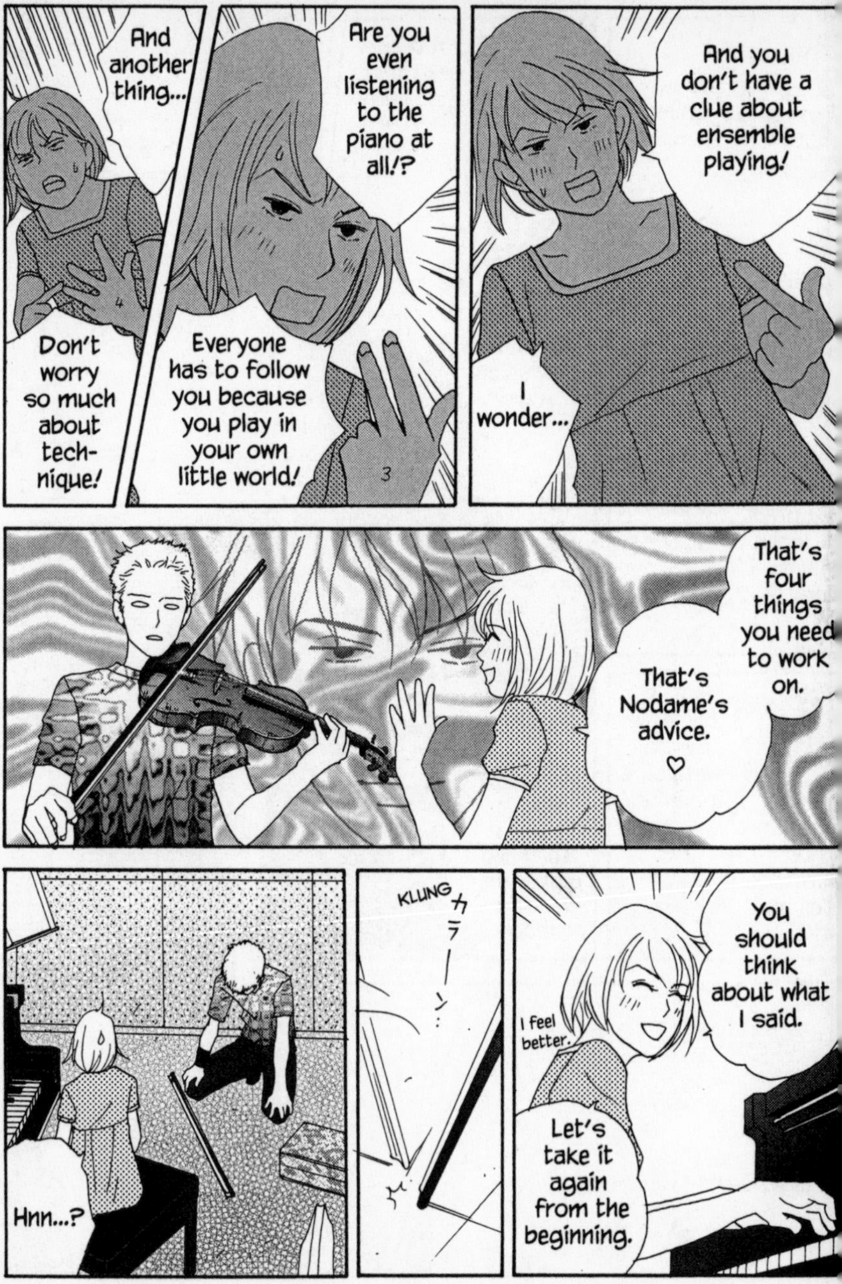
And you don't have a clue about ensemble playing!
I wonder...
Are you even listening to the piano at all!?
Everyone has to follow you because you play in your own little world!
And another thing...
Don't worry so much about tech-nique!
That's four things you need to work on.
That's Nodame's advice. ♡
You should think about what I said.
I feel better.
Let's take it again from the beginning.
KLUNG
カラーン…
Hnn...?

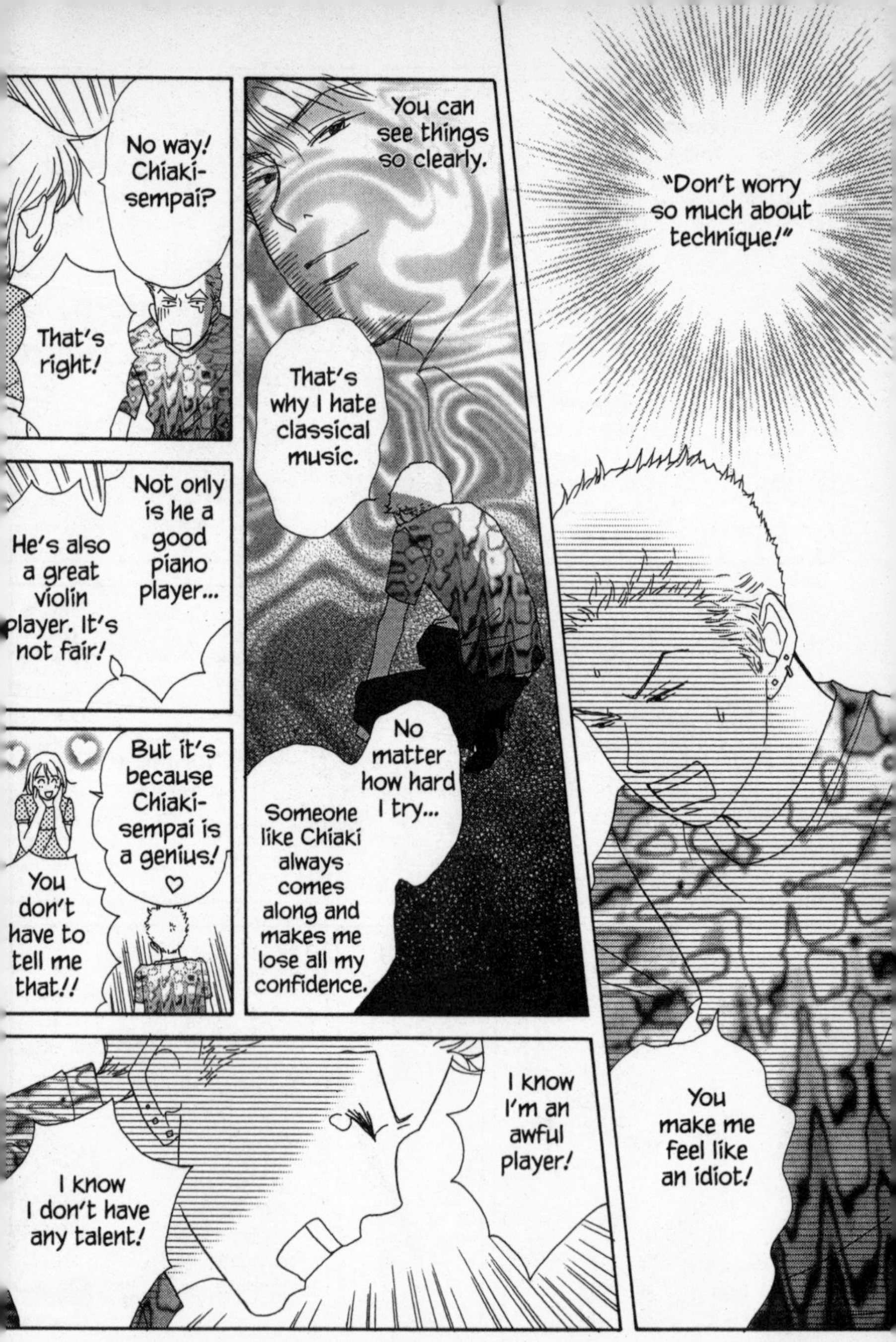
"Don't worry so much about technique!"
You make me feel like an idiot!
You can see things so clearly.
That's why I hate classical music.
No matter how hard I try...
Someone like Chiaki always comes along and makes me lose all my confidence.
No way! Chiaki-sempai?
That's right!
Not only is he a good piano player...
He's also a great violin player. It's not fair!
But it's because Chiaki-sempai is a genius! ♡
You don't have to tell me that!!
I know I'm an awful player!
I know I don't have any talent!

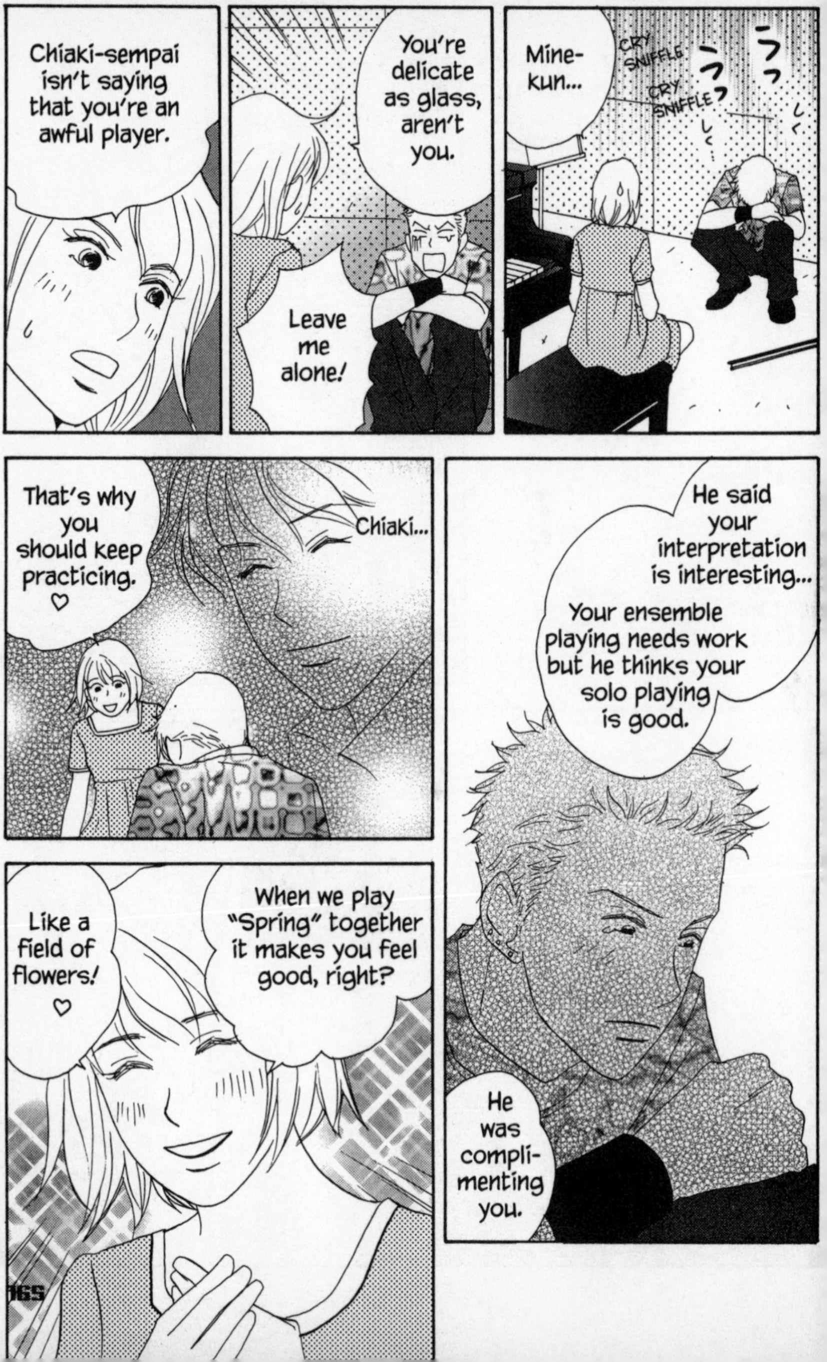
Mine-kun...
CRY SNIFFLE
CRY SNIFFLE
You're delicate as glass, aren't you.
Leave me alone!
Chiaki-sempai isn't saying that you're an awful player.
He said your interpretation is interesting...
Your ensemble playing needs work but he thinks your solo playing is good.
He was complimenting you.
That's why you should keep practicing. ♡
Chiaki...
When we play "Spring" together it makes you feel good, right?
Like a field of flowers! ♡

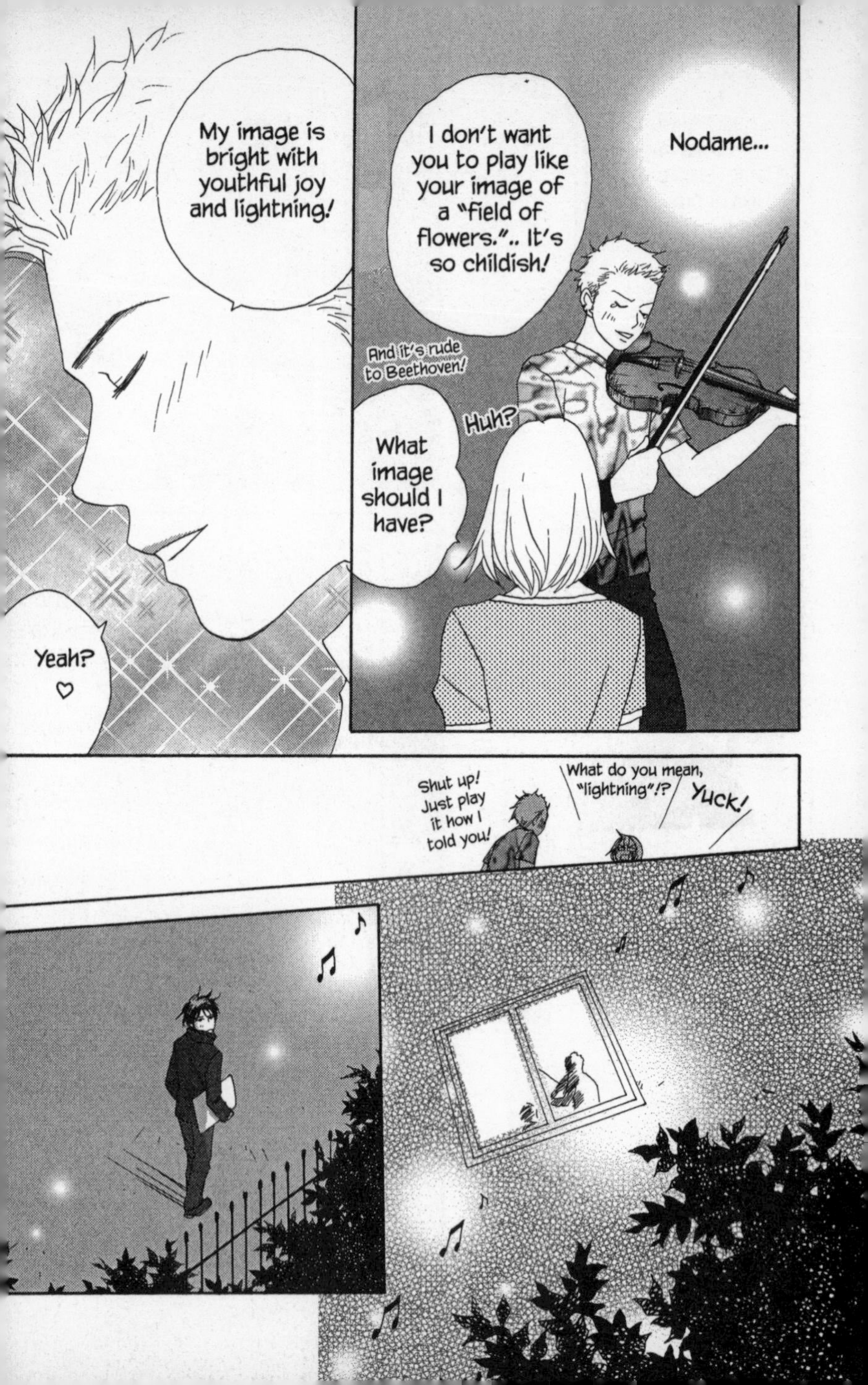
Nodame...
I don't want you to play like your image of a "field of flowers.".. It's so childish!
And it's rude to Beethoven!
Huh?
What image should I have?
My image is bright with youthful joy and lightning!
Yeah? ♡
Yuck!
What do you mean, "lightning"!?
Shut up! Just play it how I told you!

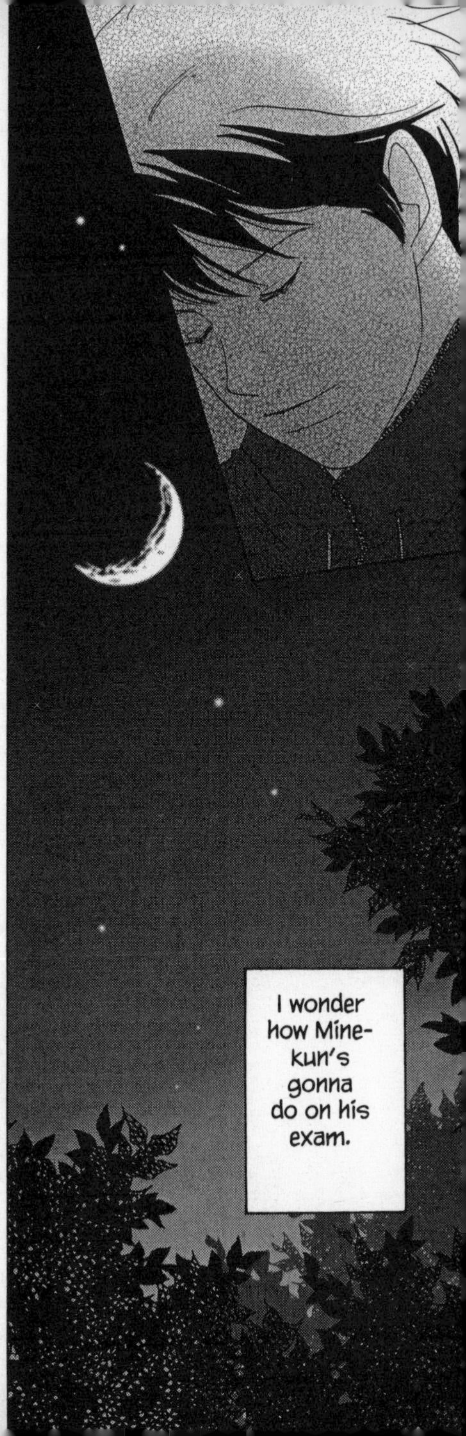
I wonder how Mine-kun's gonna do on his exam.
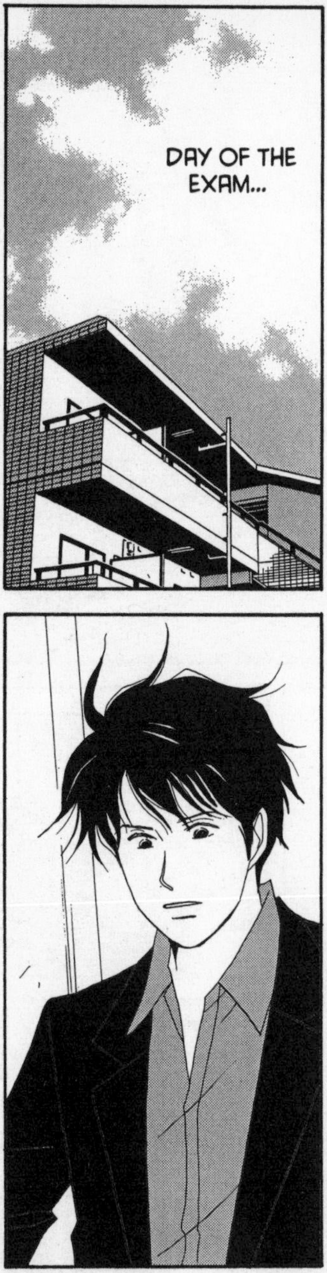
DAY OF THE EXAM...

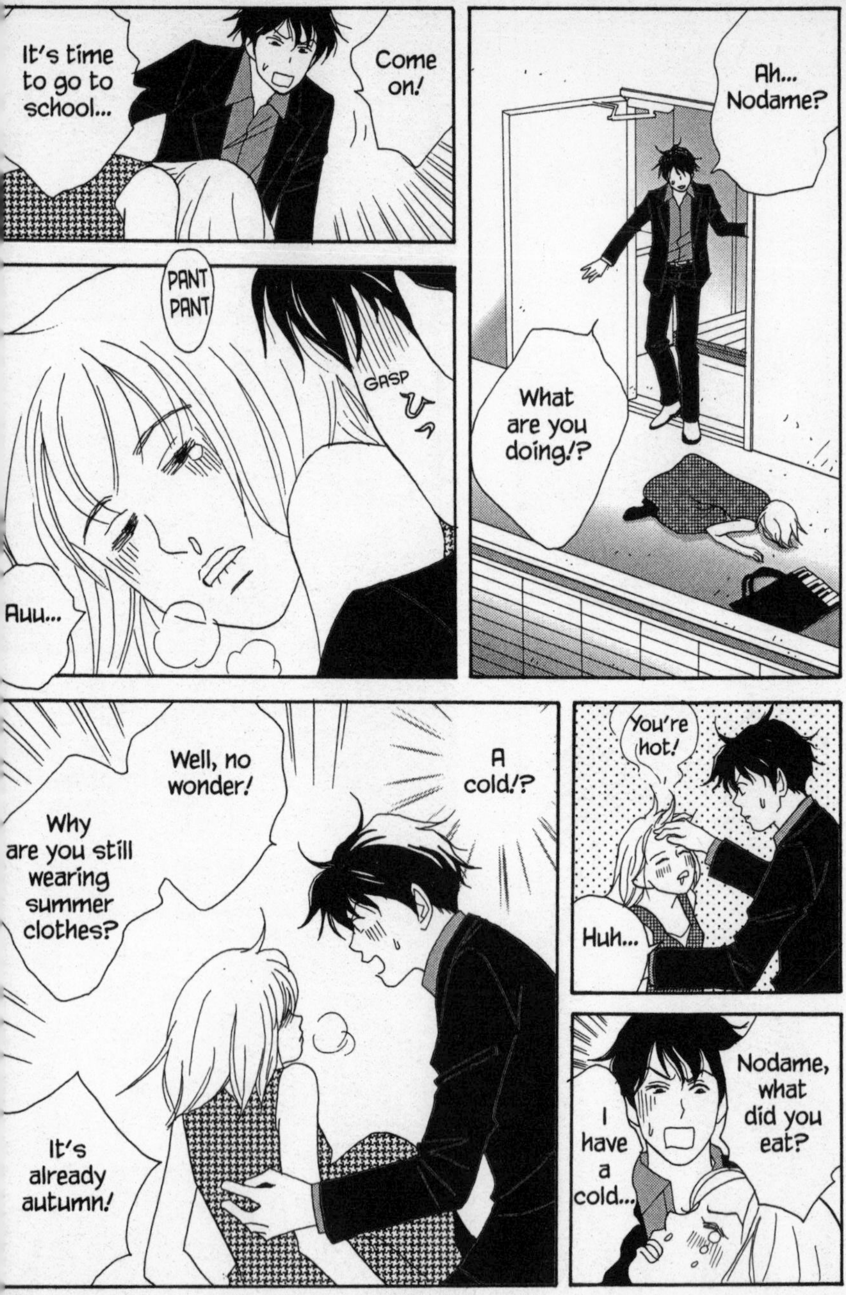
Ah... Nodame?
What are you doing!?
Come on!
It's time to go to school...
PANT PANT
GASP
Auu...
You're hot!
Huh...
Nodame, what did you eat?
I have a cold...
A cold!?
Well, no wonder!
Why are you still wearing summer clothes?
It's already autumn!

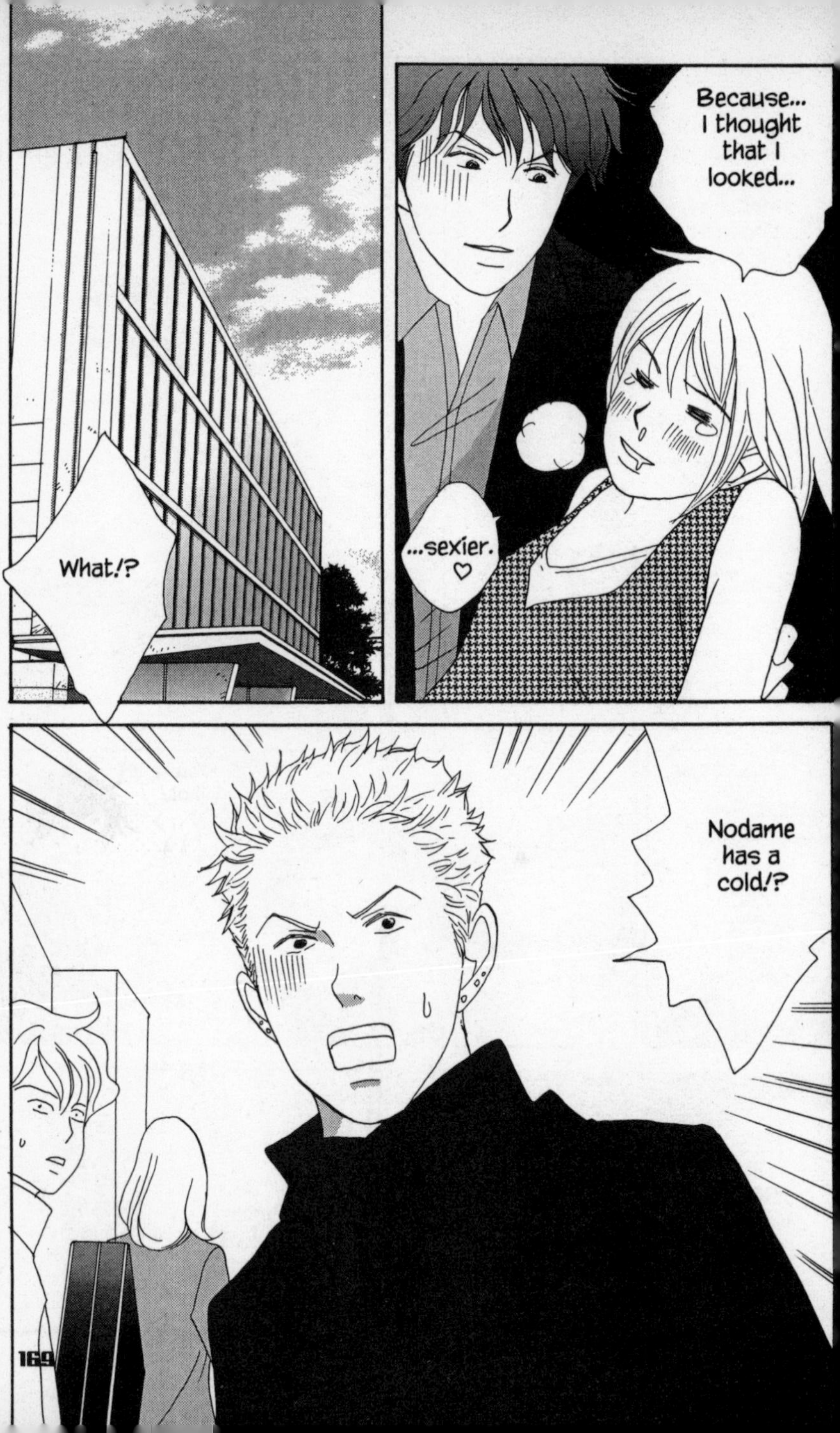
Because... I thought that I looked...
...sexier. ♡
What!?
Nodame has a cold!?

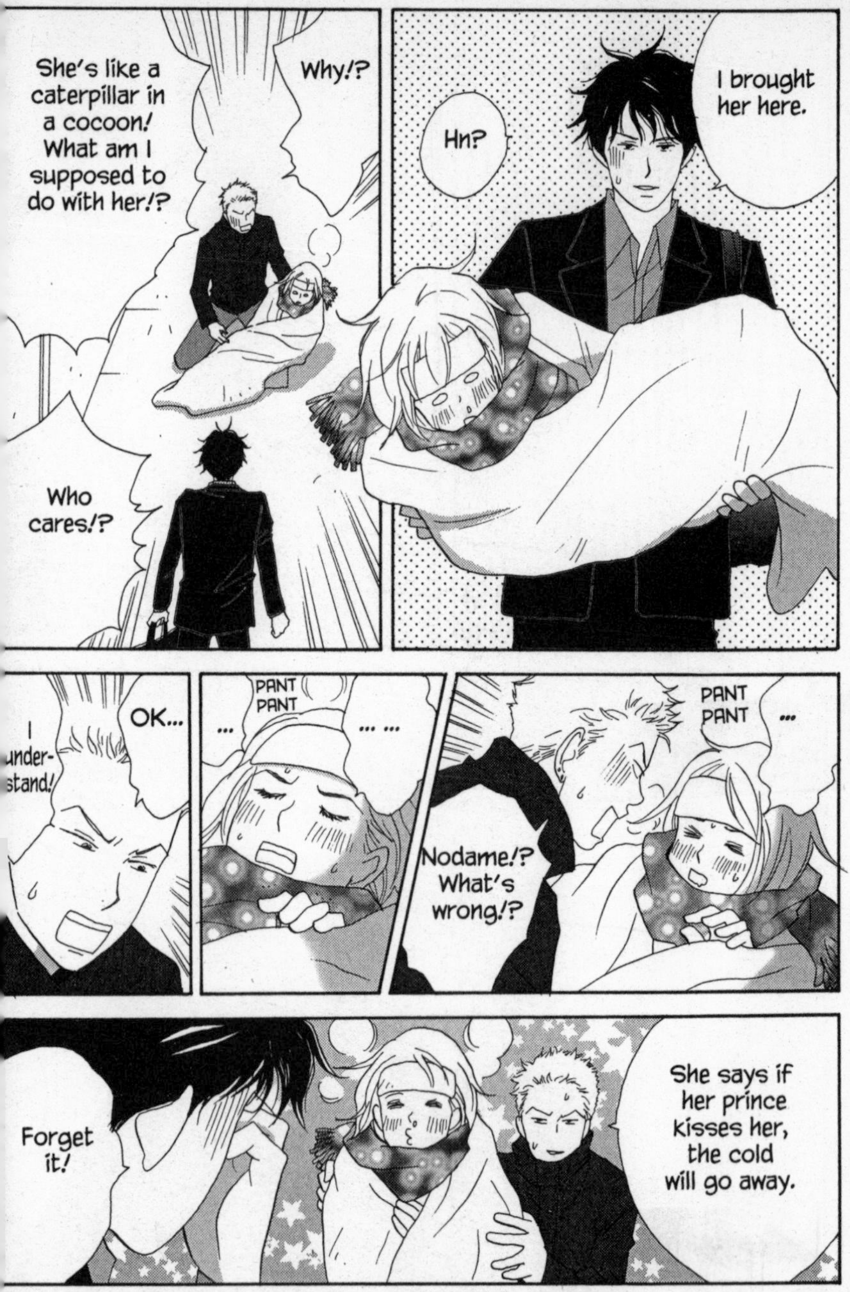
I brought her here.
Hn?
Why!?
She's like a caterpillar in a cocoon! What am I supposed to do with her!?
Who cares!?
...
PANT PANT
Nodame!? What's wrong!?
... ...
PANT PANT
...
OK...
I understand!
She says if her prince kisses her, the cold will go away.
Forget it!

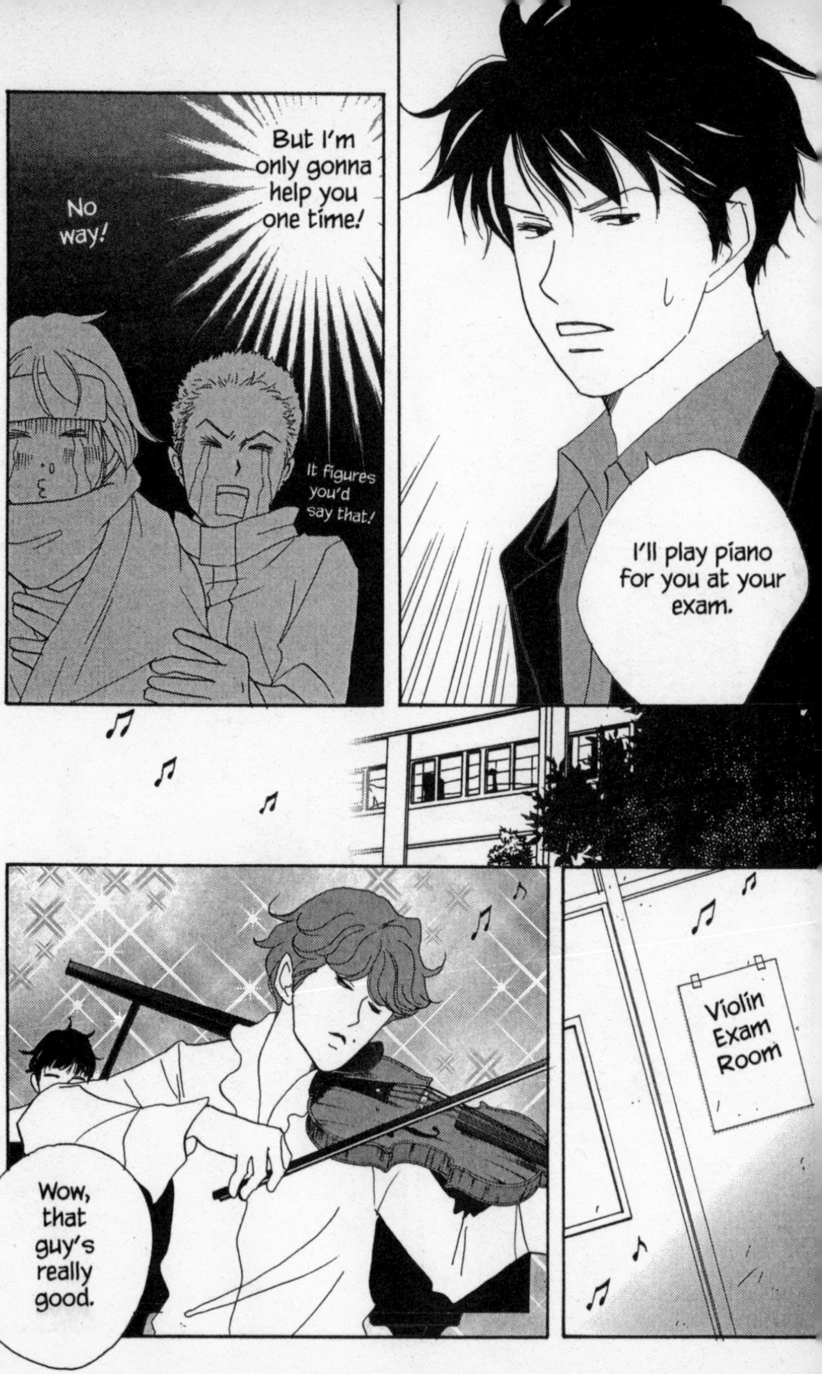
I'll play piano for you at your exam.
But I'm only gonna help you one time!
No way!
It figures you'd say that!
Violin Exam Room
Wow, that guy's really good.

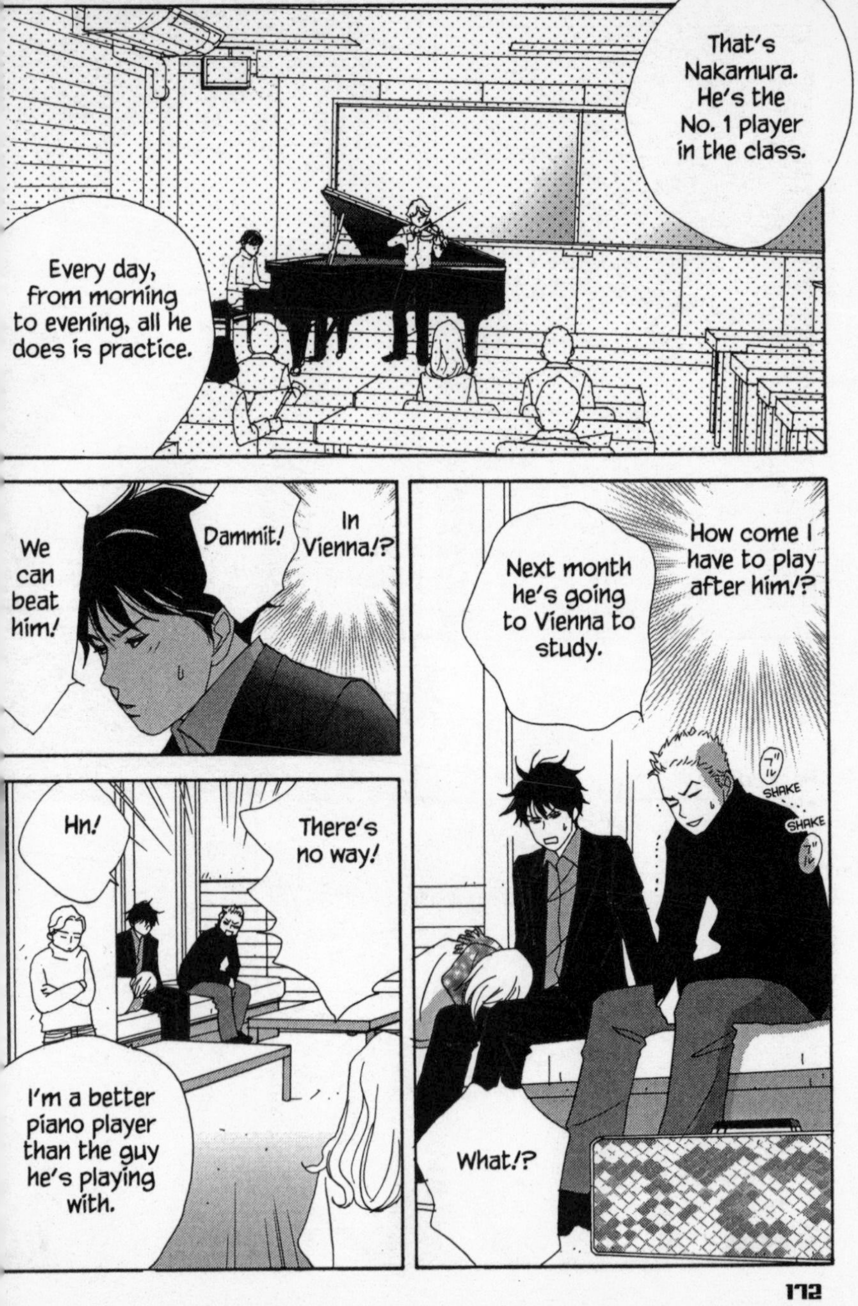
That's Nakamura. He's the No. 1 player in the class.
Every day, from morning to evening, all he does is practice.
How come I have to play after him!?
Next month he's going to Vienna to study.
ブル
SHAKE
SHAKE
ブル
What!?
In Vienna!?
Dammit!
We can beat him!
There's no way!
Hn!
I'm a better piano player than the guy he's playing with.

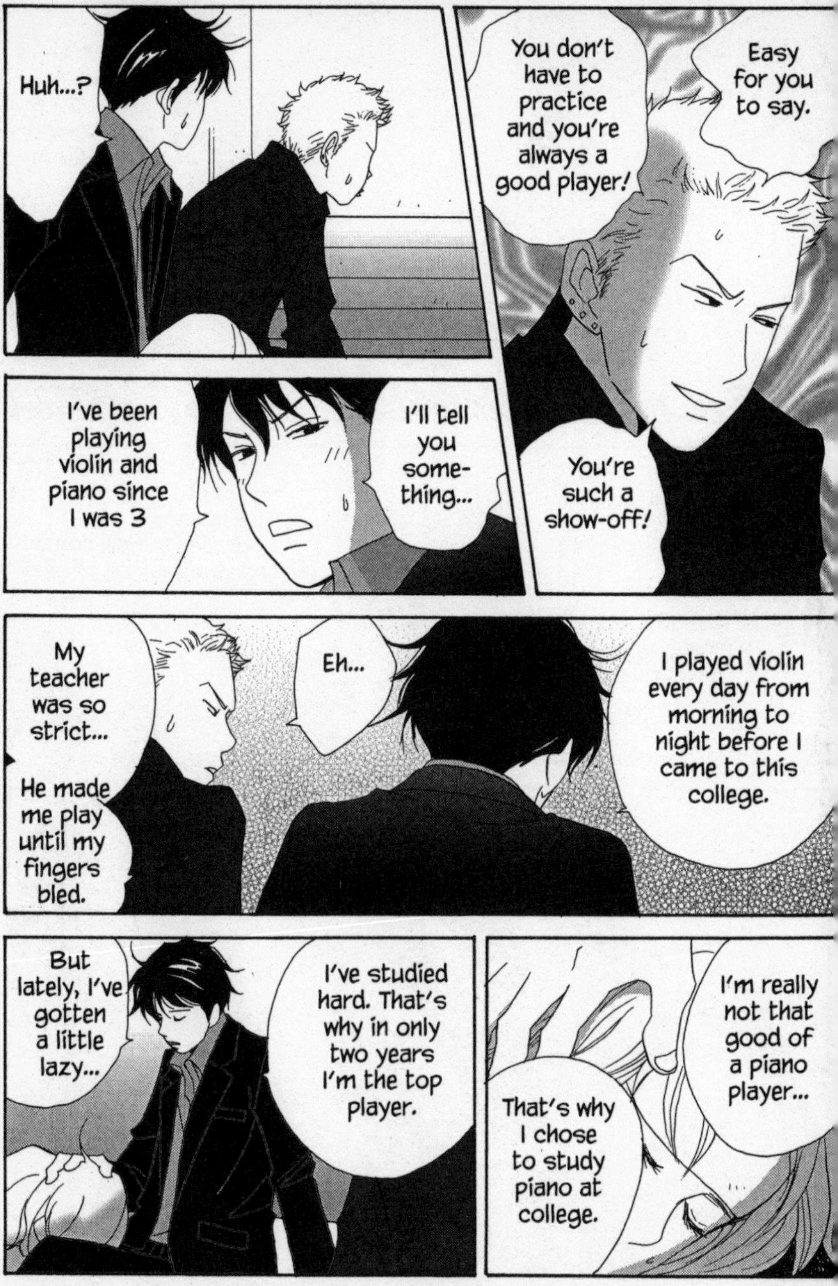

Easy for you to say.
You don't have to practice and you're always a good player!
You're such a show-off!
Huh...?
I'll tell you something...
I've been playing violin and piano since I was 3
I played violin every day from morning to night before I came to this college.
Eh...
My teacher was so strict...
He made me play until my fingers bled.
I'm really not that good of a piano player...
That's why I chose to study piano at college.
I've studied hard. That's why in only two years I'm the top player.
But lately, I've gotten a little lazy...

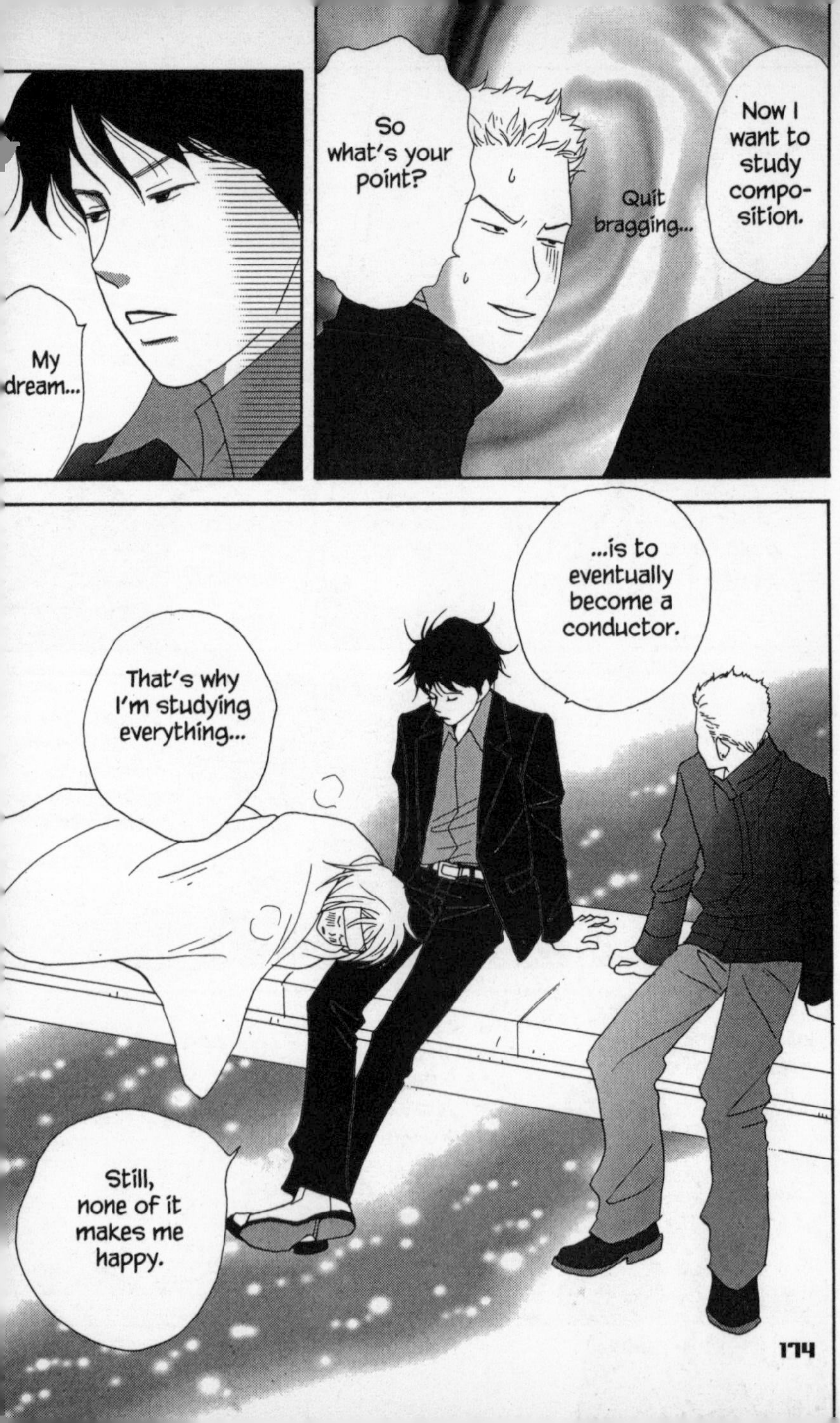
Now I want to study composition.
Quit bragging...
So what's your point?
My dream...
...is to eventually become a conductor.
That's why I'm studying everything...
Still, none of it makes me happy.

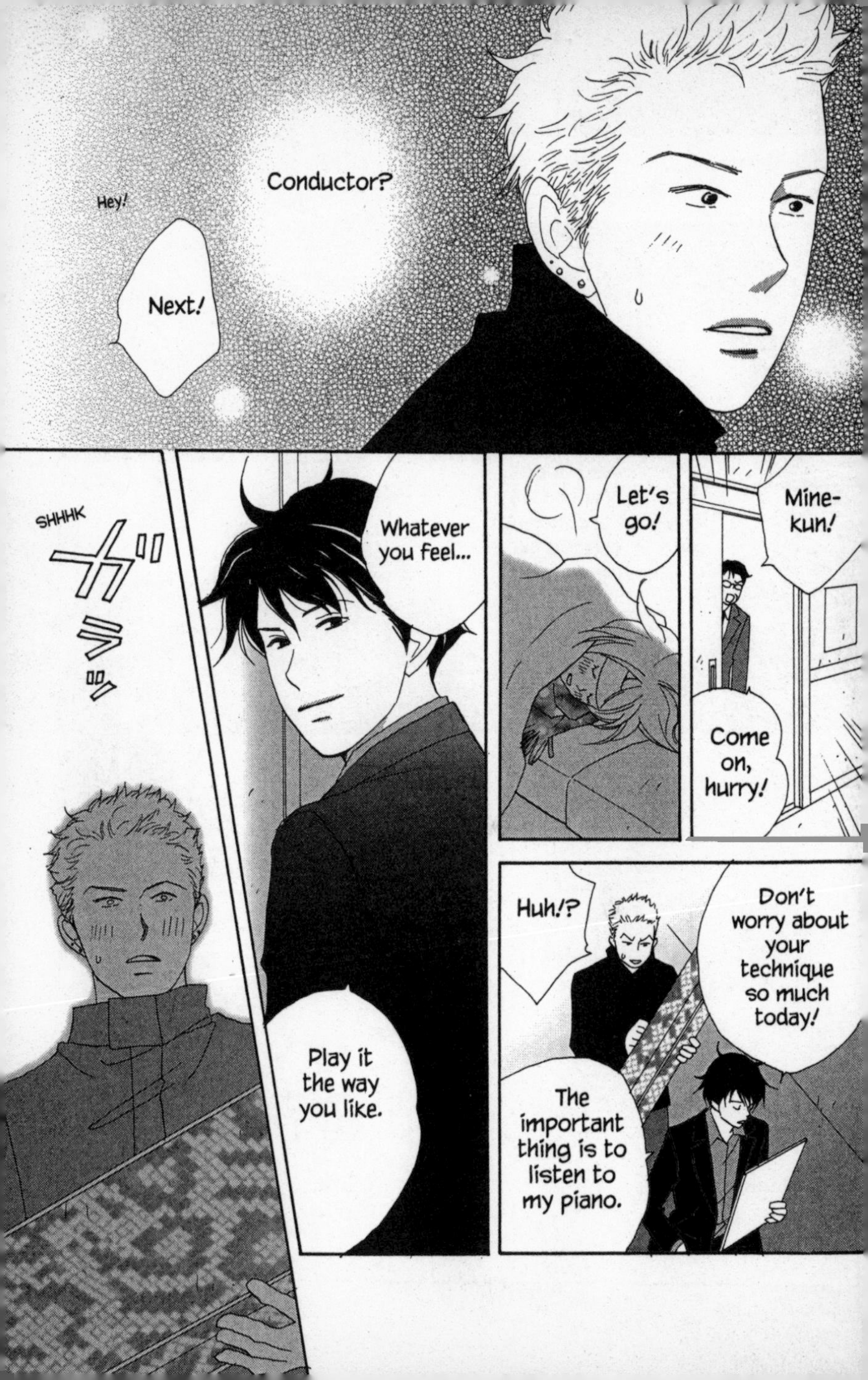
Conductor?
Hey!
Next!
Mine-kun!
Come on, hurry!
Let's go!
Don't worry about your technique so much today!
Huh!?
The important thing is to listen to my piano.
Whatever you feel...
Play it the way you like.
SHHHK
ガラッ

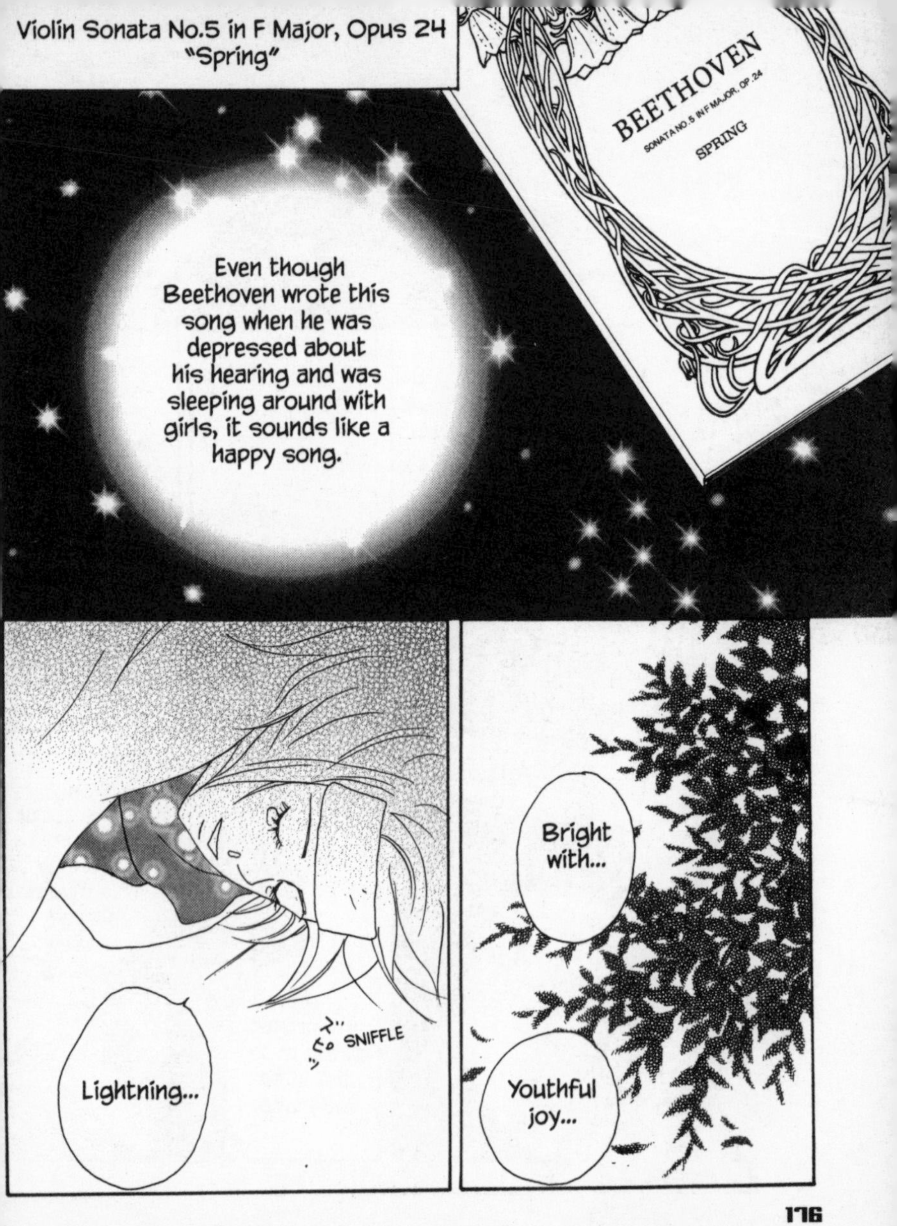
BEETHOVEN
SONATA NO.5 IN F MAJOR, OP.24
SPRING
Violin Sonata No.5 in F Major, Opus 24 "Spring"
Even though Beethoven wrote this song when he was depressed about his hearing and was sleeping around with girls, it sounds like a happy song.
Bright with...
Youthful joy...
SNIFFLE
Lightning...

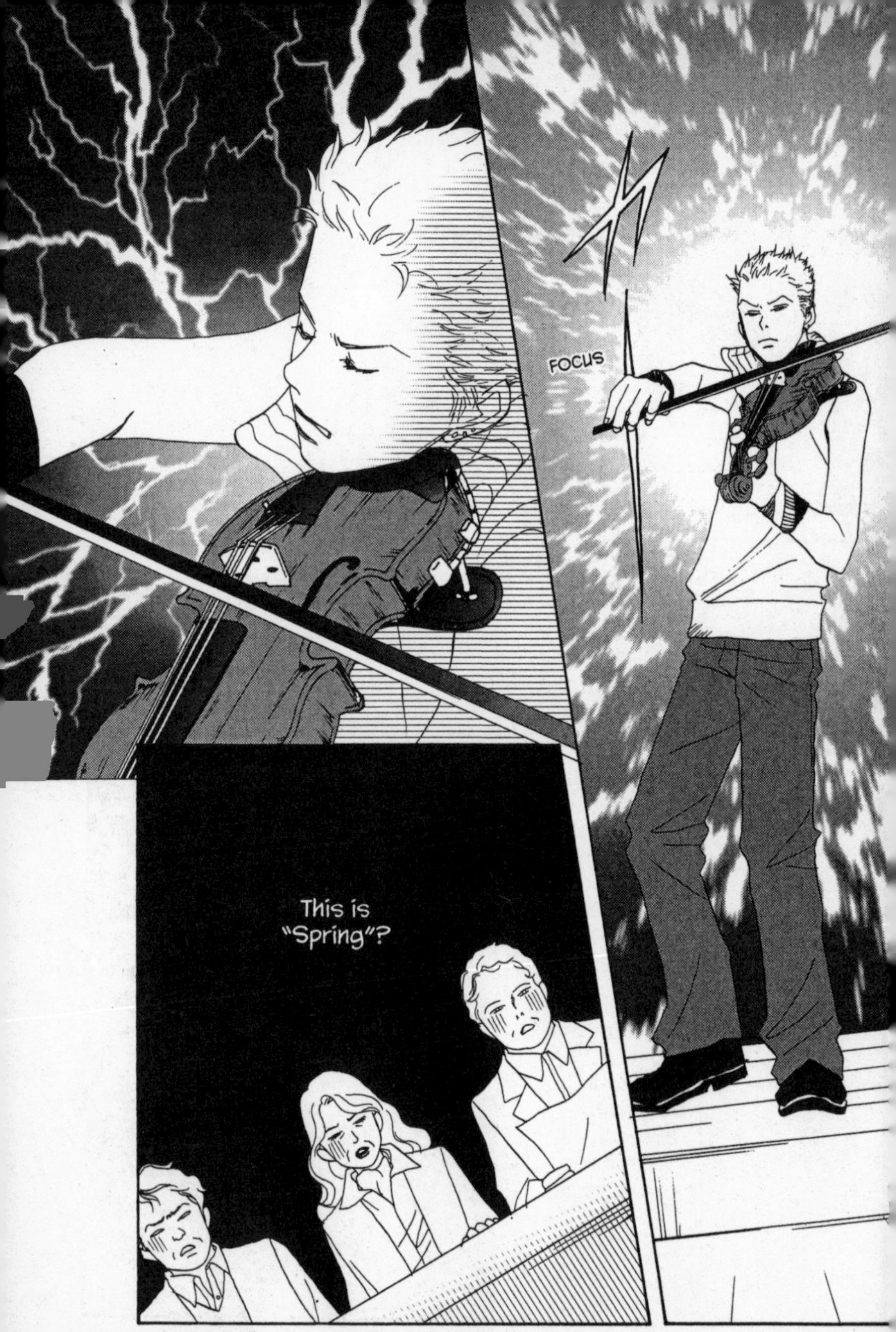
FOCUS
This is "Spring"?

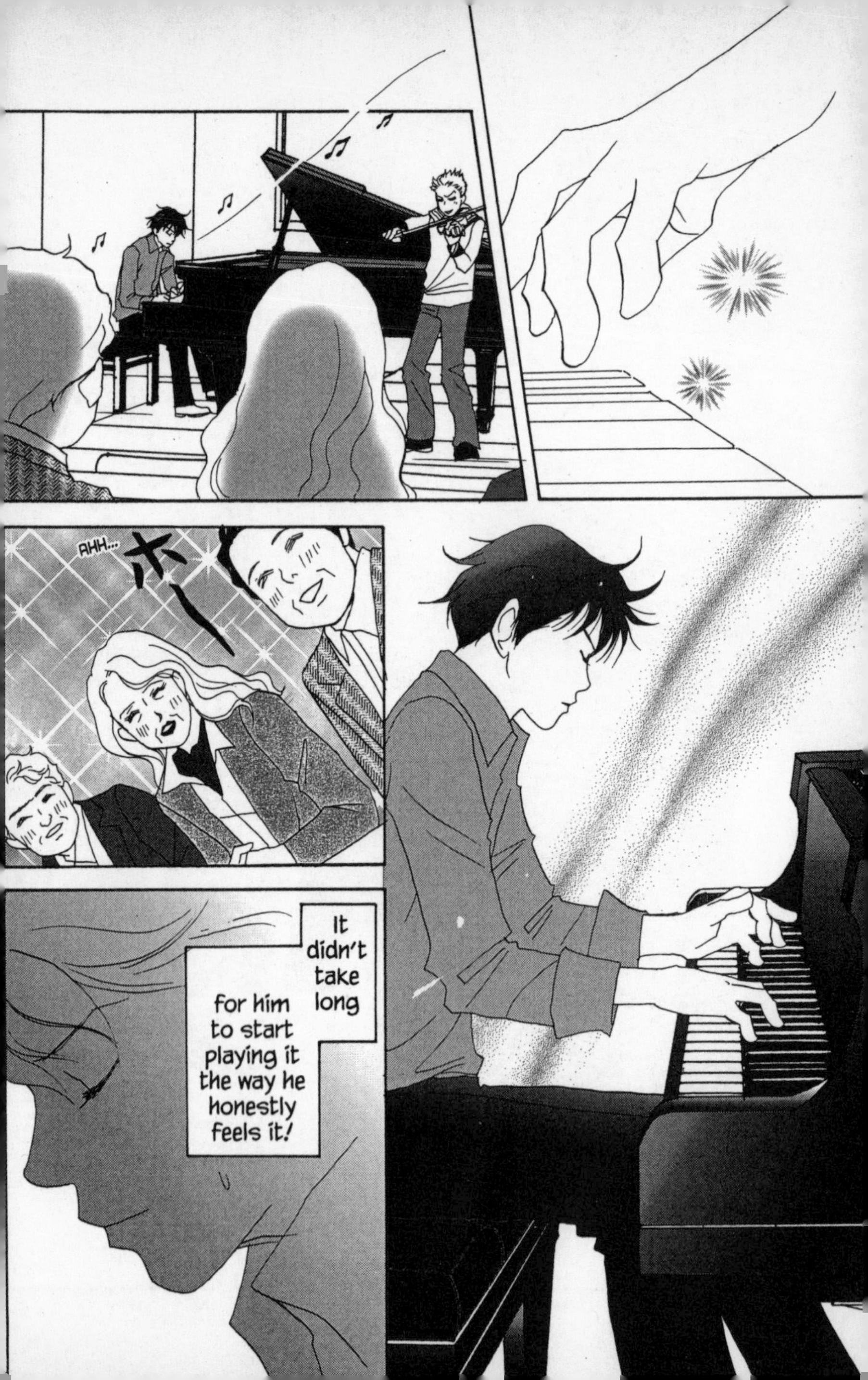
AHH...
ホー
It didn't take long
for him to start playing it the way he honestly feels it!

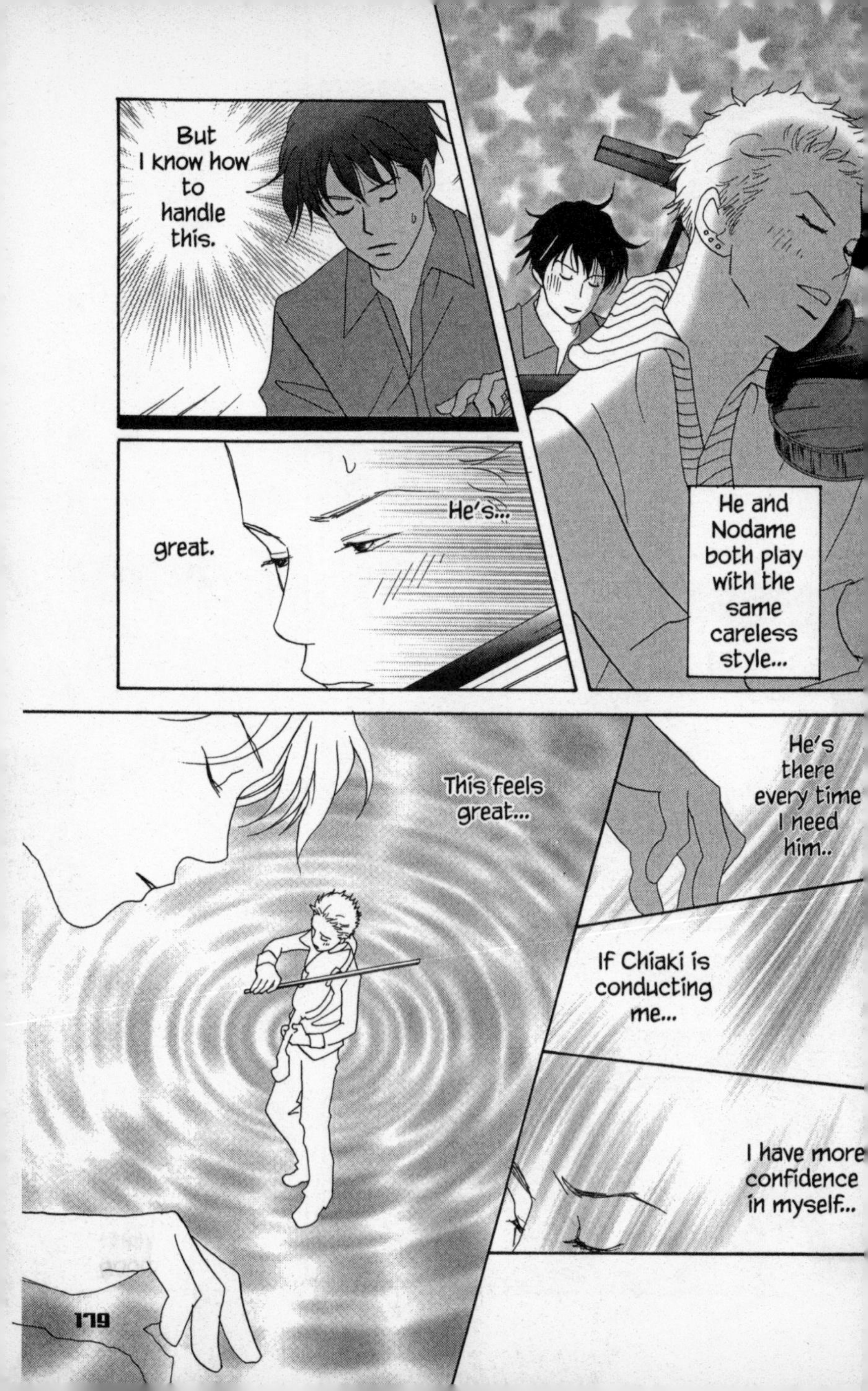
He and Nodame both play with the same careless style...
But I know how to handle this.
He's...
great.
He's there every time I need him..
If Chiaki is conducting me...
I have more confidence in myself...
This feels great...

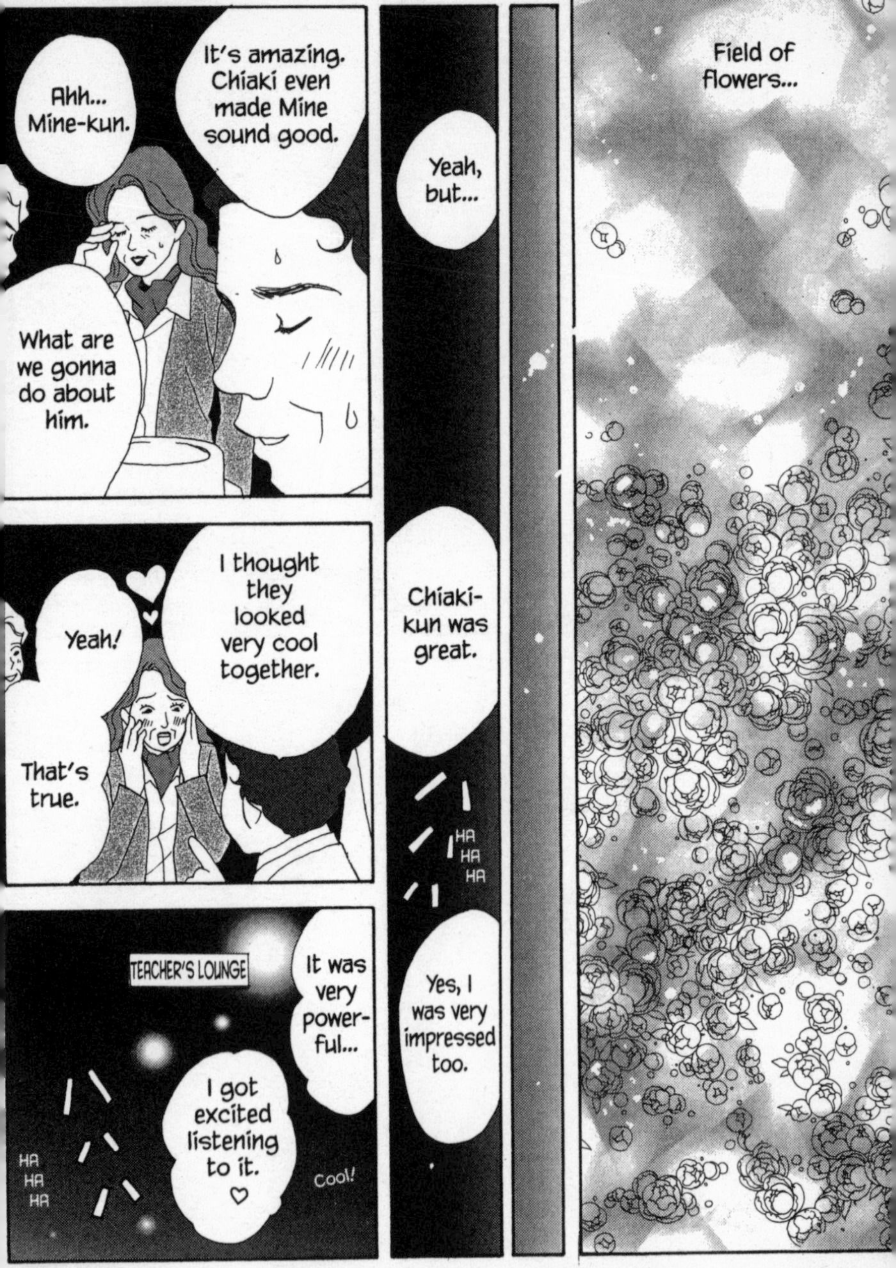
Field of flowers...
Yeah, but...
Chiaki-kun was great.
HA HA HA
Yes, I was very impressed too.
It's amazing. Chiaki even made Mine sound good.
Ahh... Mine-kun.
What are we gonna do about him.
I thought they looked very cool together.
Yeah!
That's true.
It was very powerful...
TEACHER'S LOUNGE
I got excited listening to it. ♡
Cool!
HA HA HA

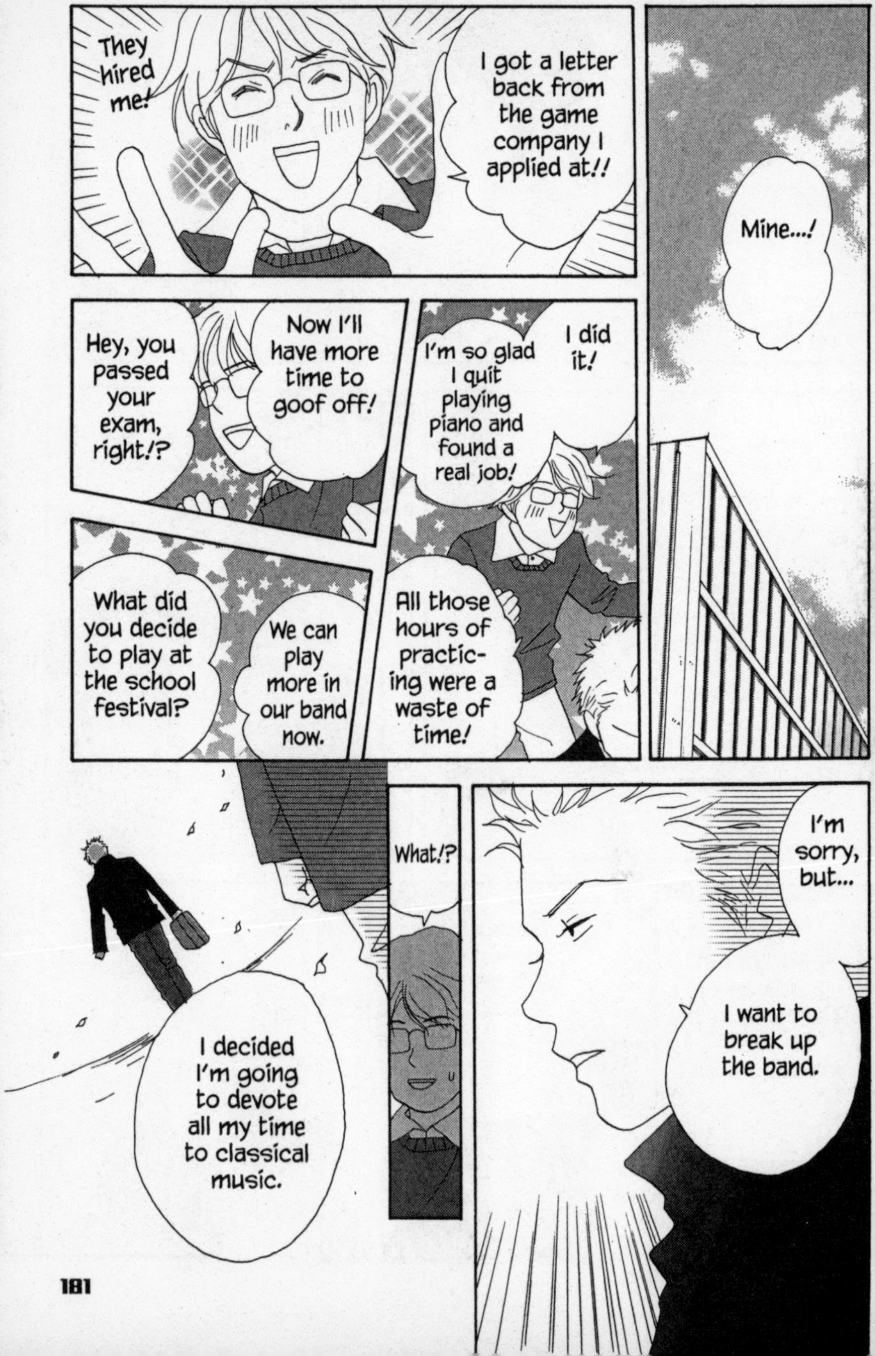
Mine...!
I got a letter back from the game company I applied at!!
They hired me!
I did it!
I'm so glad I quit playing piano and found a real job!
All those hours of practic-ing were a waste of time!
Now I'll have more time to goof off!
Hey, you passed your exam, right!?
We can play more in our band now.
What did you decide to play at the school festival?
I'm sorry, but...
I want to break up the band.
What!?
I decided I'm going to devote all my time to classical music.

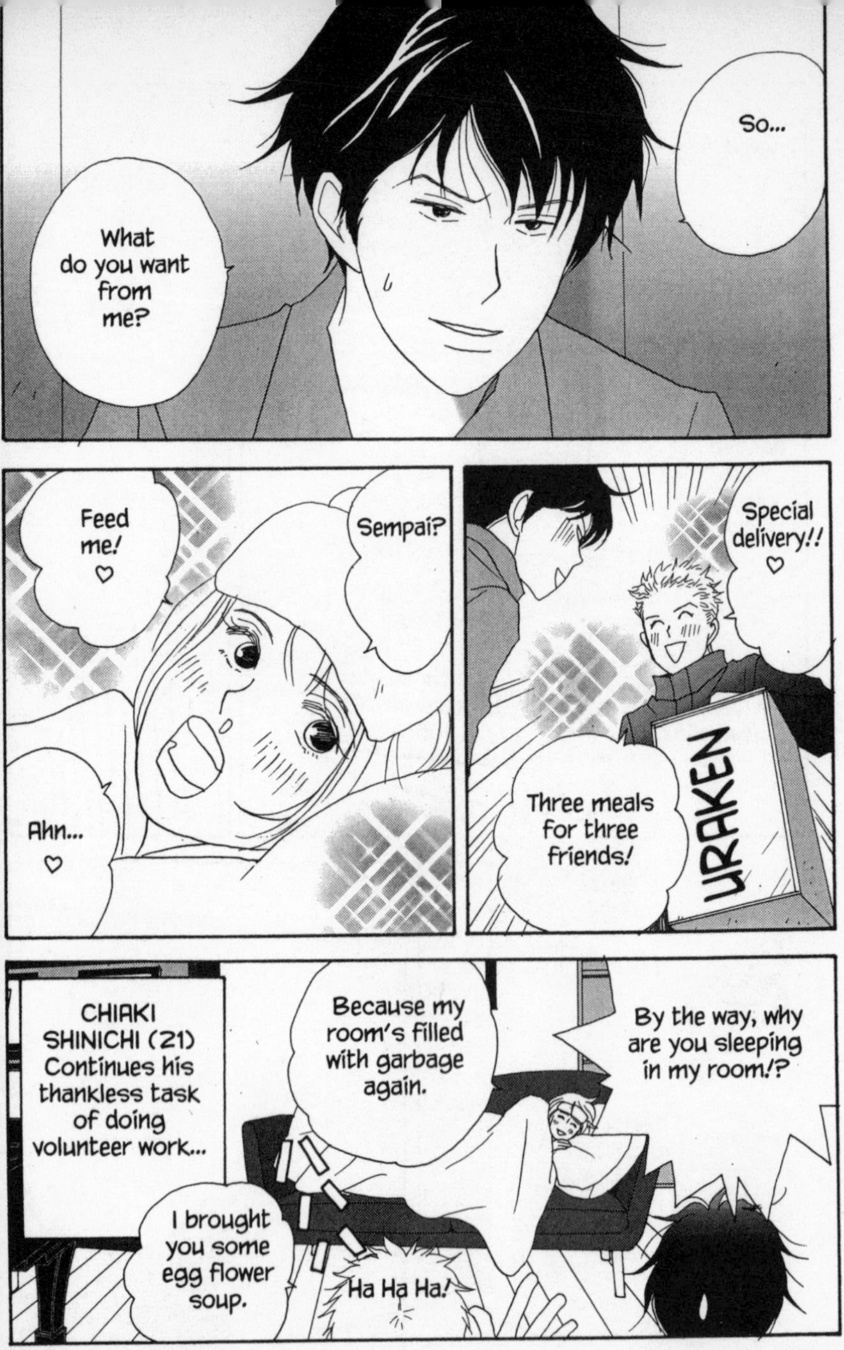
So...
What do you want from me?
Special delivery!! ♡
Three meals for three friends!
URAKEN
Sempai?
Feed me! ♡
Ahn... ♡
By the way, why are you sleeping in my room!?
Because my room's filled with garbage again.
CHIAKI SHINICHI (21) Continues his thankless task of doing volunteer work...
I brought you some egg flower soup.
Ha Ha Ha!

Special Thanks

Thank you, all the current music students
who helped me with gathering information!!

Volume 1 assistants
Nodame, Makiron, Yukiko-chan
Anan-chan, Reina-chan
Hoshino-kun...

Thank you for the tasty food
Nodame's Mother-sama (Ariake dry seaweed, thanks!)
Hoshino's Mother-sama (sake, thanks!)

Best wishes to everybody!

I can't play piano...
Tomoko Ninomiya

I welcome readers to send in your own experiences
with music. ♡

Nodame Cantabile 1

We look forward to hearing your opinions
and impressions about *Nodame Cantabile.*
Please send to the following.

=Address=
Del Rey Manga
1745 Broadway, Room 1830
New York, N.Y. 10019

Translation Notes

Japanese is a tricky language for most Westerners, and translation is often more art than science. For your edification and reading pleasure, here are notes on some of the places where we could have gone in a different direction in our translation of the work, or where a Japanese cultural reference is used.

The Lunch Box, page 8

A lunch box is a complete prepared meal you can buy in a handy carrying box. Similar to takeout food in America, you can eat it at your own convenience, but it is found at markets and convenience stores instead of restaurants.

But I'm gonna eat lunch first.

Japanese Department Stores, page 8

A department store in Japan can be compared to a mall in America. Different shops can lease space in the same building. Some department stores have a food section with vendors selling bread, lunches, candy, etc. A department store with a large food section is a joy to find because the shops usually offer many samples to try.

Mozart's jokes, page 18

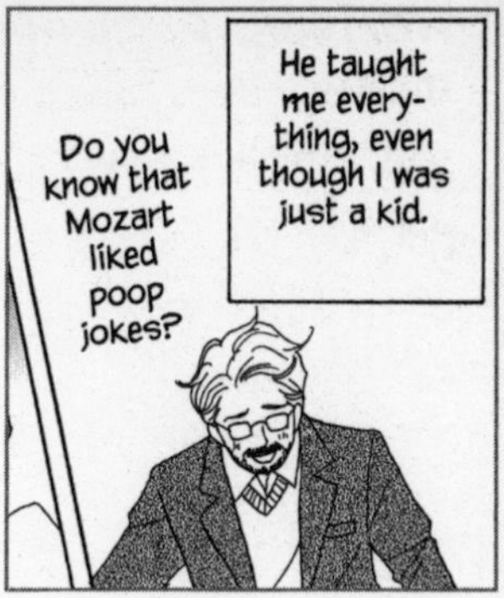
He taught me everything, even though I was just a kid.
Do you know that Mozart liked poop jokes?

Sebastiano says that Mozart liked "sukatoro," and Shinichi repeats "Sukatoro?," not knowing what it means. This is a Japanization of the word "scatology," which we know is the study of feces. Mozart did in fact make a lot of rude references to feces in his letters, but they seemed more like the immature jokes of a genius than a sexual preference.

The Hanshin Tigers cheer, page 19

The Hanshin Tigers is a popular baseball team in Japan. The student is singing their cheer in operatic style.

Fart song, page 27

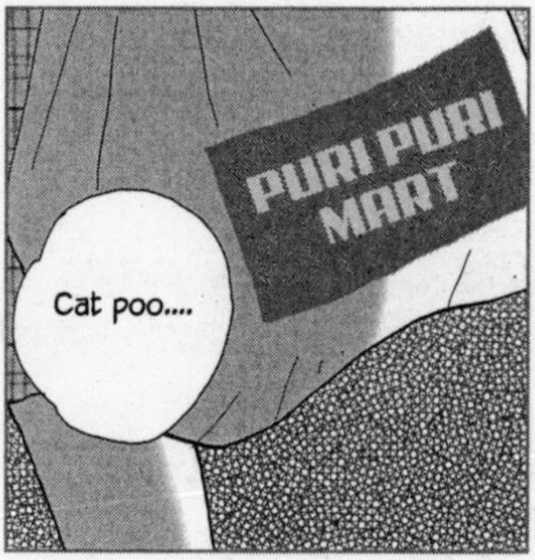
PURI PURI MART
Cat poo....

Nodame will be writing a children's song about farting. The Japanese FUN refers to animal poop, and this seems to be Nodame working out ideas for the song.

Mansions, page 39

In Japanese, an apartment can be referred to as a "mansion," which is very different from the English meaning.

Harisen, page 44

Shinichi refers to Eto as "hari-sen," which is a puffer fish in Japanese.

He can't be any worse than "puffer fish" Eto was.

Hey now!, page 46

Nodame and Tanioka are writing a children's song about farting. The reason Tanioka says "hey" sounds rude is because in Japanese it's also a way of saying "fart."

But the "Hey! Hey!" still isn't right.

The Ope-ken, page 48

Ope-Ken is the opera club on campus.

What's in the bag?, page 52

In Japan, residents must purchase special trash bags that indicate the type of trash that's inside.

OKYO GARBAGE COLLECTION BAG

Kinopia, page 56

Kinopio is a play on "Pinocchio," using the Japanese word "kino-ko," which is the mushroom on the VHS box.

Koshien, page 60

Koshien is an amateur baseball team that she apparently likes. The soil from their ball field is a keepsake.

Tarako, page 102

Tarako is a fish egg that the Japanese put inside rice balls.

Yonesuke, page 105

Yonesuke is a variety show host in Japan. Nodame's comment is similar to what Yonesuke would announce on his TV show.

Chicken Capri-style, page 105

Shinichi said the chicken is "capri-style," which is probably a play on "capriccio," meaning an improvised dish.

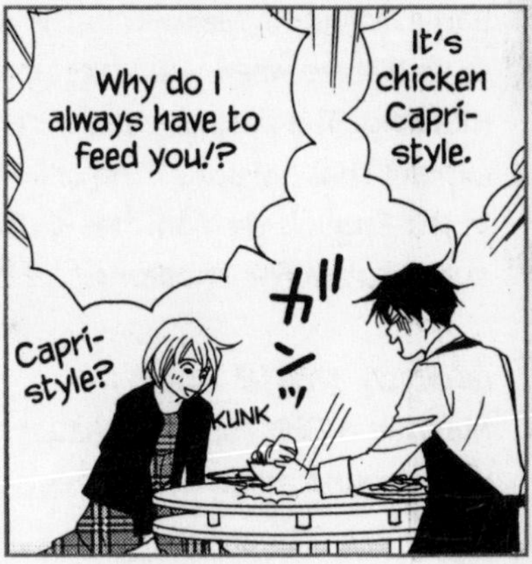
It's chicken Capri-style.
Why do I always have to feed you!?
ガン
Capri-style?
KUNK

Celebrate with a Snapper!, page 115

In Japan, snapper is expensive and eaten in times of celebration when something good such as a wedding or graduation has happened.

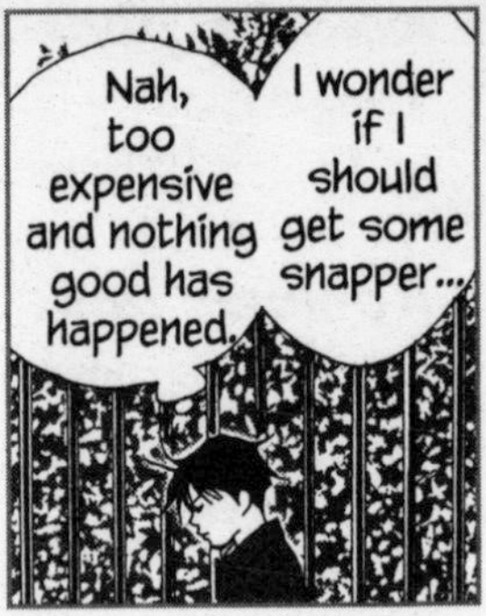
I wonder if I should get some snapper...
Nah, too expensive and nothing good has happened.

No-DUMMY!, page 122

The parenthesis in this bubble says "Nodame" because when Shinichi opened the door he rudely yelled "Mekuso," a play on Nodame's first name, Megumi. Mekuso is the stuff in your eyes when you wake up in the morning. The parentheses were meant to explain that "Mekuso" meant "Megumi." In the English version, "No-DUMMY" is substituted for "Nodame."

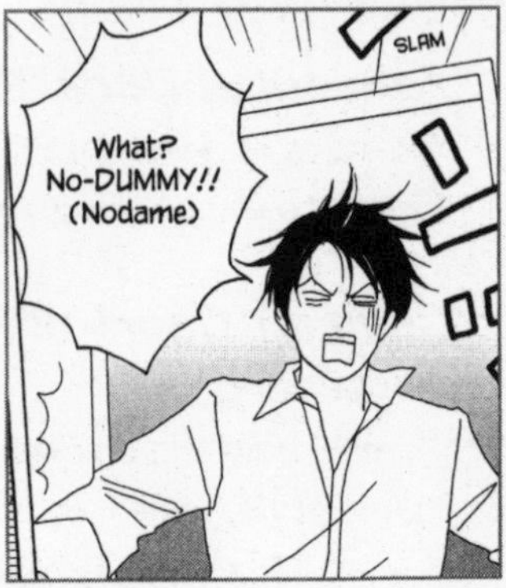
SLAM
What? No-DUMMY!! (Nodame)

Mabo, page 139

Mabo is a Chinese-style sauce with ground meat and spices.

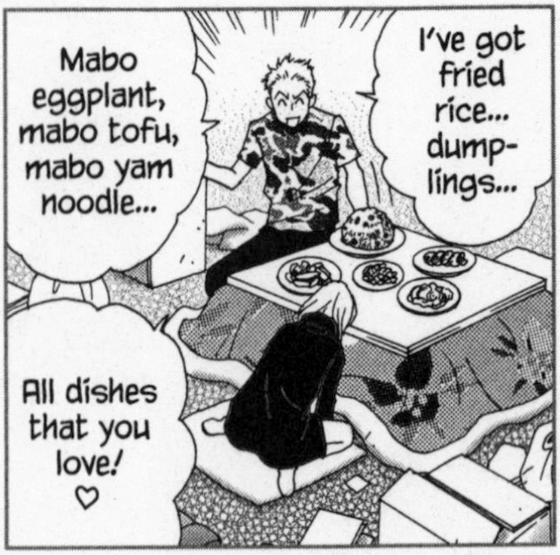
I've got fried rice... dump-lings...
Mabo eggplant, mabo tofu, mabo yam noodle...
All dishes that you love! ♡

We're pleased to present a preview from Volume 2.
This volume is available now.

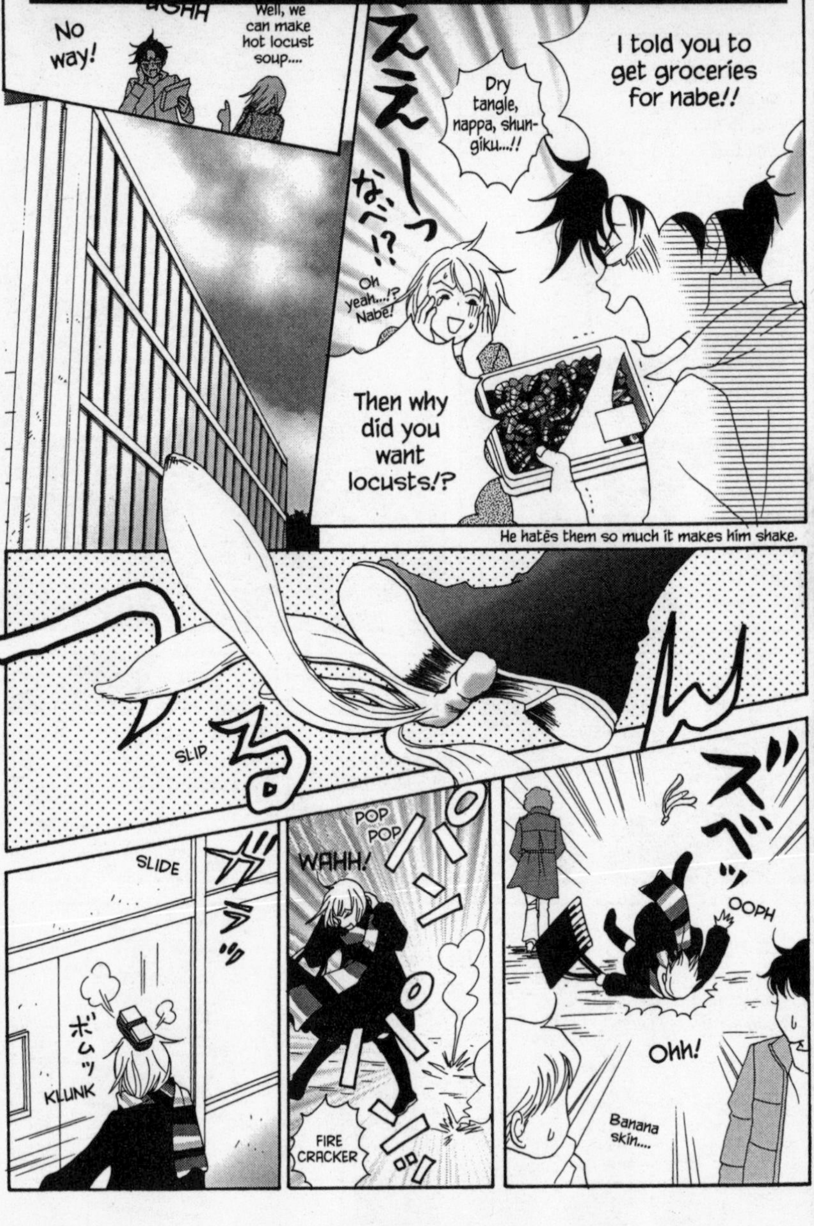

I told you to get groceries for nabe!!
Dry tangle, nappa, shun-giku...!!
えぇーっ なべ!?
Oh yeah...!? Nabe!
Then why did you want locusts!?
He hates them so much it makes him shake.
No way!
Well, we can make hot locust soup....
つる
SLIP
ズベッ
OOPH
Ohh!
Banana skin....
POP POP
WAHH!
FIRE CRACKER
SLIDE
ガラッ
ボムッ
KLUNK

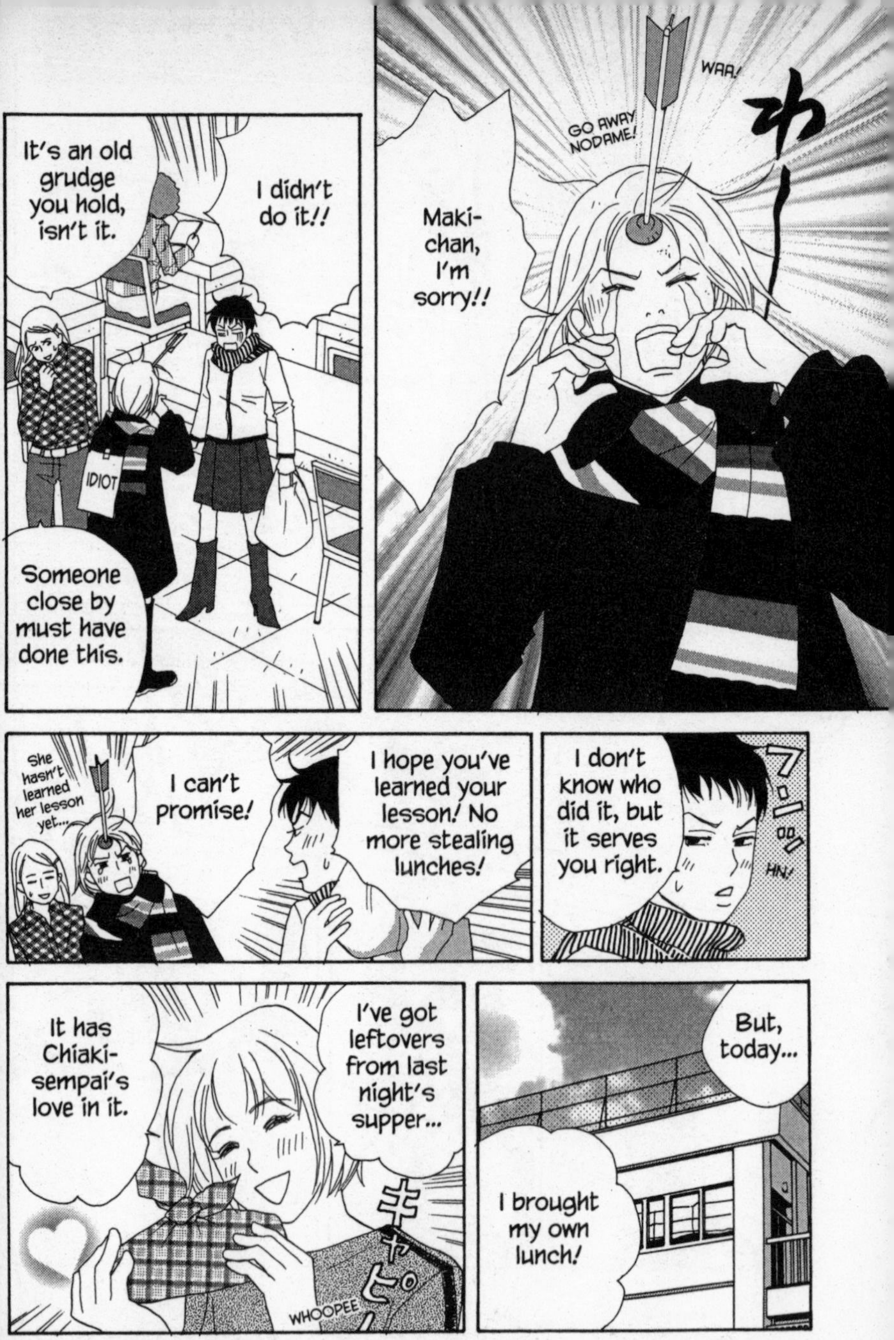
WAA!
GO AWAY NODAME!
Maki-chan, I'm sorry!!
I didn't do it!!
It's an old grudge you hold, isn't it.
IDIOT
Someone close by must have done this.
I don't know who did it, but it serves you right.
HN!
I hope you've learned your lesson! No more stealing lunches!
I can't promise!
She hasn't learned her lesson yet....
But, today...
I brought my own lunch!
I've got leftovers from last night's supper...
It has Chiaki-sempai's love in it.
WHOOPEE

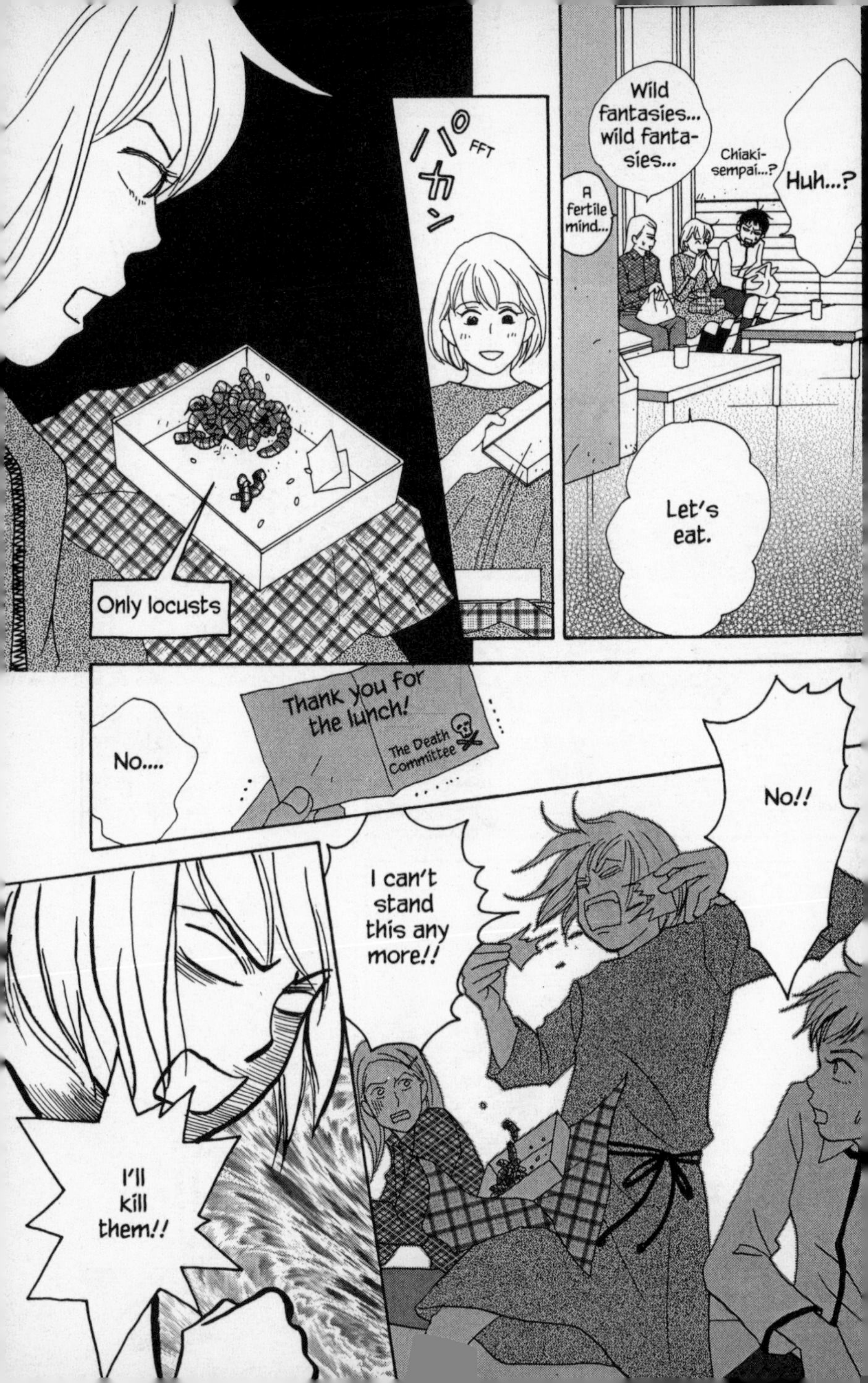
Huh...?
Chiaki-sempai...?
Wild fantasies... wild fanta-sies...
A fertile mind...
Let's eat.
パカン
FFT
Only locusts
Thank you for the lunch!
The Death Committee
No....
No!!
I can't stand this any more!!
I'll kill them!!

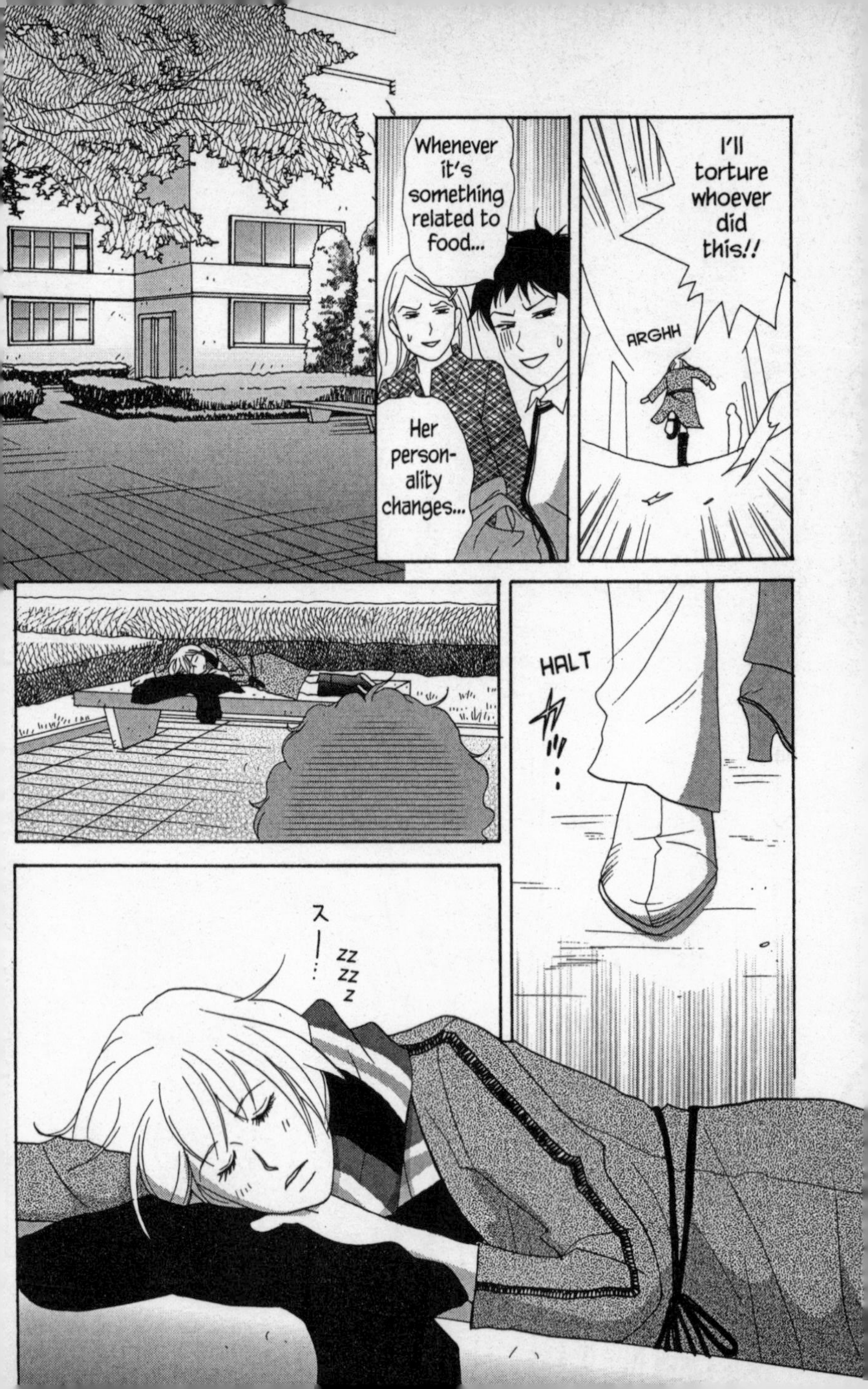

I'll torture whoever did this!!
ARGHH
Whenever it's something related to food...
Her personality changes...
HALT
スー…
ZZ ZZ Z

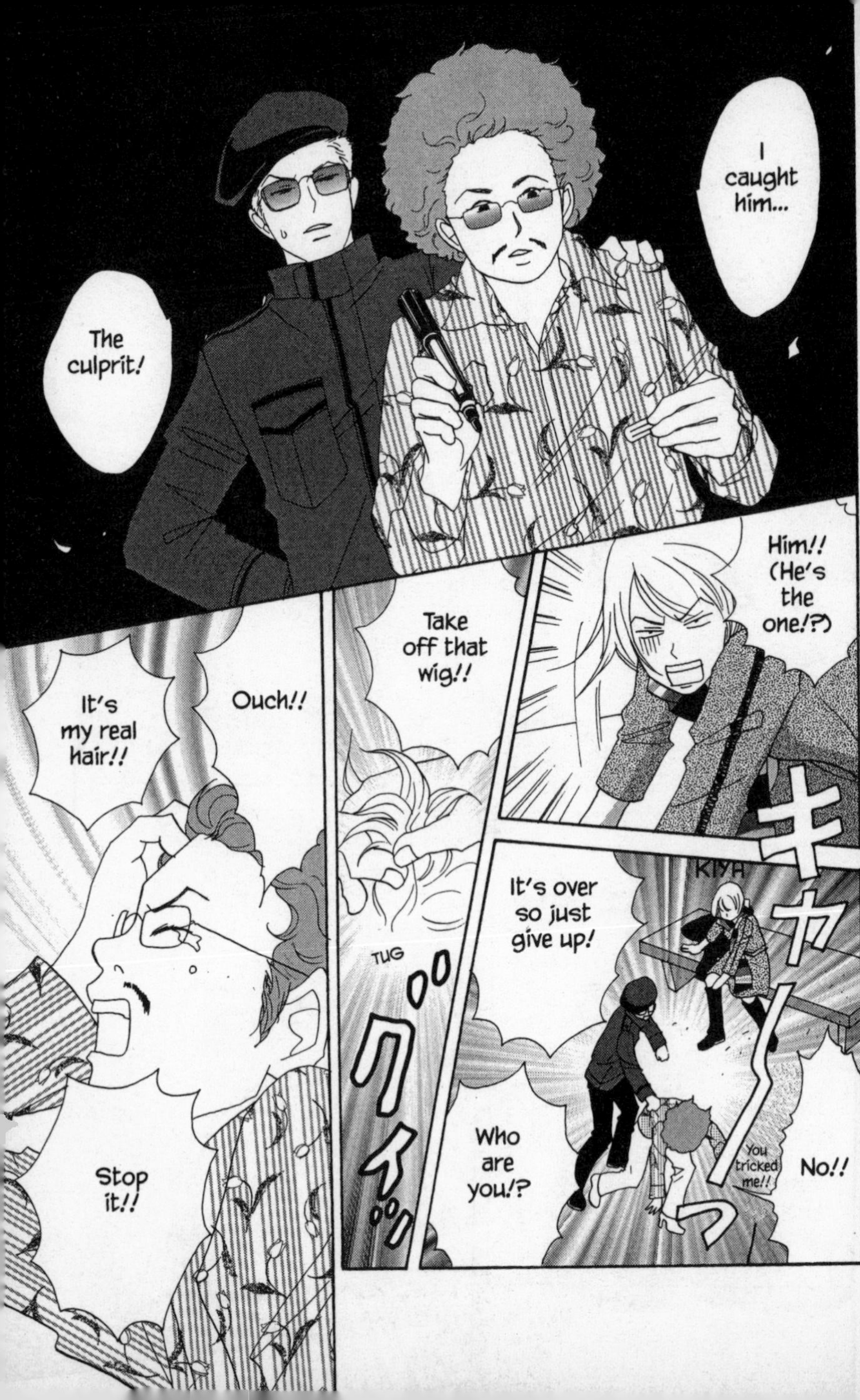
I caught him...
The culprit!
Him!! (He's the one!?)
キャーっ
KIYA
It's over so just give up!
No!!
You tricked me!!
Who are you!?
Take off that wig!!
グイッ
TUG
Ouch!!
It's my real hair!!
Stop it!!

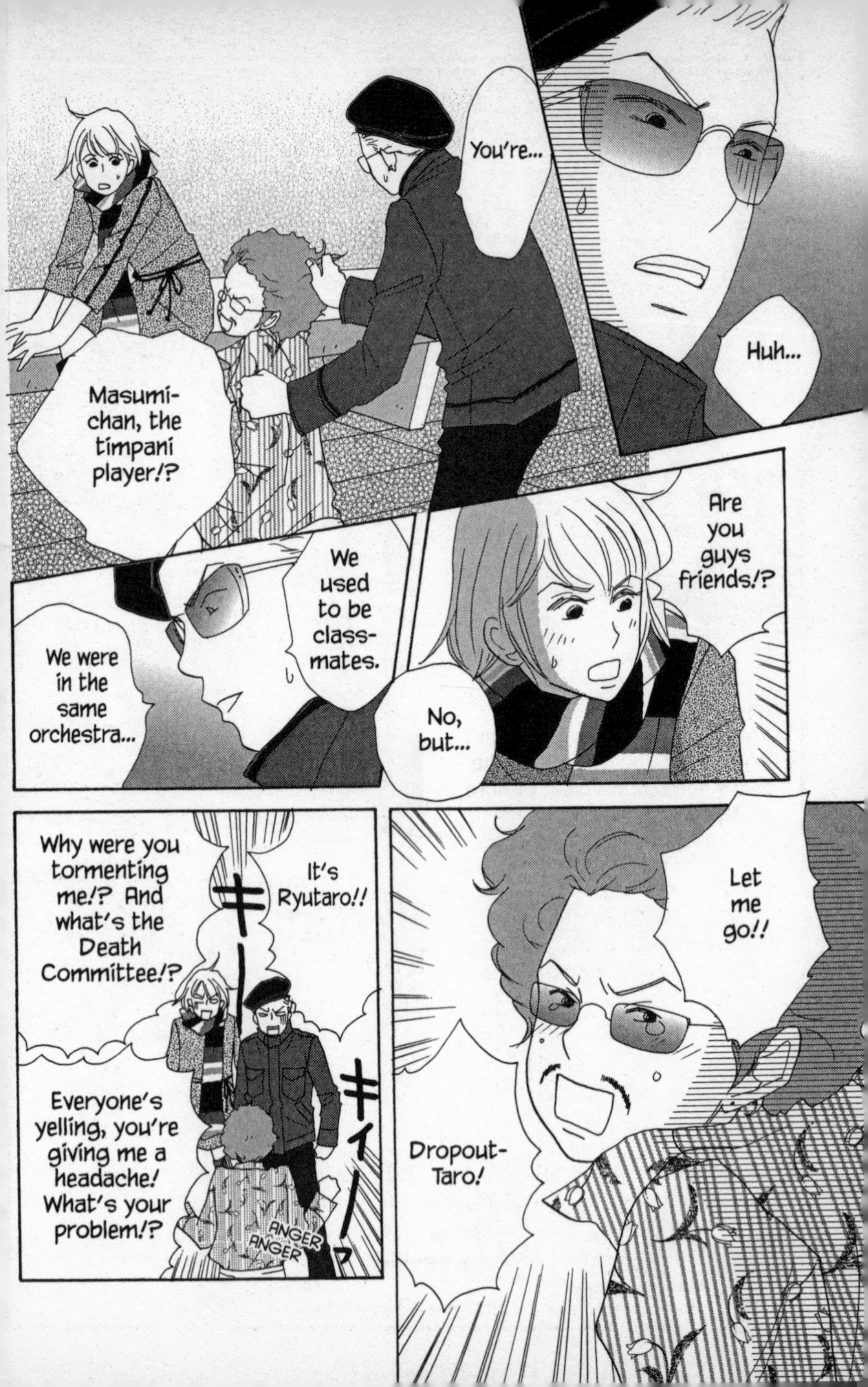
You're...
Huh...
Masumi-chan, the timpani player!?
Are you guys friends!?
No, but...
We used to be classmates.
We were in the same orchestra...
Let me go!!
Dropout-Taro!
It's Ryutaro!!
Why were you tormenting me!? And what's the Death Committee!?
Everyone's yelling, you're giving me a headache! What's your problem!?
ANGER
ANGER

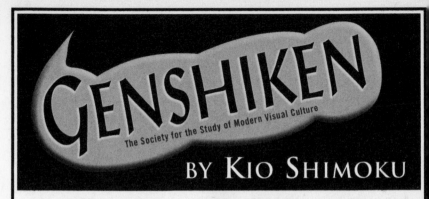

GENSHIKEN

The Society for the Study of Modern Visual Culture

BY KIO SHIMOKU

ARE YOU OTAKU?

It's the spring of freshman year, and Kanji Sasahara is in a quandary. Should he fulfill his long-cherished dream of joining an otaku club? Saki Kasukabe also faces a dilemma. Can she ever turn her boyfriend, anime fanboy Kousaka, into a normal guy? Kanji triumphs where Saki fails, when both Kanji and Kousaka sign up for Genshiken: The Society for the Study of Modern Visual Culture.

Undeterred, Saki chases Kousaka through various activities of the club, from cosplay and comic conventions to video gaming and collecting anime figures—all the while discovering more than she ever wanted to know about the humorous world of the Japanese otaku!

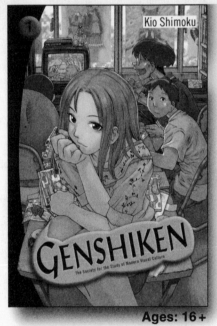

Ages: 16+

Special extras in each volume! Read them all!

BY TOMOKO HAYAKAWA

It's a beautiful, expansive mansion, and four handsome, fifteen-year-old friends are allowed to live in it for free! But there is one condition—within three years the young men must take the owner's niece and transform her into a proper lady befitting the palace in which they all live! How hard can it be?

Enter Sunako Nakahara, the horror-movie-loving, pock-faced, frizzy-haired, fashion-illiterate hermit who has a tendency to break into explosive nosebleeds whenever she sees anyone attractive. This project is going to take far more than our four heroes ever expected; it needs a miracle!

Ages: 16+

Special extras in each volume! Read them all!

Guru Guru Pon-Chan

BY SATOMI IKEZAWA

WINNER OF THE KODANSHA MANGA OF THE YEAR AWARD!

Ponta is a normal Labrador Retriever puppy, the Koizumi family's pet. Full of energy, she is always up to some kind of trouble. However, when Grandpa Koizumi, a passionate amateur inventor, creates the "Guru Guru Bone," which empowers animals with human speech, Ponta turns into a human girl!

Ponta dashes out into the street and is saved by Mirai Iwaki, the most popular boy at school! Her heart pounds and her face flushes. Why does she feel this way? Can there be love between a human and a dog?

The effects of the "Guru Guru Bone" are not permanent, and Ponta turns back and forth between dog and girl.

Ages: 13+

Special extras in each volume! Read them all!

VISIT WWW.DELREYMANGA.COM TO:
• View release date calendars for upcoming volumes
• Sign up for Del Rey's free manga e-newsletter
• Find out the latest about new Del Rey Manga series

By Hiroyuki Tamakoshi

Kouhei is your typical Japanese high school student—he's usually late, he loves beef bowls, he pals around with his buddies, and he's got his first-ever crush on his childhood friend Kurara. Before he can express his feelings, however, Kurara heads off to Hawaii with her mother for summer vacation. When she returns, she seems like a totally different person . . . and that's because she is! While she was away, Kurara somehow developed an alternate personality: Arisa! And where Kurara has no time for boys, Arisa isn't interested in much else. Now Kouhei must help protect his friend's secret, and make sure that Arisa doesn't do anything Kurara would regret!

HIROYUKI TAMAKOSHI

Ages: 16+

Special extras in each volume! Read them all!

BY AKIRA SEGAMI

MISSION IMPOSSIBLE

The young ninja Kagetora has been given a great honor—to serve a renowned family of skilled martial artists. But on arrival, he's handed a challenging assignment: teach the heir to the dynasty, the charming but clumsy Yuki, the deft moves of self-defense and combat.

Yuki's inability to master the martial arts is not what makes this job so difficult for Kagetora. No, it is Yuki herself. Someday she will lead her family dojo, and for a ninja like Kagetora to fall in love with his master is a betrayal of his duty, the ultimate dishonor, and strictly forbidden. Can Kagetora help Yuki overcome her ungainly nature . . . or will he be overcome by his growing feelings?

Ages: 13 +

Special extras in each volume! Read them all!

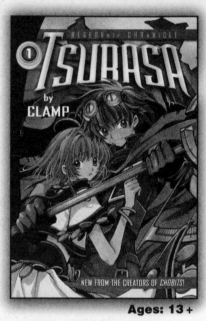

TOMARE!
[STOP!]

You are going the wrong way!

Manga is a completely different
type of reading experience.

To start at the *beginning,* go to the *end!*

That's right! Authentic manga is read the traditional Japanese
way—from right to left. Exactly the *opposite* of how American
books are read. It's easy to follow: Just go to the other end of
the book, and read each page—and each panel—from right side
to left side, starting at the top right. Now you're experiencing
manga as it was meant to be.